Caribbean Exchanges

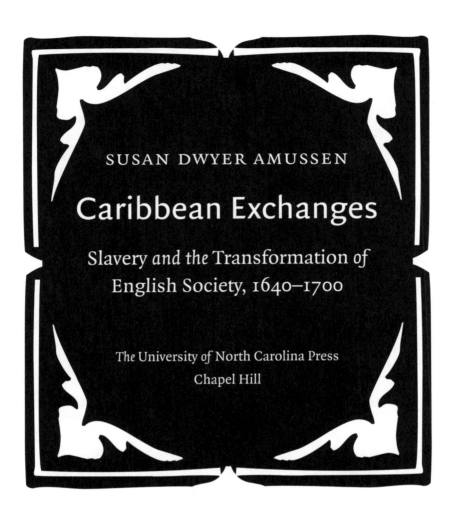

SUSAN DWYER AMUSSEN

Caribbean Exchanges

Slavery and the Transformation of
English Society, 1640–1700

The University of North Carolina Press
Chapel Hill

Designed by Kimberly Bryant
Set in Quadraat by Keystone Typesetting, Inc.
Manufactured in the United States of America

The paper in this book meets the guidelines for permanence and
durability of the Committee on Production Guidelines for Book Longevity
of the Council on Library Resources.

Library of Congress Cataloging-in-Publication Data
Amussen, Susan Dwyer.
Caribbean Exchanges : slavery and the transformation of English society, 1640–1700 /
Susan Dwyer Amussen.
p. cm.
Includes bibliographical references and index.
ISBN 978-0-8078-3165-6 (cloth : alk. paper)
ISBN 978-0-8078-5854-7 (pbk. : alk. paper)
1. Slavery—Great Britain—Colonies—History. 2. Slavery—West Indies, British—History.
3. Social change—England—History—17th century. 4. England—Social conditions—17th
century. 5. England—Civilization—Caribbean influences. I. Title.
HT1165.A68 2007
306.3'620941—dc22
2007008869

cloth   11 10 09 08 07   5 4 3 2 1
paper   11 10 09 08 07   5 4 3 2 1

for David

Contents

Maps and Illustrations

Maps

Illustrations

Acknowledgments

It is a cliché to say that scholarship is a collaborative enterprise, but the cliché is repeated because it is true. While it is impossible to acknowledge all the help and support that have allowed me to bring this project to a conclusion, I want to mention the most obvious.

When I began this work, a faculty development grant from the Union Institute and University funded my first research trip to Barbados and Jamaica. Several years later, I received a sabbatical leave from Union Institute and University, during which I began the first draft of the book. Writing continued with a Mellon Post-Doctoral Fellowship at the Huntington Library in 2002–3. The luxury of the collegial and beautiful surroundings of the Huntington provided an ideal environment. Roy Ritchie and the library staff were unfailingly helpful; I am particularly grateful to Linda Zoeckler for her help with some of the art historical research. Finally, a visiting fellowship at the Yale Center for British Art at the end of 2004 provided an opportunity to focus my attention on the paintings I had been collecting; my conversations there, and especially the opportunity to study the center's portrait of Elihu Yale and the Duke of Devonshire with Julia Marciari-Alexander, Cassandra Albinson, and Gillian Forrester, were extraordinarily helpful in providing this historian with a somewhat reasonable vocabulary with which to discuss art.

Historians love archivists and librarians. The work for this study has been carried out at the National Library of Jamaica; the Jamaica Archives; the Barbados Central Library; the Barbados Archives; the Barbados Museum and Historical Society; the Public Record Office of the National Archives in London; the British Library; the Somerset Archives and Record Office; the Huntington Library; the Beinecke Rare Book and Manuscript Library, Sterling

Memorial Library, and Yale Center for British Art at Yale University; the Newberry Library; the National Portrait Gallery Heinz Archive; and the Courtauld Institute. The librarians and archivists in all those locations were unfailingly efficient and helpful—even in Spanish Town, when a visiting scholar was oblivious to riots. Matt Pappathan and the librarians at the Gary Library of the Union Institute and University were amazingly efficient.

Many parts of this manuscript were presented in various forms at conferences, and my thinking has been sharpened and clarified by the responses of the audiences at the Union Institute Faculty Scholarship Conference, Northeast Conference on British Studies, New York University Atlantic Seminar, Anglo-American Conference of Historians, University of California at Riverside, Huntington Library Early American Seminar and Huntington Library Early Modern Seminar, the Shakespeare Association of America, Vann Seminar at Emory University, Yale Early Modern Studies Colloquium, Attending to Early Modern Women Workshop with Kim Hall, Dartmouth Early Modern Studies Seminar, and Renaissance Colloquium at the University of California, Davis.

One of the pleasures of the scholarly life is the way that human interactions feed our work. To the Union learner—whose name I do not remember—who unwittingly set me on the path that led to this book, I am deeply grateful. I would not have been able to pick up on her question were it not for the conversations I was engaged in with my then colleagues, learners, and graduates. They were unfailingly encouraging as I struggled to find a shape for the questions that emerged. In particular, Leslie Hill, Arthur Jones, Judith Arcana, Minnie Bruce Pratt, and Michael O'Neal offered not only encouragement but substantive suggestions that helped move me forward.

Colleagues at the Huntington—especially Dan Howe, Josh Piker, Lara Kriegel, Elliott West, Barbara Donagan, and Chris Kyle—offered intellectual encouragement as well as practical support as we dealt with illness far from home. Michael Shapiro unintentionally started me on the hunt for plays, and Margaret Ezell gave me important leads about late seventeenth-century drama. Professor David Buisseret generously shared his transcription of John Taylor's "Multum in Parvo"—a gift that saved enormous time.

As someone who has worked in a nontraditional institution primarily with students outside of history, the professional colleagues who stayed in conversation with me have been particularly important. This is a partial list, but Margaret Hunt, Frances Dolan, Keith Wrightson, Cynthia Herrup, Judith Maltby, Jennifer Morgan, Kim Hall, Tom Cogswell, Lori Ann Ferrell, Paul Monod, and Deborah Valenze each at particular times helped me stay connected with my research and with the field. It meant more than they could imagine to have their friendship and colleagueship.

This manuscript has benefited from several excellent readers. David Underdown is my first reader, always, and my writing owes much to him. Jennifer Morgan read Chapter 2; Grey Osterud helped me reshape the manuscript in ways large and small. Carla Pestana provided an extraordinarily helpful and detailed reading of the whole manuscript. Paul Monod and Deborah Valenze read the epilogue and helped me think about what came next. The anonymous readers for the University of North Carolina Press saved me from errors trivial and profound. I am deeply grateful to Jerome Handler, who initially suggested I contact my editor, Elaine Maisner. She has been encouraging and wise in the ways she has helped me reshape the manuscript. Years ago a colleague told me that you should want a good copyeditor; I was lucky to have Jay Mazzocchi's eagle eye to catch infelicities and confusions. Needless to say, any errors that remain are my responsibility.

Writing a book is never separate from life. The ten years during which I have focused on this project have had many ups and downs, and it would have been impossible if it were not for the family and friends who have put up with me, provided me with alternative activities, and occasionally listened to me talk about it. Gretchen Pritchard, Sally Fleming, and Liz Cox have been stalwart friends; through their work in New Haven, they have kept me connected to the problems of this world, as well as those of the past. My reading group has frequently reminded me of the importance of good writing. The Reverend Professor Harlon Dalton—with his legal and theological knowledge—reminded me that this was a good idea. The choir at the Episcopal Church of St. Paul and St. James and the Tuesday night pottery class at the Creative Arts Workshop have provided creative outlets with more immediate satisfaction than writing. Gretchen and John Amussen are perfect siblings, interested but not impressed; John was also an anchor as I dealt with hospitals and doctors in Los Angeles. My stepmother, Jane Munro, has used her experience as a scholar and poet to encourage me through the revision process. Marion Pritchard and Simone Rubin-Underdown have provided play and distraction. I am fortunate to have been raised by parents who loved words and books. Diane Amussen has never let me abandon the questions of race and gender, and always reminds me that they are living questions; she has also helped with the index. Robert Amussen has always been concerned about the writing process. Both have believed I could finish this.

Finally, David Underdown has offered love, support, encouragement and sharp questions from the beginning. I could not have done this—or any of my scholarly work—nearly as well without that magical combination. As I would throw out outrageous hypotheses, he would say, "How will you prove it?" I have not proved my more outrageous theories, but I hope he will think I have done a pretty good job on the ones I have stayed with. Even as my own energy began to drag, he maintained his enthusiasm. The dedication of this work is a small token of my love and thanks.

Caribbean Exchanges

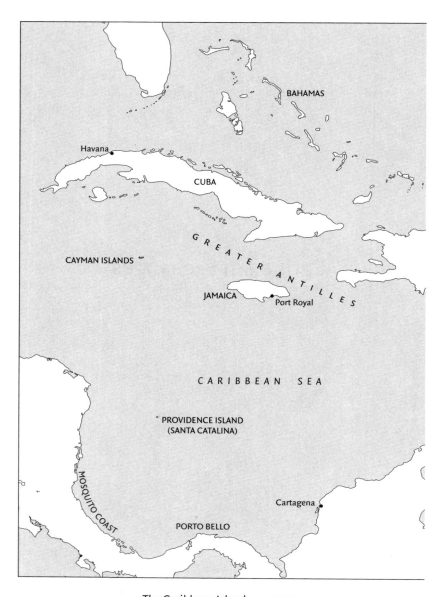

The Caribbean Islands, ca. 1700

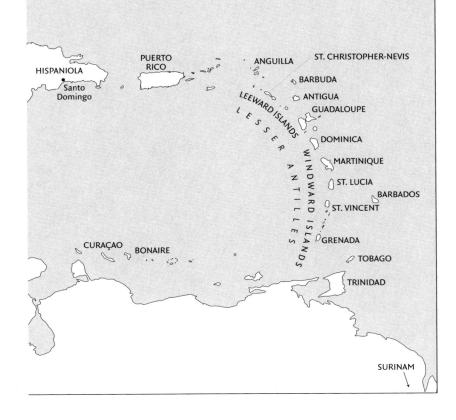

ATLANTIC OCEAN

HISPANIOLA

Santo
Domingo

PUERTO
RICO

ANGUILLA

ST. CHRISTOPHER-NEVIS

BARBUDA

ANTIGUA

LEEWARD ISLANDS

GUADALOUPE

DOMINICA

MARTINIQUE

ST. LUCIA

BARBADOS

ST. VINCENT

L E S S E R   A N T I L L E S

W I N D W A R D   I S L A N D S

CURAÇAO

BONAIRE

GRENADA

TOBAGO

TRINIDAD

SURINAM

Introduction

The English Caribbean and Caribbean England

The reflexive cultures and consciousness of the European settlers and those of the Africans they enslaved, the "Indians" they slaughtered, and the Asians they indentured were not, even in situations of the most extreme brutality, sealed off hermetically from each other.

PAUL GILROY, *The Black Atlantic: Modernity and Double Consciousness* (1993)

In May 1692 the parish clerk in East Coker, Somerset, recorded the baptism of "Thomas, Wm Helyar Esq. Blackamoor." The clerk was apparently so startled by this unusual event that he inserted a note above the record reinforcing Thomas's identity: "A black of William Helyar Esq." Two years earlier, John Helyar had promised to send his brother William two young "Negro" children by the next ship to serve as household servants or slaves. John was in Jamaica, at their father's plantation, Bybrook, some fifteen miles north of Spanish Town. William was in East Coker, about thirty-five miles south of Bristol, where their father William was the squire. The Helyars did not baptize slaves in Jamaica, but, like other families, they baptized slaves in England. We do not know whether John only sent Thomas, whether another child was sent but died before being baptized, or if the second child made it

---

Spelling has been modernized. The year is taken to begin on 1 January.

to England but for some reason was not baptized. Whether alone or with another child from the plantation, Thomas's journey from Bybrook, home to about 110 slaves and less than a dozen white servants, to his new home, a pretty Somerset village of some 500 inhabitants, covered more than 4,500 miles; the cultural distance is immeasurable. The village was dominated by Coker Court, the home of the Helyars, on the hill just above the church where Thomas was baptized. Thomas was probably the only person of African ancestry in the parish. We do not know what news reached Bybrook about Thomas after his arrival in England; he disappears from the record after his baptism. Nine years later, however, Dr. John Hall, then overseer of Bybrook, ended a letter to the same William Helyar with a short note stating that "Betty, a Negro, asks if her son is living with you and sends her love."[1]

Betty's voice and Thomas's journey remind us that people, black and white, enslaved and free, were at the heart of the colonial enterprise in the seventeenth century, and that their journeys entailed multiple Atlantic crossings. The remarkable element of this exchange, from the sending of Thomas to Betty's message, is that the correspondence has survived. Colonel William Helyar kept almost all the correspondence relating to his Jamaican property, providing us with a remarkable account of the building of a plantation. The traffic between England and its Caribbean colonies involved not only the English men (primarily) who went to make their fortunes in the West Indies, but also often the slaves they brought back to England.[2] Yet while this traffic was of growing significance in late seventeenth-century England, it has been largely invisible in the work of historians of England in the period.

In this book I try to understand the significance of the experience, not only of John Helyar but also of Thomas and his mother Betty, by exploring a series of linked questions. What did the English have to do to become slaveholding planters in the seventeenth-century Caribbean? How did they change? What was the impact of this on individuals, as well as social groups? How did the interactions between slave owners and slaves shape the attitudes and actions of each group? And finally, what did the English bring home from their experience in the West Indies? Social relations in England differed from those in its Caribbean colonies in ideas about law and punishment as well as meanings of gender, work, and society; those Caribbean ideas returned to England along with the sugar that became the colonies' primary export. This process began in the seventeenth century, long before it has usually appeared in discussions of the impact of the empire on England. I will concentrate on Barbados and Jamaica, the two most important of England's Caribbean colonies. In order to bring attention to the process of becoming a slave society, I will focus primarily on the period between 1640 and 1700. By slave society I mean a society with a majority slave population, dependent on the work of slaves, and organized in all ways to sustain the system of slavery. In the 1640s, Barbadian planters began to produce sugar on a large scale as they transformed the island into a slave society. By 1700 both Barbados and Jamaica had fully organized the institutions—legal and social—of a slave society, but the institutional and social transformations took place at a different pace from the economic ones. The development of the sugar economy was so rapid that the supporting institutions took time to fully develop. Such dates are inevitably arbitrary, but the laws that governed slavery in Jamaica and Barbados throughout the eighteenth century were passed in 1696 and 1688, respectively; the last plot for a slave rebellion in Barbados in the eighteenth century was discovered in 1702. By the beginning of the eighteenth century, Barbados and Jamaica had settled legal, political, and social institutions.[3]

As is usually the case with such projects, this is not where I began. More than fifteen years ago, I began to study the nature and meaning of violence in early modern England. One day, talking to a group of nonhistorians, I described what I saw as the relative absence of sexualized violence in seventeenth-century rape narratives: the most common defense against a charge of rape was not consent, but that no sexual activity had taken place.[4] I puzzled aloud at how that set of ideas about sexual violence had changed to the twenty-first century one with which we are familiar. Someone asked me about the impact of the rape of slave women by their masters on this process. I had never thought about this, so I gave an evasive answer; but the question stayed with me, and I began to explore the early history of British slaveholding in the Caribbean. I was immediately struck by three things. First was the rapid development of large-scale slave societies, with majority slave populations, after the introduction of sugar to Barbados in the 1640s, and the conquest of Jamaica by the English in 1655. To someone familiar with the rhetoric of law and liberty so prevalent in seventeenth-century England, it was remarkable how quickly—and apparently easily—the English took to large-scale slave owning. Second, the traffic between the West Indies and England was two-way, with many men spending some years in Jamaica or Barbados and then returning to England. This made the experience of the West Indies a more real and visible feature of English society than that of England's mainland colonies. Finally, in spite of the wealth and products provided by England's Caribbean colonies, they play a minor role in studies of seventeenth-century England, aside from occasional references to the arrival of sugar from the Caribbean or discussions of the colonial dimensions of the wars of the late seventeenth century. Few seventeenth-century British historians pay much attention to English involvement in the slave trade since the time of John Hawkins, or to the relationship between the English Civil War in defense of liberty and the constitution and the development of slavery in the colonies—where planters debated not freedom, but whether slaves should be treated as real estate or chattels. The combination of these features of the seventeenth-century Caribbean and recent historiography stimulated the central questions around which this book revolves.

In the course of research and writing, my questions kept splitting and expanding. What changes—in agriculture, work, law, social relations—were necessary for the English to become slaveholders? How did the English work those things out? And what, if anything, of the social and cultural world of the colonies was brought home? What—aside from goods—was sent from the Caribbean to England? What did it mean for Thomas to live in East Coker? How did Betty and her fellow slaves respond to their treatment by the Helyars? What did the English in England learn from the social relations of a slave society? Were there elements of social relations in England that developed from the social relations of slavery? What difference has the history of slavery and slaveholding made in the history of England? What happens when we view English colonial expansion not just as an economic process, but as a source of social and cultural change within English society? We can speak more easily about what happened in the colonies, but I will argue that slaveholding also had a profound significance for English society.

People in the seventeenth century did many things that we now find morally repugnant: they held public executions and mutilations, for instance. The enslavement of other people certainly fits this category. It differs from other such behaviors because the consequences of that enslavement remain major social and political issues in both the United States and Britain. The job of the historian is to create a "fruitful memory." That means that I am primarily concerned with understanding the ways in which slaveholding developed and its impact on people and social organization. By the end of the seventeenth century, the economy fueled by sugar and slavery was so pervasive that most merchants and investors in England (and indeed the rest of Europe) were in some way implicated in it. Only when slaveholding is contextualized and all its social and cultural consequences explored can we begin to respond imaginatively to the legacies of the actions first undertaken by the merchants, slave traders, and planters of the seventeenth century.[5]

While this project inevitably involves issues of race, the legacy of slave-holding is much broader than race alone. It has had a deep impact on the development of ideas of gender, of labor, and of work. There is little that multinational corporations today could teach the seventeenth-century traders of the Royal African Company about how to manipulate power to support their business interests. The sugar plantation was a far more advanced and complex industrial enterprise than any in England at the time, involving not only specialization but also shift labor and "just-in-time" production. Finally, slaveholding marked a new expansion of the use of state power in defense of private property, and the treatment of people as property. Following the trail of the early planters, we may find that many features that are defined as distinctively "western" can be traced to the sugar economy of the seventeenth and eighteenth centuries. This is in some ways a familiar argument. More than fifty years ago, Eric Williams argued that sugar provided the capital that was used for the industrial revolution. But discussion about the role of slavery in the industrial revolution has been primarily from an economic standpoint.[6] The social and cultural impact of the sugar economy lacks the concrete and measurable quality of economic data, but it is no less significant.

Historians need to pay attention to this history of slaveholding and the exchange with the Caribbean, not just because of present concerns (though these are important) but also because when they are excluded our understanding of early modern England is only partial. I have always been interested in the nature of social hierarchies and social relations, and I know how easy it is to naturalize relations of domination and thus make them invisible. I began my career studying the (then) almost invisible history of women in the early modern period. Most historians have now accepted that there indeed were women in the sixteenth and seventeenth centuries, and they have come to view the history of women and of gender divisions as a central aspect of early modern history. To study slaveholding, then, is in many ways a continuation of my intellectual journey.

The study of slaveholding, however, does present some significant challenges. First, because of the nature of the historical record, Betty's concern for her absent son must stand in for that of many parents missing their children; we might imagine her anxiety without the letter, but her voice has survived only because an overseer was willing to add the query to his letter. Furthermore, we do not have Thomas's account of his experience. By the late eighteenth century it is possible to say more about the impact of slavery on slaves in the colonies and in Britain, but in the seventeenth century we catch only glimpses of them.[7] While we cannot tell the story directly from the perspective of enslaved people, there are many sources that show slaveholders learning to manage their human property. These record the impact of power on the powerful, as well as on the powerless, and allow us to denaturalize the history of power. One of my central contentions is that owning people did not come "naturally" to the seventeenth-century English: slaveholders had to learn to do it. The seventeenth-century historian William Camden highlighted the novelty of slavery for the English by suggesting that Hawkins and other English sailors had only taken to slave trading because they had learned slavery from the (evil) Spanish. In the Caribbean, the English had to create new institutional and legal structures, reorganize work, and change their relations with each other. This was a profoundly historical process. Nor was slavery an inevitable by-product of European contact with Africans: while there were stereotypes of Africans quite early, they did not require that Africans be enslaved. Some studies of race have suggested that English racial thinking about Africans was modeled after their views of the Irish, yet for all their cruelty to the Irish, the English never considered enslaving them.[8]

The history of slavery and settlement is familiar to historians of the colonial Americas; it is less so to historians of England and Britain in the seventeenth century. Yet because the slave population of the mainland colonies grew more slowly than that in the Caribbean, the impact of slavery on white women has been located more in the eighteenth than in the seventeenth century.[9] Furthermore, few colonial historians have concerned themselves with what happened when people went back to England. As an English historian, I bring different perceptions and assumptions from those of colonialists. Furthermore, the history I am describing here is an "English" history as much as a Caribbean one. In saying that, I take issue to some extent with both recent approaches to the "British dimension" and Atlantic history. The "British dimension" is primarily a constitutional structure, not a social or cultural one: while there was one king over England and Wales, Scotland and Ireland, the three kingdoms were separate, and England was the one that mattered. People in the Caribbean made clear distinctions between the English, Scots, and Irish—they did not refer to the "British." The seventeenth-century empire is an English one.[10]

In recent years, there has been increasing emphasis on the concept of Atlantic history, fostered both by institutional support and some critical publications. My approach is consonant with what David Armitage has called "cis-Atlantic history"—and indeed the reciprocal relationship between two separate areas of the Atlantic is central—but I worry that the term "Atlantic" draws our attention away from the English character of this story, and its impact on people in both England and the Caribbean. It also erases differences between societies on both sides of the Atlantic. I share the interest of those writing Atlantic history with the interactions of the various peoples in the Caribbean and the attention to the ways in which ideas created in the Caribbean were returned to England. The Atlantic helps construct a set of dynamic relationships that are important in understanding developments in the colonies, and it also discourages excessive English exceptionalism. My focus is on the settlers in the Caribbean who still thought of themselves as Englishmen (and the ones whose records we have are primarily English and men) who happened to be living in the Caribbean and sought recognition as such.[11] Their insistence on their Englishness was accompanied by a growing realization that while they were English, life was significantly different in the Caribbean and that difference needed to be explained. But many of the tensions between the government in London and the colonies, and between absentee plantation owners in England and their representatives in the West Indies, reflect the ways in which things were assumed to be the same as in England and known by those in the West Indies to be different. The islands were simultaneously English and not English. While the concept of the Atlantic is useful for comparative purposes—and I have relied heavily on research done in the field—I have not found it interpretively useful in approaching the questions I address here.[12] My approach bears a greater similarity to that of Catherine Hall for a later period, with an understanding that the histories of colony and metropole need to be placed in one analytic frame, as separate histories that are deeply intertwined. Equally important is Paul Gilroy's conception of the Black Atlantic as the place where "the constitutive relationships with outsiders that both found and temper a self-conscious sense of western civilization." Both these approaches are interested in the Atlantic as a site for the operations of power.[13]

This project also contributes to our understanding of the development of the concept of race. This exploration brings with it serious challenges. The process of coming to see skin color as a central marker of identity began in the seventeenth century, and the process of construction illuminates the choices made at different points. Race as we know it was an emergent category in the seventeenth century, beginning to be actively constructed but not yet fully formed. Thus race based on skin color coexisted with other methods of defining difference; Europeans with dark hair and dark complexions were often referred to as "black." Seventeenth-century ideas of race are not only different from those of today but also from those of the later eighteenth century. The biological racism of the late eighteenth century—often represented through the work of the Jamaican historian Edward Long—was not present a century earlier. Recent scholarship has emphasized race as a social construct that emerged (variously) in the seventeenth and eighteenth centuries. While the images of Africans and of blackness in England were often negative, I will argue that it was slaveholding that pushed the English to move toward systematic racial thinking. It is important to watch this process but also to understand the alternative concepts that existed in the Caribbean.[14]

It is now 2007. I cannot write this without some awareness of the role of race in contemporary society on both sides of the Atlantic. In the United States, there has been public debate about the payment of reparations for slavery; in the United Kingdom, a series of widely publicized cases has put institutional racism on a wider agenda than it had been before. On both sides of the Atlantic, there is a lively discussion of racial identity. I live in New Haven, Connecticut, a city with a large (and largely poor) black population. To some extent this project seeks to understand how the world we live in came to be. The present offers important challenges, especially around the use of language. Over the past fifty years, language has been a central part of the self-definition of the descendants of those enslaved in the Caribbean and North America, as well as those who have come to Britain from her former empire. I have used the language of the seventeenth century in preference to modern usages. The seventeenth-century English usually referred to people of African descent as "Negroes," a Spanish word that both acknowledged the Spanish history of enslaving Africans and distanced the English from the people they enslaved. The use of the word "Negro" helps reinforce the distance between our expectations and seventeenth-century approaches to skin color and identity. The other seventeenth-century term, which I have also used, is "black." This word then, as now, was ambiguous, and in England (though less so in the Caribbean) it referred simultaneously to people of African descent, American Indians, and those from South Asia. At the same time, in England the descriptions of Charles II as a "Black Boy" and similar uses of "black" remind us of the ambiguous and arbitrary nature of all language that seeks to create categories of people.

These questions and my approach to them span many scholarly conversations. These include those about the "British dimension" and the "Atlantic world"; race and empire; whiteness; the origins of racial categories; the relationship between gender and race; the meaning of identity; colonial settlement; and the development of slavery. Each of these has a voluminous literature, which has influenced me and helped me clarify my own thinking. But they are not, by and large, literatures that are in conversation with each other. My notes will suggest the works that have been most important to me, but in order to make this subject more accessible to readers, I have focused on telling a story rather than responding to other scholars. This does not diminish either the importance of their work or my debts to them.

THE CHAPTERS THAT FOLLOW will provide a map of the process of planting in its multiple dimensions. The first chapter will examine English society, as well as its interactions with the rest of the world, especially through trade, as a framework for the early history of Caribbean settlement. The second chapter will look at the descriptive narratives of the islands written in the seventeenth century, to see what was most striking and novel for the English in the West Indies. These narratives—particularly those of Richard Ligon in Barbados and John Taylor in Jamaica—help define the central areas of difference between England and the islands, the subjects we need to understand to grasp the impact of the West Indies on England. The third chapter will examine planting, as both an economic and social process. What exactly did the English do? How did they develop the economy of the islands? And how did they build plantations?

The islands were more than 4,500 miles from London, and they needed some kind of government. The settlers were notoriously independent and resisted the application of royal power throughout the late seventeenth century. In doing so, they used the rhetoric of law and liberty. The fourth chapter will look at two central dimensions of the emergence of government in the Caribbean colonies. First are the tensions between planters and the royal government about authority and the use of the language of liberty by the settlers to defend their own rights as English men. Second, while they insisted on the importance of liberty, the planters slowly developed a legal system that denied liberty to a significant portion of the population, both white servants and enslaved Africans. While both service and slavery were understood in seventeenth-century England, the initial understandings of these relationships proved inadequate for the needs of the planters. The fifth chapter will step back from the formal legal structures to look at hierarchy and order on the one hand and resistance on the other. Neither slaves nor servants accepted their position without question, and the late seventeenth century is replete with not only tensions around hierarchy—between race and class, for instance—but also with resistance and attempted rebellion by both servants and slaves.

The sixth chapter will bring these issues back to England. John Helyar sent Thomas to East Coker; many other planters brought slaves home with them, as did sea captains. In addition, by the 1690s a black page was a desirable accoutrement of the lady of fashion in London. Some of these black attendants ran away, and in attempts to recapture them we have a picture of an emerging black community in London. Black attendants appear in paintings—mostly of the upper aristocracy—with increasing frequency. At the same time, the planter himself came to be a familiar if troubling character on the London stage, while a few moralists began to offer a critique of the practice of slavery. As the concluding epilogue will show, these and the more material exports from the colonies provide an important base for the development of eighteenth-century English culture.

Trade & Settlement

England and the World in the Seventeenth Century

They which go down to the sea in ships, and occupy by the great
waters, they see the works of the Lord and his wonders in the deep.
RICHARD HAKLUYT, quoting Psalm 107, in Dedicatory Epistle
to *Voyages and Discoveries* (1589)

The English who ventured to the Caribbean built on English social forms to
create new societies. Those societies emerged in a strange environment
where the English encountered indigenous people while they brought Europeans and Africans to settle. As they responded to rapidly changing economic opportunities as well as social and political conditions, they built on
English traditions and ways of thinking about the world and its peoples. To
understand the society they constructed, we must first look at the society
they came from. The English, whether propertied adventurers or poor and
desperate, arrived in the Caribbean with assumptions about how societies
should be ordered, what could be expected of peoples from other societies,
and the purposes of colonization. Together these ideas shaped their initial
experiments and the social order they created.

England in the Early Seventeenth Century

English society in the seventeenth century was marked by rapid growth of
population and increasing social polarization. The population doubled be-

tween 1540 and 1640. The rising demand for food brought prosperity to those who owned arable land but impoverishment to those who did not. English agriculture became increasingly productive with the enclosure of common fields and the adoption of new crop rotations. The combination of expanding productivity and a growing population led to structural under- and unemployment: those who worked for wages found it more difficult to find work, while they paid more for food. Many English officials were concerned about overpopulation, and as late as the 1620s there were still occasional years of severe dearth, when small harvests and high prices caused widespread hunger. The vagrants who traveled the country seeking work were seen as threats to social order. For both projectors and officials, settler colonies were a solution to the problem of vagrancy and overpopulation.[1]

The increasing profitability of agriculture created not only unemployment at home but also surplus capital for investment, especially in trading ventures in Europe and eventually the colonies. Merchants first attempted to strengthen England's position as a trading nation in Europe by maximizing the profits of the cloth trade. Although these efforts were unsuccessful, they signaled England's growing engagement in the European economy and reinforced the emerging political importance of commerce. For England, as for other European nations in the sixteenth and seventeenth centuries, the first and always most important purpose of colonies was to provide the mother country with valuable products to trade on the European market. Tobacco, and increasingly from the 1650s, sugar, served as leading products for English merchants reexporting colonial products. This approach to trade was a success: by 1700 colonial goods accounted for 34 percent of imports to England, and 45 percent of exports were reexports. Over time, English manufacturers and merchants also came to depend on the export of English goods to the colonies. All of these developments—in both European and colonial trade—contributed to England's increasing consumption of material products. More and more people in England consumed goods they did not produce—from food and drink to cloth and furniture. This "consumer revolution" gave many people a stake in England's colonies and their produce.[2]

It is a mistake to think of such exchanges entirely in terms of goods; people traveled with their values and expectations. The English people who migrated to the colonies had varied attitudes toward work, which had profound effects on their experiences in settling the "new world." On the one hand, the English shared with other Protestants a belief in the dignity of all "callings," work in the world that glorified God. On the other hand, not everyone was expected to have the same calling; status and skills differed. Hard work at whatever calling—whether as a landowner who managed property or a laborer who worked for him—was considered a sign of virtue. Yet manual work always had less status than work of the mind. In the 1570s Sir Thomas Smith defined those who did not work with their hands—lawyers and clergy, for instance—as "gentlemen." All women were expected to work: wives of farmers, tradesmen, and gentlemen managed the household and its many productive tasks; servant women and poor women did a wide range of domestic and industrial work and, in times of harvest, toiled in the fields alongside men. Even the wives of gentlemen and nobles carried out and supervised their households' domestic economies and in some cases provided medical care in the wider community. The work of the housewife, whatever labor was entailed, was a sign of her virtue: she was paying attention to her household rather than seeking pleasure.[3]

The issue of who worked, and who did what kind of work, became a persistent challenge in the Caribbean. Some of the early settlers in Barbados, as in Virginia, came from gentry families and were unwilling to work with their hands. But even men who would have expected to work in England assumed they would have an easier life in lands that promised quick riches. The gradual establishment of a system of labor based on slavery did not end disputes over status or work among the English.

English society in the seventeenth century was hierarchical. The hierarchy was rooted in the household, which was ruled, at least in theory, by a benevolent father; the household served as a mirror of the state, ruled by a beneficent king. In the context of the household, subordination was a function of age as much as status. One of the primary forms of education and training was "service," living as a servant or apprentice in another household. Almost everyone in English society spent some part of their youth away from their parents' home in such service. While those in service were bound by contractual obligations to their masters, they were in other ways free—able to testify in court, for instance, or enter into marriage. Most people moved from service to a position of greater independence when they married. For women, marriage and maternity signified social adulthood. For men, independence was a precondition for the full membership in civil society: independence required ownership of property or a business, as well as the establishment of a family and household. Those who did not have property left service when they married and worked for wages as laborers.[4]

While servants might be exploited and abused, they were protected by the observation of neighbors and by law. Indeed, one of the notable characteristics of English society in this period was the ideological role of law and the law's purview across all social relations. The legal system required the participation of many people of various social ranks. In each English county, quarter sessions met four times a year to try criminal cases. While the largest landowners, as justices of the peace, had the most power, many others had important roles, serving on grand and petty juries and appearing as witnesses to crimes or as constables, offering an account of crimes in their village. For better or worse, courts were never hard to find, and there was nearly always a court with jurisdiction over any conflicts. Borough and manorial courts adjudicated local conflicts, church courts dealt with conflicts over morals as well as marriage and probate, and at the assizes the king's justices tried serious criminal cases. In theory, at least, no one was above the law. In practice, law effectively, if imperfectly, limited the ability of those who were richer and more powerful to exploit or mistreat those below them. Subordinates were disadvantaged relative to their superiors, but they were not without recourse.[5]

English law limited the power of the state as much as that of individuals. "Law and liberty" were watchwords of English politics throughout the seventeenth century. Liberty meant, most immediately, that English men were free and possessed rights guaranteed by law. That law itself was participatory, quite broadly in its local enforcement and to a more limited extent in Parliament. In practical terms, English men expected to have their property exempt from taxes, and their households from pressing and quartering of soldiers, without the consent of Parliament. The central political question that emerged at midcentury was how far the king was bound by the expectations of his people, and how his behavior could be constrained. The king's power was effectively limited by his income and the small size of his bureaucracy: he had to rely on volunteer local officials to carry out his will. Whatever the theory, in fact the king could not act without the consent of most of the governing class. Still, the tensions between theoretical royal power and practical royal dependence on the governed were the source of repeated conflict.[6]

The prevalence of "law and liberty" in the political discourse of the seventeenth century generated an implicit notion of freedom that became more salient as the English simultaneously complained of "slavery" to various governments and relied more heavily on slave labor in the colonies. As a legal concept, freedom was rooted in feudal tradition, when a man who was free of obligations to a feudal lord could be a full participant in society. In the late sixteenth century, freedom was connected to the liberties guaranteed by the common law and Magna Carta and represented by the idea of the "Ancient Constitution." While the Ancient Constitution was a historical fiction, the notion of a government defined by long-established law was central to ideas of legitimacy. In England, slavery was a metaphor frequently used as the antithesis of freedom to condemn the illegitimate use of power. In the 1620s Thomas Scot had insisted that the presence of courtiers in Parliament would lead to "slavery and ruin," while other Parliamentarians argued that the Duke of Buckingham "would make us all slaves." Charles I insisted that he would "never command slaves but free men." In the early years of the English Civil War, Lord Robartes saw Parliament as the only way to keep the English "free men" and urged the army to fight to protect England from becoming a land of "peasants and slaves."[7] "Slavery" in this sense referred to the use of power in particular political structures: the absolute powers of the French king, for instance, enslaved the French people; so, too, did the English Major-Generals during Cromwell's Protectorate. Liberty was protected by the rule of law and restraints on executive power. In Barbados and Jamaica, however, slavery was a real set of social relations that denied not only freedom but also personhood to a class of people. The relationship between these two dimensions of the term "slavery" was a fundamental question that the English and their colonists faced and more often avoided.[8]

The English gained a perspective on their freedom through trade with other European countries, which brought them into contact with foreign peoples. When seamen and merchants traveled, they noticed differences between their country and the others. English liberty seemed to be based in England's common law, which was more participatory than the Roman law that dominated the rest of Europe. Trade also brought foreign merchants to live in England. These merchants were only the latest migrants to England. The "English" were the product of a series of invasions of Romans, Germans, Danes, and later Normans into a British and Celtic land; through centuries of intermarriage, the differences had largely disappeared. Throughout the Middle Ages, groups of foreign merchants had settled in London and other ports. In the sixteenth century, Protestant refugees from the Continent had settled both in London and East Anglia. These new arrivals had not constituted a significant challenge to English identity: they were European and Christian. After the Reformation, English nationalism and identity came to be entwined with Protestantism and, particularly after the defeat of the Spanish Armada in 1588, national pride was attached to martial valor. The stirring patriotism of Shakespeare's *Henry V* was not just a literary conceit; in 1628 Sir Dudley Digges boasted in Parliament that "in Muscovy one English mariner with a sword will beat five Muscovites that are likely to eat him." The political upheavals of the seventeenth century did not diminish the importance of Protestantism to national identity. The inscription on the Monument, erected in memory of the Great Fire of London (1666), attributed the fire to "a horrid plot for extirpating the Protestant Religion and old English liberty, and introducing popery and slavery."[9] Trade had made the English familiar with other Europeans and sharpened their sense of national identity.

The English knew little about people outside Europe. Through much of the sixteenth century, the most important source of their limited information was The Travels of Sir John Mandeville, a mid-fourteenth century account of the peoples of the world. Mandeville's Travels brought together a wide range of sources, some accurate and some spectacularly imaginary, and suggested that the far-flung reaches of the earth—from Africa to Asia—were peopled by fantastical societies bearing little relation to those of Europe.[10] In the late sixteenth century, English travelers began to publish accounts of journeys, peoples, and places in Africa and the New World, based now on the very real voyages that were taking place at the time. Sporadic accounts of particular voyages were followed by more systematic and far-reaching reports, most notably Richard Hakluyt's Principal Navigations of the English Nation in 1589. Hakluyt's compilation went through two editions and revisions before his death in 1616, after which the project was carried on by Samuel Purchas. These works, along with other travel narratives, were very popular at the start of the seventeenth century.[11]

These newer accounts included more complex portrayals of the rest of the world, with cultures having both positive and negative characteristics and familiar and unfamiliar aspects. They still included extraordinary tales of the peoples encountered on journeys, with bizarre customs described by Mandeville attributed now to real societies as well as to mythical ones. The most far-fetched tales were credible because there were few witnesses.[12] If Africa and Asia were unfamiliar, Ireland was not, especially since the Irish wars of Elizabeth's reign. The Irish had long been seen as uncivilized, though not incapable of civilization. In some accounts, the Irish had the same characteristics of barbarism, as well as some of the same bizarre customs, as Africans: they were wild and fierce fighters, yet lazy when it came to work. Although they were Christian, their Catholicism was suspect in Protestant England. The stereotypes of the Irish that emerged in English culture are similar to stereotypes about inferiors in many places. They were applied to the Irish in Ireland and followed them when they were transported to the

West Indies as servants. In this sense, the Irish were the first uncivil, racial "other" for the English.[13]

Traders returned from other parts of the world with material goods as well as stories. The goods, exotic and everyday, were often visible only in localized contexts: west country fishers who brought fish from the Grand Banks were unnoticed by merchants elsewhere. However, some notable voyages brought not just goods but foreign people to London, where publishers often printed accounts for wider distribution. In 1535 Richard Hawkins brought a "savage King" from Brazil to London; twenty years later, John Lok returned from Guinea with five Africans, with the aim of teaching them English so they could return to Africa to facilitate English trade there. Sir Walter Raleigh's expedition to Roanoke in 1584 returned with two Indians, from whom Thomas Harriot developed an alphabet and lexicon of the Algonkian language. The famous arrival of Pocahontas in 1616 was thus part of a tradition of bringing people from distant lands back to England to promote trade and diplomacy.[14] English traders in the late sixteenth century ranged from Muscovy and the Levant in the East, to Africa in the south, and the Spanish and Portuguese Americas to the west. The first English slaving voyage by John Hawkins took place in 1562–63, when he carried some 300 slaves from Sierra Leone to Hispaniola to sell to the Spanish. Some English people, then, had come into contact with people from all continents. The increasingly complex portrayals of the people found in other parts of the world mark a process of trying to make sense of difference. The accounts still include some fantastical elements, but other dimensions are clearly grounded in observation. The terms in which difference was defined—religion, culture, skin color, language—were fluid for a time and only became fixed through the process of building societies with ongoing relationships with those of other cultures.[15]

Those of us living in the twenty-first century easily think in terms of "race," which we define in terms of skin color and hair and facial features, or as a matter of ancestry. Yet the language of race as we know it was rare in sixteenth- and seventeenth-century English usage. That is not to say that skin color was not noticed, but it was not thought to define other aspects of character or personality. Even the term "race" was itself new and used most often to refer to a family or lineage, not to skin color. Insofar as race was connected to lineage, it was also deeply marked by gender. The meanings of skin color and the meanings of race were initially two separate sets of ideas. English participation in the slave trade and slaveholding later linked these ideas, but in the beginning they were distinct. And, for a time, difference was defined through other sets of terms.[16]

Throughout the Middle Ages, Europeans had believed that all people were descended from Adam and Eve and therefore were of one blood. The observed differences between peoples were understood as differences of religion, law, and culture, not matters of body or innate capacities. The primary distinction was between Christians and non-Christians. Distinctively racialized ideas did not appear until late in the sixteenth century, and even then they were not yet dominant. In 1578 George Best first described the skin color of inhabitants of Africa as the result of an infection that was passed on to children, "so all the progeny of them descended are still polluted with the same blot of infection"—an explanation that links skin color closely with religious ideas of sin and pollution. It was not until 1625, in Samuel Purchas's continuation of Hakluyt's work, *Hakluytus Posthumus*, that an English work clearly linked the sons of Ham—Noah's son, who according to biblical tradition was cursed for having viewed his father's nakedness —to Africa and used the association to justify slavery. Although the curse on the sons of Ham was a familiar part of European thinking, earlier commentaries had occasionally located Ham's descendants in Asia, rarely Africa, and they had not connected Ham's sin to slavery: slavery was the result of military defeat or religious difference. The link between Africans, slavery, and sin was forged in the context of England's growing international involvement in slavery.[17]

The concept of "race," as well as the word itself, was emerging during the sixteenth century. Race referred to a group defined by common ancestry or origins. The focus on ancestry meant that it was often used to refer to people of elevated rank, as in "a noble race" or "a race of Kings." Initially, belonging to a "race" was a sign of privilege. The voyages of exploration provoked new questions and provided the basis for beginning to think in new ways about how human beings might be divided. Writers tried to link geography and culture, positing an association that ultimately became part of new concepts of race. When people were described as "black" or "red" or "white," it might just as well refer to the color of their hair as of their skin.[18] In some cases, the valences of the terms "white" and "black" as they came to be associated with race were entirely contrary to expectations: Cary Helyar, on his first arrival in Barbados, trumpeted the virtues of the island by admiring an old man "that when he came hither was all white with age, and now is turned black again." Although he was ninety-three, he looked no more than fifty; aging had been reversed in the beneficent climate of the West Indies.[19]

The absence of an idea of race as skin color does not mean that negative ideas about Africans, or about "blackness," were absent from early seventeenth-century English culture. Whether English people saw the world as divided by religion or civilization, Africans were on the other side and by definition inferior to the English. However, because of the assumption that all humans were descended from the same ancestors, it was not entirely clear that such negative characteristics were innate or inherited. The negative associations of blackness prominent in English culture at this time were equally confused in their relationship to actual people. White was the color of virtue, black the color of evil; white usually signified beauty, and black its absence. These meanings, like all moral and aesthetic attributions, were mutable in their application. Most importantly, they were not necessarily used to reflect on people of African descent, precisely because there was no consensus that skin color was the critical determining feature of character. These rhetorical traditions formed the basis for the eventual negative associations between those of African descent and blackness, but the process of constructing those associations was slow and complex.[20]

As the English became increasingly involved in the world through trade, they encountered people of different cultures. One of the central tasks they faced was to find ways to categorize them. This was a gradual process, and the emergence of what we now think of as "race" as the most critical divider occurred in relationship to a specific set of social relations in the Caribbean colonies.

Settling Colonies

For the first century after Christopher Columbus's arrival in the Americas, the Spanish and Portuguese were the only Europeans to build permanent settlements there. The more important colonies were on the mainland, from Mexico and Florida in the north to Peru and Brazil in the south. The Spanish also had settlements of varying importance on the islands of the Greater Antilles. Santo Domingo, on Hispaniola, became a major administrative center with a university, and it was initially the meeting point for convoys returning to Spain. In response to incursions by French, English, and Dutch ships, the Spaniards by the early seventeenth century had moved the most important activities—especially for provisioning and gathering the fleets—to Havana, Cuba, which was more easily defended.

During the first third of the seventeenth century, northern Europeans began to move from piracy and privateering to settlement. The first permanent English outpost in the western hemisphere was Virginia, settled in 1607 and sponsored by a trading company; Bermuda was settled in 1612 after being discovered in a shipwreck in 1609; and in 1620 a group of Protestant separatists settled Plymouth Plantation. At the same time, the French were beginning to settle on the coast of Acadia and in the St. Lawrence Valley. Between 1625 and 1635, Caribbean settlements were established by the English in St. Christopher, Barbados, Nevis, Antigua, Montserrat, and Providence Island and by the French in another part of St. Christopher, as well as Guadeloupe and Martinique. The Dutch settled New Amsterdam (later New York) on the mainland, as well as the Caribbean islands of St. Martin, St. Eustasius, and Tobago; they conquered Curaçao from the Spanish in 1634 and sought to seize Brazil, as well. The shift from privateering to settlement in the southern regions of North America and the Caribbean can be attributed primarily to the influence of one amazingly profitable commodity: tobacco. Tobacco demonstrated that cash crops could produce wealth just as much as gold and silver mines. While not all the colonies of this period survived, the flurry of activity reflects the emergence of a model of colonization based on plantation agriculture. It reflected the two concerns that would shape Caribbean development for the rest of the century: trade and war. Neither was new to the region, but the settlements intensified them.[21]

Barbados

In 1625 an English ship under Captain John Powell landed on Barbados, where, according to Simon Gordon, one of the sailors, "[they] did hunt and take hogs without discovery, or hearing of any people upon the said island." The island was uninhabited; its Carib villagers had been killed or removed by the Spanish, and the island was overrun with hogs, the descendants of pigs left by Portuguese sailors to provide meat for ships. In 1627 Gordon and others returned to Barbados with a group led by Powell and sponsored by English merchants to "settle and plant." Like most other early English settlements in the Americas, the settlement of Barbados was the result of private enterprise. English ships had been sailing the Caribbean for more than half a century, harassing the Spanish on behalf of themselves or the English Crown. Some of these ships had sold slaves captured or purchased in Africa to the Spanish settlers; others bartered for goods from the Spanish colonies. Many years of trade, piracy, and privateering in the Caribbean had made English merchants aware of the region's economic potential, and they sought to profit directly from the colonial plantations.[22]

At first sight, Barbados was not a promising site for a colony. The island had the advantage of being uninhabited, but it was small and isolated. No more than fourteen miles across and some twenty-two miles long, it contained 166 square miles. Finding such a small island in the Atlantic was a navigational challenge, especially before sailors could track longitude at sea, a technique that was only developed in the eighteenth century. Barbados is the easternmost island of the Caribbean, eighty miles from its nearest neighbor. The temperate climate compensated for its small size and isolated location. The trade winds provide Barbados with almost constant sea breezes that moderate the climate. The south equatorial current made it an easy trip from either Madeira or the Cape Verde Islands—the usual stopping points on the journey from England. The Atlantic coast of Barbados is rough, but the more sheltered south and west coasts of the island provided good land for planting as well as sheltered harbors at Speightstown and Carlisle Bay (Bridgetown) that were to be crucial to Barbados's prosperity. Hills in the northeast portion of the island were not well suited to planting but could be used for raising stock or fruit. Little of this landscape would have been visible in 1627, however, as the island was covered with dense forest.[23]

English settlers arrived in Barbados under Powell's leadership early in 1627, sponsored by a joint stock company led by the Dutch-English merchant Sir William Courteen. The company sent settlers and supplies, so that by 1629 there were over 1,600 settlers on the island. The first colonists were employees paid by the company who gave the company any crops that they grew. Courteen and his associates acted without any royal grant to protect their interests. Unfortunately for them, they were not the only ones who wanted profitable colonies in the Caribbean, and in July 1627 one of Charles I's courtiers, the Earl of Carlisle, received a proprietary patent to the "Caribee Islands" from St. Eustatius to Barbados. Carlisle was working with another group of London merchants who had begun settling St. Christopher in 1626. Eight months later, in February 1628, Charles I gave a second courtier, the Earl of Pembroke, a patent to several Caribbean islands, including Barbados. Although Carlisle quickly persuaded the king to confirm his right to Barbados, the tangle of conflicting interests in London shaped the political and economic fortunes of the island for thirty years. According to the merchant Thomas Paris, in early 1628 the only settlers on the island represented the Courteen-Powell group, which also had the only political organization there. At the same time, in London the two earls were vying for the right to govern and profit from the island. In June 1628 the first of Carlisle's representatives arrived. The situation remained chaotic, with conflict in both the island and London. At times two and even three men claimed authority as governor. Settlers found themselves punished for their allegiance to a particular proprietor, abused by power-hungry governors, and bribed to support different factions. They learned to manipulate the situation by sending complaints home along with their produce. To gain control of the island, Carlisle's deputies granted settlers title to their land. By 1629 the Earl of Carlisle had gained control of the island, and his patent continued to be the usually accepted source of power; but the Pembroke patent provided occasional challenges, and later those acting for Carlisle fought among themselves.[24]

For fifteen years, between 1630 and 1645, the island's development followed two separate but parallel tracks, one focused on political and organizational development, the other on economic survival. The political developments involved apparently unrelated intrigues in London and Barbados. To gain favor in Barbados, rival contestants for power promised planters secure titles to their land and political privileges. These promises were the basis for the emerging government of the island. In 1630, after a rebellion by a former governor and indentured servants, Governor Henry Hawley formed a Council made up of leading planters, who ensured that the governor's policies would be amenable to those with the most land. In 1638, in the midst of yet another power struggle, Hawley called together "burgesses" to represent the freeholders to sit in a "Parliament." All freeholders with more than ten acres were allowed to vote, giving an electorate of some 1,500 planters. In 1641 that Assembly was formally integrated into the government of Barbados and given the right to initiate legislation. This structure of a governor aided by a Council, with a legislative Assembly, provided the continued basis for colonial government and for assertions of Barbadian interests in England.[25]

While the proprietors and settlers struggled to establish a secure political structure, the settlers also struggled to find a successful export crop. Virginia, just becoming economically successful when Barbados was settled, was their model. Virginia was sponsored by a merchant company. Its first few years were marked by disaster caused by disease and starvation. Soon, however, colonists were growing food for themselves and cultivating tobacco, for which the mid-Atlantic climate was ideal. In 1624 Virginia shipped 200,000 pounds of tobacco to England, and by 1638 the quantity had increased to 3 million pounds. Tobacco production required land, which the English seized from the Indians, and labor, which had to be imported. By the 1620s planters in Virginia had two sorts of workers. First were indentured servants shipped from England—poor people, including vagrants, petty criminals, and servants, who arrived in Virginia with the obligation to serve a master for a period of years. After 1619, with the importation of enslaved people of African descent, planters had a new source of labor. Although in the early

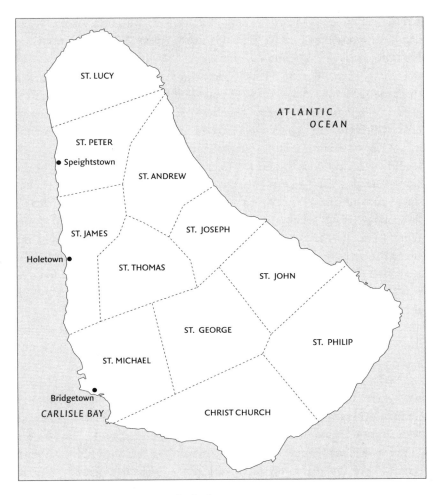

Barbados, ca. 1700

years the boundaries between slavery and freedom were less clear than they later became, chattel slavery was established as an important form of bound labor. Indentured servants and slaves performed most of the labor a tobacco plantation required. By 1625 the population of Virginia was 1,300; it doubled during the next four years, and by 1640 it had reached about 8,000.[26] Virginia demonstrated that export crops could be a source of colonial wealth. Settlers in Barbados, with their attention to a cash crop and exploitation of bound labor, followed Virginia's example.

English men in Barbados did not always apply great energy to their search for a successful crop; like the early colonists in Virginia, many of the first arrivals expected wealth to come without effort. During the early years, supplies were shipped from England. In 1627 Captain Henry Powell had brought plants and a group of Arawaks from Guinea to live freely on the island and teach the settlers how to grow tropical foods. The plants brought from the mainland included sweet potato and cassava, which became the island's staple foods for its first twenty years, as well as tobacco and sugarcane, which became its cash crops. According to Powell, the Arawaks came voluntarily, as their tradition said that they had formerly inhabited the island. Powell's promise of freedom to the Arawaks was soon violated by the settlers in their drive to exploit labor. The Arawaks on Barbados were enslaved and only freed in the 1650s, when Powell intervened on their behalf.[27] The colony was beset by the same problems that afflicted early Virginia. When Henry Colt visited Barbados in 1631, he was unimpressed: while the island itself was fertile, "would it were my own," it was not being adequately exploited. Colt arrived in the midst of a drought, a time that was known as the "Starving time." He attributed the hunger not to drought but to "sloth and negligence." In ten days of travel around the island, he "never saw any men at work." Barbados was wild; the powerful used force to get their way, and few rules governed interactions among people or groups. Colt noted that the "manifold quarrels" often had "slight beginnings."[28]

The first cash crop grown on Barbados was tobacco, but it was considered too coarse to be successful on the European market. John Winthrop complained to his son Henry in 1629 that the tobacco from Barbados was "very ill conditioned, foul, full of stalks and evil colored, and . . . taking the judgment of divers grocers, none of them would give five shillings a pound for it."[29] In 1631, ostensibly to encourage the Barbadian settlers to plant other crops but also to prevent a complete collapse of the tobacco market from oversupply, the Privy Council limited the import of tobacco from Barbados and placed a duty of one shilling per pound on it. Tobacco would not be Barbados's ticket to wealth. Planters grew wheat for basic provisions, but the salt winds damaged the crop. Throughout the 1630s there were also efforts to encourage cotton production—Colt noted that "the trade of cotton fills them all with hope"—and there was a brief boom in cotton prices. The boom was short-lived, as cotton required more capital than tobacco and much of the land in Barbados was unsuitable for its growth. While neither cotton nor tobacco provided the great riches that colonists dreamed of, both remained minor export crops, along with indigo and ginger, for the rest of the century. By the 1640s the colony was self-supporting, and some planters were beginning to make larger profits. When Thomas Verney settled in

Barbados in 1639, he obtained 100 acres of land and promised his father to pay back soon whatever was laid out in expenses; while he does not identify the crop he will grow, his expectations were not unreasonable.[30]

Sugar, which became the island's staple crop, had arrived on the island with the Arawaks, and its potential profitability was first mentioned in 1638. In 1643 the first known shipment left the island, and by 1644 sugar was seen as the new source of wealth. In 1647 Governor Winthrop of Massachusetts was told that Barbados was a promising market for food imported from New England, as "they would rather buy food at very dear rates than produce it by labor, so infinite is the profit of sugar works."[31] From 1650 onwards, the wealth of Barbados depended primarily on sugar, and its society was shaped by the ways the planters organized the production of that one commodity. In the first years of sugar production, Barbados planters had tenant farmers produce sugar to be milled centrally; in the 1650s, Barbadian estates began to move to the integrated sugar plantation, with its system of gang labor that was to be characteristic of production in the English sugar islands from that point on.[32]

In spite of all these political and economic difficulties, the population of Barbados grew throughout the 1630s. Even without a successful cash crop, settlers had enough to eat. The society the colonists began to build was initially similar to that of England, framed by a hierarchy based on wealth. Some new arrivals, like Thomas Verney, came from established gentry families and could purchase property. Other English men came as indentured servants. There was a relatively small number of slaves of African and Indian descent. By 1640 Barbados had about 10,000 inhabitants. About one-fourth were landholders, many with very small holdings. As late as 1644, there were only 800 African slaves in Barbados. Most of the work was done by the many indentured servants from England, Scotland, and Ireland, bound to serve a master for a term of years—usually four—in return for their passage. At the end of their service, they received a bonus, usually of money or its equivalent in goods; in Virginia that bounty was land, but on the small island of Barbados the land was soon all taken up.[33]

The population was predominantly male: in 1635 only 6 percent of those leaving London for Barbados were women. In the 1640s, even before sugar came to dominate the Barbadian economy, the number of slaves began to grow: in 1645 it was reported that planters in Barbados had purchased more than 1,000 enslaved Africans that year, "and the more they buy, the more they are able to buy, for in a year and a half they will earn (with God's blessing) as much as they cost." The expansion of sugar production intensified the demand for slaves, but the increasing reliance on slaves cannot be attributed solely to sugar production. By 1660 the population of Barbados was about 40,000, half of whom were enslaved Africans.[34]

Comparing Barbados to the other English colonies in the Caribbean helps to identify the sources of its success. The colonies in the Leeward Islands developed more slowly than Barbados; their settlers had less capital than the leading Barbados planters and their location made them more vulnerable to attack, first by the Spanish and later the French and Dutch, as well as the native Caribs. As in Barbados, settlers in the Leewards began with tobacco cultivation, then turned to other crops, including indigo and later sugar, as the basis of their export economy. St. Christopher, with its volcanic soil, produced better tobacco than did Barbados. Throughout the seventeenth century, the Leeward Islands had fewer English colonists, smaller landholdings, and fewer servants and slaves.[35]

The case of Providence Island, far to the west near the coast of modern Nicaragua, is particularly illuminating. The Providence Island Company was led by Puritan grandees in England, who sought simultaneously to place an English colony in the center of Spanish power and to build a model godly society. The company, whose leaders were notable for their defense of property rights in Parliament, saw the settlers as employees and provided them no independence or security of property. As a result, the island attracted few settlers and was unable to protect itself from a Spanish attack. It was conquered by the Spanish in 1641. Its spectacular failure, according to Karen Kupperman, highlights the factors that fostered successful colonies. In addition to the need for a solid economic base, essential conditions included secure land tenure, a form of representative assembly to take care of public works and defense, and civilian control of the military.[36]

By the early 1640s, Barbados had met all these pre-requisites for survival and growth. The settlers had gained effective title to their holdings in the 1630s, and that title was affirmed by the Assembly in 1643. The rents paid to the proprietors were becoming less burdensome. The government included a governor, a Council, and an elected Assembly, ensuring that political decisions protected the interests of at least the largest landholders. The cultivation of sugar had begun, and while the extent of the wealth that sugar was to offer was by no means evident, its promise was visible. The island was protected by a militia, which was controlled by the great planters. Nonetheless, tensions between the island and England continued. The planters, seeing themselves as Englishmen, wanted autonomy; authorities in England wanted control.[37] These tensions were exacerbated by the distance between the island and England and the time necessary for communication between them. In good weather, a ship might travel to Barbados in less than eight weeks, but the return voyage against the trade winds was much slower; it was rare for an exchange of information to take less than six months. Throughout the century, it was difficult for anyone in England to exercise real control over the island. Decisions made in England often reflected profound ignorance of conditions in the West Indies, and the difficulty of curbing the power of the great planters fostered widespread corruption.

Much as the planters in Barbados may have wished it otherwise, their fate was still closely connected to events in England. The power they developed during the late 1630s enabled them to take advantage of the political disorder in England during the 1640s. Finally tasting financial success, they decided that they would gain more by not joining either side in the Civil War. In 1644 the Assembly voted to cease discussions with Carlisle and his trustees. Although it briefly reappeared in 1650, proprietary government, which treated the island as a possession of a particular person, was effectively over.[38]

During the years that followed, Barbados's strategy of neutrality led to toleration of both religious and political diversity. The island's elite included men whose political sympathies in England had been both Royalist and Parliamentarian; in religion, in addition to Anglicans of various stripes, it also included Jews, Catholics, and later Quakers and other Dissenters. Richard Ligon, who lived in Barbados from 1647 to 1650, remarked that anyone who used the words "Roundhead or Cavalier" was punished by having to invite all those who heard him to his house for "a shot [of alcoholic liquor] and a turkey."[39] The goal was social harmony and economic success, not political uniformity. The French priest Father Antoine Biet remarked that "all are given freedom of belief, provided that they do nothing to be conspicuous in public."[40] The business of Barbados was making money, not politics or religion.

Political conflict in England, and the changes of government brought by the Civil War, Commonwealth, Protectorate, and Restoration, inevitably affected Barbados. The planters' shared goals were to trade freely and to govern themselves, but different factions advocated different paths to those goals. While some thought their independence best protected by a wealthy proprietor, others thought direct control by the English government would be better. Many feared any interference in the life of the island. Those with ties to Parliament hoped for advantage after the execution of the king, while a growing contingent of Royalist exiles sought to protect their property.

Rumors of plots against the island's independence were rife. In 1650 the Royalist faction gained power and expelled the leading Parliamentarians. Soon after, in a gesture of conciliation, the Assembly voted to accept Francis, Lord Willoughby, as the proprietary governor of Barbados. Willoughby had served first Parliament and then the king in the Civil War. He had leased the proprietorship of the island from the Earl of Carlisle and received a commission to be governor from the king. As an exile, Willoughby would be resident; thus it was assumed that while his title was proprietary, he would protect home rule. Willoughby promised to respect existing property rights, and the Assembly granted him a duty on all exports to support the government.[41] The planters of the Parliamentary faction, however, returned to London and promptly persuaded Parliament to retake the island. An expedition arrived in Barbados in October 1651, and after a blockade and a series of raids, Barbados surrendered in January 1652. One key to the expedition's success was the defection of Thomas Modyford, a former Royalist, to Parliament; Modyford would become an early governor of Jamaica. The terms of the surrender gave up Barbados's claim to political autonomy, but granted it commercial freedom, particularly the right to trade with any country "in amity with England."[42]

The defeat of Willoughby and the Royalists marked the final end of proprietary government on the island; thereafter, Barbados was governed under the direct control of London. From this point on, the official records of the island become far more complete, allowing us to reconstruct the patterns of colonial society and trace its development in greater detail. In October 1652 the new governor, Daniel Searle, called a meeting of the General Assembly and reissued the laws of the island, ensuring that a legal system was in force. These laws were described as a recapitulation of existing laws and practices, a confirmation of local customs. The legal system mirrored that of England, with modifications to suit the differences between the two societies.[43] After 1652 there were no major changes in the political organization of the island, though this did not mean a lack of political conflict. Barbados had a governor who was responsible to the central government, a Council made up of leading planters and merchants, and an Assembly made up of two representatives from each parish. Laws were enforced by a system of courts parallel to those in England, although in disputed cases appeals were sent back to England. Although the governor was appointed from London, the planters thought of their Assembly as parallel to the House of Commons. Their distance from London made it easy to ignore the power of the central government.

Though all factions had wanted home rule, they did not achieve it. The settlers learned this sooner than they would have wished. Throughout the 1640s, Barbados merchants had traded freely, particularly with the Dutch. The surrender agreement had sought to protect that trade; however, it was ignored by the governments of the Commonwealth and Protectorate, who saw trade as a way to enhance English power. In 1651 the Rump Parliament passed the first of several Navigation Acts, which required that goods coming in to English territory be carried in English ships and manned by crews that were at least half English. The act was particularly designed to limit the Dutch carrying trade to and from the colonies. The Navigation Acts gave English merchants a monopoly on trade to the island and put the planters in their power. The situation was exacerbated after the Restoration, when the Navigation Acts were extended to cover exports as well as imports. The control of trade imposed by the Navigation Acts was never entirely effective, but it was to be a subject of frequent complaint for the rest of the century. Both the planters and the English government sought an increase in trade, but their different interests led to ongoing conflicts. More immediately, the first Navigation Act was one of a number of irritants that led to the first of several wars between the English and the Dutch, which profoundly affected the Caribbean.[44]

By the middle of the 1650s, Barbados was the jewel of the English colonies, producing great wealth for its planters. It had an established society and government and a flourishing economy. But because of high levels of mortality, Barbadian society was always in flux, and fortunes were lost as well as gained. The relatively small size of the Barbadian elite fostered corruption and competition as well as sociability. The attempt to transplant English society in all its dimensions remained a fragile enterprise.[45]

Jamaica

The English conquered Jamaica in 1655, extending their colonial presence into the center of the Greater Antilles. In 1654 Cromwell's government had launched an expedition with the aim of gaining a foothold in the Spanish Caribbean. The commanders of what was called the Western Design, Admiral William Penn and General Robert Venables, chose to attack Hispaniola. The expedition stopped in Barbados for ten weeks in early 1655, where it collected ammunition and supplies, as well as 3,500 additional soldiers. The expedition against Hispaniola was the greatest military disaster of the Protectorate; the soldiers were ill-trained, ill-equipped, and badly provisioned, and the defenses of Santo Domingo had been wildly

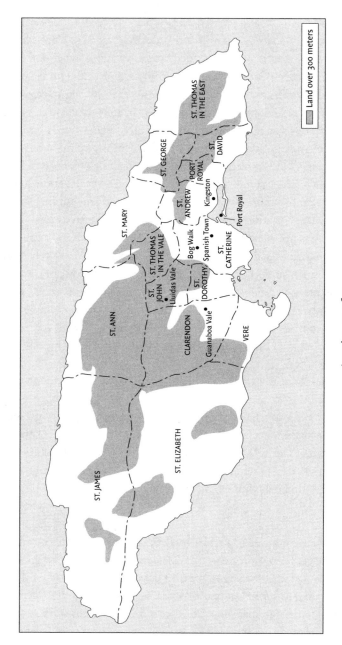

Jamaica, ca. 1690

Land over 300 meters

ST. JAMES

ST. ELIZABETH

ST. ANN

ST. MARY

ST. GEORGE

ST. THOMAS IN THE EAST

ST. THOMAS IN THE VALE

ST. JOHN

Lluidas Vale

CLARENDON

Guanaboa Vale

VERE

ST. DOROTHY

Bog Walk

Spanish Town

ST. CATHERINE

ST. ANDREW

PORT ROYAL

ST. DAVID

Kingston

Port Royal

underestimated. At least 1,000 soldiers died, primarily from hunger and disease. After the debacle in Hispaniola, Penn and Venables sought to salvage their reputations by turning to the smaller—and lightly defended—nearby island of Jamaica. The Spanish authorities in Jamaica gave up without a fight, and within a week of landing the terms of surrender were established. The Spaniards had the right to leave the island, carrying only clothing and provisions; non-Catholics who were willing to accept English rule were allowed to stay. Since a large group of Spanish settlers did not accept the terms of the surrender but retreated to the north of the island, the full conquest of Jamaica took several years. The struggle with the remaining Spaniards, and the slaves who had been freed by or had escaped from departing Spanish planters, was a guerrilla campaign fought primarily when groups encountered one another while hunting cattle on the open savannas. There were also more focused struggles against the Spaniards who had left Jamaica for Cuba, then made several attempts to recapture the island. English control was secure by April 1660. Throughout the conquest, disease was a more potent enemy than the Spanish: some 5,000 of 7,000 soldiers who had initially landed died in the first year.[46]

Jamaica is significantly larger than Barbados—142 miles long and 50 miles across at its widest. Its 4,411 square miles make it the third-largest island in the Greater Antilles, after Cuba and Hispaniola. Mountains, rising to 7,000 feet, run east to west and divide the island, making some parts unsuited for agriculture but also creating a cool region close to the tropical coasts. The land on the north side of the mountains is more fertile, but the north coast is less than 100 miles from Spanish centers in Hispaniola and Cuba; the initial English settlement was concentrated in the south and east, which was better protected from French and Spanish attack. The flat savannas of the south were suitable for raising livestock, which the Spanish sold more for the hides than for meat; the wild hogs were slaughtered to provide lard for mainland colonies. Plantation agriculture was less developed. Fruits—cacao, bananas, plantains, and citrus fruits—were grown primarily for local consumption, as was a small amount of sugar. The Spanish cacao walks and sugar plantations were mostly destroyed during the conquest.[47]

Despite its size, the fertility of its soil, and its strategic location, Spanish Jamaica was a failing colony. Its population was small, only about 1,500 people when the English arrived. While the makeup of the population in 1655 is unclear, in 1611 there were 700 whites, 100 free Negroes, almost 600 African slaves, 75 Arawaks, and 75 foreigners in Jamaica. Numerous attempts by colonists and governors to develop the island's potential—using lumber for shipbuilding, for instance—received no support from Spain. Few settlers were sent from Spain, and the ships bearing slaves for the Spanish colonies bypassed Jamaica, so the population was never able to move beyond subsistence. The settlers and their slaves harvested the products of the land more than they cultivated it. Because of the Spanish use of the convoy system, relatively few ships arrived in Jamaica, and the island's produce often rotted before it could be exported. The Spanish emphasis on precious metals meant that an island with no mines would never receive investment. In 1655 Jamaica was a weak colony whose strategic and agricultural potential had never been exploited.[48]

The conquest of Jamaica represented the culmination of the effort begun by the failed Providence Island Company earlier in the century, taking English colonization into the center of Spanish power, but it brought problems of its own. The terms of surrender required the Spaniards to leave, but the refusal of many of them to do so, and their alliance with bands of former slaves, shaped the subsequent history of the island. The African bands sought to defend both their freedom and land on which to support themselves; the Spaniards wanted the island back. The English found the chief city of the island, Villa de Vega, which the English called St. Iago de Vega and later Spanish Town, empty of goods, and they burned much of it. The freed slaves had taken shelter in the Lluidas Vale, a fertile valley surrounded by mountains. The English did not find the Vale until 1660, when they made their final push to complete their conquest of the island. Even then, the communities of freed Spanish slaves, known as Maroons, remained unsubdued; they retreated further into the mountains, continued to harass the English planters, and later provided refuge for enslaved Africans who escaped the plantations. Warfare against the Maroons, as we shall see, continued well into the eighteenth century. The Spanish resistance to the English was centered on the north coast, where the colonists could be resupplied from Cuba and receive provisions from their former slaves in the Lluidas Vale. While the army continued to fight a remnant of Spanish colonists and former Spanish slaves, English soldiers and settlers were beginning to plant in Jamaica.[49] By the time the Spaniards were defeated, English Jamaica was able to feed itself.

The process of settlement foreshadowed both the persistent conflicts that defined Jamaica's development and the English settlers' attitude toward exploiting the land. Initially, the army merely consumed what was available. When Major-General Robert Sedgewick arrived in Jamaica in October 1655, he found a miserable situation: the surviving soldiers were weak, many of the provisions had spoiled, and the soldiers had destroyed some 20,000 head of cattle, as well as fruits and locally grown provisions. There was plenty of good land available, but they had planted nothing, "so great a disinclination the officers and soldiers in general had for planting, or even to provide common necessaries and conveniences for themselves." Soldiers expected to be fed, not to feed themselves. Eighteen months later, the situation had improved: at least the army was in good health, although there was still an "averseness and disinclination for planting." Those who had joined the army from Barbados and other islands with the promise of land were particularly resentful that the officers were using them as unpaid servants on the land they settled.[50]

The transformation of Jamaica from a military camp to a colonial settlement was set in motion by a decision of the Council of War in Jamaica in October 1656 to divide the island for planting. The council assigned each of the regiments a portion of the "plantable land" where they were quartered; soldiers received thirty acres each. In 1656 the Council of War also recorded the arrival of several women to settle in the island, joining those who had traveled with the invasion force. In 1657 and 1658, settlers were recruited from Bermuda, Nevis, and Virginia with offers of generous land grants and help with defenses. Those who came with many servants got more land; in 1657 Bartholemew Harvey asked to get land in Liguanea (modern New Kingston) because there was not enough available for him at Port Morant to employ his servants. While Harvey came with many servants, the abundant land of Jamaica always held the promise of more opportunity than Barbados for men of small means.[51]

The ongoing war with the Spaniards and the Maroons meant that Jamaica remained militarized as settlement proceeded. Not all the military forces engaged in Jamaica were official. In 1657 the threat from the Spaniards led the English commander, Colonel Edward D'Oyley, to invite the buccaneers living on Tortuga to settle in Jamaica.[52] As a freelance navy, they provided an additional defense against Spanish attack, and they also brought the promise of riches from piracy. They stimulated the Jamaican economy, both by their booty and, more legitimately, by their demand for provisions.

The military and economic advantages of the alliance with the buccaneers were counterbalanced by serious drawbacks. The amounts of money won in prizes was more limited than people's dreams. In his account of Jamaica following his return to England in 1662, D'Oyley reported that planting was hindered both by the frequent demand for soldiers in military expeditions and the offers of employment in privateering. Men often expected unimaginable riches, "scorning the dull and tedious work of planting, whilest every-one thinks to get the basin and ewer in the lottery." Even more disastrously, when the men sold their land, they spent all their money in the alehouses and then left the island for Virginia to escape their debts. The possibility of easy money—whether from stories of sugar wealth from Barbados or ac-counts of a few successful privateering expeditions against the Spanish—undermined the willingness of not only former soldiers but also some new arrivals to do the hard work of building a society. In addition to the challenge posed by the Maroons, Jamaican society would long be torn between the quick riches of piracy and the slower profits of planting.[53]

Privateering, War, and Trade

The privateers were not merely a romantic sideshow in the Caribbean; by conducting trade through war, they were part of government policy. When peace was signed in Europe, they continued to harass trade for their own benefit. Their primary goal was to seize goods and make money, whether or not they had the support of any government. They flourished with the almost continuous wars of the second half of the seventeenth century. Since all the major European powers had colonies in the Caribbean, the region was em-broiled in most wars. The English governors of Jamaica and French gover-nors of Hispaniola offered letters of marque legitimating the attacks on the ships of the enemy of the moment. The English Republic fought the first Dutch War from 1652 to 1654; Charles II's government fought the Dutch again from 1665 to 1667. Although commercial interests in England were increasingly concerned about the power of the French, Charles II maintained his alliance with France and fought a third Dutch war from 1672 to 1674. In 1678 English policy was reversed, and opposition to French power remained central to English foreign policy for over a century.[54]

England was at war with France from 1689 to 1697; war resumed in 1702. Whenever war broke out in Europe, privateering and other raids between the islands grew in intensity. However, it was not until the Nine Years War of the 1690s that battles were officially fought in the Caribbean. The buccaneers were a blunt instrument, as they did not always stop action when the govern-ments at home signed treaties of peace. Sir Henry Morgan's famous expedi-tion against Porto Bello in Panama was highly successful but especially embarrassing because it took place in 1671, a year after peace had been signed between England and Spain. While the distance of the Caribbean from Europe allowed Morgan to argue that he had not known of the peace, the Spanish government was not happy.[55]

While the most important aspect of Barbados's location was its relationship to the trade winds, Jamaica benefited from its strategic position on the main route taken by the Spanish treasure fleet on its journey from Cartagena by way of Havana or Hispaniola back to Spain. As a result, privateering and piracy remained part of the Jamaican economy through the end of the seventeenth century. Until the 1680s, the attempts to control the privateers were half-hearted: Morgan, one of the most successful privateers, was even named governor of Jamaica in 1680. Only when Jamaican sugar production became a source of significant profit in the 1680s did Jamaica's leaders find that the safety of shipping was more important than the profits of piracy. Until the great earthquake of 1692, Port Royal was not only a major naval station and trading center but also a resort of privateers known for its rum shops, prostitutes, and thieves.[56] The Caribbean gold rush was now in Jamaica, and in the first thirty years of its settlement by the English, Jamaica had the same "anything goes" culture as had Barbados in its early years.

The Western Design marked a new phase in English colonial policy. For the first time, a colonizing enterprise took place under the direct control of the government, instead of through a private company or patentee. The already strong commercial focus of English foreign policy became stronger. This orientation was not changed by the Restoration of Charles II: a number of proposals were sent to the king to ensure that he understood the value of the colonial policy developed by the Protectorate. The king accepted these proposals, and in 1662 he sent his first governor to the island. Jamaica moved from a military to a civilian government, although martial law was regularly imposed for either political advantage or military necessity. While privateering remained a local industry, the land available also drew many settlers to raise both cattle and sugar. Yet there was always an edge to this: Orlando Patterson has suggested that Jamaica was marked by the "neglect and distortion of almost every one of the basic prerequisites of normal human living."[57]

Trade became the central focus of competition between the European powers, and the protection of trade was pursued by war. While the Spanish were the longest-established colonial power, they viewed the islands with their agricultural economies as secondary to the mainland colonies with their mines. For the French, English, and Dutch, however, whose territories had no mines, the production of staple crops for export to Europe joined trade in Spanish contraband as a source of colonial wealth.[58] This emphasis on trade reflected the economic theory of mercantilism, which saw the wealth of a country bound up in its products. The goal of every nation was to maintain a favorable balance of trade. Because it was assumed that the wealth of the world was fixed, the only way to gain wealth was to seize a larger slice of the pie. Colonies were thus an essential part of economic strategy. Competition—both in Europe and the American colonies—was now as much about the products of the land as the possession of land itself.

From 1660 onwards, the central commodity of the English Caribbean was sugar. The English produced sugar the way the Spaniards mined gold and silver; this was an extractive economy, where planters got as much as they could as quickly and cheaply as possible. Sugar was the most important export from the Caribbean and the most valuable colonial commodity. In 1660 England imported approximately 8,000 tons of sugar, primarily from Barbados, and probably exported about half of that; by 1700, England imported about 23,500 tons of sugar and reexported only about 40 percent of it. Consumption of sugar in England soared from 4,000 tons to 14,000 tons in a period of forty years; at the same time, the population of England and Wales was stable if not shrinking, which means that per capita sugar consumption almost tripled.[59]

The increasing consumption of sugar reflected the increasing production of sugar in the West Indian islands and the consequent decline in its price. Sugar was also connected with the consumption of a number of other exotic items—coffee, chocolate, and tea—for which statistics are less readily available. The addition of sugar was a distinctly European contribution to the preparation of these beverages, dependent as it was on the arrival of sugar on the market at the same time as the new drinks. The coffeehouses that sprang up in London—and later in provincial cities—sold not only coffee but also chocolate, which was produced in Jamaica and elsewhere in the New World. Newspapers announced meetings at both the Barbados Coffee House and the Jamaica Coffee House, underlining the connection between the colonies and the sweetened drinks. Samuel Pepys drank chocolate in the morning and at social occasions. Over time, chocolate lost out in popularity, first to coffee and then to tea, both of which were less expensive. Yet in the late seventeenth century, sugar and chocolate provided constant reminders of England's Caribbean colonies.[60]

At the same time that England developed a sweet tooth, sugar became increasingly important to English trade. This trade engaged many investors, often small ones. In 1686 some 700 merchants shipped goods to the West Indies, and 1,283 imported goods from the West Indies. These were often small-scale investments—almost 60 percent of those shipping goods to the Caribbean shipped less than £50 worth, and over 40 percent imported less than that amount. Family members of West Indies merchants frequently traveled to the islands, where they would, like John Helyar, represent the family's interests. The increase in trade led to a vast expansion of English shipping, port facilities, and other ancillary activities. In 1686, 275 ships entered English ports from the West Indies, and 219 left for the islands. The tonnage of ships involved in the American trade doubled between 1663 and 1686; in the 1680s, historians estimate that some 10,000 men were employed directly in transoceanic trade.[61]

The production of sugar required a large labor force. The English, like other Europeans, used enslaved Africans to labor on colonial plantations. This trend fueled the expansion of the slave trade, which provided additional profits to English merchants. English involvement in the slave trade grew rapidly in the second half of the seventeenth century. Between 1651 and 1700, English ships carried over 350,000 Africans into slavery in the Americas. Slaves themselves were only part of the exchange; slave ships took goods to trade in Africa and required food and other supplies for their voyages. The slave trade thus had a broad impact on the economy.[62]

As English trade expanded, ships traveled not only from major ports like London and Bristol but also from small ones like Exeter, Lyme Regis, and Whitehaven. Shipbuilding grew into a major industry; quays were constructed and served by small boats, porters, and car men. Colonial plantations, as well as trading ships, purchased provisions. Much of the meat and grain consumed in the islands was imported from England and Ireland, as well as from the New England colonies. Cloth, furniture, and most of the necessities of daily life were imported. In 1686 Barbados and Jamaica each imported an average of over £3 10s. worth of goods for each white resident; the English colonies on the mainland, in contrast, imported less than £1 worth. The islands were dependent on England for the manufacture of much of the machinery of sugar refining—the grinding mills, boiling coppers, and so on. Sugar was shipped to England in a semirefined state—it kept better that way—and was further processed at English sugar refineries. By 1695 a petition alleged that there were nearly thirty sugar refineries in England; there had been fifty in the 1650s. While it is impossible to determine the exact number of people in England whose livelihoods were in some way dependent on the West Indies, it was clearly a substantial and growing number and of unmistakable importance in port and manufacturing cities.[63]

THE ENGLISH EXCHANGE with the rest of the world began with trade. The desire for staple goods to trade fueled the settlement of the Caribbean colonies, and the sugar grown in those colonies in turn revolutionized English trade. The ease of documenting the volume of trade masks the complex process involved in building the societies that produced sugar. Growing and processing sugar in the West Indies drew upon and reshaped English ideas of identity. Within twenty years, African slaves constituted a majority of the population of Barbados; Jamaica was a slaveholding society from the start. With the expansion of slavery, English men and women used skin color increasingly to define character and ability. The rapid growth of the slave labor system meant a profound shift in social relations. Slavery transformed English ideas of law and order, gender, work, and property. The English settlers in the islands felt themselves beleaguered, surrounded on the one hand by hostile slaves, on the other by competing European powers. However much their goal was to recreate England, the production of sugar by slaves required them to create something new. They constructed a world where the wealthiest exercised power untempered by reciprocity, social relations were deeply exploitative, and no attempt was made to mask the use of naked force in social control. In the islands that provided sweetness to Europe, life for most was "nasty, brutish, and short."

Islands of Difference
Crossing the Atlantic, Experiencing the West Indies

Great herds of cattle mutually sporting themselves . . . you shall
find the strong and sturdy bull, the swift and nimble Spanish horse, the
harmless lamb, the furious boar, and the lascivious goat all feeding
and mutually sporting together in great abundance.

JOHN TAYLOR, "Multum in Parvo"

The journey to the Caribbean brought English people to islands that were
startlingly different from their homeland. The world they encountered was
foreign in both trivial and profound ways. The plants, birds, and insects
were strange. The staple foods and drinks were unfamiliar. Agriculture
involved not just new crops but a radically different way of organizing
work. Social relations—interactions within and across class and gender—
ostensibly mirrored those in England but never quite matched them; English
expectations were an utterly inadequate guide to colonial behavior. Everything in the West Indies was complicated by the presence of a large and
growing group of enslaved Africans. The accounts of journeys to Barbados
and Jamaica, as well as descriptions of the islands sent home by settlers and
newly arrived officials, are saturated with perceived difference and strangeness. They mark what in the colonies was remarkable or significant from the
perspective of England. Even as these accounts became more formulaic, they
remind us of how much the world of the seventeenth-century Caribbean

differed from that of England. In doing so, they identify the aspects of society that we must examine as we seek to understand how the English changed as they settled the islands.

These accounts were not necessarily accurate: they express the authors' hopes and dreams, and sometimes their anxieties and doubts, as much as describe what they actually found in the Caribbean. Newcomers to the West Indies, like other European travelers to the New World, sought to place what they saw in the context of familiar ideas, but they found their preconceptions challenged by new experiences. The genre of English travel writing often focused on the surprising, the exotic, and the bizarre. In 1665 John Style asserted, contrary to all expectations about the tropics, that English agriculture could be replicated in Jamaica. Henry Colt, arriving in Barbados in 1631, was less flattering, commenting on the gnats that made sleep impossible.[1] Thomas Verney attempted a more balanced approach, marveling at the "fruits that this land doth bear," while complaining of the "land-crabs" that so completely covered the roads at certain times of the year that they bit through shoes; even worse, the crabs were poisonous.[2] Governor Jonathan Atkins in Barbados found it difficult to describe the unfamiliar hurricanes to his English reader, so he created a battlefield: "It is a mutiny or contention of the winds from all quarters issuing, as if they were to dispute for victory one over the other, and comes accompanied with such vehement rains that the one washes the way upon the buildings for the other to ruin them." Sir Thomas Lynch, arguing for the advantages of Jamaica, asserted in 1683 that the island "is subject to no storms or hurricanes as the Windward Islands are."[3] Such differences are unusual: many reports about the islands treated Barbados and Jamaica in similar ways, giving little sense of the differences between them; the variations in the accounts depend less on the island than on the perspective of the writer. Almost all asked readers to pay attention to a world that was, for the English, profoundly strange. That strangeness was sometimes beneficent beyond imagination, but it could also be disturbing.[4]

All these descriptions had polemical purposes. Promoters wrote home to seek support for particular colonial policies; their descriptions come with suggestions attached. Royal governors who were expected to send annual reports on the state of their islands sought to show how they had carried out instructions, so their accounts were often repetitive and formulaic. Occasionally, especially at the beginning and end of their tenure, governors wrote of what they saw and what they thought the government at home should know. Some tried to challenge the reputations of the tropics. This was part of the message, for instance, when Cary Helyar described Barbados in 1659 as a fountain of youth: "It makes old people grow young again when they come hither." Sir Hans Sloane also noted the longevity of people in the islands: "The air here, notwithstanding the heat, is very healthy, I have known blacks one hundred and twenty years of age, and one hundred years old is very common amongst temperate livers."[5]

Two surviving seventeenth-century accounts are particularly useful, as they offer not formulaic description but acute observation, great detail, and an individual perspective. Richard Ligon's *A True and Exact History of the Island of Barbados*, published in 1657, is one of the most famous and influential accounts of a Caribbean colony published in the seventeenth century. It details his voyage to Barbados in 1647 and his experiences during the three years he spent on the island. While Ligon draws on earlier accounts of Africa in his descriptions of Africans in both the Cape Verde Islands and in Barbados, his own observations are perceptive and detailed. When *A True and Exact History* was reprinted in 1673, it was purchased by the clerk of the Committee of Trade and Plantations for his reference library; the work was also frequently cited by other writers.[6]

John Taylor's "Multum in Parvo," on the other hand, was never published. Taylor arrived in Jamaica at Christmas 1686 and spent less than six months on the island. In spite of his short stay, he collected an extraordinary amount of information. By the time Taylor wrote, the "Description" of a place was an established genre, and his work echoes Ligon's *History*. The repetition of information—and misinformation—suggests Taylor was familiar with other works on Africa and the Caribbean, including Ligon's. The manuscript begins with an account of Taylor's family, upbringing, and early life as a mathematician. His voyage to Jamaica and his voyage home are presented in the form of a ship's log; the log surrounds the more conventional "Present State of Jamaica." While the whole was prepared for publication, it is possible that it was preempted by the far more famous work by Sir Hans Sloane, *A Voyage to the Islands of Madeira, Barbados, Nieves, St. Christophers and Jamaica, with the Natural History of the herbs and trees, Four-footed beasts, Fishes, Birds, Insects, Reptiles &c. Of the last of those Islands* (1707). Sloane had published a Latin account of the plants of Jamaica in 1696. While Sloane and Taylor present the natural history of the island in similar ways, Taylor engages with social organization and local culture more fully than does Sloane.[7]

Both Ligon and Taylor were from minor gentry families; they identified with the planters yet were dependent on their goodwill. These men's social observations reveal the sharpened perceptions subordinates always have about the operation of power. Ligon and Taylor wrote as much about their own journeys and experiences as about the islands; they were as interested in social relations as in natural history. Both books are full of detail, thoughtful, and opinionated, as well as frequently self-contradictory. They offer an account of difference and strangeness that upholds the order of society but also interpolates observations that—if taken seriously—undermine it. A parallel analysis of their accounts, with references to others, provides a useful framework for examining both the journey and the world that English men found when they arrived in the West Indies.

We know frustratingly little about Richard Ligon himself. He was born in about 1590, a younger son of a younger son. The Ligons, a Worcestershire gentry family, were connected by several marriages with the aristocracy. As a junior member of a cadet branch of the family, Richard had to make his own way in the world; his inheritance lay in the family's connections more than money. From the text of the *History* we know that he had spent time at court; he also served as a man of business for members of the aristocracy. He was knowledgeable about music and counted the English composer John Coprario as a friend. Frequent references to the rules of drawing and painting related to proportion and color indicate serious study of art. Ligon was involved in the schemes for draining the Lindsey Level in Lincolnshire, and his property there was seized by rioters during the 1640s. During the Civil War, he served as a royal official in Devon and was in Exeter when the garrison there surrendered.[8] The difficulty of establishing biographical detail results from his relative obscurity, which may help explain the sharpness of Ligon's observations: as one on the margins of elite society, he was acutely aware of social signals. In 1647, following the end of the Civil War, Ligon was destitute; he decided to leave England for some foreign opportunity. A fellow Royalist from Exeter, Thomas Modyford, the son of a wealthy merchant and former mayor, offered him a place on a ship to the West Indies.

We know more about Taylor than Ligon because he begins with an autobiography. He was born in 1664, the posthumous son of a minor gentleman on the Isle of Wight who could trace his ancestry and property to just after the Norman Conquest. In 1685 Taylor interrupted his studies of mathematics to fight against Monmouth in support of James II, but he was bored by military life after the rebellion was over and returned to London to study mathematics and chemistry. In 1686 he published his *Thesaurarium mathematicae; or, The treasury of mathematicks*, a thorough textbook covering all the practical uses of mathematics. He also married that year. Soon after, when his wife was pregnant, Taylor had an argument with his father-in-law and decided to leave England to make his fortune in the West Indies.[9] Both Ligon and Taylor left England at moments of personal crisis, and both had resources that helped them on the journey.

Ligon and Modyford sailed from London in June 1647, bound first for the island of Sao Tiago in the Cape Verdes and then on to Barbados. In his first efforts to accommodate his experience to the familiar, Ligon relieved the tedium of the journey at sea with watching the "sport" of the fish, which he likened to hunting. In the Cape Verdes they were to purchase "Negroes, horses, and cattle."[10] The Cape Verde Islands were Portuguese colonies, a frequent stop on journeys to Brazil and the West Indies: ships sailing to the West Indies from the Cape Verdes picked up the South Equatorial Current and made a rapid crossing of the Atlantic. The islands were first settled in the late fifteenth century; the European population was always outnumbered by African slaves. The population of the Cape Verde Islands also included a large and growing mixed, or "Crioulo," component. Although the islands produced cotton and some sugarcane, their primary importance was as a supply depot for water, food, and livestock for ships crossing the Atlantic. Cape Verde also had a flourishing slave market.[11]

Ligon had a number of adventures in Sao Tiago that show how he saw himself in the world; they register the expectations of an English gentleman in his relations with women, the poor, and foreigners. First, some serious problems were caused by a "Portugal" on the ship. Bernardo Mendes de Souza claimed to own one of the islands and to be related to the governor, Padre Vagado; he promised the merchants financing the voyage favorable trade deals. He was evidently a member of the islands' Portuguese elite, since he later entertained his shipmates at the governor's palace in Praia. A change in his behavior as they approached the islands made the "gentlemen" on board uneasy, and with the assistance of Spanish-speaking sailors they discovered a plot to extort money from them. Throughout Ligon's account, Mendes de Souza is referred to as a "Portugal," rarely by his name. He is identified by difference, but that difference is among Europeans.[12]

Ligon also recounts several incidents involving African and English women. The first African woman he described was the mistress of the governor of the island. In his view, she was a woman "of the greatest beauty and majesty together: that ever I saw in one woman." After dinner, he wanted to hear her speak "partly out of curiosity, to see whether her teeth were exactly white, and clean, as I hoped they were." Ligon was impressed by her teeth, which really were white: the visual contrast between black and white was, as we shall see in Chapter 6, a frequent element in paintings of Africans. He was also struck by her graceful carriage: she walked "with far greater majesty and gracefulness, then I have seen Queen Anne." She was the "rarest black swan that I had ever seen." This is the language of courtly compliment, incongruous following the questions about her teeth. In context, calling her a swan is a reminder of her otherness. Ligon was impressed, but the muddled language shows his confusion.[13]

Some days after his encounter with the governor's mistress, several of the passengers on Ligon's ship went ashore, bringing with them "diverse women" to wash their clothing. While the women were ashore, Ligon reports, "The Portugals, and Negroes too, found them handsome and fit for their turns, and were a little Rude, I cannot say Ravished them; for the major part of them, being taken from Bridewell, Turnbull Street, and such like places of education, were better natured than to suffer such violence; yet complaints were made, when they came aboard, both of such abuses and stealing their linen."[14]

The account reveals significant aspects of Ligon's thinking. First, Ligon had a strong sense of rank. He distinguished between "gentlemen," "passengers," and "women." The gentlemen paid a premium for better accommodations and food, the passengers were paying their own way, and the women were either being transported or traveling to be sold as indentured servants. Furthermore, Ligon thought the "women," because of their poverty and history of sexual activity, were either prostitutes accustomed to rough treatment or so morally compromised that sexual abuse of them did not constitute rape. The women's complaints remind us that while Ligon spoke for the status quo, he did not speak for the women. Ligon left England with a view of women shaped by expectations of the social hierarchy; in this case, class trumped national or racial identity.

Ligon and the other gentlemen of the company felt no obligation to defend the honor of the women—honor pertained not to all women, but only to some. Idealized femininity was selective. However, in response to the women's descriptions of the valley where they had done their laundry, the gentlemen went ashore the following day. In an encounter that revealed contrasting cultural expectations, the local authorities assumed that they had come to avenge the honor of the women on their ship and were astonished to learn that they were merely sightseeing. The social distinctions that mattered so much to Ligon were invisible to the Cape Verdeans, while the Cape Verdeans' conception of collective honor was alien to the English. Having dealt with the authorities, Ligon and his companions arrived in the valley, where they saw a fountain and he watched "nymphs" filling their casks with water. Two especially stood out for their "perfections of nature . . . of such shapes, as would have puzzled Albert Durer, the great Master of Proportion, but to have imitated; and Titian, or Andrea de Sartas, for softness of muscles, and curiosity of colouring. . . . A word or two would not be amiss, to express the difference between these and those of high Africa, as of Morocco, Guinny, Binny, Cutchow, Angola, Ethiopia, and Mauritania, or those that dwell near the River of Gambia, who are thick lipped, short nosed, and commonly low foreheads."[15]

Because of his admiration for their beauty and grace, Ligon accosted the two young women and gave them some ribbon, for which they thanked him with a toast of water, but they were too shy to speak. (It did not occur to him that there might be linguistic difficulties.) He was surprised that after seeing the governor's mistress, he could be overwhelmed by the younger women's beauty: "Had not my heart been fixed fast in my breast, and dwelt there above sixty years, . . . I had undoubtedly left it between them for a Legacy."[16]

Ligon acknowledged that it was odd to spend so much time describing young women; he explained it by his former study of art and the absence of anything else to describe on the island. Ligon wrote as a titillated voyeur, regarding the African women as spectacles. The courtly language of his description especially suggests an ironic detachment. He expected the people of Africa to be different and was surprised when they met his criteria for admiration. His portraits offer an awkward combination of the stereotypical and the individual. He was not struck by all the women he saw, just some. He did his best to distinguish among them. He described the women as individuals and noted the differences between people from different parts of Africa. In other words, Ligon was able to recognize that African women were not all the same. Even if, as is possible, the two young women at the fountain were of mixed ancestry, he saw them as African. He was aware of skin color, but he did not see skin color as the defining characteristic of identity.

Ligon's brief stay in the Cape Verde Islands allows us to see him at the beginning of his journey, with English attitudes intact. He saw the world as an English gentleman and had little respect for the poor women on his ship; he certainly saw no reason to defend their honor. He was curious about African women, but in a voyeuristic way; he could see them as individuals and could see beauty in them. The distinctions among Europeans were as significant for him as those between Europeans and people of other races. This set of perceptions was challenged in the world of the West Indies.

As Ligon's ship approached Barbados, "the nearer we came, the more beautiful it appeared to our eyes." Ligon's first impressions were mixed. He commented on both the beauty of the island and the number of ships in

Carlisle Bay, "so quick stirring, and numerous, as I have seen it below the bridge at London." When Ligon arrived, Barbados was in the midst of an outbreak of yellow fever so deadly that within a month "the living were hardly able to bury the dead."[17] In spite of the epidemic, Ligon's patron, Thomas Modyford, decided that Barbados was the appropriate place to retrieve his fortunes.

Taylor's journey began less desperately than Ligon's. He had enough money to purchase passage for several convicts, who he would sell in Jamaica as indentured servants, and he traveled with introductions to various Jamaican worthies. Taylor, like Ligon, narrated the journey as a set of adventures, although it was fairly uneventful. Five days after his ship left Gravesend, while anchored off Dungeness, it was hit by a "violent storm," and the ship lost its topmast and foreyard. As the crew struggled with the storm, they discovered that the seventeen convicts who were being transported to be sold as servants had filed through their leg irons in order to escape. For the rest of the journey, the convicts were closely confined whenever the ship was close to land. By 1686 the transatlantic journey was almost routine, so Taylor's ship stopped at Madeira, the Portuguese-controlled island off the African coast, for only four days to take on wine and water. As they sailed from Madeira, Taylor mused on the habits of the sea birds he watched, wondering particularly where they slept and bred when they were, like him, so far from land. His musings were interrupted when the convicts, who had been given some freedom on the ship, broke into the stores, stole sixteen bottles of claret, and got very drunk. For Taylor, the convicts' behavior helped explain the harsh treatment of servants in Jamaica.[18]

Taylor records only one death among the convicts sent to Jamaica. Travelers were not always so lucky. In 1682, when Thomas Lynch arrived as governor of Jamaica, he wrote, "It is hardly possible to be alive and to have had more misfortunes than I have had this voyage." Early in the four-month journey, his wife suffered a miscarriage; she became acutely ill when they stopped at Madeira for water, and he had left her there on her deathbed. He became ill as soon as the ship entered the tropics. When he arrived in Jamaica, he could not walk and had to be "led" to his first ceremonial engagements; he was so ill that he could hardly move for six days.[19] As the journey became more common, the anxiety that accompanied it became ritualized. Hans Sloane, sailing with the Duke of Albemarle in 1687, suffered from sea sickness. To alleviate boredom, he made careful observations of the fish and birds and studied accounts of the early voyages across the Atlantic, as printed by

Hakluyt and Purchas. His journey to Jamaica took two and a half months, with stops of two days in Madeira and ten days in Barbados.[20]

We lack accounts of the experience of those who, like the transported felons on Taylor's journey, traveled in more confined quarters than Ligon, Taylor, and Sloane. Mortality on the passage from Europe to the West Indies was relatively low, especially compared to the voyage from Africa. The mortality rate among enslaved Africans on the "middle passage" was almost 25 percent. On voyages from Africa to the Caribbean, disease moved quickly through densely packed ships, affecting animals as well as people. In 1676 Abraham Lloyd reported the loss of 134 of the 172 donkeys in only twenty days; "a losing journey so far," he noted laconically. The stresses of the African journey on everyone involved are suggested by Lloyd's log four years later, when the mate and boatswain both threatened to leave the ship in Africa without "a rational word." They appear to have panicked about ever getting home.[21] In contrast to the threat of disease and insurrection on the journeys from Africa, the major challenges to those traveling from Europe were those posed by storms, or raids by pirates.

The Caribbean Environment

One of the first things newcomers noticed when they arrived in the West Indies was the warm weather. On Christmas Day, Taylor noted, "we had brave, fair, warm weather full as hot now as 'tis in England in the midst of summer."[22] According to Ligon, for eight months of the year the weather was "very hot, yet not so scalding but that servants, both Christians and slaves, labour and travail ten hours in a day." He alleged that unlike in England, work in the heat was possible because "we do not find that faintness that we find here, in the end of July, or beginning of August." The other four months were more moderate, with weather like that of May in England. Winter could only be identified by more frequent rain and thunder. Taylor described Jamaica's weather as "moderately temperate," rarely any hotter than July in England. Sloane, too, sought to reassure readers that the climate was not excessively hot but well suited to agriculture. Richard Blome countered common perceptions of the West Indies, reporting that Jamaica was "more temperate than in any of the Caribbee Isles" because it was more northerly. Thomas Lynch and Blome argued for the superiority of Jamaica as a destination, asserting that it was not subject to hurricanes; Taylor reported that hurricanes were less common there than in the Windward Islands. According to Sloane, the only time the heat was unbearable was "during the dog days" just before rain. The rains were "very violent and lasting when they come, the drops are very large." The air was "healthy."

The productivity of the land was even more remarkable than the warm weather. Thomas Verney reported to his father that the land in Barbados bore fruit "every month in the year."[23] In 1667 John Scott waxed lyrical about the island's natural and human riches: "Barbados is the crown and front of all the Caribbee Islands towards the rising sun; being the most east of any, and lies more conveniently than any of the rest for a seat of war, being most healthful, fruitful, and stored with all things of its own innate growth which are necessary for life; the greatest mart of trade not only of the Careebs, but of any island in the West Indies, being inhabited with many wealthy planters and merchants."[24] In 1690 Governor James Kendall was similarly effusive, suggesting that the land was shaped by the planters' work: "It is the beautifullest spot of ground I ever saw, the inhabitants very industrious." According to Sloane, "The outward face of the Earth seems to be different here from what I could observe in Europe."[25]

Jamaica, with its more varied terrain, was rarely described as simply as Barbados, but the descriptions were equally enthusiastic. John Taylor described Liguanea as "the pleasantest place on all the island, being continually plantable green and flourishing for seven miles together . . . trees are always loaden with ripe and delicious fruits, the earth filled with choice herbs and roots, and the circumambient air filled with odorous perfumes and the warbling music of ravishing voices, echoing from the slender pipes of the ambitious nightingale." Indeed, Liguanea was so lovely "that the muses themselves never enjoyed such shady sweet and delightful bowers." The fertile soil yielded a bounty of both European and American produce; "no part of America can outvie it." Liguanea not only sustained itself but also provided much of the fresh food for Port Royal.[26]

As they described the agriculture of the islands, newcomers made every effort to make it comprehensible in England. In the early years of settlement, observers commented on the prevalence of wild hogs in both Barbados and Jamaica. The map included in Ligon's *A True and Exact History* depicted the practice of hunting hogs, although Ligon reports that by 1650 the hogs in Barbados were all enclosed. The conquest of Jamaica created a new frontier; in 1664 "old soldiers" in Jamaica survived by hunting hogs, which they sold to merchants, seamen, and planters. Taylor provided detailed descriptions of how the meat was "jerked," or dried, to preserve it for use on the long voyages back to England.[27] Hunting was, of course, a familiar sport. Yet the context was different: while in England the game laws were steadily limiting access to hunting, in Jamaica hunting served as an entry into the colonial economy. When Ligon's old patron, now Sir Thomas Modyford and an experienced sugar planter, arrived in Jamaica in 1664 as governor, he reported that the profit from hunting hogs allowed some men to purchase servants and slaves and begin planting.[28] At about the same time, another observer noted that "the interest of this Island, as of all new settlements, is daily changing, provisions and all sorts of goods of the country produce being infinitely increased." Under Modyford's governorship, "people began vigorously to apply themselves to planting by the example and encouragement of the Governor." Producing provisions for subsistence and sale was soon joined by planting and cultivating sugar for export.[29]

By 1675 an anonymous official report described Jamaica as "underpeopled" and the settlement still in its infancy, but noted that there were seventy sugar works in operation and another forty in "a great state of forwardness." The author continued: "The soil is . . . naturally apt for all commodities those parts of America afford; also well shaded with fair and goodly woods, and timbers of diverse sorts, large pastures with pleasant streams, and incredible numbers of cattle, as well horses and kine, as the lesser sort, viz. sheep, hogs, and goats etc. . . . . The country affords great quantities of fish, fowl, and other conveniences at present, which gives great hopes of perpetuating and improving their condition to posterity."[30] This edenic vision of prosperity and plenty countered stories of cruelty and disease, promising riches for all.

While pastoral farming and hunting were familiar to the English, the cultivation of the "commodities those parts of America afford"—sugar, ginger, indigo, cacao, and pimento—were entirely new. Both Taylor and Ligon provided detailed descriptions of the growing and processing of sugar and rum; Taylor also described the cultivation of cacao, ginger, indigo, and cotton.[31] All these crops presented major challenges; English men had to learn how to produce them in a tropical environment and to obtain and organize the labor that plantation agriculture required.

To English eyes, the islands seemed so strange that many improbable tales were given credence. Taylor wrote that at night, the winds in Jamaica blew "at one and the same time from every part of heaven off the land." This had been reported to the Royal Society in 1668; two years later, that report was used to construct a set of queries about Jamaica given to Sir Thomas Lynch on his way to serve as governor. These included:

- Whether in the harbor "there grow many rocks, shaped like Bucks and Stags horns"?
- Is it "true that at the Caymans, the brackish water be wholesome for men, insomuch that many recover there by feeding on tortoises, and drinking no other water?"
- Does the urine of those who have eaten the fat of tortoises, which is green, turn "yellowish green and oily"?
- When crops are grown in saltpeter ground, does tobacco flash as smoked?
- Is it true that animals rarely or never drink?
- Is it true that in the Maggotty Savanna rain breeds maggots in 30 minutes, and is it healthy to live there?[32]

However absurd some of these questions seem, the publication of such assertions in the *Philosophical Transactions* of the Royal Society, and the society's interest in researching them, shows the conflation of the exotic and the bizarre in ideas about the islands.

The flora and fauna of the islands provide a central focus in all accounts. Richard Ligon did not tell tall tales, but he described the major plants and animals on Barbados in terms of difference. For instance, he places Barbadian birds in relation to those of England.

> The biggest is a direct buzzard, but somewhat less than our grey buzzards in England, somewhat swifter of wing; and the only good they do, is . . . kill the rats. The next to him in bigness is the larger turtle dove, and of them, there is great store in the island: 'tis a much handsomer bird, both in shape and color, than ours in England, and is very good meat. Next to her is the lesser Turtle, a far finer bird than she, but of a contrary shape, for this is of the shape of a partridge, but her plumage gray, and a red brown under the wings; a prettier bird I do not know.

Of the gray kingbird's song, he writes, "I have not heard any like her, not for the sweetness, but the strangeness of it, for she performs that with her voice, that no instrument can play, nor no voice sing, but hers." She sings in quarter tones, "her song being composed of five tones, and every one a quarter of a note higher than the other." This phenomenon surprised Ligon because his friend John Coprario had told him that no one had successfully used quarter tones in music. Ligon found himself confounded and entranced—and occasionally irritated—by the peculiarities of the islands. The ants were far more numerous than anything expected in England; Ligon noted that it was easier to keep them out of a hammock than a bed and described the various expedients used either to trap them or to observe their behavior.[33]

Taylor was also struck by the wildlife; his account includes descriptions of animals, birds, and fish. While some wildlife was relatively familiar, other varieties were quite remarkable. The sloth, Taylor reported, moved so slowly that its motion, though constant, was imperceptible. The colored plumage of birds was amazing. The "marcough" (macaw), "a most beautiful bird," was "of a green color, having his beak white, and of the same form like a parrot and his head and breast is adorned with beautiful azure, crimson and yellow shining feathers." The hummingbird was "the most beautiful creature in the whole creation," next to the bird of paradise found on the Mollucas. Taylor alleged that the female shark protected her young from predators by swallowing them and "conveyeth them down into a certain recepticule which nature hath for that purpose prepared in her belly, where they are preserved, and when she thinketh fit she throws 'em out again, and they swim after her."[34] Taylor was so confounded by the strangeness of Caribbean creatures that he could not distinguish the fabulous from the fabricated.

English visitors expressed ambivalence about the unfamiliar foods the islands afforded. According to Ligon, cassava bread, made from the ground roots of the cassava plant, "has not here the full taste it has in England." The corn meal product called "lob-lolly" (similar to grits) was served to servants but was hated by slaves.[35] Some local fruits were delicious. Thomas Verney described the "best fruit," the pineapple, as "luscious" and suggested that this was the fruit with which Eve had tempted Adam! Because it was so difficult to transport, few in England had ever tasted it, so Ligon carefully introduced his readers to the pineapple, "for in that single name, all that is excellent in a superlative degree, for beauty and taste, is summarily included." His explanation of how it was eaten combined the exotic and the erotic. The rind, which he describes as beautiful, had to be removed "like a Thief, that breaks a beautiful cabinet, which he would forbear to do, but for the treasure he expects to find within." The juice of the pineapple was mild, but when you bite the fruit "it is so violently sharp, as you would think it would fetch all the skin off your mouth; but, before your tongue have made a second trial upon your palate, you shall perceive such a sweetness to follow, as perfectly to cure that vigorous sharpness."[36] Such intensely sensuous experiences suggested both pleasure and danger.

In Port Royal in 1687, according to Taylor, the markets were "plentifully supplie[d] with good and wholesome meats" and "much variety of excellent fish, and choice fruits to adorn their tables, furnish their lady closets with sweetmeats and banquets with plenty of curiosities . . . neither are they wanting as to suitable quelquechoses for regallas [entertainments], as cheesecakes, custard, tarts, etc. which are here made as curious as those sold by our pastry cooks in London." The only thing you could not buy was bread. While the foods of Port Royal were familiar, local foods required an explanation. As Taylor surveyed Jamaica's wildlife, he often described the taste of various creatures. The flying fish is "very fat, and eat much like a new-caught pilcher." The flesh of the green tortoise "eats just like our English veal." The flamingo was excellent, especially "his wing is counted as a great rarity being broiled, for it tasteth more delicate than marrow." On the other hand, pelicans and "soldier," or hermit crabs, were "but mean diet," given primarily to slaves. Taylor noted that while the "wealthy planter lives here in full enjoyment of ease and plenty," the same was not true of his English servants, who were fed "only on old salt Irish beef, pork, old stinking salt fish, and cassava bread." A similar diet was given to "Indian slaves," while Negro slaves were given a small area of land on which to grow their own food, so that planters only had to provide "small supplies of salt fish etc." in "hard times."[37] The plenty of the island was not equally available to its inhabitants.

The strangeness of the food in Jamaica prompted Sir Hans Sloane to reflect on the wide varieties of foods eaten by humans. He emphasized that many staple English foods, such as meat, flour, cider, and ale, decayed quickly in the tropical climate. Meat butchered in the island had to be consumed rapidly, before it began to rot. Beef, pork, and fish were salted and preserved. Everyone in Jamaica, including servants, "both whites and blacks," had three pounds of salt meat or fish a week—a more generous ration than that described by Taylor. Raccoons, rats, and snakes were sold in the markets and eaten without repugnance. Most people—that is, servants and slaves—ate primarily local foods. Cassava, while closest to European bread, "is very different from that in Europe." Plantains, potatoes, and yams were also staples. Chocolate was drunk in the morning, but Sloane found it "nauseous, and hard of digestion"; he was puzzled that infants and children in Jamaica drank it "as commonly as in England they feed on milk."[38]

Thomas Tryon, in his *Friendly Advice to the Gentlemen-Planters of the East and West Indies* (1684), turned the strangeness of the foods into an argument for his vegetarian diet. He complained that the medicinal virtues of pineapple were not properly appreciated because they were mostly eaten between meals, "to pleasure wanton appetite and depraved senses." He argued that the chief mistake settlers made was trying to maintain an English diet; instead, he suggested, they should eat native plants, herbs, and fruits that are "easy of digestion." Indeed, in any location the best diet was a local one. Following such a diet, he argued, allowed Brahmans in India to live to age 120. He concluded that intemperance, not climate, was the chief challenge to the health of inhabitants of the tropics.[39]

Caribbean Society

Descriptions of the islands use the strangeness of the flora, fauna, and foods as a prelude to the strangeness of social relations. While nature was largely beneficent, the strangeness of society provoked more anxiety. Society was described in relation to the familiar, but it was undeniably different. According to Ligon, Barbados society consisted of "masters, servants, and slaves"—though Ligon himself fit into none of the groups he listed, and free white laborers are conspicuously absent. This was not a stable society: planters built their houses "in the manner of fortifications" in case of an "uproar or commotion" by slaves or Christian servants. According to Ligon, servants were treated worse than slaves because masters had no interest in preserving their health.[40] The instability of Barbadian society resulted not just from its newness but from the distinctive set of social relations that sustained its increasing economic prosperity.

When he arrived in Barbados in 1647, Ligon's patron, Thomas Modyford, was able to buy half of a settled plantation of 500 acres, with some 200 acres in sugar, twenty-eight servants, and ninety-six slaves. By purchasing an established plantation, Modyford avoided the cost and time needed for clearing and settling one. Ligon helped Modyford manage the plantation. They arrived in the middle of the "sugar revolution." While sugar was among the crops carried by the Arawaks that Henry Powell had brought to the island in 1627, the first concrete evidence of sugar production comes from the early 1640s. English planters quickly embraced this new export crop. The early years of sugar production required much experimentation, but in less than twenty years, Barbados changed from a society with many small planters working at a subsistence level, assisted by white indentured servants, to a plantation economy centered on large estates worked by African slaves. Historians estimate that the population of Barbados rose from about 10,000 mostly white inhabitants in 1640 to a total of about 40,000 in 1660, half of whom were slaves. Ligon knew that a transformation was under way: when he first arrived, "the great work of sugar-making" was new to the island and, "the secrets of the work being not well understood," they only made bad sugar; by the time he left in 1650, sugar production was better understood and Barbados was producing more marketable sugar.[41]

Sugar production required a complex set of skills, and sugar plantations were industrial complexes. Because sugarcane spoils if it is not processed rapidly, West Indian planters built their own mills and boiling houses. Ligon provided detailed descriptions of sugar production, diagrams of a sugar mill, and a calculation that showed how someone who arrived in Barbados with £3,000 could, within a few years, purchase a plantation for £14,000 that would soon be making an annual profit of £7,516. While actual enterprises rarely realized the profits Ligon's calculations project, the wealth generated by sugar in Barbados in the early years was staggering. In Jamaica, sugar production began soon after the conquest, brought by Modyford when he became governor. According to one observer, "a sugar work with 60 Negroes is capable of making more profit than one with a hundred in any of the Caribee Islands, by reason the soil is new."[42] For Ligon and many other observers, the potential for wealth was the reason to go to the Caribbean.

The promise of wealth had problematic as well as benign implications. Ligon provides the first version of the story of the Indian woman Yarico, who rescued an English man from her people; when the ship that rescued them came to Barbados, the man "forgot the kindness of the poor maid" and "sold her for a slave, who was as free born as he."[43] Taylor believed that life in Jamaica was driven—and corrupted—by greed. It began with the conquest of Jamaica: "The sacred hunger of gold is that which spurs men on to the most desperate attempts which can be proposed or imagined: what is that which makes monarchs disagree, but ambition, and avarice? This gold was the bait which stirred up Oliver [Cromwell]." Taylor develops his critique through a series of three ghost stories featuring men in the "enchanted places" of Jamaica who have visions of Spanish gold that mysteriously vanishes. In the first, hunters turned from a cave with bound chests to catch a wild boar, only to find the cave had disappeared. In a second incident, a man saw two jars on the road and found them too heavy to lift, so he assumed they contained Spanish dollars. He went to get a drink of water, but when he returned the jars were gone, although the marks they had made in the sand remained. In the third and most intriguing story, the first English child born in Jamaica—now grown to manhood—was in the woods with a companion when they saw a man in Spanish dress. They followed him to a large Spanish-style house, where he and a Franciscan friar stood by a table laden with gold and silver. When one of the English men claimed all the gold and silver, everything vanished: the Spanish man, the Franciscan, the house, and the treasure. In addition to these stories of disappearing treasure, Taylor reported "apparitions of Spanish Cavaliers," sounds of music from a ruined monastery, and visions of houses in the woods. While the enchantments are not always about greed, Taylor suggests that men were too easily tempted by the lure of riches—and that wealth was not what it seemed.[44]

Ligon was less interested in moral judgment than Taylor and more concerned with showing that social relations in Barbados replicated those in England. He worked hard to place various people in Barbados into familiar categories. Ligon praised the masters effusively; indeed, he could not "say half of what they deserve. They are men of great abilities and parts." The management of their plantations, which required careful planning and provision for numerous workers, was an indication of both their managerial abilities and their good intentions. While great wealth could be acquired in Barbados, it came, Ligon insisted, from hard work. The planters' dispositions were "compliable in a high degree to all virtues, that those of the best sort of Gentlemen call excellent," including hospitality, helpfulness, and civility to one another. Ligon described in great detail the elaborate feasts provided by leading planters to their neighbors. They were English gentlemen who happened to be in Barbados.[45]

Taylor was not as sure as Ligon about the hard work done by the planters, although he was greatly impressed by their wealth. In Port Royal "the merchants and gentry live here to the height of splendor." But moral disorder prevailed: "debauched wild blades" and a "crew of vile strumpets and common prostitutes" filled the town "with all manner of debauchery." In Spanish Town, the inhabitants "spend their time in ease and pleasure, having English servants to manage their chief affair[s] and supervise their Negro slaves, which not only wait on them, but also do their work both in their houses and plantations, bringing great profit to the planters." In Liguanea, "the garden of Jamaica," the planters "live extremely happy by the enjoyment of each other's company." They enjoyed a full range of sports, from hunting to archery, and lived "in full enjoyment of ease and plenty." Likening the colonial masters to the English gentry, Taylor remarked on the "sweet pleasures which the country gentry enjoy." But he observed pointedly that the Caribbean planters' "ease and plenty" came at the expense of others, "not considering his poor slaves . . . for by the pains of their vassals they become rich." Taylor knew that the pleasures of the masters came at a price.[46]

The work of the planters, according to both Ligon and Taylor, was managerial. Overseeing the work of the plantation entailed ensuring that all tasks were accomplished at the appropriate time, that there was enough provision for the slaves, and that the mills were in adequate shape for making sugar. The actual work of weeding, planting, harvesting, and making sugar was done by English servants and African slaves.

The harsh treatment of servants in Barbados was notorious in England before Ligon wrote, publicized through letters sent home by settlers and indentured servants who migrated there voluntarily, as well as through accounts of people who had been kidnapped and sold as servants.[47] This well-deserved reputation complicated Ligon's admiring portrait of planters. Cruelty to servants was, he argued, an individual rather than a systemic failing. "Those [masters] that are merciful, treat their servants, well . . . and give them such work, as is not unfit for Christians to do. But if masters be cruel, the servants have very wearisome and miserable lives. . . . I have seen such cruelty there done to servants, as I did not think one Christian could have done to another." Cruel masters did not provide adequate clothing, shelter, or food, required excessive physical labor, and punished servants with frequent severe beatings. Others decided that they would be more successful if they treated their servants with kindness. Some masters provided servants with no "bone meat" (fresh as opposed to dried meat), or did so only when cattle died; others provided bone meat as often as twice a week. Servants responded to bad masters by plotting rebellion. In his description of one such plot, Ligon reported that the servants "were not able to endure such slavery." His thinking involved two sets of categories, which he expected to be parallel: non-Christians and Christians, and slave and free. Cruel masters behaved toward Christian servants in a way that would have been unacceptable in England. Indeed, as we shall see in Chapter 4, they probably treated their servants no better than they did their slaves. In Ligon's estimation, servants' treatment was "worse" than that of slaves. African slaves, he thought, did not deserve the respect and rights due to Englishmen, so treating servants like slaves was a greater insult.[48]

Ligon tried to defend the planters from accusations of cruelty to servants, but Taylor was shocked by the condition of servants in Jamaica. He began his discussion of the treatment of servants by saying that planters were "very severe" to their English servants. They were not forced to work the fields as slaves were, but "they are kept very hard to their labour . . . so that they are little better than slaves." While the masters lived "at ease," the servants worked hard outdoors, "almost burnt up with the sun and stung to death by tormenting insects." Their food was inadequate, their housing "mean," their clothing "poor." Servants were rarely given adequate clothing and shoes. Women servants received proper clothing only if they were "kept in the planter's family" as well as "handsome and kind"—that is, sexually available. In one such case, Taylor remarked pointedly, "her master clothes her well and her mistress bestows many curses on her and blows to the bargain." Sexual exploitation was not unique to Jamaica, but Taylor saw it as a major problem there. When English servants were sick, masters took less care of them than of slaves, "and when dead, no more ceremony at their funeral than if they were to bury a dog." By various stratagems, the four years' service—"or rather slavery"—owed by servants was often extended, so that "many never become free men." Their treatment made them effectively slaves. Taylor was certain that servants "repent their rash adventures in coming from England."[49] The judgments of cruelty and beneficence were subjective, and it is impossible to be sure at this distance exactly what was meant; but both Ligon and Taylor were distressed by the treatment of servants, which violated commonly held English standards.

Ligon argued that slaves, like most servants, were well treated by their masters. This assertion is part of his argument for the benevolence of Barbadian planters. Yet Ligon's account of the slaves and their treatment is full of paradox and contradiction. For instance, he confidently announced that slaves, unlike servants, did not rebel. This was somewhat surprising, he noted, since Africans are a "bloody people." Ligon gave three reasons for their failure to rebel: first, slaves were kept away from weapons; second, they were kept in "such awe and slavery, as they are fearful to appear in any daring act"; and finally, because they came from different areas of Africa, they could not understand each other and thus could not conspire together. Yet he recounted one planned rebellion on a plantation, and another on a slave ship on its way from Africa to Barbados. The good treatment he alleged in general was combined with an awareness of cruelty and poor treatment in numerous particular cases.[50]

Ligon was so surprised by the planters' refusal to allow the slaves to become Christian that he mentioned it twice. In order to sustain his argument, almost everything Ligon wrote about slaves is given a stated meaning opposite to its apparent significance. Thus, his account of a plan by slaves to destroy a plantation by arson ends up demonstrating the loyalty of the slaves: not only did some of them reveal the plot, but they also refused to be rewarded for doing that which they considered their duty. Ligon could not ignore what he saw, but he could not fully acknowledge that slaves wanted their freedom.[51]

Situated in the midst of an account of natural strangeness, Ligon's account of the enslaved population of Barbados circles around strangeness. A keen observer of customs, he recorded some of the slaves' cultural practices. For instance, he reported that enslaved men wanted wives and insisted that their masters have as many female as male slaves, so all could be married. Once married, men were jealous. Because they believed that the birth of twins could only result from a woman having sex with two men, mothers of twins were assumed to have been unfaithful and were hanged by their husbands, he reported. Ligon found the Africans' notion of resurrection peculiar: they believed that on their death, they would return to their homeland. Ligon maintained that because of this belief, slaves who feared punishment would commit suicide. In fact, suicide was almost unknown in African societies; Ligon's account reflects the beliefs of most African religions that the souls of the dead return to their ancestors.[52]

Ligon's misinterpretation highlights the pressure that Caribbean slavery placed on African culture. His distortions are telling ones. The suicides Ligon reports—and the resistance to enslavement they represent—demonstrated to Ligon the desire for liberty among the enslaved. Yet Ligon was blind to the implications of this desire for his benign interpretation of slavery. The beliefs about the mothers of twins and about resurrection that he recorded threatened planters with a loss of property. Ligon focused on the peculiarity of slave beliefs and the clever ways in which planters responded to protect their property.[53]

In the process of describing the strangeness of enslaved people, Ligon made critical contributions to the development of racial stereotypes. The word "pickaninny" to describe slave children—a term used by their mothers —is recorded for the first time in Ligon's account. He offers many images that later became part of the stereotypes of enslaved Africans in the English Americas. "They are a happy people, whom so little contents." They were deeply devoted to their music, made by drums that provided a surprising amount of tonal variation: Ligon was unaware of the spiritual role of drums in African cultures. They were physically strong, both in their work and in swimming. "Religion they know none, yet most of them acknowledge a God." Although they wore few or no clothes, they were modest and chaste: "They never cast their eyes toward the parts that ought to be covered."[54]

These representations, developed as Ligon tried to make sense of unfamiliar people in a strange world, were not entirely negative. They drew on both previous European descriptions of West Africans and his own observations of Africans in the Caribbean. His view was ambivalent: he admired some aspects of the emerging Afro-Caribbean slave culture and acknowledged the talents of individual slaves, but he could not place them in the same category as English men. For instance, Macow, the chief musician of the plantation, heard and saw Ligon playing the theorbo, a lute-like instrument; several days later, Ligon found him trying to build his own version of the instrument, so he gave Macow further instruction, concluding, "I say this much to let you see that some of these people are capable of learning Arts." A slave called Sambo was curious about the workings of his compass, so Ligon explained the principle of magnetic north. Sambo was fascinated and asked that he might become a Christian, since he thought "to be a Christian was to be endued with all those knowledges he wanted." Ligon protested that he was unable to do this, since the slave owners feared that if slaves became Christian, they would gain their freedom.[55]

In spite of his particular descriptions of individual slaves—all of whom, importantly, were men—Ligon's account is full of generalizations. He speaks of the slaves as "these people." They are, "the most of them as near beasts as may be, setting their souls aside." Ligon's tendency to see slaves as a group more than as individuals is especially evident in his descriptions of the bodies of enslaved people. While in the Cape Verdes, Ligon had described individual bodies; in Barbados, the physical characteristics were of the group: "The men . . . are very well timber'd, that is, broad between the shoulders, full breasted, well filleted, and clean legged, and may hold good with Albert Durer rules. . . . But the women not." The women failed to meet his aesthetic standards because their hips were too narrow. His assessments were not just aesthetic; body types were judged like horseflesh, for their strength and power.[56]

Perhaps the most profound transformation of Ligon's view is revealed by his fixation on black women's breasts. While his description of African women in the Cape Verde Islands was voyeuristic, in Barbados it became pornographic. The strangeness of Barbados permitted Ligon to write about enslaved women in a way that would have been unthinkable in relation to English women of any class. Unlike the two young women he had admired in Sao Tiago, whose breasts he described admiringly as "round, firm, and beautifully shaped," the slave women's breasts were novelties. Young women's breasts were large, but "strutting out so hard and firm, as no leaping, jumping, or stirring will cause them to shake any more, than the brawnes of their arms." The reference to the strength of their arms reminds readers of their work. All this changed with age, when labor and child-bearing had taken their toll. Then—in one of the more frequently cited passages from his work—Ligon reported, "Their breasts hang down below their navels, so that when they stoop at their common work of weeding, they hang almost down

Crossing the Atlantic, Experiencing the West Indies [63]

to the ground, that at a distance you would think they had six legs." The image of long breasts is common in descriptions of African women, and animal comparisons were not unheard of; Ligon moves to imagining a new beast. African women were another of Barbados's bizarre animals.[57]

Ligon does not mention white women on Barbados, and he makes only rare references to Indian women. In his account, African women stood for women on Barbados. Enslaved women were defined by their labor in two ways. First, women's work—in this example, weeding—is the point at which they were viewed. Furthermore, their sagging breasts resulted from nursing, part of their labor as "breeders" for their masters. These women were without individuality; Ligon recognized only their labor and their sexuality. In this, Ligon was not unique, but his work encapsulates the dehumanization and objectification of enslaved women by the planters. Ligon did not always echo other descriptions of Africans; for example, he did not draw on the tradition of describing black men's genitals as extremely large. As people of African descent came to be defined by their origin, their differences from white people were most clearly marked in women's bodies.[58]

This telling inability to assimilate black women to English men's expectations was a common feature of seventeenth-century accounts and imaginings of the Caribbean. In Henry Neville's utopian myth of political origins, *The Isle of Pines*, published in 1668, the original settlers—one man and four women—are stranded on an island; the women include a Negro slave. In the man's sexual paradise, there is always a woman who is not pregnant available for sex. The man's favorite is the woman who had the highest status in England, "my master's daughter"; he could only sleep with the slave in the dark. Neville, like Ligon, saw enslaved women as less than human.[59]

Taylor, like Ligon, was fascinated by the culture and the bodies of enslaved Africans. He wrote at some length about their work, their treatment by their owners, and their culture. By the time Taylor visited Jamaica, the system of assigning slaves plots of land on which to produce their own food was well developed; these "provision grounds" saved planters money, since they did not have to import foodstuffs for their labor force. The slaves built shelters that Taylor called "wigwams" (thus confusing African slaves and the indigenous people of North America) and planted subsistence crops, which they cultivated during their "leisure." This "free" time was limited, since they worked for their masters from sunrise at four in the morning until eleven and then again from two in the afternoon until dark. They had time to rest on Saturday afternoons and Sundays, as well as on holidays. Taylor describes how the slaves worked to preserve and create a culture independent of their masters. In the evenings, he reported, they built a fire and made music and danced around it "in an antic manner, as if they were all mad"; then they all slept on the floor around the fire "in a confused manner." He was particularly intrigued by their singing and dancing, which he described on three different occasions, referring repeatedly to its apparent "confusion" and the mixing of men and women. He found the music curious—slaves "howl instead of singing." Like Ligon, Taylor reports slaves' belief that when they die, their soul returns to Africa; when they buried their dead, they provided the body with all the food and other goods necessary for the journey. Taylor repeats a story Ligon told about how a planter convinced his slaves that suicides would not return home. For Taylor, as for Ligon, slaves were strange people.[60] Yet neither Taylor nor Ligon acknowledged the underlying—and profoundly unsettling, even subversive—implications of the beliefs and behaviors they found so strange.

Like Ligon, Taylor was especially fascinated by slave women. He reported that they suffered no pain in childbirth and were back at work the next day, and that their children were able to walk at the age of four months. The children were white when born, "but soon change yellow, and in one months time become coal black." Mothers were very "kind and tender" to their infants. Like Ligon, Taylor focused on long hanging breasts that "are not like our English women," repeating the image from other travel writers that the breasts were so long that they often nursed their children over their shoulders. This image emphasized the sharp distinction between English women and enslaved African women. Despite their peculiar physique, Taylor thought their behavior similar to that of a dutiful English wife; they were "kind and honest" to their husbands.[61]

Taylor was well aware of slaves' suffering but found it difficult to face and write about. When newly enslaved Africans arrived, he noted, they "seem in much to grieve and lament their loss of their country freedom, and their now captivity, which they sing and bellow forth in their own language in a mournful manner." Taylor ignored the evidence of continued resistance and argued that enslaved Africans soon adjusted; they learned the tasks allotted to them, and "being set to work they willingly submit." This supposed submission is belied by Taylor's detailed descriptions of the harsh punishments meted out to slaves; he maintained that strict discipline was necessary because, if slaves were treated with too much kindness, "they would sooner cut your throat than obey you." The fear of a slave insurrection runs through his account, and he devoted an entire section to recent rebellions on Jamaica. Like Ligon, Taylor reported that planters prevented rebellion by mixing together slaves from different regions of Africa, so that in addition to speaking different languages, they "hate one another." This advantage would, he thought, disappear with the emergence of the Creole slaves, who spoke the same language and did not carry old enmities. In any case, he acknowledged, "'tis common for men to strive for freedom." Taylor could see injustice and even momentarily recognize that slaves were "men," but he would not challenge the status quo.[62]

Like Taylor and Ligon, Sir Hans Sloane remarked on the varied origins, peculiar culture, and strange bodies of slaves. Masters and traders who evaluated the productivity of various groups thought that slaves from Guinea were "the best slaves," while those from the East Indies or Madagascar were "good enough, but too choice in their diet." Sloane reported that Africans believed their souls returned to Africa after death, and that they placed high value on fidelity in marriage. He was sufficiently interested in slave culture to include the music of several songs he had heard them sing. Like Ligon and Taylor, Sloane was especially intrigued by the bodies of enslaved women, observing that after they nursed their children their breasts "hang very lank ever after, like those of goats." The animal analogy places the women outside normal human society. Sloane also repeats a common misunderstanding of physiognomy, suggesting that slave children's flat noses resulted from the practice of women carrying babies on their backs. Finally, Sloane notes that slaves, like sailors, were referred to as "hands."[63]

Sloane's depiction of slaves was as complex as Ligon's: he admired their fidelity, ridiculed their superstitions, and compared the women to animals. Indeed, he acknowledged, as had Ligon, "there are as honest, faithful, and conscionable people amongst them, as among those of Europe." Sloane, like Ligon, saw individuals, not just racial and cultural groups. The slaves' desire for freedom was implicit, but not acknowledged. Observers like Ligon, Taylor, and Sloane found it impossible to understand slaves, whose lives, beliefs, and behaviors were unfamiliar and seen only in the context of an institution that was also unfamiliar. The presence of so many people from different cultures, in an unaccustomed social structure, was at the center of everything that rendered the islands so unlike England.[64]

Some English observers were more critical of the social structure that was developing in the islands. Thomas Tryon, as we shall see in Chapter 6, denounced the cruelty of slavery. John Style, trying to develop a plantation in Jamaica during the late 1660s, deplored the development of slavery not because of its effects on slaves but because of its influence on slave owners. The estates, which were "for the most part managed by Negroes," he argued, "altogether destroy the Christian interest." Style suggested that if the slaves were converted to Christianity, they might be better subjects to the king than their current masters.[65] Both Tryon and Style had larger goals that framed their descriptions: Tryon sought religious and dietary reform, while Style sought to re-create English society in Jamaica. These English critics, who placed themselves outside the social order of the islands, articulated more directly what remained implicit in many other commentators' accounts.

Ligon's and Taylor's richly complex descriptions of the islands illuminate central problems that plagued English settlement in the Caribbean. The distance between the Caribbean and England was as much cultural as geographic. The harsh treatment of servants and the entire institution of slavery made the English uncomfortable. The social structure that emerged in the colonies did not simply replicate that of England; it constructed new relationships and identities. While landowning and service might be accommodated to English society, slavery could not. Slavery was a feature of classical society, and of the Turks and others in the Mediterranean who enslaved English men, not of England.[66] Ligon's account demonstrates that the construction of racial identities, for both the English and those they enslaved, was a process—it did not happen all at once. And the colonial social order was shaped by fundamental contradictions that were both disturbing to observers and causes of disorder in the islands. The tensions within Ligon's account reflect a dialogue between his desire for a familiar world and his sense that Barbados was neither similar to England nor simple to comprehend. He longed for clarity and certitude, but he was forced to recognize ambiguity and interpolate counterevidence. The more English colonial society developed, the more profoundly different it became.

Caribbean Contradictions

The views of slavery and race held by English men in the Caribbean changed as the social structure of plantation economies became more settled. The very categories through which these men understood the world shifted. By the time Taylor traveled to Jamaica in 1686, the English had increasingly clear expectations about the nature of blacks as distinct from whites. Not only did Ligon's perceptions of Africans change as he crossed the Atlantic, but his terms of comparison also changed. He increasingly defined his reference group, which set the standard for civility, as European rather than English. He observed, for example, that the Indians "have more the shape of the Europeans than the Negroes." Still, he insisted on the possibilities of virtue among slaves.[67] When Ligon was constructing stereotypes of enslaved Africans that persisted for centuries, he was also implicitly defining whiteness. His identity became more firmly fixed as a white European man. Before he had contact with enslaved people, he made sharp distinctions between himself and "a Portugal"; once in Barbados, he grouped himself with Europeans over against "Negroes" or "slaves." Race, gender, and class were inextricably linked in Ligon's mind. When he first set out from England, he saw English women as sharply divided by class; the poor women being transported on his ship were so lacking in virtue that when they were "abused" on the Cape Verde Islands, rape seemed to him an oxymoron. As he developed a conception of race, it was fundamentally marked by gender—and gender became increasingly sexualized. In the Cape Verdes, he described African women with the language of courtly love; in Barbados, his view of enslaved women lost any ironic romantic tinge and became highly objectified. Ligon could not bring slave women into his understanding of womanhood but made them into entirely separate creatures. The invisibility of English women in Ligon's Barbados makes it difficult to track this process in detail, but the outlines are clear.[68] Enslaved women were marked by race in that they were fundamentally different from European women, while enslaved men, in Ligon's view, shared intelligence and creativity with white men, even though they had little knowledge and were sometimes "savage." We can see in the process of enslavement the simultaneous development of whiteness as a concept, the increasing sexualization of ideas about enslaved women, and a racial division of labor that served to distinguish enslaved women from white women more than enslaved men from white men.

The peculiar tensions of society in the West Indies that Ligon chronicled became commonplace in accounts of the islands. A 1684 report on Barbados for the king argued that the island had four kinds of people, adding to Ligon's categories of masters, servants, and slaves that of "freemen" who had served out their time as servants but had no land and worked for wages. Jamaican society was more complex than that in Barbados because some Indians and Africans who had been on the island before the conquest stayed there; the Spanish eventually left, while Maroon resistance continued. Some discussions of Jamaica refer to Indians who had been enslaved. According to Taylor, they only served their owners if treated well; Indian slaves on the island were "subtle" and would either "get off the island or else murther themselves."[69]

By the late seventeenth century, the distinctive framework of colonial society in the Caribbean was becoming clear, although these differences had not been assimilated in England. According to a 1664 report to the Council for Foreign Plantations, "People are the foundations and improvement of all plantations, and that people are increased principally by sending of servants thither." Blacks purchased on the coast of Africa "are the principal and most useful appurtenances of a plantation and are . . . perpetual servants." The distinction between black and English servants indicates the emerging racial categories of the islands. Significantly, the report does not use the word "slave," substituting "perpetual servant"; the term "slavery" was repugnant to the English, even as they expanded the slave labor system and commodified black people as "appurtenances of a plantation." Whites were necessary both for their occupational skills and for purposes of defense and protection.[70]

The high mortality on the islands meant that a constant stream of servants was needed, and the 1664 report focused on how to provide a regular supply of them. Reports of kidnapping poor people into service in the islands harmed the reputation of the colonies. Moreover, merchants complained that the practice allowed "rogues" to live on board ship for a month and then complain that they had been lured with false pretenses and demand to be put ashore—a request that was often granted, given the increasingly common presumption that English men were free to make contracts rather than subject to sale and involuntary servitude. The solution offered by the 1664 report, which echoed the proposal made by Sir Thomas Modyford at the same time, involved the transportation of convicted felons, vagrants, and poor children lodged in English workhouses; a register of all servants who arrived in the colony and whom they served would prevent runaways as well as especially egregious abuses. The Caribbean islands could serve formally— as they already did informally—as a depository for England's undesirables.[71]

Filling the islands with England's rejects led to predictable problems that many observers reported. Felons and vagrants were disinclined to hard work. Complaints from Barbados and Jamaica about the character of servants increased over time. In 1672 the Council of Jamaica sought to deal with "divers thefts, felonies, and other enormities" in Port Royal committed by transported convicts. In 1676 the governor of Barbados argued that the servants who were shipped to the island were not worth the little they cost: "The most that come is from Ireland, and they grow weary of them for they prove commonly very idle and they do find by experience that they can keep three blacks who work better and cheaper than they can keep one white man." In 1688 the governor reported that servants were unsuitable material for building colonial society:

> The most of the Christian servants of this island are brought out of the several gaols of England, Scotland, and Ireland, or such whose lewd lives and conversations have taught them all manner of villainy, and reduced them to such miserable conditions of fortune that to prevent their starving they are forced to come servants to these colonies, where they cannot be maintained without work, many of which, having not been used to any thing of that kind, will not set themselves to it, but run away from their masters, steal and purloin from them what they can.[72]

Such white servants presented serious challenges for planters and governors. White servants were supposed to constitute a useful component of the labor force and an essential prop to social order, but they seemed to be a source of idleness and disorder instead.

While these laments about the supply and poor quality of white servants echo and complicate the contradictions Ligon articulated, they also hardened the expected division of labor. There were only two types of servants: blacks and whites. Race was the significant mark of division. In England, the most basic divisions of labor and authority had followed lines of gender. In the Caribbean, by contrast, there were relatively few white women servants, and black women worked in the fields alongside men. In the eyes of English men, black women were seen more in racial terms than in relation to white womanhood, and their bodies were sexually objectified. Race became increasingly salient as the colonial economy developed. White men who were unused to hard work and relatively free from coercion were less productive than Africans; slaves worked harder and were cheaper to maintain. In this context, the racial hierarchy was complicated, and it was not at all clear that all whites ranked above all blacks. By the end of the century, even skilled jobs on plantations were filled by slaves. The labor regime of mature plantation slavery had emerged.

These workers, black and white—however idle or ignorant, subtle or resistant—built the English colonial economy. The most crucial challenges facing planters were figuring out how to manage plantations and building a new social structure. As they developed a hugely successful agricultural regime, planters found themselves constantly trying to explain to those they left behind not only the situation on the islands, but also how it differed from that in England. Such explanations had to use existing categories, which built an odd combination of familiarity and difference into what they wrote. The sugar plantation and the social structure that supported it involved enormous transformations of agricultural production, labor organization, social hierarchy, and law. It is to this process of transformation that we now turn.

A Happy & Innocent Way of Thriving
Planting Sugar, Building a Society

If you did but see what brave estates are gotten by very much meaner
principles than we begin upon, you would say it is a brave thing to have elbow
room enough and that planting is a happy and innocent way of thriving.
CARY HELYAR, 1671

None of the descriptions of the Caribbean Islands that circulated in late
seventeenth-century England prepared those who came to establish and
manage colonial plantations for the challenges inherent in the undertaking.
The foundation of the economy was as new as the environment was unfamiliar. Workers had to be recruited or purchased, replaced frequently
because they died at alarming rates, and disciplined in backbreaking work.
Everything from methods of production to prices and profits was uncertain.
The only thing planters could be sure of was that the best possibility of
financial success lay in the cultivation, processing, and export of sugar.

Barbados, which in 1626 was densely wooded, was completely cleared
and planted with sugar within fifty years; Jamaica rapidly developed an intensive regime focused on sugar that complemented pastoral farming. The
English learned how to grow tropical crops, partly from people with previous experience but primarily through their own experiments. After the
English conquered Jamaica, Barbadian planters and the servants and slaves
they brought taught these skills to their counterparts on the larger island. In

addition to learning new agricultural methods, English settlers had to build all the relationships and institutions that hold society together. Few servants attained the freedom and independence that they longed for when they promised to exchange years of labor for transatlantic passage. The people who arrived on the islands involuntarily faced even bigger challenges. Africans had to learn new methods of agriculture and the rudiments of a new language as they adapted to their enslavement. The English had to work out how to manage slaves. This process involved improvisation in many aspects of life, and initially everything seemed unpredictable. By 1700, however, both islands had well-established agricultural and social systems, along with entrenched, albeit corrupt, governments.

Building a plantation required land, labor, and time. Initially, English settlers in both Barbados and Jamaica received land in return for clearing it and bringing servants to cultivate it; later arrivals had to purchase land.[1] There was rapid turnover in ownership of plantations, which became available when the owners returned to England or when they died. (For example, Richard Ligon's patron, Thomas Modyford, purchased his plantation from someone returning to England.) Few records that document the process of establishing a plantation have survived, but one significant set of records from a seventeenth-century plantation in Jamaica enables us to reconstruct its history over the first half-century of its development. The plantation called Bybrook was owned by the Helyar family of East Coker, Somerset, from 1661 to 1713. Cary Helyar (1633–72) first settled in Jamaica in 1664 as a merchant. In 1670 he purchased Bybrook, which was then uncleared land located near the current town of Bog Walk. In 1671 he convinced his older brother, Colonel William Helyar (1621–97), to invest in the plantation. William Helyar sent his young godson, William Whaley, to work with Cary; when Cary died a year later, Whaley inherited his share of the plantation. When Whaley himself died in 1676, the colonel gained complete ownership of the plantation. For some ten years, Bybrook was managed—or mismanaged—by agents. In 1686 Helyar's son John went to Jamaica to oversee the plantation; he returned home between 1688 and 1690, went back to Jamaica in 1690–91, and then returned to England permanently. The Helyars finally sold the plantation in 1713.

In spite of Cary Helyar's optimism, for most of the half-century Bybrook was owned by the Somerset squire and his heirs it constituted not a source of riches but a drain on their money; it was only profitable during the brief period that John Helyar managed it. The plantation's difficulties were typical of those that many planters encountered, and its uncertain fortunes paralleled more general trends in the Caribbean colonies. Absentee landlords rarely made money, at least during the seventeenth century; enterprising and unscrupulous men who were on the spot found ways of profiting at the owners' expense. Furthermore, while wealthy Barbadian planters made a great deal of money on sugar in the 1650s, the market contracted somewhat in the 1660s and 1670s.[2]

William Helyar's papers document his difficulties and his determined, if often unsuccessful, efforts to surmount the challenges that running a colonial plantation entailed. He kept almost all his papers relating to the enterprise—letters, accounts, and letter books. The letters he exchanged with a variety of correspondents dealt with matters ranging from sugar production and shipping to legal conflicts. While primarily concerned with plantation business, they often comment on the many differences between the colonies and England and the manifold problems English planters encountered in Jamaica. Most valuably for our purposes, the letters attempt to explain the complex realities of a planter's life and the perils facing absentee landowners. They draw attention to the remarkable, strange, and even discomfiting aspects of the society that planters were constructing in Jamaica. These documents provide a useful lens through which we can understand how English planters figured out how to manage agriculture, organize labor, and control their estates after they returned to England.

Planting

Few planters enjoyed the success they all dreamed of. Cary Helyar's brave words about reaping a fortune from a small investment ring hollow in retrospect, even had he not died so soon after buying Bybrook. Planters faced numerous obstacles, whether they went into sugar production when land was still relatively inexpensive or waited until the plantation regime was more securely established. The production of sugar was an extremely complex process; Barbados planters lamented in 1687 that it was "a design full of accident."[3] There were many points where things could and often did go wrong: weather damaged the crop, equipment broke down, and illness took an excessive toll among the slaves. The various elements of sugar production all required capital investment, making successful entry possible only for those who, like Thomas Modyford, began with capital. The work of planting was complicated by the unfamiliar and often fatal diseases prevalent on the islands. The required management skills went far beyond the methods of estate management that were customary in England.

Barbados was already a populous, although not particularly prosperous, colony at the time that sugar was introduced in the early 1640s. Land had been cleared and plantations established. The introduction of sugar led to a relatively rapid consolidation of holdings; as Ligon wrote, "small plantations in poor mens hands, often twenty, or thirty, acres, which are too small to lay to that work, be bought up by great men." In the early 1640s, there were about 10,000 landholders in Barbados; by 1679, nearly three-quarters of those had disappeared, and there were only 2,639. In 1680 the 175 largest planters—those with more than sixty slaves—controlled half of the land on the island; these men constituted just 6.6 percent of the planters, but they owned 54 percent of all the slaves. Almost all the available land was under cultivation.[4] Barbados was dominated by the large planters, and small landholders had few opportunities for upward mobility. When Modyford was named governor of Jamaica in 1664, he brought a large party from Barbados to Jamaica to settle and to plant sugar. The recruits included many of the small landholders who saw better prospects in the new colony than in Barbados. Thus sugar came to Jamaica almost as soon as the English did. Although the larger size and more varied terrain of Jamaica provided more opportunities for small planters and for the cultivation of other crops, sugar and the wealthy men who owned sugar plantations came to dominate the island.[5]

Cary Helyar, like many younger sons, turned to trade to earn his living. He had been engaged in international trade before he settled in Jamaica in 1664, the same year that Modyford became governor; by 1669 he was one of Modyford's partners in the slave trade. When Cary purchased his plantation on the banks of the upper Cobre River, Modyford provided advice and expertise, as well as lodging, while he developed his property. Bybrook, in Sixteen Mile Walk, was about fifteen miles north of Spanish Town in a fertile and well-watered valley. According to Sir Hans Sloane, "some of the best and securest plantations of the island" were located in the vicinity.[6]

Cary Helyar's letters contain many detailed explanations of agricultural products and processes, which were necessary because of the unfamiliarity of tropical agriculture. In September 1670, Cary planted six acres of cacao after procuring trees from a nursery. Almost as soon as the cacao was planted, he began to write to his elder brother about planting sugar. Cary explained the crop's growing cycle and processing, as well as its economics. Sugar could be the source of great wealth, and the land at Bybrook was ideally suited to sugar production. But it required major investment in both slaves and a mill. Initially, Helyar regarded that expense as relatively trivial. He suggested that the sugar could be milled at Modyford's, noting, "It is the custom here that he that has a mill will grind his neighbor's sugarcanes and make his sugar at halves." The only cost Cary anticipated was that of cutting and bringing the canes. Cary insisted his plan was not a gamble, but "a known and experienced truth. I have had as able planters as any in this island upon our land to see it, and they all conclude it is excellent land for canes and the river . . . the envy of all that see it." Cary believed that soon they could build their own mill, which would then be used by their neighbors.[7]

Cary Helyar planted cacao just as a blight destroyed most of the cacao in Jamaica—a blight caused, it was alleged, by a curse placed on the crop by the slaves who had lived there under the Spanish. A year later, the "old cacao trees" showed no signs of recovery, although some new ones appeared to be flourishing. Cacao would not become a dependable staple crop.[8] The blight altered Cary's plans. Within six months of his original proposal to his brother, he had second thoughts—"I have since often disputed it with myself"—because it moved too slowly. Given the situation of their plantation near the river, he suggested, they should plant sugar and build their own mill right away, grinding sugar for others and keeping half the produce. This letter enclosed a calculation of costs and potential income. The proposition entailed the purchase of eighteen more slaves and of expensive and complex machinery, requiring an outlay of £423 on William's part. At the same time, Cary would not give up on cacao, for that crop "affords no trouble or labor after they are set, a little keeping clean excepted." Cary captured the Jamaican approach to wealth as he concluded, "While our patience is employed to expect the fruit of these [cacao], our hands may be employed to bring to pass this work of more speedy profit, and methinks there's the best sowing of money which comes up and bears soonest; if you did but see what brave estates are gotten by very much meaner principles than we begin upon, you would say it is a brave thing to have elbow room enough and that planting is a happy and innocent way of thriving." Cary's vision of sowing money and reaping profits was shared by many English planters. He then described precisely what was needed for the mill, so that supplies could be sent from England as soon as possible. With sugar and rum, Cary promised, they could make £30 an acre; while they did not have as many slaves as Mody-ford and could not work so quickly on such a large scale, their location was far better.[9]

In early 1672, Cary promised his brother that the profits of the plantation would be sufficient to settle a second plantation, "for as Negroes will beget Negroes, so one plantation will beget another." He suggested that William Whaley, who was keeping the plantation accounts, could himself build up an estate "according to the custom of the country": one began with two or three slaves and an overseer and planted tobacco, ginger, and achiote (a plant whose seeds produced a red dye), as well as provisions for the plantation and stock to provide meat, dung, and sometimes energy for the sugar mill. An acre of ginger, Cary asserted, would produce a year after planting and provide a 20 percent return. The profits from ginger, tobacco, and other specialty crops would enable Whaley to buy another slave, "so that in 7 years time it will produce a hopeful business. . . . This sir is what my eyes see every day, so it is no new thing." Alas, Cary died less than six months after writing this letter, and the plantation suffered through prolonged disputes about his estate.[10]

Cary Helyar's plan was not a certain road to riches, but it was not an impossible one. Francis Price, who patented his lands at Worthy Park in 1670, founded a Jamaican estate that survived into the late twentieth century. Price started with less capital and fewer political connections than Helyar, but he lived until 1689. His estate finally became profitable in the early eighteenth century when his son Charles managed the sugar plantation. Had Cary lived ten or fifteen more years, his experience as a merchant and his political connections would have helped to build a profitable enterprise. Luck in the demographic lottery of the islands was critical to success.[11]

Like most planters, Cary Helyar began his plantation with some capital, but he had to borrow money in order to build it rapidly. In 1659 a letter from Barbados explained the high levels of debt in the island: "Those persons who settle upon plantations in the West Indies have no considerable estate to purchase slaves, cattle, etc. when they begin to plant, but what by their industry and labor they make out of the earth."[12] In 1681, when the governor of Jamaica, the Earl of Carlisle, discussed the possibility of a royal plantation on the island, he noted that the usual computation was that it cost £5,000 to build up a plantation of 1,000 acres, which would yield £1,000 a year—but he acknowledged that no one had actually done it.[13] Those who had enough money were more likely to follow Modyford's course in Barbados and buy an existing plantation; for poorer men, the gradual method was indeed more common.

Two notable features of sugar production were especially important to English planters. First, it took fourteen to eighteen months for sugarcanes to mature. The laborers who were not employed in the fields while the crop was growing had to be put to other tasks. Cary Helyar wisely used his slaves to clear more land while the canes ripened; his white servants built the sugar mill and boiling house. Second, when the ripe canes were cut, they had to be processed within three days, or the sugar would spoil. The timing of sugar production was quite awkward: a real emergency followed a long period with little demand for labor. The need for rapid processing required that sugar plantations become industrial plants. The model that Cary initially suggested in his letters to William—of centralized mills processing cane from several plantations—never took root in the English islands, though it was common in Brazil and had briefly flourished in Barbados. Each plantation had its own sugar mill, boiling house, and curing house, as well as workers to maintain them; this in turn led to the concentration of landholdings. Both labor and equipment had to be available when the canes were ready for cutting. Letters sent back to England frequently noted how profits were hampered because of problems in the mill or a shortage of workers. It was hard for those who had not been to Jamaica to understand that in making sugar, timing was everything.[14]

Cultivating and processing sugar demanded a substantial number of skilled workers. The process of growing and harvesting cane was labor-intensive. First, parts of old canes were placed in holes or trenches, where they sprouted. After about two months, the field was weeded and carefully fertilized, and new plants were inserted in any places where the canes had not sprouted. As the canes grew up, they became too dense to weed, so it was important that the field be well weeded at the outset. After about fourteen months, the canes were ready for harvesting. By then they were about eight feet tall, and when ripe the canes turned a blue-green that Ligon called "deep popinjay." After they were cut, the canes themselves were ground, and the juice distilled and dried to make sugar. The tops were used to feed cattle.[15] Each step had to be done at the right time and in the correct way: some steps—especially cutting canes—were extraordinarily laborious, while others—like the boiling of the juice—were highly skilled. Work on the plantation required both careful supervision and experienced management of labor.

Bringing new cane fields into production and constructing the mills to process sugar took several years. Taylor described the process of preparing to plant. First the slaves cut down the trees and burned the stumps. After it had rained, they hoed the land and planted several pea crops in succession for at least a year, while the tree roots decayed. In the second year, they planted potatoes and yams to provide provisions. Only in the third year would the land be ready for canes.[16] By the time the crop ripened the next year, the mills had to be ready for operation. Equipment was procured from England; skilled English craftsmen—millwrights, smiths, carpenters—assembled the grinding machinery and built the boiling house. This process accounts for the slow development of sugar in Jamaica. Cary Helyar, planning his plantation in 1670–71, was one of the earliest to begin sugar production. In 1675 there were only seventy working sugar mills in Jamaica. The first sugar from Bybrook was shipped to England in 1676, though earlier crops had been sold locally.[17]

The intensive sugar cultivation required to produce a profit quickly exhausted the soil. The planters treated sugar production as an extractive process. In the early years, planters in both Barbados and Jamaica could cut the cane and get a second and even third crop from new shoots that emerged from the stalks. After twenty years or so, however, the soil became depleted; each sugar crop required planting new canes and spreading manure. By 1679 the soils of Barbados had been sufficiently depleted by years of overproduction that they needed regular applications of fertilizer. Colonel Henry Drax, in his instructions for his overseer that year, provided more than a page of detailed discussion of the production and application of various fertilizers. In addition to animal dung, Drax used the residue of sugar production. One basket of fertilizer was to be divided between every two cane holes; Drax seemed to think he was lucky not to have to provide a basket for every cane.[18] He also had lime kilns, whose yield reduced the acidity of the soil. In the 1670s, planters in Jamaica boasted of the greater fertility of their soil than that of Barbados, but their advantage was short-lived. By the late 1690s, overseers in Jamaica wrote repeatedly of the need for heavy fertilizing in order to maintain productivity.[19] Sugar was the dominant crop, and the intensity of farming depleted the once rich soil.

William Helyar never saw the great riches Cary promised him. Cary died of a fever only six months after he developed his plan for the plantation, and he left his share of the plantation to William Whaley. Whaley himself died four years later. Neither Whaley nor his successors had the political connections necessary to protect the property. Furthermore, the estate suffered from the major problem associated with absentee ownership: finding a competent and honest manager. After Whaley's death, Helyar arranged a three-way management team for Bybrook, for if one manager died, "I know not what might follow"; one of the three died soon after. This team of overseers was replaced by a distant relative, Thomas Hillyard, who not only used an accounting trick to keep all the profits for ten years but also reported on the island that he owned the plantation; on a map from the early 1680s, it is identified as "Hillyards" (see Figure 1). When John Helyar arrived in Jamaica in 1686, his first task was to regain possession of the plantation. Under his management, the plantation was profitable for several years, but after his return to England it again lost money.[20]

Bybrook failed to make a profit because of a combination of premature mortality and corruption, two major features of West Indian society in the seventeenth century. Illness and death were among the most significant challenges to planting. The mortality rate for new arrivals in the Caribbean— European as well as African—was extremely high. Smallpox, dysentery, and yellow fever, as well as hunger, were endemic on slave ships; such illnesses were exacerbated after arrival in Jamaica by both hunger and overwork. Europeans carried no resistance to tropical diseases and died of them in great numbers. Both Cary Helyar and his nephew William died less than a week after contracting fevers. Although, as we have seen, many observers from Cary Helyar to Sir Hans Sloane praised the healthfulness of the islands, they did so first naively and then defensively; John Helyar told the truth when he wrote of "hot countries where a man does not live out half his days."[21]

The diseases that were endemic to the islands and the level of chronic mortality were scarcely imaginable to those in England. During the late seventeenth century, mortality in England was falling, at least outside London. The chronic mortality in the islands was matched in England only episodically, during major epidemics. Disease and death are a constant background in planters' letters home. As his correspondents in Jamaica frequently reminded Colonel Helyar, the illnesses affected productivity even if they were not fatal. In 1676 the bricklayer Dodge "hath not been able to lay a brick this twelvemonth by reason of his lame leg, and a distemper which we here call the yaws, which is usually caught by being naught with Negroes." Later that year, Whaley wrote that "I am daily troubled with the fever and cough, as also Mr. Atcherly who had a hard bout of it being taken in sick in few days after he arrived." Whaley noted that one cure for the fever was a trip to the Cayman Islands, which had a different climate and only turtles for food. Whaley, who regularly worried that William Helyar would predecease him, died after only five years in Jamaica, twenty years before his godfather. In 1677 the plantation was "exceeding sickly and fatal"; in recent months, four white men and two white women had died. Many of those who survived had suffered repeated illnesses. During his first stay in Jamaica, John Helyar wrote that "I am confident that no one that ever came to Jamaica has had so

FIGURE 1. Map of Jamaica (detail), ca. 1684, showing St. Iago
de la Vega (Spanish Town); the Helyar plantation (just to the east of
"Vale") is labeled "Hilliard" (National Archives)

much sickness as myself, for I have had three fevers, and three bellyaches." His boast was sadly inaccurate, since in the same letter he reported the death of John Everard, who had traveled to Jamaica with him.[22]

THE WEALTH PRODUCED by the islands came at an enormous human cost to the English and to those they enslaved. Slave owners expected newly arrived slaves in the Caribbean to live just over seven years; about a quarter of them died in the first three years, while they were being seasoned. In the first year at least, it is possible that English mortality was as much as four times higher than that of slaves, as a result of African resistance to malaria. The English had little knowledge of tropical diseases or how to treat them effectively. Some slaves arrived with medical knowledge, and they were more successful than European doctors in treating yaws, but their remedies for more fatal diseases, like those of the English physicians, were only sporadically effective.[23] The yellow fever epidemic Ligon observed in Barbados was only the beginning. In 1664 Sir Thomas Modyford reported that a ship had arrived from England with much disease, but that Barbados itself was "(now) very healthy."[24] Malaria, which was not present in seventeenth-century Barbados, was endemic in Jamaica, although the various fevers were not yet carefully distinguished. When Modyford arrived in Jamaica later that year, he wrote that the mountains were healthy, but in the valleys and near the mouths of rivers it was "feverish": these were places where malaria flourished.[25] In 1683 Governor Edwin Stede reported that he had suffered for two months from the "dismal and epidemical distemper of this country," the bellyache, which had been worse this year than usual. The bellyache is the most mysterious of the diseases of the islands; it caused intense intestinal cramping, and sufferers often lost the use of their limbs.[26] John Taylor fell ill with a fever almost as soon as he arrived in Jamaica and was confined to his room for over a month; he recovered, but just a month later he got the dry bellyache and "lay as on a rack of torture and extreme misery." Since recurrences of the bellyache apparently caused paralysis, he determined to leave the island.[27]

The fevers and bellyache were chronic conditions, at their worst from July to September. Their impact was exacerbated during epidemics that decimated both the European and African populations. In 1685 and early 1686, Barbados suffered not only from the usual fevers but also from smallpox; the governor adjourned both the Assembly and Council and reported home that the epidemics had cost "many of our best . . . [along with] great numbers of our more ordinary people, as well as blacks." It was mortal not just to the usual victims—children and slaves who lacked resistance—but "even [to] men and women grown" who had been born in the island. Smallpox returned to Barbados in 1695.[28] In 1691 the governor of Jamaica, the Earl of Inchiquin, wrote to the Council that "people die here very fast and suddenly, I do not know how soon it may be my turn, for I find I decay apace, insomuch that I must desire his Majesty leave to recruit myself with a little English air."[29] In 1693 Governor James Kendall in Barbados wrote that in three years in this "Region of Death," two-thirds of those in his party and half the inhabitants of the island had died; the regiments preparing to attack the French had been decimated. They celebrated the end of the epidemic with a day of thanksgiving.[30] A malaria epidemic followed the disastrous Jamaican earthquake of 1692, adding to the sense of doom felt by inhabitants.[31] In 1694 the fever in Barbados was particularly virulent near Bridgetown; the governor had already buried three of his servants, and five more were ill.[32]

For those who survived, the high mortality rate on the islands provided opportunities as well as challenges. The demographic lottery of the West Indies often left widows with substantial estates. Marriages to widows offered men one of the few avenues to wealth. In 1696 a Jamaican planter wrote resentfully to another that "I never could hear that you ever was able to live great, had it not been by the fortunes your good ladies brought you." In contrast, the writer had earned everything he had by his own labor.[33] The social mobility that men attained through marriage often came at the expense of heirs: new husbands might take over a widow's property as their own and keep it from her children by a previous marriage, particularly if the woman died. Heirs who were underage, or not living on the islands, were particularly vulnerable to such maneuvers.[34]

The unrelenting experience of illness and disease, which disrupted families as well as fortunes, was a central aspect of life in the seventeenth-century Caribbean. Several writers suggested that the source of illness lay in the behavior of the planters rather than the atmosphere of the islands. Many new arrivals attempted to explain sudden deaths in terms familiar from England: for example, in 1680 two ladies, including Modyford's daughter-in-law, were said to have died after dancing and catching a chill.[35]

Such explanations did not usually work very well, as something was fatally different on these tropical islands. Thomas Tryon argued that the problem was that Europeans insisted on eating rich foods and drinking strong liquors instead of the light foods, mostly fruits, that were native to the area. From a different medical perspective, Sir Hans Sloane suggested that long life was possible for "temperate livers."[36] Sloane and another Jamaican doctor, Thomas Trapham, provided guides to treatment, based on the humoral theory of medicine; slaves brought with them herbal traditions that were sometimes effective. The lack of knowledge about disease transmission, however, meant all explanations and treatments were inadequate. In early 1700, after one ship in Barbados was rendered useless for the defense of the island because nearly the whole crew that had sailed from England had died, a treatise attempted to explain the causes of the illness. It remarked on the "filth, dung, and dirt" in the streets; it noted that infection passed to those who slept in beds and sheets used by those who had previously died; and it recommended that the swamp be drained. Most significantly, it argued that slaves were the primary purveyors of infection in the town, especially because they slept in the streets and fouled them, so it advocated the removal of all slaves from Bridgetown. These observations moved from practical and accurate assessments of the sources of infection—swamps, dirty sheets, and feces—to social analysis, assuming that slaves were primarily responsible for disease.[37] English observers linked the new diseases with the slaves whose presence was also part of the novelty of the islands.

The problems encountered by the Helyar plantation—the cost, labor, and time required to plant, cultivate, and process sugarcane for export; the prevalence of disease and death that lowered productivity and put a sudden stop to many promising careers; and, consequently, the real difficulty of making the enterprise yield sustained profits—were typical of those English planters experienced. The rarity of success in planting was the source of great social tensions among white men. The publicists for the islands, including Ligon, promised riches, and those who arrived with money usually prospered, as did those with connections to those in power. For the rest, life was more difficult. The situation was particularly acute in Barbados, where the shortage of land provided few opportunities for English men to build up estates. In 1669 one writer lamented the plight of poor men there, who "continually eat the bread of carefulness, and lie down to rest with sorrow, never enjoying themselves, wives or children, for they can call nothing their own."[38] Those white servants who survived the period of their indentures found their prospects for acquiring property severely limited; enslaved Africans had no prospects at all.

Working

Slavery and race reshaped the organization of labor and the meanings of class and gender for everyone in the West Indies. Work was clearly divided by race: while field labor and skilled sugar trades were the work of slaves, skilled labor in the "English trades" belonged to English craftsmen. While many craftsmen traveled to Jamaica as indentured servants, the relatively high value of their work when they arrived in a colony that was chronically short of skilled labor created conflicts; frequently it gave them greater leverage in their relationships with landowners than they would have had in England. White servants and craftsmen made a greater distinction between themselves and slaves than between themselves and landowners. The refusal to "slave it" was common among white servants in the West Indies.[39]

The large labor force that sugar production required posed problems for planters that went far deeper than farmers' perennial concerns about weather and prices. The supply of labor was a constant source of anxiety, especially given the heavy mortality on the islands. Sugar required both skilled workers, who maintained the machinery of the mill and supervised the boiling and curing process, and unskilled ones, who planted, manured, and weeded the crop. Skilled workers in trades practiced in England—carpenters, masons, coopers, potters, and the like—were for most of the seventeenth century drawn from the white servants. The skilled work that was unique to the Caribbean—boiling and curing the sugar—was done primarily by slaves. Slaves also performed all the work in the fields. For example, in 1672 Whaley wrote that "the Negroes are dumbling down trees as fast as they can in order for the planting of more canes. Henry Hodges and the rest of the white people, servants and hired men, are about the mills as fast as they can." The white servants requested by those managing the Helyar plantation over the course of some thirty years include carpenters, masons, sawyers, smiths, and doctors. The smiths, Whaley noted, should "bring bellows and iron with them fit for to work and not to buy it here." It was considered inappropriate for English servants to work in the fields, except when a plantation was being established; field work was for slaves. This distinction was reinforced by planters' practice of punishing disobedient white servants by sending them into the fields to work alongside African slaves. White women were always exempt from field labor, but this gender distinction was not made in the work assigned to slaves. On the Helyar plantation, at least, white men maintained a monopoly over skilled work outside the sugar mills through the seventeenth century; only in 1701 did a letter suggest that slaves might be trained in skilled trades not related to sugar processing.[40] The division of labor by race ensured the value of the skills of white servants and offered them a degree of protection from excessive labor.

White Servants

The persistent shortage of skilled English workers led to relatively high wages for artisans. Cary Helyar and his successors sought to have such servants bound to the plantation for a term of years. In March 1672, Cary asked for a variety of workmen: "If you cannot get any in the country, Mr. Warren may employ such in London as will bring him enough, not by those base means of kidnaping, but by good honest indenture."[41] Cary initially asked for "a sawyer, a smith, a carpenter, and a mason, by which we shall save much money"; in 1671 one of the workers on the plantation suggested workmen from East Coker who might want to come. In 1675 Whaley was still asking for skilled craftsmen. "Let them be traders" (tradesmen), he complained; "other people can get them, and it is strange to me you can get none, it hath been five hundred pounds out of our way this year, for want of carpenters and masons." When he had to hire carpenters, he paid them £3 a month and provided 7 pounds of meat each week. The shortage of skilled labor in Jamaica is a constant refrain in the letters sent back to Somerset.[42] Planters, managers, and officials in the Caribbean were convinced that their English counterparts did not comprehend how difficult it was to run an industrial enterprise without an adequate supply of skilled workers.

It proved exceedingly difficult to recruit English workers because it rapidly became evident that those who went to America as servants rarely shared in the wealth that sugar produced. As the "sugar rush" failed to deliver its promised rewards, correspondents increasingly emphasized the need for hard work, the perils of the enterprise, and the difficulty of creating wealth in a distant land. Accounts of the practical problems supplanted descriptions of the exotic environment. Those who sought to attract investors wisely warned that quick profits were unlikely. Propertyless men who came with unrealistic expectations caused problems for those who recruited and employed them. In 1675 Whaley complained about the workers recently sent by Helyar: "Some of them stands us in good stead, but then you send one riff raff or other that is not good and fit for nothing."[43] Two of the men "thought to come here to do nothing." One of these was William Dampier, better known for his later career as a buccaneer and explorer. He thought he had come as a bookkeeper and refused to do any outdoor work; Whaley supposed "he would have money for doing of nothing." In 1677 Helyar's nephew William asked permission to discharge the clerk William Foyle, who refused to work. He added, "If you were here to see what I do amongst the servants I am sure you would not be so forward in sending them here without they more fitter and do better service than those which are here already." Exaggerated expectations were not unique to those coming to Bybrook; in 1677 Helyar's correspondents reported that the brother of Thomas Hillyard, who himself later defrauded Helyar, "hath idly spent and wasted his estate through the ambition he had in keeping and spending his money with such as were above him."[44]

While all were expected to work, status distinctions still mattered. In 1686 John Helyar was relieved when his cousin Giles left Jamaica: "I cannot in honor put [him] to mechanical employ & as for greater, in truth I do not see he is capable of unless he were of a mind to undergo the tutoring."[45] The salience of status is clear in the declining career of Cary Helyar's ne'er-do-well cousin, Jack. Cary had promised that if Jack came to the colony, he would be put to work: "We can tame any body here, and make them work and that too in the field with the Negroes and be allowed nothing but two salt mackerel a week, but Indian fruit enough . . . we have degrees of work for the good and bad, but no idlers." Jack began his sojourn in Jamaica by pledging his cousin's credit to buy drink. Later, in spite of promises to reform, he was sold as a servant to pay his debts, suggesting that whatever taming might have been attempted was unsuccessful.[46]

As population growth slowed in late seventeenth-century England, the pressure for emigration decreased. At the same time, the circulation of reports regarding the ill-treatment of servants made Barbados and Jamaica especially unappealing destinations for poor English men. The difficulty William Helyar had in recruiting servants may have been compounded by local conditions. In 1677 Helyar reported the accounts by "Bristol men" of "their hard usage, and want of provisions there"; in addition, "some letters have lately come hither to this parish from some of the servants complaining in the same manner." The Helyar plantation was notoriously hostile to the presence of white women, for whom they had no work. The colonel's refusal to accept "women of her rank" led one woman to dress as a man to accompany her husband. After she arrived, Whaley complained: "We have two women in the plantation the Doctor's wife and the potter's, two filthy lazy sows good for nothing."[47] In East Coker, people apparently realized that service in Jamaica would entail continued subordination to the Helyars rather than offering an opportunity to attain wealth. As those who had stayed behind heard about the plight of their relatives and friends who had gone out as servants, villagers became more reluctant to emigrate.

These problems of recruitment represented a major concern for planters in the Caribbean. Complaints about the shortage of white servants are a constant theme in reports to London. White servants played two equally important roles. One was the contribution made by their skills; the other was their role in helping to defend the islands and control the slaves. The improvement of English economic conditions meant that coerced rather than voluntary migration was ever more important as the source for servants. Indentured servants were increasingly drawn from the social as well as the geographical margins of Britain. As early as 1674, a memorial from Barbados to the Crown argued for free trade between the islands and Scotland—limited by the Navigation Acts—in order to increase the supply of white servants. Scots servants would be willing to go to the English sugar islands, where their labor would be profitable and they would serve the king by defending the islands.[48] Two years later, the governor of Barbados argued that the depopulation of England should not be blamed on the island, because there was no encouragement for immigrants, "there being no land for them nor anything but hard service for small wages. The most that come is from Ireland, and they grow weary of them for they prove commonly very idle."[49]

In 1680 the governor of Barbados complained of the number of white servants and laborers who had left after their term of service for South Carolina, Jamaica, Antigua, and the other Leeward Islands where they could obtain land, "this Island having none to give." In 1681 a new governor sought legislation to ensure an adequate supply of white servants and asked the Assembly to pass a bill "to restrain bad Masters and overseers from cruelty to their Christian servants." In 1684 the Grand Jury of Barbados complained again of the shortage of servants, "many going off so soon as they become free to other places who encourage them by having some small quantity of land free in consideration of service, which cannot be here done being a small island and wholly taken up and managed." The scarcity of labor was exacerbated by the death of so many from "the epidemical distemper of the bellyache."[50] Although Jamaica looked better from a distance, it too suffered from a shortage of English servants. In 1679 the Earl of Carlisle argued that Jamaica had 20 percent fewer white servants than it needed, which made the island vulnerable to attack; the servants who arrived barely replaced those who had died.[51]

The islands' elites were heartened by the transportation of a significant number of Monmouth rebels in 1685 and 1686, especially because the rebels had been sentenced to colonial servitude for ten years, rather than the usual obligation of four years. Barbados quickly revised its laws to allow such extended service; the Assembly in Jamaica, in one of its regular arguments with the governor, took somewhat longer to do the same. After the Revolution of 1688, the Crown decided to offer a pardon to the rebels. Many planters had trained the rebels in the more skilled jobs on plantations, it was alleged, so they asked that instead of immediately freeing the servants, they be allowed to reduce the rebels' term of service to seven years to ensure proper training of replacements.[52]

Concern about the scarcity of white servants continued throughout the 1690s. In 1695 Governor Francis Russell wrote from Barbados that there was "a great want of white servants . . . our fatal sickness here hath thinned them very much & to white servants when they come out of their time there is no encouragement, for they have but about forty shillings for all their services, and no other encouragement given them to stay upon the island." At the end of their term, most of them left for more promising places.[53] Early in 1697 a London merchant delighted Jamaican representatives with a proposal to bring 250 tradesmen to the island. They offered encouragement but suggested a postponement of the journey until the autumn so that the men would not arrive during the sickly season. Later that year, Barbadian agents in London noted that the Council had proposed "transplanting" former soldiers to the island and that Barbados had created incentives for bringing servants, including legal redress for servants against cruel masters.[54] The following year, the Council of Barbados again reported that it had offered incentives for people to bring white servants to the island, but that they were limited by the lack of available land.[55] English servants expected more than a life of perpetual wage labor in the sugar islands.

Negro Slaves

The planters' obsession with white servants obscures their increasingly limited role as colonial development proceeded. As early as the 1670s, Barbadian planters wrote that Irish servants were not very useful, and "our whole dependence therefore is upon Negroes." White men were necessary "to keep their vast number of Negroes in subjection & defend their islands against foreign enemies."[56] This dependence was rarely acknowledged because doing so undermined planters' claims to independence; in practical terms, it also limited their power. Finally, it made white claims of superiority to enslaved Africans more awkward. In the 1690s West Indies merchants in London admitted that there was no work for farmers in the islands because agricultural labor was done by slaves; however, English farmers could find employment as overseers and "in the nature of a guard to keep the Negroes in awe, that they do not rebel."[57] The labor of slaves drove the prosperity of the islands. In 1684, as Thomas Tryon explored the evils of slavery, he had a planter admit the cruelty but excuse it by asking, "How would we live as we do without slaves?" As the Council of Jamaica put it in 1692, "All our estate here, or the increase or preservation, depends wholly upon the frail thread of the life of our Negroes."[58]

Slaves often represented more than half the capital tied up in a plantation. The purchase of slaves, their work, their health, and the control of their behavior were thus matters of obsessive attention to planters like the Helyars. Yet the word "slave" rarely appears in their letters; instead, there are constant references to the purchase, work, health, and management of "Negroes." On the one hand, the silence about slavery indicates that the institution of slavery was taken for granted in the West Indian colonies. Jamaican planters followed the practices adopted in earlier English colonies, especially Barbados. Barbadian planters had copied the practice of slavery from Virginia, as well as Spanish and Portuguese colonies in the Americas. Everyone in the Caribbean assumed that growing sugar meant owning slaves. On the other hand, the failure to describe slaves as such suggests that owning slaves made the English uncomfortable: their dependence on slaves emphasized their vulnerability. However well established the institution was in the colonies, slavery had no counterpart at home, and its legitimacy was doubtful if the question of its legal basis was faced squarely. In their correspondence with England, planters, merchants, and officials tended to assume the existence of slavery rather than to justify or even explain it. Referring to African slaves as "servants" elided the differences between free and chattel labor. Finally, the repeated use of the term "Negro" instead of "slave" served to foreground the workers' origins, rather than their legal status.[59] The distinction between free and enslaved labor rested on what came to be defined as race.

One of the more puzzling questions about the emergence of slave societies in the seventeenth-century English Caribbean is why the English turned to slavery as the foundation of their labor system. While the institution had classical precedents, slavery did not exist in England at the time, and the watchwords of English politics were "liberty" and "freedom," though these were always in tension with the practice of subordination in a hierarchical society. Slavery was practiced in Spain and Portugal, as well as in their American colonies, but these were not England's models. While England had forms of bound labor in apprenticeship and had experimented with using slavery as a punishment in the sixteenth century, slavery had not taken root.[60] The two most recent scholarly analyses of the rise of the slave system agree, despite their significant disagreements, that in the long term—and possibly the short term as well—the planters' decision to rely on enslaved Africans was not an economically advantageous one. David Eltis has argued that it would have been less expensive and easier for Europeans to enslave other Europeans—vagrants, convicts, and prisoners of war—to work in the colonies, and that the failure to do so reflected a strong historical disinclination to enslave people who were seen as members of the same group. While England, as well as France, Spain, and Portugal, used convicts for forced labor in various contexts, this practice always fell short of perpetual slavery.[61] Robin Blackburn disagrees with Eltis on the availability of sufficient European labor; the turn to African labor enabled the more rapid development of the plantations. At the same time, he argues that relying on free labor would over the long term have provided more stimulus to the English economy. English planters in Barbados and Jamaica were not so interested in the long term as they were in obtaining a prompt return on their investment. Slaves cost more to purchase than indentured servants did, and the capital that planters invested in slaves might be severely diminished if too many died. But slave labor was more productive, and if slaves lived more than a year or two, the profits were considerable.[62]

Whether the English were merely reluctant to coerce their fellow Europeans or unable to recruit them in sufficient numbers, planters regarded slavery as vital to their enterprise. Equally important, they never considered allowing Africans to occupy any other position. From a very early point, Africans were expected to be slaves—"perpetual servants," in the language of the 1664 report to the Council—while whites were accorded the status of servants. Slaveholders like Cary Helyar, without weighing alternatives, found the purchase of African slaves the easiest way to build a large labor force in a short period of time. Once that choice was made, it was clear that the management of slaves required new skills and attitudes. English planters who purchased enslaved Africans went about constructing a slave labor system without stopping to consider the social and political consequences.[63]

William Helyar's correspondents regularly discussed the purchase of slaves. The size of a plantation's workforce was defined by the demands of the harvest. Cary Helyar, with his experience in the slave trade, prided himself on his ability to choose slaves who were fit to work. In 1670 he reported the arrival of "a parcel of good Negroes"; fortunately, he shared the control of the sale with Thomas Modyford. A year later he wrote that he was waiting for the next "good Negro ship," although he had been able to buy a couple of Negroes on the island. As Cary put it, "The more Negroes the greater income." In planning to build another plantation, he thought that William would not have to invest additional money to buy slaves to work it: after all, he wrote optimistically, "Negroes will beget Negroes." Slaves were chosen, Ligon wrote, much as were "horses in a Market: the strongest, youthfullest, and most beautiful yield the greatest prices." The choice of slaves, like that of horses, involved skilled judgment. Cary was willing to pay £25, well above the usual price, for a "choice Negro woman" who was, he presumed, fit for childbearing as well as field work.[64] Whaley did not buy any slaves off one ship because "they were very sickly." Slaves were essential parts of the capital of the plantation; indeed, in one letter Whaley joined Negroes and coppers (the vats used for boiling sugar) as the objects of capital expense. In a letter written shortly before his death, Cary Helyar calculated the value of the plantation. He valued the whole at £1,898 8s. 3d., of which slaves accounted for £1,100, or about 58 percent of the total. When Whaley died, his slaves were valued at £2,288, more than 75 percent of his property.[65]

The purchase of slaves was a matter of obsessive interest to all the planters in the islands, and they regularly lobbied the authorities in England in favor of policies that guaranteed their access to a plentiful supply. When sugar was introduced in Barbados, slaves were sold to the island by Dutch traders as well as English merchants. After the passage of the first Navigation Act in 1651, English traders gained a monopoly of the legal slave trade. Following the Restoration, the trade was lodged first in the Company of Royal Adventurers in Africa and then, from 1672 to 1698, in the Royal African Company. For forty years, planters were largely dependent on these companies. The supply of slaves was never adequate and was often interrupted by war and conflict. Independent traders, called interlopers, smuggled additional slaves but never enough to fill the demand. The companies not only defended their own monopoly but also at various times gained the right to provide slaves to the Spanish colonies, thus forcing English planters to compete against the Spanish.[66] The leading planters in both Barbados and Jamaica were often agents of the company; they gained a better chance of purchasing slaves and profited from their sales to other planters. Their use of political power to advance their interests against those of the small planters—who were often indebted either to the company or directly to the large planters—was the source of major political conflicts in the islands.

As government officials in Barbados and Jamaica frequently reminded their superiors in London, slaves were an absolute necessity for the prosperity of the islands. As early as 1660, Barbados planters complained that slaves were now twice their earlier price.[67] In 1673, a year after the Royal African Company was chartered, there were complaints about both the supply of slaves in Jamaica and the price: the Jamaican planters thought Barbados was favored because of the debts already owing to the company.[68] Two years later, the Council of Barbados complained that the shortage of slaves for sale was so severe that the price had risen from £16 to £20–£22; even "infirm" slaves were being sold for £15.[69] In 1680 planters in Jamaica argued that since interlopers could sell slaves for £14, the company ought to sell them for no more than £17; furthermore, they could easily sell 3,000 to 4,000 slaves a year. Interest rates of 20 percent for the first six months and 15 percent thereafter made it impossible for poor planters ever to pay for the slaves they purchased.[70] In 1683 Jamaican planters complained that the company had sent no slaves at all that year; the governor allowed interlopers to provide slaves so that planters could purchase a few.[71] In 1698 the Council of Barbados insisted that the company offer more slaves for sale on "easy terms." Only the representatives of the company, such as Jamaica's governor Sir William Beeston, defended its practices; in 1700 he maintained that while the Royal African Company had sold slaves at £24 each or less with up to a year's credit, the independent merchants who were increasingly taking over the trade were selling them for £34 and offering no credit at all.[72]

The actual number of slaves brought to the West Indies was higher than these gloomy pronouncements suggest. Between 1661 and 1700, more than 245,000 slaves arrived in the English sugar islands, the vast majority in Barbados and Jamaica. During that same time, the slave population of Barbados rose from 12,800 to 50,000 and that of Jamaica from 500 to 42,000. Thus more than half the slaves brought to the islands had already died, many prematurely of disease or overwork. The planters' repeated complaints reflect the unpredictability of the supply of slaves rather than an absolute shortage. The market price of slaves varied enormously. In Barbados, for instance, the average price of a male slave rose from £10 8s. in 1692 to £23 10s. in 1695, and fell to £9 8s. in 1699; the number of slaves imported ranged from over 8,000 in 1683, down to 679 with the disruption of war in 1690, and up to over 4,000 in 1697. Because of the high mortality, slaves never reproduced themselves, and planters relied on new arrivals to keep their plantations going. Through the seventeenth century, approximately 90 percent of the slaves in Jamaica had been brought from Africa; those born in the Caribbean remained few in number until mortality rates among slaves declined.[73]

The health and fitness of such valuable and productive property was a matter of concern, especially when the owner managed a plantation. While Cary Helyar was alive, none of the Bybrook slaves died; Whaley repeatedly reported on the "good health" of the slaves, once despite the fact that "we have had a very sickly year of it amongst our white people." An illness that killed four slaves in 1675 is the first mention of slave deaths in the Helyar correspondence. The attention that Cary and Whaley had taken in the purchase and care of their slaves was rewarded.[74] But such good fortune could not last. When a hurricane of October 1689 wiped out the plantain walks at Bybrook, the slaves "were like to starve," especially because the hurricane's destruction made all provisions on the island more expensive. Although Bybrook suffered relatively little damage in the catastrophic earthquake of 1692, the destruction of Port Royal led to a shortage of supplies; three years later, the overseer reported that Bybrook had lost many slaves "since the earthquake." In 1698 John Austin reported that "the Negroes continue dying still," even though the slave houses had been moved to "as fine and healthful a place as the plantation affords." When Robert Hall took over the management of the plantation, he complained that recently "little care [was] taken, especially of Negroes who come at a great charge have been starved to death & mules and cattle likewise."[75]

William Helyar believed that good treatment of slaves was essential to the profitability of the plantation. As an English gentleman, he had an essentially paternalist attitude to his dependents. In 1678 he urged his overseers to treat them "with that humanity that every good man will afford even to his very beast." And he added, "What is it that those poor creatures will not do for a master that will treat them a little kindly?" The lists of slaves sent to Helyar at various times underline his concern with the slave workforce. Several list slaves by name; all distinguish between various levels of health and ability. Thus Hall's inventory of April 1700 identifies "those very old" or "very old very little labor they do," and "pretty able Negro men some of them but indifferent disordered by ill management and want of plantation provisions" and "several very weak and low in strength." Although women were generally expected to do the same work as men, Hall acknowledged that the ten slave women who were nursing "cannot be supposed to do much."[76]

Helyar's paternalism was, however, largely irrelevant in Jamaica. The health of slaves was threatened in two ways, neither of which was addressed by his admonitions. First was their condition when they arrived in the islands. The mortality of enslaved Africans on the middle passage is well known; in the 1680s, some 23 percent died during the journey. While mortality declined over time, conditions on the ships represented "probably the purest form of domination in the history of slavery as an institution."[77] Even those slaves who survived the voyage were often weakened by it. In 1685 the

Barbados Assembly complained that the slaves being sold in the island were sicker and weaker than formerly: "In those days we purchased a better sort of Negroes." Now planters had to keep more slaves to do the same work.[78] Slaves who were already weakened by the scarcity of food and water, prevalence of disease, and lack of exercise on the transatlantic journey could not cope well with conditions in the West Indies.

On plantations in Barbados and Jamaica, slaves' health was further undermined by the heavy work planters demanded and the inadequate food they provided, as well as by the diseases prevalent on the islands. The work slaves did was backbreaking and unending. Planters ensured that slaves were always working. Strict discipline was necessary to keep slaves at work, and idleness was regarded as a threat to order. Planters resisted mechanical improvements that might have lightened the load of labor. The key determinant of the number of slaves that planters kept was the number needed during the harvesting and processing of sugarcane; the rest of the work was designed to keep slaves busy outside the times of greatest demand.

Planters themselves acknowledged the problem of inadequate food. Edward Littleton, writing against the 4.5 percent duty levied by the government on sugar, maintained it impoverished the planters, so slaves "must fare and work the harder. And that their masters cannot now allow them, and provide for them, as they should and would." As he drafted instructions to his overseer in 1679, Colonel Henry Drax insisted that his slaves be adequately fed, since an adequate diet was necessary for health. Yet he was more concerned about security than about slaves' well-being. His instructions included advice to have sugar shipped to Bridgetown either late at night or early in the morning, to avoid "the heat of the day . . . [which] is destructive both to horses and horned beasts, and also the acquaintance of other carters."[79] It is not clear whether he thought other carters would encourage theft or foment plots against owners; both would jeopardize his profits. Drax sought to protect his cattle from the heat and his slaves from corruption.

Littleton and Drax both attest to the toll that labor in the islands took on slaves. Littleton suggested that a planter with 100 slaves would have to purchase at least six new slaves each year to keep up the numbers. Drax, who left his overseer with more than 200 slaves, assumed that maintaining that number would require the purchase of between ten and fifteen slaves each year, which estimates chronic morality at between 5 and 7.5 percent. If an epidemic, "which I beseech the great God of mercy to defend you from," devastated the slave population, the purchase of twenty or more slaves would be required. Drax suggested that one way to provide enough food for the

slaves was to plant a variety of provisions, including plantains, sweet potatoes, guinea corn (millet), and cassava; if a pest or disease attacked one
crop, the others would provide adequate nourishment. In addition to the
crops grown to nourish both slaves and animals on the plantations, Drax
ordered that his slaves be given one pound of fish, or two mackerel, and two
quarts of molasses weekly. Slaves who worked as task overseers and head
boilers received double the normal allowance. Tobacco, palm oil, and salt
were distributed occasionally.[80]

Drax's instructions about slave provisions were unusual in their detail and
generosity. According to Ligon, when he first arrived on the island slave
provisions were limited to plantains, cassava bread, maize, and potatoes,
though by the time he left the provision of two mackerel a week had become
more common. The shortage of land in Barbados made many planters reluctant to devote much of it to slave provisions, though there were often limited
provision grounds. In Jamaica, however, the easy availability of land led
planters to have each slave family grow their own food on a plot of land—
according to Taylor, half an acre. This arrangement shifted the burden of
providing food from the planter to the slave; planters had to provide extra
food only in times of serious drought; over time, it also helped create commercial opportunities for slaves. Cassava, guinea corn, and plantains were
the staples of slaves' diet. Salt beef and salt fish were imported from England;
sometimes grain or other foods were brought from New England. In 1696
the Helyars sent two barrels of herring from Bristol to Jamaica; in 1700 Robert Hall wrote that he needed a barrel of herring each month for the slaves,
while the "family"—the white servants—consumed a barrel of beef every two
weeks. The beef and herring should be shipped from England, he argued,
because the prices were lower there than in the islands. The cheapness of
provisions suggests their quality: in 1690 the Council of Jamaica decided that
rotten food taken off naval ships should be sold as slave provisions.[81]

Drax spent less time specifying the food for his servants, whom he called
his "family of whites," than for his slaves. They clearly occupied a superior
place in the order of the plantation. Every Sunday they were called to a service
of morning prayer with the overseer. When they were punished, they were to
be placed in the stocks, while slaves were to be whipped. This difference
reflected the different offences for which Drax assumed that white servants
and slaves would be punished: servants were more likely to be drunk, slaves
to be thieves. The superior status of servants relative to slaves is made even
more obvious by their control over tools, which were issued and inventoried
by "white overseers" to prevent theft by slaves.[82]

Slaves did all the field work, planting and dunging the canes. They also did most of the processing: they fed the canes into the mill, ladled the juice into the large coppers in which it was boiled, skimmed the impurities from the boiling juice, transferred it to progressively smaller vats, potted the sugar, placed the potted sugar in jars, and moved it to the curing house.[83] This was both skilled and dangerous work. In 1690 a slave at Bybrook, Major Needham, was killed when he fell between the grinding cases of the sugar mill. Such accidents were common. Edward Littleton described the dangers: "If a stiller slip into a rum-cistern, it is sudden death; for it stifles in a moment. If a mill-feeder be catched by the finger, his whole body is drawn in, and he is squeezed to pieces. If a boiler get any part into the scalding sugar, it sticks like glue, or birdlime, and 'tis hard to save either limb or life."[84]

At the height of the harvest, the mills and boiling houses ran "at all hours of the day" and night from one o'clock on Monday morning until late Saturday night. Speed was critical to the entire process: the canes had to be crushed as soon as possible after harvesting, and the juice had to be boiled within a few days of crushing. All the slaves on the plantation worked intensively and unremittingly throughout the harvest period. Their work was specialized, and that of the boilers and stillers extremely skilled. Sugar processing was an industrial enterprise on a scale completely unfamiliar to the English. The machinery had to be well maintained and, because of the importance of timing, replacement parts had to be on hand. In the seventeenth century, the work of maintaining the equipment was primarily done by white servants, particularly carpenters, millwrights, and smiths, although slaves were also beginning to carry on these trades, especially in Barbados. All the rest of the work of the plantation was organized around the harvest. Drax suggested that the various building projects on the plantation be scheduled so that "not one days time either of planting, weeding, or making of sugar" was missed. The detailed description Drax provided about the production process underscores the complexity of the plantation as an agricultural and industrial enterprise. He assumed that relatively few people understood the system as a whole, and that even a man he trusted to manage the enterprise in his absence knew only parts of it.[85]

The exploitation of slaves involved direct, personal coercion as well as labor. This aspect of social relations in the sugar islands is rarely visible in planters' correspondence; the language of servitude masked the most brutal realities of enslavement. The human dimensions of relations of domination, although seldom discussed, occasionally leaked out in planters' correspondence with their associates at home. The most common of these involved the sexual exploitation of slaves. White masters frequently had sexual relationships with enslaved women, especially in Jamaica. This phenomenon, which violated racial boundaries while enacting and reinforcing hierarchies of power, was a predictable outcome of the relative scarcity of white women in the island colonies. Such relationships could never be consensual, though some were long-term. Whaley's treatment of the paternity claim by a mulatto woman owned by his friend and patron Thomas Modyford against the deceased Cary Helyar suggests that such a situation, however common, was embarrassing to explain to people in England. Whaley began his report to William Helyar with a convoluted apology: "Sir, here happened a business the other day which causes me to write that which I never intended to acquaint you withal, until I delivered it by my own mouth." He followed this evasion with an excuse: "It happened when your brother was living, he being as indeed in these hot countries most men are, a little venereal given." Only then did Whaley tell the story. For several years, Cary Helyar had kept a mulatto mistress. She had borne him two children; one had died, and the other was now about five. Cary had given the woman a small pension just before he married, when he "turned away this wench." Three years later she claimed that the promised pension had not been small, but £32 per year for life, and sued Whaley for £140—four years of support, as well as £12 damages for not receiving the money in a timely manner. Whaley triumphantly reported that he had successfully defended the estate from her claims. However, at the instigation of Modyford, Helyar later provided a regular pension for the child.[86]

What is remarkable about this report is, first, that the legal dispute between the mulatto mistress and the deceased planter's estate occurred at all. The slave woman, who is never identified by name, ought not to have been able to go to court because she had no civil identity. Yet Whaley never argued that the case was inappropriate, although he did his best to discredit the story. In this early period, the law and practice of slavery were more flexible than they later became. Over time, while sexual relationships between masters and slaves certainly continued in Jamaica, suing for child support became unimaginable. This woman's ability to bring suit depended at least in part on the support of her owner. Although the woman was a slave, she held a privileged position in the Modyford household: she waited on Sir Thomas Modyford's daughter. As many black women discovered, work in domestic service that brought them into direct contact with white men made them especially vulnerable to sexual coercion.[87]

A second significant feature of this case is the variety in the descriptions of the woman in question, which underlines the fluidity of notions of race during the development of slavery. Whaley began his report to Helyar by defining "mulatto"—he did not assume that this term or concept was familiar in England. Whaley and Modyford wrestled, in different ways, with distinctions within the category "Negro." Racial categories figured in the dispute over the value and admissibility of sworn testimony about the woman's relationship with Cary Helyar that was offered in court by her mother and her mother's husband. In perhaps the most interesting exchange Whaley recounted, he tried to discount the testimony of the woman's mother: "I told the judges she was a Negro, and her oath was not valuable. [Sir Thomas] made answer she was a Brazil Negro, and had lived with him seven years in Barbados, and after married that man." To Modyford it mattered, at least rhetorically, that the woman testifying had not just been brought from Africa but had come from Brazil and had lived in Barbados for some time.[88] While Whaley and Modyford each had strategic reasons for their arguments, both their rationales were marked by tension between the assumption that all "Negroes" were the same and the recognition that some were different from others. This case shows how complicated thinking about identity was during the time when the slave system was being constructed and reminds us that the interconnections between race and gender extended beyond work to sexuality, reproduction, and legal power.

Negro slaves on Barbados and Jamaica engaged in a constant tug-of-war with their white masters. The provision grounds they cultivated certainly saved the planters money, but they also provided slaves with a more independent subsistence and a measure of control over their own work. On Sundays and holidays, slaves enjoyed their leisure time and carried on their own recreations and celebrations. Although slaves were not allowed to be baptized as Christians, they were not expected to work on the staple crop on Sundays and religious holidays. Christmas was observed with some fanfare, which soon became a matter of local custom: in 1690 the Council of Jamaica ordered that the slaves be taken care of "as usual" over Christmas. Their music and dancing was observed with fascinated wonder by English visitors. Ligon described how "in the afternoons on Sundays, they have their music" and "to dancing they go, the men by themselves and the women by themselves." Taylor wrote that they "gather together in great companies, going to visit their countrymen in other plantations, where according to their own country fashion they feast, dance, and sing (or rather howl like a beast) in an antic manner, as if they were all mad."[89] Modern scholars, like seventeenth-century observers, recognize these practices as African in origin. But what social scientists now see as cultural continuity and concerted resistance to enslavement seemed to contemporary English people signs of backwardness and inferiority. These commentaries contrasted the "antic"—bizarre and grotesque—recreations of the slaves to the more civilized pastimes of the white population, serving to remind readers that slaves were a strange, wild, and rude sort of people. It was these perceived and ascribed differences between slaves and white people that justified, in English eyes, the work slaves did and the treatment they received.

Trading

Life on the plantations was often quite isolated; sociability, as well as trade, was centered in the towns. William Whaley remarked to Helyar that "it is not one newcomer in ten that fancies living at a plantation for they cannot live without the company." At about the same time, William Dampier, whom Helyar had sent to assist Whaley, accused Whaley of spending time in Spanish Town, "sometimes in business and sometimes for his pleasure," while he thought of "nothing but how to abuse me."[90] The isolation of the plantations was a cause of danger as well as discontent. In 1694 a privateer attacked the Jamaican plantation of Widow Barrow, "plundered all her Negroes, household goods and all she had, Tortured her to confess if she had money and then took away with him her maiden daughter, Mrs. Rachel Barrow of about 14 years." The attack succeeded, Governor Beeston wrote, because of the sparse settlement of the north of the island: "In at least 25 or 30 miles space, there was not above 130 men of all sorts, and therefore not possible in any wise to defend themselves."[91] The isolation was less striking in more densely populated Barbados, but even there residents outside the towns often lived in widely scattered houses.

The islands' wealth depended as much on the exchange of information as goods. Planters and servants went to the towns because there they found connections to the wider world. Yet even the towns were a long way from the centers of trade and power in England, and the communication links on which they depended were often tenuous. For instance, the Earl of Carlisle received three letters, dated 25 March, 4 April, and 31 May, on 26 August 1679.[92] That same year, the Assembly of Jamaica offered arguments against the constitutional reforms proposed by London to institute a government similar to that in Ireland, where all legislation was initiated in London. One of their arguments was entirely practical: exchanges between London and Dublin could be completed in two weeks, not the year that had to be expected with the Caribbean.[93] Those who had not been there rarely grasped the full implications of the delays in communication on life in the islands. The difficulties of communication also affected those in England, like the Helyars, who sought to manage their plantations from a distance.

The Jamaican Assembly was excessively pessimistic in suggesting it would take a year for an exchange of letters, but it was rare for correspondence between England and the islands to take less than six months, and eight to ten months was more common. There were whole times of year when no ships sailed, particularly during the late summer, when Atlantic hurricanes posed a great danger. Not only did letters take a long time to arrive, they often did not arrive at all. Those in the islands routinely sent two or three copies of their letters by different ships in the hope that at least one copy would reach its destination. Thus Cary Helyar's letter of 10 September 1671 of that year began by saying "the foregoing" was a copy of his last letter, though the copy in the Helyar papers does not include it; an addition to that letter is dated 23 October, by which time Cary had received William's letter of 25 May. A letter from Richard Trew mentioned by William in his letter had not arrived.[94] The situation was particularly acute in wartime. In 1695 Governor Beeston described the misadventures of one letter:

> In my last which was by Capt. Willmot I acquainted your Lordships with all things then necessary in relation to this island, but we have late news from New York that he and Capt. Lance died about Cuba, and the *Winchester* unfortunately lost in the Gulf of Florida, and the rest designed to Virginia there to refresh and recruit, having lost many men by the sickness they brought hither, and for that reason I now send Mr. Blathwayte the duplicate of that letter supposing it may get home before the original.[95]

The difficulties of communication compounded the serious problems faced by absentee owners. Before the eighteenth century, the islands lacked systems of control to protect the interests of nonresident planters. The Helyars' experience with Thomas Hillyard from 1678 to 1686 is instructive. The original agreement was that after the expenses of the plantation were deducted, Hillyard would get one-third of the profits of Bybrook. However, he interpreted the agreement to mean that he would take one-third of the income and then charge all the expenses to Helyar. To further his scheme, he failed to send detailed accounts. The Helyars sent additional servants and furnished funds for the purchase of more slaves when Hillyard repeatedly demanded them, but Hillyard complained that the supply of labor was still inadequate, and eventually Helyar discovered that Hillyard was selling servants and slaves. Sailors returning from Jamaica also reported that Hillyard was selling the plantation's best sugar on his own account and using the profits to settle his own plantation. As early as 1681, Helyar had drawn on the knowledge he had developed as a plantation owner to offer negative comparisons between the coarse, and therefore less profitable, sugar that Hillyard shipped in the name of Bybrook and other Jamaican sugars arriving in Bristol. In early 1686 an exasperated Helyar wrote, "You cannot think me so blind here, but that we see what you do do [sic], what is become of all the sugar you made this year, you have sent me but about £70 the least that ever you sent yet." By August of that year, Helyar had discovered the full extent of the fraud, which he laid out in a letter. He hoped that the exposure of Hillyard's corruption would encourage him to make restitution and to give full possession to his son John Helyar, who had now arrived on the island. But it took another year for John to gain full control of the property, and that required an arbitration in which Hillyard, instead of paying Helyar back, was himself paid off to release the plantation from his claims. As John Helyar noted ruefully in an early letter from Jamaica, "Thomas Hillyard has made it his business to mind his own interest before yours."[96]

The difficulties caused to absentee owners by distance and a lack of information about events on the islands were sufficiently well known that when Colonel Henry Drax left Barbados in 1679, he built into his instructions detailed provisions for relatives and friends on the island to oversee the plantation and its accounts. In 1695 the executors of Barbara Newton complained of the difficulties they faced in getting payments of more than £6,000 owed to Newton by two men on a lease of her plantation; five years later they were trying to collect some £30,000 owed by another of Newton's debtors. In 1702 the Council of Barbados described the criminal career of one Edward Burke, who arrived as a "bought servant" of Tobias Frere, Esq. When his master died, he stayed on the plantation and convinced Frere's son Tobias to give him a lease and make him guardian of his son. Burke never paid any rent, and after both Tobias Jr. and his son had died, he refused to turn the plantation over to the heir, a nephew of Tobias Sr. "Capt. Burke now still lives upon the plantation and will come to no account, nor yield possession," the Council remarked, adding that he "seeks to be made one of the Council to keep Tobias Frere the nephew from having the benefit of the law against him, and to keep him out of the possession of his just right." Burke used his connections in England to get himself named to the Council, taking advantage of the lack of local knowledge among those in London.[97]

English people who had no direct interest in colonial plantations found it difficult to understand the situations represented in letters, which contributed to the planters' and officials' frustrations. In the midst of a testy exchange with his superiors in London in 1678, Sir Jonathan Atkins, the governor of Barbados, complained about how letters could be misread: "Letters are but characters, and take no more impression than according to the character the persons to whom they are directed will put upon them, which commonly is according as they apprehend the sense of them, either as they understand or are inclined to believe. This I find to be the common fate of letters of business; familiar epistles move in another circle, they usually encounter kindness."[98] Communication was hampered not only by the distance but also by the difficulties of enforcing decisions over 4,000 miles, by competing agendas, and by profound misunderstandings.

Communication was critical to the exchange of goods and money between England and the islands, which was the lifeblood of the entire colonial project. The shape of trade was determined by the Navigation Acts, which required all legal trade to be carried in English ships. This requirement, as well as the 4.5 percent duty on sugar, were subjects of almost constant complaints in Barbados and Jamaica. When Sir Thomas Modyford went to Jamaica as governor in 1664, he wrote home that he had promised free trade to settlers but was not sure whether he had the power to do so. Three years later, Lord Willoughby insisted that the survival of Barbados depended on free trade with Scotland in order to obtain a supply of servants. In 1676 a complaint from the Council of Barbados about the Navigation Acts was considered in London, but rejected; the Council argued that it was inappropriate—and set a bad precedent—if colonists "should presume to petition your Majesty against Acts of Parliament which are the laws they must live under, & call them grievances." Yet, that same year another observer noted that the "Act for Trade and Commerce" had, "by bringing all their commodities to one market . . . brought down the price of them to so low an ebb" that planters could not earn enough to pay the costs of production.[99]

The interests of the planters were at odds with those of merchants, who enjoyed a monopoly on and guaranteed supply of colonial products. The interests of London won out over those of the islands. But this debate is important because it reveals the increasing gap in perceptions between those in the islands and those in England. The issues involved arose partly from the well-understood differences between producers and merchants, but the central role played by the government in the regulation of colonial trade made the entire matter fraught with political significance. The government's determination to control trade policy pushed the planters to define their position clearly and defend it carefully. As early as 1655, the Barbados planters presented the situation in stark language: if forced to trade only with English ships, "the planters may then seem to be but as so many slaves to the merchants employed and appointed to drudgery." With all the political charge that such language carried in the aftermath of the Civil War, they asserted that they were Englishmen "and would be as free as any English subjects and ought to enjoy those common liberties and privileges due to them without restraint."[100] This contrast between slavery and freedom stands in ironic contrast to the actual social relations of the islands. The emphasis on the planters' liberty and freedom as English subjects remained a major theme in political relations between the colonies and the Crown. It was as difficult to decide how to manage law and government as it was to manage the cultivation and processing of sugar.

Right English Government
Law and Liberty, Service and Slavery

They [are] so well acquainted with
their own laws that they keep copies of them.
GOVERNOR JONATHAN ATKINS,
10 November 1678

In 1695 the Assembly of Barbados reminded Governor Russell of the pleasure
they had taken in his appointment as their governor and of their expectations
of government, while providing a summary of their conflicts with his pre-
decessors. In doing so, they placed themselves in relation to an ongoing
English debate about liberty and authority. They welcomed, they said, "a
person to Govern us who was descended of a family famed for moderation:
who had always carried it evenly betwixt the prerogative and the just liberties
of the people, true lovers and asserters of the right English Government. . . .
We received you as the redeemer of our just rights and liberties as we were
English men; which had been too much trampled upon by some former
Governors."[1] By the time they wrote this, the Barbados planters had also been
disappointed in Russell. In their view, the governor should balance his prerogatives with the rights of the people. But government in the islands never
measured up to what the planters expected of "right English government."

In designing a government for the colonies, English colonists thought
they knew what they were doing. Many had participated in the English legal

and political system as jurors and voters, if not as holders of local offices. They knew what government should look like. Yet the process of establishing a legal and political system was fraught with conflicts among English colonists, as well as between them and authorities in London. A functional constitutional and legal framework was constructed only after a long struggle in both islands, although the challenges colonists encountered and the political conflicts in which they engaged differed somewhat in Jamaica and Barbados. As they defined the relationship between the islands and England, planters focused on their rights and liberties as Englishmen, while authorities in London focused on their own authority over the colonies.[2]

Yet plantation society in Barbados and Jamaica was not structured along the same lines as that in England, and the island colonies were far away from the capital. Nothing worked quite as planned. Familiar institutions proved woefully inadequate for colonial conditions, or they worked in unaccustomed ways. The courts, functioning in relatively sparsely populated and isolated islands, were corrupt and inefficient. Over the whole system of government and law loomed the problem of slavery. The law of service, which defined relations between masters and those who worked for them, could not meet the demands placed on it by the development of the slave labor system: a whole new set of laws relating to slavery had to be created and tailored to plantation conditions. The legal structure of slavery was not complete until the end of the century, long after both islands had become functionally slave societies. The liberties of Englishmen and the law of slavery, then, evolved simultaneously and as part of the same process.[3] Thus, it is important to examine constitutional development and legal structures simultaneously; although they often appear to involve separate issues, their development was profoundly intertwined.

Constitutional Structures

The processes of establishing government in Barbados and Jamaica followed different paths, since the island colonies were founded in very different ways. Barbados was originally settled under a proprietary patent, and for most of its first twenty-five years it had a governor appointed by the patentee. After the execution of the king, direct control from London was established. After the Restoration, King Charles II assumed the powers of the proprietors to himself, though he made Francis, Lord Willoughby, who held a lease of the patent, governor of "Barbados and the rest of the Caribbee Islands." In 1663 Willoughby persuaded the Assembly of Barbados to grant the king a tax of 4.5 percent on all commodities exported; in exchange for assuming this obligation to the Crown, planters' titles to land were confirmed, and any obligations to pay rents to the proprietors were removed. From this point onwards, Barbados was a royal colony. This constitutional situation, while stable, created chronic political disputes. The islanders complained about the Crown's control of the 4.5 percent, which they thought should pay for the government and defense of the island. They also sought to enlarge the power of the Assembly at the expense of the Crown and the governor.[4]

Jamaica was conquered by an English army, so there was never any dispute about the locus of control. However, the transition from military to civilian rule and from the imperatives of conquest to the demands of settlement was protracted and incomplete. After the Restoration of Charles II, a civil government was instituted, with a governor appointed by the king. Initially, the governor was assisted by an elected Council, which established the framework of government. It set up courts, enacted laws, and served as a court of appeal from other courts in the island. In 1663 the Council decided to call for elections to an Assembly. The Assembly met in early 1664 and immediately claimed legislative power, insisting that only those laws that it had confirmed were in force. It also asserted that no revenue acts could be passed without its participation, preemptively claiming rights that its members feared they might not have. From 1664 the structure of Jamaican government was parallel to that of Barbados. However, Jamaica's location and history of slave resistance, as we shall see in the next chapter, meant that its governors frequently declared martial law.[5]

The constitutional structure of the islands generated persistent conflicts. Tensions inherent in the colonial relationship were compounded by the distance between England and the islands. The colonists saw themselves as Englishmen and expected the rights and liberties that all Englishmen enjoyed. This expectation, which they usually expressed in terms of the power to write their own laws, conflicted with both royal and parliamentary authority. They also resented what they saw as their obligation to pay taxes twice: the export duties on sugar were paid to the Crown, but they also had to levy taxes to support the governor and pay the militia. Colonists were convinced that authorities in London did not understand their needs, as the king insisted on one set of laws and repeatedly rejected laws they had written. An examination of these endemic conflicts helps identify the points of difference and the lessons that had to be learned to govern the islands.

The most common conflicts centered on the location and extent of authority. In both Barbados and Jamaica, a royal governor held local authority;

he governed with the assistance of a Council, with periodic meetings of an elected Assembly. The governor's power came by virtue of a royal commission, which set out the tasks he was to undertake and the policies he was to follow, as well as necessary changes in colonial law and practice. These "Instructions," which often run to twenty or thirty pages of manuscript, were drafted by a committee responsible to the Privy Council in London. This supervisory group went through various reorganizations, name changes, and shifts in membership, but its location in the Privy Council reflected the importance of the colonies. In the early 1660s, the Privy Council was assisted by a "Council for Foreign Plantations"; in 1672 it was replaced by the "Council for Trade and Plantations." In 1675 the work of these committees was shifted to a subcommittee of the Privy Council called the Lords of Trade. In 1696 the Lords Commissioners of Trade and Plantations, commonly known as the Board of Trade, was established. The names of the various offices in charge of colonial affairs indicate their mission: to promote trade in order to increase England's wealth. Colonies, or "plantations," were central to that effort. In pursuing that objective, these subcommittees of the Privy Council vigorously defended the royal prerogative.[6]

The problems relating to authority can be seen in the process of passing laws in the islands. Legislation was passed by the Assembly and then approved by the Council and governor before being sent to England for royal assent. This process was cumbersome and inefficient. Laws were assumed to be in force for two years before they needed royal assent, but if there were any questions, it might easily take more than two years for approval to come through. In Barbados, the Assembly began passing laws when it first met in 1638. The earliest laws whose text survives are those passed in 1652, shortly after the island's surrender to Parliament's forces. These laws, published in London in 1654, codify previous laws and make frequent reference to prior legislation; they were not primarily new laws.[7] The laws passed between 1652 and 1661 are now missing, so the continuous series of Barbados laws begins in 1661.

In Jamaica, the first civil government quickly enacted several ordinances, especially for raising revenue; between 1661 and 1664, when the first Assembly met, laws were enacted by the governor and Council as needed. The first laws in Jamaica were directly copied from the 1654 edition of the laws of Barbados; for the first year or so, most laws depended on the Barbados model. In the preamble to a law regarding debtors in 1662, the Council made explicit its reliance on other colonies as models, saying, "Acts of this nature are allowed and practiced by well-constituted governments of Barbados and other Caribee Islands." In 1664 Governor Modyford sent twenty-seven laws back to England for approval by the king. In 1670 he reported that while the Earl of Clarendon had told him they were approved, he had never received the official royal assent, so he sent another copy of the statutes.[8]

Reading the correspondence between the islands and London about law, the distance that divided the participants is striking. The geographical distance compounded the differences in points of view that arose from divergent experiences and priorities. The commission to Lord Willoughby to serve as governor of Barbados in 1663 required him to send any laws passed in Barbados to London for approval; he apparently never did so.[9] When Sir Jonathan Atkins was appointed governor in 1672, his commission not only repeated the requirement that he send all laws he passed for approval, but it also asked that he send all laws already in force in the island to London for review. This apparently simple request was not answered until 1679, after seven years of increasingly impatient correspondence between London and Barbados. In June 1678 Atkins complained that he had received a duplicate copy of a letter he had already answered. Atkins had to contend with the attitudes of the planters; the Assembly would not allow Atkins to send original copies of the laws, so he was having them copied.[10] Four months later, he wrote that the planters worried that "if their laws might be taken away, their proprieties might follow them."[11] Their ability to make laws and govern themselves was central to their understanding of themselves as Englishmen and to protecting their property.

The following year the Lords of Trade sent Atkins a furious letter, suggesting, on the basis of complaints from merchants in London, that he was not doing enough to protect the king's interest.[12] Atkins dashed off a preliminary response within four days. His answer concluded, "My lords, I must finish with a request that you will please to consider me as the King's Governor here, and that you are pleased to put the opinion of Merchants, or people that are concerned in this Island in balance with me, 'tis something hard to bear as your letter expresses, they tell you their own interests and it may be not the King's, which when 'tis required I shall faithfully do."[13] When the laws finally arrived, the Lords of Trade concluded they offered adequate protection to the king's authority, "and for good of his subjects inhabiting there, . . . although some of the laws therein contained are not consonant to the laws of England." Most dissonant were the laws regarding the trials of slaves; limitations on the rights of the accused were justified, the

Lords of Trade decided, because of the large numbers of slaves, and their "being a brutish sort of People."[14]

The testy correspondence between Atkins and London illuminates the anxiety about sovereignty in Barbados, where colonists worried they would lose rights they thought they already had. In Jamaica, by contrast, the great fear was that they did not have the rights they thought they should have. As inhabitants of a conquered island, the planters worried that the king could and would claim the right to govern arbitrarily. The Assembly repeatedly asserted that all laws and customs of England applied to Jamaica. In 1670 Modyford declared, "Right reason which is the common law of England is esteemed and of force amongst us, together with Magna Charta and the ancient statutes of England, so far as they are practicable."[15] The question was, who decided what was "practicable"? The claim that English law was in force in the islands was one element in the recurring conflicts between London and Jamaica. In 1676 a letter from London responded to that assertion by arguing that the situation in the colony made such liberties dangerous: "The laws in England favor not any guards or standing forces. The statutes here have taken away the power and authority of the Council board . . . which considering the remoteness of that frontier place, might leave all in confusion."[16] The defense of the island, and the need for executive authority, militated against the full adoption of English laws, and English liberties, in Jamaica. A year later the Lords of Trade asked that the formula describing the enactment of laws be changed. The laws had been approved "by the Governor, Council, and Assembly"; the Lords insisted that the proper formula was, "Be it enacted by the King's most excellent Majesty and with the consent of the General Assembly." The Council further insisted that fines collected should not be assigned "for the public use of the island" but instead should be paid only "to the King's most excellent majesty."[17] The Lords of Trade sought to claim maximum authority for the Crown and its representatives, while the Jamaican formulations had located sovereignty in Jamaica rather than London.

In 1678 the government in London reinforced its claim to authority by attempting to reorganize the structure of Jamaican government. It asserted that the constitution of Jamaica could be altered simply by changing the terms of the governor's commission—confirming the worst fears of the planters that they lacked the rights of Englishmen. The new structure, modeled on that of Ireland, dramatically reduced the colony's independence. All legislation was to be initiated in London and then approved by the Assembly in Jamaica. The governor of Jamaica could only call a meeting of the Assembly when given permission by the king, although he could request permission to hold an assembly in an emergency.[18]

This procedure was remarkably unwieldy. When the first set of laws developed by the Lords of Trade was presented to the Assembly in Jamaica, the Assembly carefully explained its objections to particular clauses in each bill. After several days, the Assembly presented an address to the governor, the Earl of Carlisle, complaining of the "inconveniencies which are like to redound unto this his island by this method and manner of passing laws, which is absolutely impracticable." A year later, after receiving a negative response to their initial objections, the planters protested again. After all, with Ireland, "advice and answers thence may be had in ten or fourteen days"; it had taken a year for their objections to reach London and a response to be sent back. Furthermore, "we cannot imagine that Irish model of government was, *in principio*, ever intended for Englishmen." Or, as the governor reported the Assembly saying, "they will submit to wear but never consent to make chains, as they term this frame of government, to their posterities."[19] They were English, not Irish; they would accept the new model if they were forced to, but they would not give it legitimacy. The debate circled around two separate areas of incomprehension. Authorities in London apparently failed to understand the impediments to direct rule created by distance. Even more significantly, the Lords of Trade assumed that because Jamaica had been conquered, those who settled there were entirely subject to royal authority, while the colonists assumed that they were Englishmen and as such entitled to particular rights.

The Assemblies of Barbados and Jamaica made repeated efforts to define themselves as parallel to the House of Commons. In Jamaica, Governor John Vaughan unwittingly assisted this process when he insisted that the Assembly read bills three times (instead of twice, as had been the practice) to parallel the process in the House of Commons. In Barbados in 1690, Governor James Kendall complained that "some coxcombs have made them believe they have as many privileges as a House of Commons in England, they brought me a bill of Habeas Corpus, which I rejected."[20] Furthermore, the Lords of Trade's insistence on their right to approve laws encountered resistance in part because the planters thought the government at Westminster did not understand their purpose and necessity. As early as 1674, Governor Thomas Lynch wrote from Jamaica, "many things that may seem unreasonable there, are absolutely necessary here." He suggested that the Council only pay attention to whether laws damaged either the king's prerogative or his revenue, since the laws of the islands were "municipal."[21] Governor

Atkins noted in 1678 that the laws were "occasional," and if they were not allowed to pass such laws, "before we can hear of the confirmation inevitable ruin may fall upon the place."[22]

Contention over the rights of planters against the power of the king became acute when authorities in London seemed not to comprehend the distinctive conditions of colonial settlement. In both Barbados and Jamaica, conflicts focused on particular policies that pitted the interests of planters against those of the Crown. Even consulting the growing community of Jamaican and Barbadian merchants in London did not always help. Three issues dominated ongoing policy debates. The first was revenue. In Barbados, the Assembly objected to levying taxes for the defense of the island when they had already agreed to pay export duties. In Jamaica, the Assembly routinely voted revenue only for two years, while the Council in London sought to have it voted in perpetuity. Debates about the need for extra taxes in times of crisis recurred frequently. Planters' dislike of taxes was compounded by the increasing mistrust between London and the islands. Those in London thought the planters wanted a free ride, while the planters thought they were overtaxed and that the taxes reduced the return on their investment.[23]

The other two issues were repeatedly raised in letters from London to the islands. The first, on which everyone agreed, was the encouragement of immigration by white servants. The second, more contentious issue was the conversion of the slaves to Christianity. White servants were seen as an unalloyed good, and officials on both sides of the Atlantic were eager to support them. The Assemblies of Barbados and Jamaica routinely passed legislation "for the encouragement of white servants." They made sure that penalties for mistreatment of white servants were sufficient, and provided safeguards for their wages. White servants not only brought skills but were also vital to the defense of the islands. As the planters saw themselves increasingly threatened both by French raids and slave rebellions, they expected white servants to support the social order.[24] Planters and officials alike were concerned that the English population of the islands remained inadequate to enforce their rule; the repeated measures they adopted to induce white servants to immigrate bespeak a note of anxiety.

The conversion of slaves to Christianity was a favorite project of London authorities after 1680, but it was met with hesitation and outright resistance in the islands. The refusal of the planters to acquiesce to one of London's favorite projects shows the limits of royal power and underlines the divergent perspectives of those in London and the islands. Planters' refusal to convert the slaves to Christianity allowed them to define the differences between slaves and servants as pertaining not to race or status, but to religion. White people were Christian, and therefore servants, while black people were heathens, and therefore slaves. According to Ligon, a planter confronted by his slave's desire to become Christian responded, "The people of that Island were governed by the laws of England, and by those laws, we could not make a Christian a slave." By 1681 the Assembly of Barbados merely asserted that slaves could not become Christians because of their "savage brutishness."[25]

For the next half-century, the debate on conversion continued. In London, the benefits of conversion were self-evident, while in Barbados and Jamaica, the dangers were so obvious that allowing mass conversion was never seriously considered. In 1677 the Jamaica Assembly included in one of its laws a proviso that "no slave is free by becoming a Christian."[26] The contests over masters' authority that might arise from slaves' conversion were practical as well as theoretical. When the Barbados Assembly passed a statute in 1678 against Quakers, one of the chief complaints was that though "not one of them [the slaves] understood one word of what they said," hundreds would gather to listen to Quaker preachers and have the opportunity to plot a rebellion; for all their alleged incomprehension, it did not take them long to "learn the ceremony of keeping on their hats before their masters," and thus claim social equality.[27] In 1680, as the Lords of Trade developed instructions for the new governor, Sir Richard Dutton, they asked the Barbados merchants about the conversion of the slaves. The merchants provided multiple, and mutually contradictory, arguments against conversion:

> The Conversion of their slaves will not only destroy their Property, but endanger the safety of the Island. . . . Negroes as are converted usually grow more perverse and untractable than others and will not be so fit for labor and sale as others. . . . And that in order to their being made Christians it will be necessary to teach them all English which gives them an opportunity and facility of combining together against their masters and of destroying them. That they are a sort of People so averse to learning that they will rather hang themselves or run away than submit to it and that their conversion will very much impair their value and price which will much affect the African Company who are their first Masters.

The committee took the hint and only suggested that the governor "find out the best means to facilitate and encourage the conversion of Negroes and other slaves with due caution and regard to the property and safety of the island."[28]

When Dutton actually requested the Barbados Assembly "to prepare an expedient" for the conversion of slaves, the Assembly responded that "their savage brutishness renders them wholly uncapable and many have endeavored it without any success. But if a good expedient could be found for doing it the Assembly and all good people of this island would be most willing to promote it."[29] The Jamaica Assembly only passed a bill to encourage the conversion of slaves in 1688, when the planter elite had been displaced by small planters under the Duke of Albermarle.[30] The planters' resistance to conversion continued in Barbados, and in 1695 Governor Russell remarked cynically that "the greatest obstacle I apprehend in this is their keeping the Christian Holy days, most of the planters thinking Sundays too much for being spared from work."[31] The contradictions between the slave regime and the presumed status of Christians, as well as the weak development of the Church of England in the West Indies, meant that little was done to convert the slaves to Christianity during the seventeenth century.

The reasons given against the conversion of slaves by the Barbados merchants, most of whom had experience as planters, in 1680 underline the fragility of slave society and the anxiety of the planters living as a small minority surrounded by a large population of overworked slaves. Most slaves had been born in Africa, and planters saw their lack of a common language as a protection against rebellion. Fear seems the best explanation for the contradictory arguments that, on the one hand, the slaves would use English to plot against their masters, and on the other hand, they were too lazy to learn English at all. Planters realized that their control over the islands' labor force was tenuous and did whatever they could to reinforce it.

Serious disagreements over policy arose within island society and between Caribbean planters and London merchants who represented them, as well as between the merchants and the government. At times the conflicts were between large and small planters; at others, all planters were at odds with merchants, especially the agents of the Royal African Company. The divisions became visible in Jamaica in 1688–89, after the Duke of Albemarle arrived as governor. The duke's brief tenure (he died after only nine months in Jamaica) was tumultuous. When his first Assembly refused to grant him adequate supply, he called new elections and manipulated them so that few of the old members, representing the large planters, were returned. He removed key officers and replaced them with new ones. The new Assembly immediately sent a petition to the king, complaining of the Royal African Company and its agents. The company's chief agent in Jamaica, Colonel Hender Molesworth, an old friend of Cary Helyar, had been lieutenant governor and acting governor before Albermarle's arrival; Molesworth returned to England when Albermarle's attack on the Jamaican establishment began and alerted authorities to Albermarle's activities.[32]

The new Assembly claimed the company made it impossible for small planters to buy good slaves; the best ones went either to Dutch factors trading with Spanish islands or to the planters favored by the company's agents. They resented the slave trade with the Spanish islands on two counts. First, it reduced the number of slaves available for purchase in Jamaica; second, the few islanders who were allowed to participate in the trade (by buying slaves in Jamaica and selling them in Cuba) made enormous profits, allegedly 35 percent in six weeks. The scale of the profits in the exchange is confirmed by the correspondence of John Helyar. As he waited for a resolution of his dispute with Thomas Hillyard, he wrote, "If I had three or four hundred by me I would improve it to the highest degree" in a "private business arrived on by the governor [Molesworth]." He said the return was 40 percent in the course of a month and confirmed that access to the trade was limited, but he would have been able to benefit from his uncle's old contacts and friends.[33]

Albermarle did not limit himself to such a conventional attack on the elite. In February 1688 John Towers, a member of Albemarle's first Assembly, had a horse that was to run in a race against one of the duke's horses. Since the Assembly had no business that day, he asked leave to go to the race; his friends teasingly reminded him that the business of government came before a horse race. He agreed, saying "that indeed *salus populi suprema lex*" (the health of the people shall be the supreme law). His willingness to do the business of the Assembly was misinterpreted by Colonel Needham, one of Albermarle's allies, who reported to the duke that Towers had said "*populus est suprema lex.*" The switch from "the health of the people" to merely "the people" as the supreme law was an important one, for the latter would have been seditious—although even the former phrase had been thought to have revolutionary implications in 1648. Needham was expelled from the Assembly for breach of its privilege, but he was soon made a member of the Governor's Council, where he used his position to have Towers prosecuted for seditious words. While the indictment was brought forward, the case had to be sent to the jury four times before the government got its guilty verdict. Even then it was grudging: "If the words in themselves without any relation, did import malice and sedition against the government, then they found your petitioner guilty; which, if not, then they found Not Guilty." Towers was fined £600, but that fine was revoked on appeal to King William.[34]

The planter elite resisted the attack on their power mounted by Albermarle and his allies. Jamaica merchants in London joined Molesworth and members of the Royal African Company to reverse Albermarle's actions. Fortunately for them, the crisis coincided with the arrival in London of news of Albemarle's death. On 30 November 1688, a message sent in the name of James II stopped any further acts of the Assembly or Council and reappointed Molesworth as lieutenant governor. The king made a point of returning the practice of government to that in the time of Governor Lynch; he removed some of Albermarle's appointees from office and restored the previous holders to their positions.[35] None of this changed after the Glorious Revolution: there was a strong continuity of colonial policy, and the London merchants had effectively defended their interests. The old officers were in power again, and able to run things their way.

Courts

In Albemarle's attack on the planter elite, the courts acted as agents of the executive. As we have seen, the prosecutor in the Towers case forced the jury to consider its verdict four times. Colonial governors exercised a degree of power over the courts that was rare, though not unheard of, in England. In Barbados as well as Jamaica, a jury might be repeatedly told to reconsider until it arrived at the verdict that royal officials demanded. The courts in the West Indies were modeled closely on those in England, with separate systems of common law courts (Quarter Sessions, Courts of Oyer and Terminer), which heard criminal and property cases, and equity courts, which provided remedies in cases where common law offered no relief. The governor and his Council sat as a "Supreme Court," acting as King's Bench, Common Pleas, and Exchequer; the governor was also the judge of any cases in equity. When planters were dissatisfied with the result, they could—and often did—appeal to the Privy Council in London.[36] Given the relatively small white population of the islands, the legal system provided the appearance of justice in a context of relationships that impeded it.

In 1691 a protracted conflict erupted in Barbados between Governor Kendall and a member of his Council, Colonel John Hallet. The original dispute concerned Hallet's refusal to allow his wood to be cut in order to strengthen the defenses of the island; Kendall argued that Hallet had broken his oath as a councillor and suspended him from that office. Six months later, finding Hallet still somewhat recalcitrant, Kendall asked one of the justices to begin proceedings against him. Justice St. John decided that Hallet's offence amounted to "levying war against the crown" (treason) and asked him to post a bond of £1,000, with two securities for £500. While this bond was in force, one of the governor's servants insulted a slave who was escorting Hallet's wife, and Hallet attacked the servant. A justice of the peace then decided he had forfeited his bond to keep the peace. When Hallet was tried, the Grand Jury was held four days to force them to find a true bill; one juror described repeated threats against all those involved.[37]

Both colonists and officials complained repeatedly of incompetence and corruption in the execution of the law in the islands. The small white population included few with any legal training. In 1682 Governor Dutton in Barbados complained that "there is scarcely a particular cause on this island wherein judgment hath been given by the judges in . . . Common Pleas, but there is either an injunction, or writ of error prayed for to bring it before myself for my final determination." Although he was asked to rule on whether proper procedures had been followed, he too lacked adequate legal training, having left the study of law to fight for the king in the Civil War.[38] In 1701 Mr. Thomas Hodge complained to the Council about the administration of justice in Barbados: courts met irregularly, and judges were effectively immune from any legal action. The courts served the interests of the wealthy planters who served as judges. Hodge noted that when the administration of justice in the island depended on thirty-seven people who were not trained in law, "it must unavoidably introduce many partialities and other irregularities, for there can scarce be any suit of moment in the Island, that some of these persons, or their nearest relations, are not concerned in." The situation was particularly difficult for those in England who sought to protect their rights to property on the island.[39]

The problem of corruption—what the Helyar's overseer Robert Hall called "the vice of this place"—was a frequent subject in the Helyar letters. In recommending Edward Atcherly as a supervisor on the plantation, William Whaley drew a distinction between Atcherly, who "understands the affairs of this country very well," and those lacking in experience, who "when they come to a plantation, they look and expect to find all things here as they have in England." As Atcherly himself noted, "I find not only in my neighbors but in several others honey upon their tongues, but much more poison in their hearts the which I shall be cautious of." When John Helyar arrived in Jamaica in 1686, he was wary of "Jamaica tricks," remarking that these were "only consistent with knaves, for an honest and good principled man no climate whatever can no more change him." After nearly thirty years, William Helyar had apparently learned his lesson, writing to his son John that "he that trusts a Jamaicaner is fair to be cheated"; John could only agree.[40]

In the Helyars' experience, the legal system worked to favor not only the governor but also the large planters who served as judges and justices of the peace or as members of the Governor's Council. Cary Helyar had prospered as a result of such political connections; after Cary's death in July 1672, the young and inexperienced William Whaley had no friends in Jamaica. Although the forms of the law were the same on the island as in England, the rights of an absentee owner were in practice weaker than those of employees or neighbors on the spot. Cary's will was simple, but his widow claimed additional property. New claims against the estate were presented and recognized with little evidence. As a trustee, the future governor Hender Molesworth protected the interests of Cary's widow, whose sister was rumored to be his mistress, rather than the estate.[41] The attorney who handled the case admitted that the law was manipulated. Whaley had no defenders and had "many powerful enemies to deal with."[42] The lawyer apologized: "If I am overruled next Court in all these actions . . . you or any lawyer may think it strange it being in a court of common law and confined to the rules and practice of the King's Bench at Westminster. But being a member I must not censure or reflect on its proceedings." He offered ten reasons for Helyar to accept a final settlement that was far less favorable than it should have been, ranging from the possibility of endless legal maneuvering to the influential support Widow Helyar enjoyed. At every turn, personal influence was more important than justice or legal procedure.[43] The institutions of Jamaican law were immature and easily manipulated.

Fifteen years later, when Helyar sent his son John to Jamaica to reclaim Bybrook from the rogue overseer Thomas Hillyard, he encountered similar problems. Hillyard had swindled William out of substantial profits by charging all the expenses of the plantation to Helyar's share of the income. When John Helyar gained control of the plantation, he had to pay Hillyard off instead of recouping the profits Hillyard had stolen. Even this success was due, he thought, to political connections. As he mourned the death of Sir Charles Modyford, the son of the former governor, he wrote, "I verily believe that had he died before the court, I had not the possession of the plantation till this time, & truly to speak my mind I question whether I had ever had it."[44] John was able to call on his uncle's friends and connections more effectively than those who were not members of the family, but even those connections were not enough.[45] In 1690 John sought to buy out his brother and remain in Jamaica. "I know very well what an estate will come to if the master is not here to look after it," he commented, "for to trust an estate here to attorneys and servants shall have but very lame account."[46]

The corruption of justice in the islands led to frequent appeals to London, but these were lengthy, cumbersome, and often marked by the same incomprehension so common in transatlantic affairs. When the Council asked for copies of the legal proceedings against John Hallet, Hallet told them that they must be certain to get copies not just of the formal proceedings but of all the petitions, affidavits, and other attested papers in the case.[47] The distance allowed one party to a case to obtain favors by withholding information. In 1695 John Holder Jr. received a full pardon for the murder of Francis Smith. When he returned to Barbados, he was arrested before a translation of the pardon (written in Latin) was attested to the governor. Smith's widow asserted that the pardon had been granted without full information about the "barbarous" murder of her husband, so she was granted permission to appeal.[48] This was not an efficient system of justice.

The courts provided an appearance of continuity with life in England. Their functioning, however, was a perpetual reminder that the context of the legal system mattered. What worked in England with a large group of landowners educated in the law was less successful in the West Indies. Few of the planters had the legal training that was common among the English gentry, and even legal officers were often young and inexperienced. The relatively small and tightly knit island elites could and did use the law to their own benefit, and those who sought to challenge them in the courts found that legal institutions placed few real limitations on planters' power.

Service and Slavery: Making Law

From an English perspective, the development first of indentured servitude and then of chattel slavery as the primary forms of labor in the Caribbean is one of the most puzzling aspects of the colonial project. The labor system established on colonial plantations became so widespread throughout the Americas that its sheer strangeness in relation to English society is often forgotten. Both indentured servitude and slaveholding as they developed in the seventeenth-century Caribbean entailed a radically different organization of labor from that familiar in England, requiring new legal categories and procedures that were eventually codified. Much has been written on the economic and social reasons for the adoption of slavery over indentured servitude as a primary form of labor organization. In the Caribbean context, it is equally important to understand how slavery emerged from indentured servitude (which itself diverged from the forms of labor that prevailed in England) and developed as a distinct institution.[49] Indentured servitude was more common in Barbados than Jamaica, and it also changed over time as both islands moved to ever greater dependence on slavery.

The social meanings of these two forms of labor and their relationship to each other were matters of debate in both the Caribbean and England during the seventeenth century, as they continue to be among historians today. Were servants treated the same way as slaves, or even, as Richard Ligon suggested, worse than slaves? Was indentured servitude slavery by another name? Or were indentured servants more privileged than slaves, treated as members of their masters' households and recognized as potential members of the body politic? What were the critical definitions and practices that gradually distinguished one form of involuntary labor from the other? When and how did race emerge as a crucial distinction between servants and slaves and supersede other ways of defining the difference between potentially free and perpetually unfree laborers? The documentary evidence reveals that practices and principles with regard to servants and slaves were variable, complex, and often self-contradictory; they were systematized with some difficulty in part because they were such a profound departure from labor systems familiar in England.[50]

The dynamic relationship between servitude and slavery as forms of labor organization is visible in the development of the relevant laws governing workers and establishing the power of masters. Analyzed over time, they show how law contributed to the development of racial categories while it also helped to fix those categories. Because the documents record the voices of relatively few servants and none of slaves during this period, we hear primarily the masters' points of view. The development of laws regarding servitude and slavery illuminate how planters defined their relationships with servants and slaves and how those understandings changed over time. The laws passed in the Caribbean colonies were both normative and retrospective: they articulated the values and viewpoints of the planters, which were shaped in response to the concrete problems they faced and the patterns of conflict that arose. They systematized and codified what had already become common practice. Unlike the British colonies on mainland North America, Barbados functioned as a slave society before it had a fully developed slave code. The planters therefore repeatedly revised and amended the laws as they sought to control labor more effectively. The legal structures that developed in Barbados provide an unusually sensitive guide to social relations and social conflicts on the island and to the ways in which planters sought to manage them. Jamaica had slaves before it was conquered by the

British, but English officials there copied the legal codes that had been instituted in Barbados. The laws of Barbados, as England's first sugar colony, are the best place to trace the evolution of laws governing servitude and slavery.

Indentured Servitude

Service itself was a familiar institution to the first English colonists in Barbados. It was almost universal in England, where young people typically went into service in other families during their mid- to late teens. Some youths were apprenticed for a period of seven years, while others hired themselves out on a yearly basis to perform household and agricultural labor. Legally, anyone who was unmarried, under the age of sixty, and without property could be forced into service. Relationships between masters and servants were governed by the 1563 Statute of Artificers, which was designed to sustain order by placing everyone in a household governed by a responsible head.[51] In addition to enjoining service, the law prevented masters from dismissing servants before their time had been served, provided for set wages and hours, and required those with certain amounts of land to accept children assigned by the parish as apprentices until they turned twenty-one. It stipulated that those leaving service obtain a certificate from the town or city where they had served; anyone who could not present such a certificate could be whipped as a vagrant. The statute regulated entrance to the trades both by establishing rules for apprenticeship and by excluding paupers from certain trades. Had it ever been fully enforced, it would have provided a seven-year apprenticeship for every young person as well as yearly service contracts for all unmarried, propertyless adults. Like many early modern systems of regulation, it imposed reciprocal rights, responsibilities, and duties. It was designed as much to police behavior in a context of labor surplus as to police work. The concern with ensuring social stability that the statute embodied was a response to the social, economic, and political unrest that beset England in the middle of the sixteenth century.[52]

The system articulated in the Statute of Artificers, while never fully enforced, organized labor and social relations simultaneously. At its center was the patriarchal and paternalistic idea that order was best maintained when everyone was part of a household governed by a man of property. The family was the central institution of social order, as it maintained young people and educated them to work productively. Responsibility—and accountability—ran up and down the social hierarchy. Operating within a set of reciprocal rights and obligations, servants and apprentices were governed and provided for, as they in turn obeyed their masters. This model was always an ideal; social relations never conformed entirely to its dictates. Its strictures were more stringently enforced in times of social and economic crisis, when order seemed threatened. Though never fully implemented, it constituted a powerful conceptual framework in the mental landscape for all those who emigrated from England to the Americas.

Settling, planting, and financing Barbados challenged these habits of social organization. The legal structures of service and slavery in the islands shifted over time from an emphasis on reciprocal obligations to a pre-occupation with the control of labor. Although the first Barbadian planters subscribed to an English model of service, their goal in the West Indies—to secure maximum profit—was not well served by paternalistic reciprocity. Indentured servitude and later chattel slavery, which had already been developed in Virginia, were recognized as more effective ways of organizing colonial plantations. Indentured servitude owed much to the tradition of apprenticeship, most notably in the use of a seven-year term of service. The terms of the contract modified those of a standard English apprenticeship indenture. The master provided transportation across the Atlantic rather than training in a skill, as well as room and board for the term of the indenture. At the end of their term, servants in Virginia received an allocation of land instead of admission to a guild; in Barbados, when there was no more land to distribute, servants were paid a premium instead.[53] Over time, servants who were eighteen or older when they arrived were indentured for shorter terms. Indentured service loosened the elements of reciprocity familiar in service in England, but it did not entirely abolish them.

From the first years of settlement until about 1660, indentured servants dominated the labor force in Barbados. The introduction of sugar cultivation led to a dramatic rise in the demand for labor, which was met initially by growing numbers of both English servants and African slaves. The earliest extant laws of the island, passed in 1652, included more provisions regulating servants than those dealing with slaves. These laws illustrate the change in the conception of service that took place between England and the Caribbean. Some laws still sought to protect the servants, including those restricting the importation of those under fourteen, limiting the term of service for those over eighteen, ensuring that the goods with which servants were paid were accurately valued, and punishing masters who turned off servants who were sick or old. Many more laws, however, protected the rights of masters to the labor of their servants.[54]

Perhaps the most notable aspect of the legislation from the English perspective was that offences against masters were punished by additional time in service. Some of these offences, ranging from assault to embezzlement, would have been covered by criminal law in England. In Barbados, where criminal law was weakly developed, the extension of servitude was used to enforce prohibitions on a broad range of disorderly behavior. Other laws registered the serious shortage of labor in Barbados and planters' fear that discontented servants would either run away or choose another master. To guard against theft by servants, merchants could not make deals directly with servants without the permission of their masters. Penalties were established for those who harbored servants or slaves. In a twist on the certificates provided for in the Statue of Artificers, a system of tickets was established to ensure that any servants or slaves found on the roads were there with permission; if they were without a ticket, they served an extra day for every two hours of absence.

Other provisions also focused on ensuring that masters got the service they were owed if a servant's work was interrupted; terms were extended if, for example, a servant was imprisoned for some crime or troubled his master with needless lawsuits. The penalties for trying to leave the island to escape service were particularly harsh: servants were to serve an additional three years, while the masters of ships had to enter a bond of £2,000 to ensure they did not carry off servants without the permission of their owner. All of these provisions led to conflicts over the actual term of service; in December 1652 the Assembly of Barbados provided a mechanism for resolving such disputes between masters and servants. Relations between masters and servants were markedly unstable in Barbados. The mortality rate was high; some historians have suggested that few indentured servants outlived their term of service. The island had an active market in servants, who were sold not only when they arrived on the island but also when their masters needed money, left the island, or died. Control of servants was both a social and economic necessity.[55]

The attempt to regulate marriage and sexuality among servants is especially notable. In England, live-in servants who married were dismissed, while in Barbados they served extra time. In Barbados, anyone who fathered a child on a female servant had to serve her master for three years, or provide a servant to do so, in order to compensate her master for the interruption of her work and the cost of maintaining the child. In England, the father would merely be ordered to pay toward the support of his child. Such requirements underline the very different configuration of gender and sexuality in Barbados. Although women and men servants did substantially similar work until the 1650s, the shortage of women relative to men made them particularly valuable sexual commodities. The provisions of the 1652 laws effectively "priced" sexual relations with women servants out of the reach of their fellow servants and sought to limit access to servant women's bodies to their owners or other men of property. The contrast between this regulation and the English tradition underlines the heightened emphasis on control of servants in Barbados.[56]

The punitive dimensions of the servant code in Barbados were amplified by the extensions of service that followed infractions and the limitations on servants' lives that guaranteed control of their labors. Servants in England were certainly beaten and mistreated, and those who defied their masters were punished. In England, however, service was designed to uphold order; in principle, servants had rights, and in practice many had some informal bargaining power. In Barbados the chronic shortage of labor led planters to seek more complete control of workers. The system for supplying indentured servants required planters to pay for service in advance; it was then up to them to extract the labor they had purchased. In England, masters whose servants committed crimes or were otherwise disorderly were satisfied to have them dismissed and punished by the courts. In Barbados, servants were no longer participants in a reciprocal social exchange within an ordered civil society but commodities whose labor was bought and sold without their consent.

The richest evidence about the experiences of servants comes from observations made by English sojourners in Barbados during the 1650s. Richard Ligon was so shocked by the conditions of indentured servitude in the island colony that he asserted that servants were treated worse than slaves. Ligon's discussion is useful because, as someone who was on the margins of Barbadian society, he judged the colony by English standards and remarked on the differences between the two societies. Yet the details he provides about indentured servants' lives undermine his generalization that they had been reduced to a situation inferior to slavery. For instance, Ligon described the diets of slaves and servants as essentially similar: while slaves preferred plantains to the potatoes, loblolly, and bonavist (hyacinth bean) that was the standard provision for servants, they were not fed more meat than servants. Ligon asserted that "as discreeter and better natured men have come to rule here, the servants lives have been much bettered." Owners now provided hammocks for servants to sleep in and changes of clothing so that they did not remain wet too long. Treating servants better was, he argued, in masters' best interests, and expenditures for them were a good investment. Decent conditions led servants to "love" their masters, and thus work harder for them.[57] Ligon recognized that "some cruel masters" provoked their servants through "extreme ill usage," but he regarded this situation as a result of individual faults rather than a systemic problem. Nonetheless, he observed that planters felt themselves in sufficient danger that after discovering that servants had plotted a rebellion—"the like was never seen there before"— some had built their homes as fortifications.[58]

Ligon's report was shaped by his assumptions about what social relations ought to be as well as by his observations of social conditions in Barbados, and his account was designed to promote settlement as well as stability in the colony. Ligon was a paternalist and believer in social hierarchy. Curious about people and the world around him, he was, on occasion, able to see human beings among groups of slaves or servants he might otherwise pass by, noticing that not all were contented with their situation in the colony. But he regarded the cruel masters who abused their servants as exceptions to the paternalistic norm. His work was intended to demonstrate that while earlier colonists were rude and brutal, Barbados now offered not only the opportunity to accumulate great wealth but also sociability and refinement equal to that in England. The evidence of continuing social unrest clouded this picture, disturbing Ligon's settled notions of order and ensnaring him in revealing contradictions. Servants who planned to rebel had "spirits" that did not accept subordination, yet some of the treatment they received amounted to "slavery." Colonial society was supposedly moving from chaos toward order, but some English servants were not accorded the position superior to African slaves to which Ligon felt they were entitled.

The idea of slavery is central to another important discussion of the situation and a second source for the experience of servants in Barbados during the 1650s. The pamphlet *England's Slavery: or Barbados Merchandize* (1659) was a petition to Parliament written by Marcellus Rivers and Oxenbridge Foyle protesting their experience in Barbados. The word "slavery" is a slippery one in the seventeenth-century context. It could refer to the existence of actual slaves on Barbados, yet it was also part of the wider political language of the period. As we have seen, as early as the 1620s, it had been used to refer to any government that was abusive or illegitimate. In the Parliament of 1628, Sir Dudley Digges had argued for limits on the executive by saying "that king who is not limited rules slaves that cannot serve him." In less lofty circumstances, a man arrested for drunkenness in 1634 called for "a plague of God on the slaves of Dorchester."[59] From the perspective of paternalism, the abuse of power was always illegitimate, as it threatened the ideal of reciprocal obligations thought to hold society together.

For Rivers and Foyle, "England's slavery" included the rule of Cromwell and the Major-Generals as well as their masters in Barbados. Minor gentry, with a history of Royalist activity, they had been accused of participating in a Royalist rising and, along with their alleged coconspirators, transported and sold as servants. Their chief complaints focus on political and legal legitimacy. There was no legal basis for their transportation, they argued; those transported had either never been indicted, never been tried, or had been acquitted at trial. They had been transported by merchants, including the London alderman Martin Noel, who were closely connected to the government; this, they contended, showed that they had been exploited for the private profit of the government's friends.[60]

All those transported were treated alike, with no attention to age or rank: "Neither sparing the aged of seventy-six years old, nor divines, nor officers, nor gentlemen." When Rivers and Foyle arrived in Barbados, they were sold, required to work without the distinctions they felt their rank or age deserved, beaten, poorly fed, and ill-housed.[61] The use of "slavery" in the pamphlet title, then, refers less to the conditions of service than to the illegitimacy of the process by which they were sent to Barbados. The government of the Protectorate had enslaved England; its subjection of gentry to servitude was a sign of more fundamental disruptions of social order. Rivers and Foyle, who protested being turned into "Barbados merchandize" by "England's slavery," thought their treatment unsuited to their privileged status but presumed that other English men might legitimately be required to do the work they were forced to do in Barbados. They objected to being treated as commodities, not because it was not right to treat people as commodities but because it was not right for *gentlemen* to be treated as commodities. They were possessed, rather than in a mutual relationship, and treated as subordinates by men of inferior rank. In its political context, *England's Slavery* is a strong argument for the rule of law and the differential—and deferential—treatment of gentlemen.

What disturbed Ligon, Rivers, and Foyle was the apparent breakdown of reciprocal ties between masters and servants in the harsh labor regime of Barbados, which they interpreted as degrading to English men and dangerous to the social order. The evidence usually cited for the widespread maltreatment and abuse of servants by masters is less convincing than the evidence that the plantation system itself had deleterious consequences for subordinated laborers. Ligon's assertion that the usage of servants is "much as the Master is, merciful or cruel" is probably as close to the truth as we will get. Servants were worked hard and often underfed and inadequately housed in an unfamiliar climate; they were vulnerable to tropical diseases and suffered heavy mortality. The paternalism that would have mitigated their treatment in England was absent in the Caribbean. The legal framework that defined normative practices for both indentured servitude and slavery illuminates the planters' intense drive to control their labor force. Yet servants were "temporarily unfree," not permanently so. In a system utilizing both indentured servants and slaves, English servants were increasingly necessary not for hard labor but for policing enslaved Africans. Ligon was probably right that the situation of servants, while never good, improved somewhat as the proportion of slaves in the colonial labor force increased.[62]

The uneasiness about the legal and social status of servants remained an issue between London and the island's governments, reflecting the distance in miles and mentality between the two societies. In 1676 the Council for Trade and Plantations reviewed the Jamaican law regulating servants. It reported they were "not pleased with the word (servitude) p. 26 as being a mark of bondage and slavery, And think fit rather to use the word (service) since these servants are only apprentices for years."[63] This objection was grounded in the English understanding of service as an honorable status. "Servitude" was not honorable, but the law had articulated the experience of service in the Caribbean, where indentured service did make English men a sort of temporary property.

Creating a Law of Slavery

In 1661, following the restoration of royal authority, the Council and Assembly of Barbados codified local practices regarding service and slavery. The two acts of that year reveal the increasing divergence of those institutions. The complex motivations behind the legislation were articulated in their preambles. A section regarding servants defines its purpose:

> The interest and substance of this Island consists in the servants brought to and disposed of in the same, and in their labour during the time they have to serve . . . great and often damages hath happened to the people of this place, through the unruliness, obstinacy, and refractoriness of the servants. And whereas also it much concerns the peace of this Island, that a continual strict course should be taken to prevent the bold extravagancy and wandering of servants . . . making use of all advantages and occasions to disturb the public peace, and prejudice their masters.[64]

This law largely repeated the provisions of 1652. Designed to protect masters' right to the labor of servants, it defined the problem as unruly servants, not bad masters. Masters had significantly more power than they did in England. Yet the planters still thought in paternalistic English terms, however little they acted on them. Safeguards to protect servants remained alongside the law's punitive provisions. Concern with the proper treatment of servants was an ongoing theme in the instructions to governors in Barbados. In Sir Richard Dutton's first address to the Assembly in 1680, he asked them to "prepare a bill to restrain bad masters and overseers from cruelty to their Christian servants"; the Assembly responded that "they are ready to do anything for the encouragement and good usage of Christian servants." A similar request was made in 1691. Both the members of the Assembly and the authorities in London sought to recruit enough servants to meet the policing needs of the state; poor treatment of English servants might discourage immigration.[65]

The laws related to slaves were devoid of any traces of paternalism and mutual obligation. Slaves had been present in Barbados from its early years, but their numbers only became significant after the introduction of sugar. When the laws were codified in 1652, relatively few related to slaves. Between 1652 and 1661, the number of slaves had increased so that the slave population of Barbados equaled the white population and thereafter vastly exceeded it. In response to the new situation, the planters devised a special system of justice to govern slaves. The "Act for the Better ordering and Governing of Negroes" was approved on the same day in 1661 as the act governing servants. While it apparently incorporated earlier laws, most of those have not survived.[66]

The two statutes demonstrate a sharp distinction between servants and slaves. While the law relating to servants sought to ensure labor for the planters, it assumed that servants were rational beings who controlled their own actions; they would respond to inducements and could be held responsible for their behavior. The law relating to slaves, by contrast, attempted to control their every move. While servants had some rights against their masters, slaves had none. The preamble explained why such a new legal code was needed: "Many good laws and ordinances have been made for the governing and regulating and ordering the Negroes, slaves in this island and sundry punishments appointed to many their misdemeanors, crimes and offences which yet not met the effect hath been desired and might have been reasonably expected had the masters of families and other the inhabitants of this island been so careful of their obedience and compliance with the said laws." Masters and officials had neglected to exercise sufficient authority to hold slaves in subjection. Describing Negroes as "heathenish, brutish and an uncertain dangerous kind of people," it reasoned that laws must be designed specifically to govern them. "Surely," the preamble asserts, we may "extend" the legislative power to make laws regarding slaves, since English law provided no guidance. That "surely" indicates the weak legal basis for slavery. Rather than leave slaves to the mercies of "arbitrary cruel and outrageous wills" of planters, officials should protect slaves "as we do many other goods and chattels and also somewhat farther as being created men though without the knowledge of God."[67]

In reality, the law protected planters, not slaves. Negroes, though human, were non-Christian, uncivil, strange, and dangerous, so the system of governing them was based entirely on coercion. Its provisions bespeak planters' fear of slaves' potential for resistance and rebellion. Slaves were subjected to the same ticket system as servants to ensure that they did not move about without permission. Slaves who assaulted any "Christian"—regardless of the white person's status—were harshly punished: for the first offence, they were "severely whipped"; for the second, they were whipped, had their nose slit, and were branded on the forehead; for the third offence, they suffered "greater corporal punishment" as determined by the justice of the peace. Servants faced no special penalties for assault of anyone other than their master, mistress, or overseer; they were covered by criminal law, which treated assault as a misdemeanor, punished by a fine.

Elaborate provisions related to runaway slaves. The law set penalties for those who sheltered runaways, required overseers to search plantations twice weekly for them, provided rewards for those who captured them, and established a process for keeping them until they were claimed by their masters. In an exception to the rule that no inducements were offered to slaves, Negroes who helped take up runaways could also be rewarded. The law sought to control people who tried to "steal" Negroes and take them off the island, which was done allegedly by promising them freedom elsewhere. Any official who heard of a hiding place of "fugitive or outlaw" Negroes was to raise a company of up to twenty men to seize them, "dead or alive," and receive a reward for their capture. Owners were required to inform the secretary of the island which of their slaves had fled or run away within ten days of their disappearance. Eleven clauses in the slave code related to runaways, while the code governing servants had only three. Theft and violence by slaves were also treated as serious problems. Every two weeks, Negro houses were to be searched for weapons, which were to be burned as soon as found, and stolen goods, which were to be returned to their owners.

These provisions of the law regarding slaves were recognizable in the context of English law, although they were harsher and more controlling. When it came to criminal offences, however, the familiar system of justice was totally abandoned and a new system invented. The problem, according to the statute, was that slaves could not be imprisoned because of the "danger of escape," and they did not deserve to be tried by a jury of twelve peers because of "the baseness of their condition." The loss of labor if slaves were imprisoned was left unspoken. Masters were expected to punish slaves for "small broils and misdemeanors" in the presence of the injured party; if a master refused to do so, the person against whom the offence was committed could go to the nearest justice of the peace, who would determine the appropriate punishment. In some ways, this mirrors the responsibility for governing their subordinates and the right of correction given to English men, though with slaves there is both more accountability to the person injured and a broader range of offences involved. For more serious offences, or those committed off the plantation, a slave was immediately brought before a justice of the peace. The justice served as a grand jury would in England: if he determined that the slave was "probably" guilty, he was to summon the next justice; together they were to summon three freeholders, and those five would try the offence and determine guilt. In felonies the penalty was death, just as it was for whites. For petty larcenies and trespasses, which were covered by the same procedure because it would be "tedious and chargeable" to follow the ordinary course of justice, the court of two justices and three freeholders would order the owner of the slave to provide reparation. If the owner of the guilty slave refused to provide satisfaction, the Negro was first given "corporal punishment" and then awarded to the person wronged.

These provisions created an entirely new judicial system that did away with trial by jury, which had long been fundamental to English justice. This legal provision was central to the process of defining slaves—and ultimately all people of African descent—as entirely different from white people. While following English punishments as closely as possible, the planters constructed a new system to handle offences for which there would ordinarily be a fine. Slaves, unable to hold property, could not pay fines; they could only be punished physically. If their masters failed to control them and refused to make restitution for the damage they did, slaves could be rewarded as damages to the injured party. The law designated a new legal category for slaves and designed legal principles and procedures that applied specifically to them.

Colonial authorities acknowledged and justified these remarkable departures from English practice. In discussing the laws in 1678, Governor Atkins wrote, "They being dissonant so much from the laws of England, the most of them being for strengthening their propriety in their slaves and keeping them in order, they far exceeding the white men in number and upon whom indeed they reckon their whole wealth for their land without slaves is not worth ten groats an acre, and with hands to work them may be easily computed at £20 sterling & more, there being no such thing as slaves in England . . . the severity of them being necessary here."[68] Two years later, a report by a lawyer to the Privy Council on the laws of Barbados referred to laws "not consonant" with those of England, including those

in reference to Negro slaves who for capital offences are not to be tried by jury . . . and although Negroes in that Island are punishable in a different and more severe manner than other subjects are for offences of the like nature; yet I conceive that the laws there concerning Negroes are reasonable laws for by reason of their numbers they become dangerous, and being a brutish sort of People and reckoned as goods and chattels in that island, it is of necessity or at least convenient to have laws for the government of them different from the Laws of England.[69]

Both rationales for the unprecedented degree of coercion in the colonial laws governing slavery join economic interests to power. Governor Atkins emphasized the dependence of planters' profits on their ability to command slave labor and recognized that Negroes outnumbered whites, so maintaining control of them was crucial to the entire colonial enterprise. The Privy Council underlined the fact that these "brutish" and potentially dangerous Negroes counted as property; without the rights accorded to English subjects, they could be controlled by coercive means.

The law held masters accountable for the behavior of their slaves. While English law had long sought to have masters control the behavior of subordinates in their households, servants had always been assumed to be responsible for their own acts and masters had no part in criminal proceedings against them.[70] In Barbados, masters literally had to pay for the minor offences of their slaves. This provision not only required masters to control their slaves but also recognized the vested interest of all slave owners in each master's maintaining control. Laxity in enforcing discipline or tolerance of disorder was not acceptable.

Slave owners worried much more about rebellion than ordinary crime. The law prescribed trial by martial law for any slave who planned a revolt or actually rebelled; capital punishment was the automatic consequence of conviction. Owners always suffered a financial loss when slaves found guilty were executed. Because slave rebellions were a threat to the whole system, the law provided compensation for owners paid out of the treasury when slaves were executed for rebellion. Moreover, the consequences for whites who killed slaves indicate that fear of slave resistance outweighed owners' financial interest in their property; the system offered little or no protection to slaves' lives. Masters were not guilty of murder if they killed slaves while punishing them for running away or other misdeeds, though if they killed a Negro through "wantonness" or "cruel intention" they were to be fined. Those who killed a slave belonging to another paid a fine to the treasury, as well as double the value of the dead slave to the owner. If the killing was accidental, the owner could sue the killer for damages in court. "Poor small freeholders" who killed Negroes while they were stealing goods at night were not liable. Finally, the law recognized that the rapidly growing slave population could not be governed without a substantial number of "Christians," so it required planters to have one white servant for every twenty acres of land.

The law of 1661 treated slaves as a qualitatively different sort of people than servants. While the preamble asserted that English law provided no guidance on how to govern "such slaves," the law itself used the word "slave" only once: instead, it referred constantly to "Negroes."[71] This usage, which collapses status with color, was common in the Caribbean; the term "Negro" was derived from the Spanish word for black. This terminology identifies slavery as inherent in bodies, not a product of law and a system of labor. In law and practice, planters assumed that white servants were "Christians" and British; Negroes were neither, and were by definition slaves. Barbadian planters' and officials' avoidance of the term "slaves" also suggests some discomfort with being slave owners: chattel slavery was without precedent in recent English experience, and slavery was occluded by the focus on ethnic origins.[72]

Unlike the law governing servants, the law governing slaves made no distinctions between male and female slaves. There were no special provisions, for instance, for slave women who became pregnant or for married slaves. This deliberate overlooking of gender constituted a distinguishing feature of slavery. English law frequently distinguished between women and men, based both on their different biological capabilities and the implications of marriage for civil status. Unlike white men, enslaved men had no civil status that marked them as superior to enslaved women; in legal terms, no Negro had a civil identity. Nor were enslaved women offered any protection from sexual violence, unlike female servants, who could complain of rape or name a father to receive support. Gender also made no difference in the work slaves were assigned to perform. By creating distinct gender systems for indentured servants and enslaved people, this set of practices and laws enhanced racial demarcations. Only white women were eligible for specifically feminine status.[73]

The law of 1661 was amended several times before it was completely rewritten in 1688. Most of the amendments clarified matters that had remained confused or reinforced provisions that had been inadequate. An act of 1668 declared slaves to be real estate for the purposes of inheritance, though five years later this was clarified to ensure that owners could sell slaves and that Negroes were considered chattel for purposes of paying debts. Confusion about precisely what kind of property slaves were arose because slavery itself did not fit into existing English legal paradigms. In order to make the system work properly, the nature of slaves as property was entirely determined by the nature of the transaction, a unique situation in English law.[74] In 1673 the planters sought to prevent people from unjustly claiming runaway slaves as their own property; the behavior of white people needed greater regulation in order to protect owners' property in slaves.[75]

Responding to Rebellion

In 1676 the Barbados Assembly passed a major set of amendments to the 1661 "Act for the Better ordering and Governing of Negroes." The revision was one aspect of the response to the discovery of a planned slave rebellion and addressed numerous surface dimensions of the plot.[76] The preamble to the 1676 amendment noted that the 1661 act "hath not sufficiently proved to restrain them from those wicked and barbarous actions their natures are inclined to"; the situation was so bad that poor people were allegedly unwilling to settle in the island because of the thefts and "insolencies" of the slaves. The purpose of the new law, according to the preamble, was to deter small crimes in order to prevent larger ones. Its provisions show how planters understood the sources of their collective vulnerability.

The amendments increased the punishments for slaves' offences. Any grand larceny or rape was made a capital offence, which seems redundant, since such offences were already felonies under the English criminal law that was already in force on the island. More importantly, the law added penalties for those convicted of petty larceny. The 1661 act had made the master responsible for compensating the person wronged, so the slave paid no penalty. In 1676 slaves were directly punished for petty larcenies: for the first offence, they were whipped; for the second offence, they had their nose slit and were branded on the forehead; for the third offence, they were executed. Any slave who remained a fugitive for more than a year was to be executed when captured.[77]

The 1676 act included general provisions to address problems that arose in a mature slave society. The practice of hiring slaves out was increasing. According to the act, these slaves were "by their licentious manner of living and moving from plantation to plantation and by their great acquaintance more knowing and dangerous and have more opportunity of contriving of mischief and rebellion than Negroes employed only on their masters plantation." Therefore, those who hired slaves out were to pay a tax on each slave. Allowing slaves to hire themselves out—to "exercise their own will and contrivances" by working for wages in return for paying their masters a fixed sum—was forbidden; any owner who did this would forfeit the slaves entirely.[78] To protect the incomes (and numbers) of white craftsmen and induce them to remain in the colony, Negroes were forbidden to work or be trained in skilled trades. These provisions speak not only to the sophisticated financial arrangements that some white Barbadians had adopted but also to the emergence of a skilled slave labor force. Controls on masters and privileges for artisans were necessary to ensure the protection of the slave society that Barbados had become against slaves who were capable of revolt.

The 1676 amendments attest to planters' fear of rebellion in several ways. Some of the new provisions were tailored to specific features of the plot. The conspirators planned to use musical instruments (horns and gourds) to summon their fellows to action; at least one of the slaves involved in the planned rebellion belonged to a Jew.[79] The new law prohibited masters from allowing slaves to beat drums, blow shells, or use any other loud instruments, and owners or overseers were to make regular searches for such musical instruments. Jews who were not denizened were allowed to keep only one slave each. Jews had been resident on the island since the 1650s; the concern with their slaves suggests that as merchants they were more likely to hire them out. Planters were also concerned that some whites traded with slaves for stolen goods. The law made it easier for justices of the peace to trace and prosecute this trade, which suggests planters' fear of collusion in crime and even an alliance between poor whites and slaves.

The most striking and innovative provision of the legislation explicitly addressed the problematic nature of "chattels" who could made decisions of their own—articles of property who, disconcertingly, resisted their owners' power. In order to punish and prevent rebellions that threatened the very existence of property in slaves, the law extended the range of offences for which recalcitrant slaves were executed. The new law acknowledged that without compensation, the economic losses to owners would be considerable; the loss of Negroes so executed would be "too heavy for the owners only to bear," and fear of the financial consequences might induce owners not to report offences committed by their slaves. The law therefore extended the compensation previously paid to the owners of slaves executed in cases of rebellion to owners of slaves executed for any reason. To emphasize planters' shared interest in the proper punishment of slaves, the payment was to come from the island's treasury and be funded by a tax levied on all landholders at the rate of one pound of sugar per acre. If it was determined that a slave was stealing because his or her owner did not provide "enough" food, the owner would not receive compensation. This provision simultaneously recognized the economic importance of slaves to their owners, acknowledged the threat that refractory slaves could pose to the social order, and dealt with the danger to the community that resulted from some owners' neglect.

These 1676 amendments to the slave code marked the growing maturity of the system of slavery in Barbados. By 1675 there was a market in slaves for hire to meet the fluctuating labor needs of plantations. While some slaves who worked for others were still controlled by their owner, others were required only to pay a set sum to their owner and enjoyed substantial independence. The mobility of such "slaves for hire" facilitated communication among slaves and, potentially, collective action that would undermine the social order. The law addressed the challenges of managing and controlling a colonial population in which slaves constituted the majority, as well as the contradictions inherent in holding property in persons. The Barbados records include many orders relating to payments for slaves who had been executed; these orders were primarily recorded in cases where circumstances blocked the payment to the owner, so the actual amount of compensation must have been much larger. When Robert Trument, a servant, lost his arm from a wound given him by one of his master's slaves, he, rather than his master, received £20 as the value of the slave. Alexander Cunningham petitioned for the payment of the value of his slave in 1680 but was told that he would not be paid because his accounts with the treasurer were in arrears.[80]

After 1676 there were a few minor amendments to strengthen the law. Less than two years after the law was passed, the Assembly specified that capital crimes were not limited to those listed in the act but also to "all other of like horrid and heinous nature tending to such evil consequence." Another law aimed at white colonists sought to protect owners from illegal or clandestine seizures of their slaves. But the 1676 act had provided an effective basis for managing slaves and handling the offences they committed.[81]

The system of slave management enshrined in 1676 worked, most directly, by policing slaves to ensure that any Negroes who threatened whites were punished quickly and severely. Slave culture was also policed through the prohibitions on travel, musical instruments, and other means of communication. Yet owners too were subject to scrutiny, particularly those who allowed their slaves to manage their own work or so neglected their slaves' basic needs as to induce them to steal from other whites. The planters who controlled the Assembly defined their economic interests in the island's labor system and in sugar production as the interest of the island—not just in the law of slavery, but also in the petitions against duties on sugar. The law ensured that slave owners would never suffer for the losses caused by their oppression and exploitation of slaves—the whole range of conditions, from arbitrary mistreatment to unremitting toil, that might lead slaves to resist, subvert, or rebel against white authority—by using the island's treasury to ensure their investment. While protecting the value of property was a central feature of the 1676 amendments, the Lords of Trade were not convinced that slaves were indeed valued as people whose lives were worthy of protection. In 1684 Governor Dutton arrived with suggestions for a new law to provide "sufficient punishment for those that shall wilfully and wantonly kill a Negro." The Assembly refused, arguing that existing acts provided for fines for such murders, paid to both the owner and the king. They saw no need to do anything more.[82]

Synthesis: The Slave Code of 1688

The success with which the 1676 amendments addressed the management and punishment of slaves was evident when the whole slave code was reenacted in 1688. The 1688 act formally repealed all the earlier acts governing slaves and replaced them with a comprehensive law for slavery that remained in effect throughout the eighteenth century, but it adopted most of the provisions of the 1661 and 1676 laws. As Governor Stede explained in a letter to the Council for Trade and Plantations in England, it "is indeed but a collection or compliment of the multitude of scattered laws that related thereto, which made them both troublesome and difficult."[83] The 1688 act added little to the earlier legislation; rather, it simplified their provisions and streamlined their application. For instance, the close regulation of the hire of slaves was dropped, presumably because it was too cumbersome. The land tax to fund compensation for owners who lost slaves was omitted, as was the ban on training slaves in crafts. The only new item was a fine on masters who failed to provide their slaves with clothing once a year. The law continued to focus on maintaining the property of owners and reinforcing their control over slave labor. If anything, it served the interests of owners more effectively, as it used general revenues rather than the special land tax to compensate owners of executed slaves, and it recognized emergent Barbadian practice by allowing owners to employ slaves in skilled trades.[84]

The most significant departures of the 1688 act lay not in its specific provisions for managing slaves but rather in its assumptions and language regarding slavery as an institution. The preamble echoed that of the 1661 act concerning servants, emphasizing the necessity of slave labor for the prosperity of the island; like the 1661 act concerning slaves, it described Negroes as brutish, uncivilized, and potentially dangerous. However, the 1688 act concluded that the slaves "are of such barbarous, wild and savage nature, and such as renders them wholly unqualified to be governed by the Laws, customs and Practices of our nation." This is the first official assertion that slaves were entirely outside the laws of England, without any protections due to English subjects and governed by a legal system constructed entirely in the colony. That position had been emerging in practice, but it was fully articulated in 1688.

The second significant feature of the 1688 law was that it acknowledged slavery as a status. The code was written to pertain to "Negroes and other slaves." While this language still assumes that all Negroes are slaves, it suggests that there might be slaves who are not Negroes. These were most likely Native Americans. Although there never was a systematic trade involving Amerindians as there was for Africans and in 1676 the Barbados Assembly had prohibited their importation, a few were found among the island's slave population, mostly engaged in domestic work. Amerindian slaves came primarily from the coast of Guinea or nearby islands, though some were also shipped from New England.[85] But the addition of Native Americans to the enslaved population of Barbados shifted the focus from race to the position of slaves. The law now admitted that Barbados was a society based on the labor of enslaved people.

Governor Stede, in the letter that reported the new law regarding slaves, also recounted discussions of a new law regarding servants. Stede was concerned both to "restrain cruel masters" and to control the behavior of the servants themselves. Previous governors had intervened to protect servants from abusive masters, even granting them their freedom; but, according to Stede, criminal servants were an equal if not greater problem. Servants were guilty not only of "disobedience and insolencies to their masters" but also of "embezzling and willful wasting, spoiling destroying and making away their masters goods, and many times most viciously and maliciously killing and destroying the horses, neat cattle and other live stock." The servants were mostly transported convicts, were not accustomed to labor, and had to be forced to do the work paid for by their transportation. Stede's comments reflect the increasingly punitive English attitudes toward the poor.[86] But the new proposals were never passed, leaving the legislation of 1661 governing servants in force throughout the eighteenth century.

Laws Governing Slavery in Jamaica

The laws of Barbados were developed over time to regulate colonial society and respond to problems that arose in the control of labor. Jamaica's first civil government used the laws of Barbados as the basis for its own legislation. In July 1661 the Council adopted what it identified as the "fifth, eighth, tenth, thirteenth, fifteenth, and thirtieth acts" in the "Barbados book," referring to the 1654 edition of the Barbadian laws. These laws defined the position of servants—the length of terms for indentured servants, penalties for assault by servants on masters, and penalties for impregnating a servant or marrying a servant without her master's consent. The Council also copied laws regulating the unloading of ships and requiring notice before anyone left the island, thereby controlling the movements of servants and slaves.[87] Over the next few months, Jamaica adopted laws from Barbados forbidding the keeping of servants or slaves from their masters and carrying fire or lighted pipes through fields of sugarcanes. By November 1661, the Council had instituted the system of passes for servants and slaves leaving their plantations.[88]

Three years later, when Sir Thomas Modyford called together an Assembly to make laws in Jamaica, Barbados's laws again provided the model. The law regarding servants is identical to the Barbados act of 1661, except that fines were levied in pounds sterling rather than pounds of sugar; sugar had not yet become the common currency of Jamaica. The 1664 Jamaica law, "For the Better Ordering and Governing of Negro Slaves," was also largely copied from the parallel 1661 statute in Barbados. At the time, there were fewer than 2,000 enslaved people in Jamaica, so this law was an instrument for instituting a slave labor system rather than a response to its emergence. Seeking to recreate the sugar economy of Barbados in Jamaica, Modyford provided the legal structure for it in advance. This wholesale imitation led to statements that were patently false; for example, the preamble repeated the mention of the "many good laws and ordinances" that had "heretofore" been made, which was applicable to Barbados but not to Jamaica. Most of the rest of the act is parallel; some differences appear to be clerical errors. One significant difference is that while the Barbados act refers to the right of "subjects" of England to trial by jury, that in Jamaica refers to "freemen"; because of the implications of conquest, freedom had a special salience in Jamaican political discourse. The Jamaica act added a new provision requiring the posting of notices of captured runaways in public places to prevent theft. Finally, the Jamaica statute referred repeatedly to "Slaves" or "Negro Slaves," rather than "Negroes," thus marking both their subordinate status and their race.[89]

The next two extant versions of the Jamaican law regarding slaves, from 1672 and 1674, continued these provisions but encouraged the conversion of slaves to Christianity to ensure their obedience.[90] In 1677 another version of the slave code was submitted to London for approval. It is not clear whether the 1677 act was ever approved by the king, and it therefore may have expired after two years. It was sloppily drafted, and it omitted many of the explanatory passages that justified the provisions. However, it also includes provisions that took account of conditions specific to Jamaica. One provision allowed for the destruction of abandoned plantations so they would not become havens for runaway slaves; another was concerned with slaves using boats to steal timber. The law showed greater concern for the protection of property in slaves: remarkably, when a group of slaves committed an offence, only one was to be executed "as exemplary to the rest." While in Barbados the causes of execution had been widened, with compensation, in Jamaica the shortage of labor shaped punishment. The trials of rebellious slaves were simplified; they now took place not by martial law but before the same combination of two justices and three freeholders as other trials of slaves. The act also provided more venues for publishing news of runaway slaves being held in custody and restricted the hiring of slaves as porters in Port Royal. The 1677 law was no longer merely a repetition of a formula imported from Barbados but grounded in the emerging society of Jamaica. The distinctive feature of Jamaican as opposed to Barbadian slavery—the provision grounds in which, as we have seen, slaves grew their own food crops—were mandated by the act: owners were required to provide one acre of provision ground for every five slaves.[91] Jamaica had plenty of land, which made it much easier for runaway slaves to survive and also enabled slaves to provide for their own food.

The iteration of the Jamaican slave law passed in 1696 bears the hallmarks of a mature slave society and remained in effect until 1781. It was more concerned than earlier acts with catching runaways and provided special rewards for slaves who helped do so. It defined as "rebellious" any slave who was absent from his or her master's plantation for more than a year; such slaves were deemed dangerous, and they could be killed on sight. Places were set up in each parish for trials of slaves, along with a system of record keeping for the courts that tried them. A registration system for slave sales was established to prevent confusion about ownership. As in Barbados, a market in "rental slaves" had emerged, and the act sought to ensure that slaves could not hire themselves out independently of their master or mistress. Significantly, there were now enough freed slaves in Jamaica to require provisions for their trial. In this case, race trumped status, and those slaves who had been freed were tried by the same court of two justices and three freeholders as were those still enslaved. In the criminal law, freedom made no difference to those of African descent.[92]

London officials found those portions of the Jamaican slave code that clearly departed from English principles troubling. In addition to insisting that provision be made for the conversion of slaves, in 1683 the Council for Trade and Plantations rejected one proposed law governing slaves because the penalty for the "willful or wanton" murder of a slave was only a fine. They required that "some better provision be made to deter all persons from such acts of cruelty"; in reporting this objection, Governor Lynch added that "the King is too humane to be paid for shedding man's blood." The Assembly duly obliged, and after some debate agreed on a three-month imprisonment as the appropriate penalty. Servants who murdered slaves were to receive thirty-nine lashes and serve the owner of the dead slave for four years after their current term of service had expired.[93] This was as far as deterrence went.

The laws of Barbados and Jamaica defined the powers available to masters in dealing with slaves. Over time, planters constructed a society based on slave labor and legal provisions were changed in response to practical needs. While laws never directly reflect reality, they do react to events and experiences. As the institution of slavery matured during the second half of the seventeenth century, both Barbados and Jamaica had developed legal systems that protected the property and prerogatives of planters throughout the eighteenth century.

FOR PLANTERS IN Barbados and Jamaica, "right English government" was dependent on protecting the "just rights and liberties" of English subjects. Although indentured servants enjoyed far fewer liberties than they might have in England, the powerful retained the view that all English subjects were bound up together in the proper ordering of society. At the same time that they sought to defend English rights and liberties, the planters in the West Indies developed a system of chattel slavery for people of African descent, which explicitly deprived slaves of access to English rights because of their "wild, barbarous, and savage nature." The system of slavery that they constructed in the seventeenth-century West Indies was the shadow of the rights and liberties planters protected so carefully and the political slavery they resisted so strenuously. The economic and political liberty of the planters depended on slavery. Liberty was more valued as its opposite, slavery, became a more visible reality.

Chattel slavery represented a sharp departure from English experience, and it did not emerge full-blown either as a labor system or as a social order. Planters had to learn how to own people. When most English colonists arrived in the West Indies, their only knowledge of slavery was from classical sources or from anti-Spanish and anti-Turkish propaganda. They experimented with various ways of organizing work and controlling subordinates. Slavery developed over time in the interaction of their received ideas about work, status, and authority and their own experiences in the new environment of the islands. Planters' views of servants were not much different from those of propertied English men. They were more preoccupied with the control of their labor than were masters in England, but service remained a recognizable institution. The reciprocity central to service, which became attenuated but did not entirely disappear in the West Indies, was completely absent in relation to slaves. Slaves were always treated not just as people who needed discipline but rather as laborers who did not deserve the same legal rights as white people, whether planters or servants. Heathens from Africa were subject to a different set of rules than European Christians.

By 1661 the English had established a separate judicial process to manage slaves and begun to develop different standards of punishment. It was not until 1676 that they faced the contradictions posed by chattels with volition. When slaves were held responsible for their crimes, punishing them could entail financial losses for their owners; slaves' ability to labor might be diminished, and if they were executed the property invested in them perished. Therefore, to preserve both property and authority, the owner had to be compensated by the government. The increasing concern with the practice of renting out slaves registered the further development of the market in humans. While slaves were forbidden to hire themselves out as wage laborers, some masters owned slaves in order to rent them out for profit. Planters controlled this slave labor market in order to manage the islands' large and growing enslaved population, and to avert the resulting danger of conspiracy and rebellion.

In Barbados, the experiments in legislation governing slaves made between 1661 and 1676 culminated in a law that was sufficiently effective that it remained in force for over a century and provided the basis for all later slave codes in the English colonies. Planters thought that all laborers, including servants and the English poor, had to be disciplined and closely controlled. But slaves were not merely permanent servants. Planters defined slaves as an entirely different sort of person, naturally savage and brutish, uncivilized, and not Christian. The planters' practice of referring to "Negroes" rather than "slaves" defined them by race, not merely status. Slaves and slavery lay outside the boundaries of English law. The English who developed a slave labor system in Barbados were not sure what they were doing at first. They had no English models for it. Working out a functional system took time and went up a few blind alleys. If we pay attention to these, we can not only see a palimpsest of the English experience of slave owning but also trace the process by which the English responded to the challenges posed by slave ownership and learned to manage a slave society.

"Right English government" entailed ongoing communication and consultation between authorities in the islands and those in London. This dialogue, which was conflictual as well as collaborative, centered on the nature of power. Government in the islands, far more than in England, served the interests of the wealthiest inhabitants. As officials debated the specific provisions of laws passed by colonial assemblies or measures suggested by the Privy Council in London, differences were especially apparent in the assumptions that prevailed on the two sides of the Atlantic about the treatment of servants and slaves. The objections made from London to key provisions of the slave laws proposed in the islands show how far from English experience the enslavement of other people was. So, too, the development of slave codes registers the objections to the labor system enacted, if not articulated and recorded, by those who were expected to serve. Slaves were recalcitrant, ran away, and rebelled outright. Masters deemed slaves "barbarous, wild, and savage" in part because they resisted their enslavement and refused to obey the laws designed to control them. While planters continued to seek more control over their workers, servants and slaves continued to seek freedom.

Due Order & Subjection
Hierarchy, Resistance, and Repression

Persons of turbulent minds and unquiet dispositions
LETTER FROM BARBADOS, 1683

In 1692 three white women—a Mrs. Castleton, Mrs. Hallet (the wife of Colonel Hallet, a member of the Barbados Council), and Mrs. Hallet's daughter—were riding down the street in Bridgetown. A slave belonging to Mrs. Castleton ran in front of her horse. In doing so, he pushed aside a white servant, Richard Allen. Allen called the slave a "Black Dog" and pushed back, but the slave continued "to give saucy and impudent language." Allen followed him to Hallet's house, "saying he would not be abused by a Negro." Mrs. Hallet told Allen he was a "saucy fellow and bid him stay and he should have something, and threatening words to that effect." At that point, Colonel Hallet appeared and assaulted Allen. The conflict that followed was intertwined with the battle between the governor and Colonel Hallet discussed in the previous chapter, but the interaction on the streets of Bridgetown that might otherwise have gone unrecorded reveals the daily tensions of racial and class relations and the complex processes by which they were negotiated.[1]

The accounts of this incident from multiple points of view have common elements and significant variations. In all of them, an initial encounter between Allen and a slave led Colonel Hallet to assault Allen. Several accounts allege that Allen was drunk; some detail name-calling between Allen and the slave. According to Hallet, Allen spoke to him using the time-honored claim of the poor to their betters, "telling me he was as good a man as I was, and would fight me for my plantations." Allen is described in his deposition as a "labourer"; in other accounts he was described as the governor's overseer.[2] These differing accounts point to the multiple axes of power that made the social relations of the seventeenth-century Caribbean unstable.

The slave in the conflict was never named, nor was he asked for his account of the incident. Formally, this absence echoed the exclusion of slaves from legal personhood. As the conflict progressed through the courts, the slave whose inadvertent actions initiated the confrontation and whose words and demeanor may have exacerbated it was erased; the dispute was carried on between Allen and Hallet and ultimately between Hallet and Allen's master, the governor. The slave had dutifully claimed the street for his mistress, a white woman riding with the wife of one of the island's leading citizens. In this role he pushed aside a white man. The identification of Allen as a laborer first suggests a marginal existence in Bridgetown's economy. That he was later identified as the governor's overseer indicates the low status of white servants. It was perfectly reasonable for the street to be cleared for a group of elite women. It was equally reasonable for a white man to object to being pushed by a slave. The incident attracted such attention because it was connected to existing political conflicts within the elite. The management of tensions within the elite, among the white population of different statuses, and between slaves and whites was the central focus of all forms of social control, both formal and informal.

The social order of England was impossible to replicate in the islands, even though the legal structure in the colonies resembled that of England. In England, a hierarchical society was maintained by law and paternalist custom, which promised protection in return for obedience. In the West Indies, as we have seen, law was often corrupt and planters showed little solicitude for social inferiors. For many colonists the journey to the West Indies was an attempt to gain wealth and status that was unavailable to them in England. In the pursuit of profit, almost any behavior was regarded as legitimate. The planters themselves resisted discipline, especially attempts to constrain their behavior in order to protect those subordinate to them. Paternalism toward servants was far more grudging and limited than among English landowners, and that toward slaves almost entirely absent.

At the same time that planters were unwilling to sacrifice profit to protect slaves or servants, they tried to sustain the paternalist myth that their actions were for the benefit of those subordinates. Their self-image as Englishmen made it difficult to imagine that their slaves did not want to live under English masters. They asserted that their slaves were "happy" in their enslavement, as indicated by their dancing, music, and other festivals. But slaveholders were perpetually wary of their slaves, and planters developed elaborate systems of policing to protect themselves from insurrection. The pervasive fear of slave rebellion in the islands was a tacit acknowledgment that slaves were not content in their subordination. Indeed, the whole social order did not work as it did in England. The plantation system was maintained by brutal repression of all those who resisted or rebelled against domination, no matter how limited that resistance might be.

Violence and disorder were hallmarks of life in the islands. In the earliest period of settlement in Barbados, observers remarked on "the quarelsome conditions of your fiery spirits," as well as the idleness of servants.[3] Accounts of brawls in both Jamaica and Barbados throughout the seventeenth century suggest a quick recourse to violence when disputes arose.[4] The Caribbean region was in a state of almost perpetual warfare, formal and informal. Pirates and privateers took law into their hands for their own enrichment and seized whatever they could. Indeed, it was sometimes difficult to distinguish these adventurers from merchants, planters, and officials who showed little regard for the formalities of law in their pursuit of profit. On a global scale, the European land grab in the Americas fostered a culture where the goal was to take as much as possible as quickly as possible. The violence used to control servants and slaves grew out of the systemic violence fundamental to colonial society, as well as out of fear of violent resistance.

At the center of the planters' uneasiness was the instability of the colonial social hierarchy. Orlando Patterson has suggested that for the first ninety years of its settlement, Jamaica was at most "a society in an acute state of anomie," with two groups "strangers to the land on which they met, . . . experiencing, in different ways, the dissolution of their traditional cultures." Barbados was more English, and more successful, than Jamaica, but its inhabitants also experienced the process of creating a new culture from elements of their former ones.[5] Matters of rank and precedence were constantly contested; an individual's status was determined by how much power he could exert over others, and people's relative positions were always in flux. Because order was insecure, it was fiercely defended by those who exercised power. Colonial authorities treated any dissent as if it entailed a threat to their rule, or even to the existence of government itself. Although the elite's methods of asserting and maintaining control often undermined social stability, their perception that their power was precarious was correct.

The instability of colonial society had multiple roots. Most important, the divides of race and freedom created a complex social hierarchy. The terms of subordination and obligation that defined hierarchy in England did not apply in the same ways to English indentured servants and to African slaves in the Caribbean. For white servants, it was important that they be seen as "above" all enslaved people; their subordination to masters was undercut by their superiority to slaves. Over time, as servants were more likely to be transported felons than hapless youths drawn from the wandering poor, elites were torn between their need of white servants as a group and their contempt for them as individuals. High levels of mortality undermined stable relationships within the elite and between the elite and their subordinates. The inability of many planters' families to reproduce themselves enhanced social mobility; some estates, like that of the Helyars, lost out to those who fared better in the demographic lottery. Although the chances of rapidly accumulating a fortune were not as great as many colonists hoped, the expectation of mobility undercut the creation of a stable colonial ruling class.

A Fractious Elite

Social instability made governing the islands difficult. Members of the elite engaged in conflicts on a variety of issues that created multiple factions. There were conflicts between London and the islands, merchants and planters, and large planters and small ones, as well as between agents for the Royal African Company and all other planters. Those who were allies on one issue might be at odds on another. Governors who were outsiders were enlisted by parties to local disputes; those who were insiders, like Hender Molesworth, advanced their own and their friends' interests. Planters often tried to prove their power by rejecting the policies of the governor. When neither social nor political power was stable, planters were more concerned with their own position than with the common good.

The conflict that framed the encounter between Richard Allen and Colonel Hallet had begun some eight months earlier, when Governor Kendall accused Hallet of "several high crimes and misdemeanors" that required his removal from the Council. Kendall was both the accuser and the chief witness against Hallet. As part of Barbados's preparations against a French invasion, the Assembly had passed a law for fortifying the island with trenches.

When the workers reached Hallet's land, they wanted to cut down "some small underwood and brush of inconsiderable value." Hallet refused, demanding an appraisal of his "seaside grape trees from the berries of which he yearly made some advantage" and a formal order from the governor before their destruction. He argued that "it was against Magna Carta, that any person should be disturbed or receive any injury in their estates without a compensation or satisfaction appointed." The governor was furious; Hallet had never raised this issue when the Council had discussed the law, and as a councillor Hallet had forced the execution of the law on "poor people who suffered more." When the surveyor arrived with a group of slaves to lay out the trenches, two of Hallet's "Christian servants" met them with clubs and tried to block their work. Kendall was called to the scene, and the servants told him their master had ordered them to prevent any one cutting down his wood. Hallet thought that his white servants would be more effective than slaves in challenging the governor; neither side gave slaves the power to challenge white authority. Kendall struck at one of the servants with his cane but missed, so he fired his pistol, which frightened the servants away, and the work continued. Hallet was thereupon suspended from the Council and all public offices. Six months later, when Hallet did not seem properly chastened, Kendall decided that legal action was required. Justice St. John, to whom the case was referred, decided that Hallet's actions amounted to levying war against the government, so he had him bound over to answer charges of treason and to keep the peace until then.[6] The somewhat extreme charge suggests the governor's anxiety, particularly in a time of war.

As a result of his encounter with Richard Allen, Hallet was judged to have forfeited his bond to keep the peace. When Hallet's case came before a Court of Oyer and Terminer, however, the grand jury resisted handing down an indictment. While they agreed that the alleged actions and words had taken place, the jurors—themselves property owners—were not convinced that they were "said or done rebelliously maliciously or seditiously." The solicitor general told them they were to judge only matters of fact, not the intentions of the accused; the words "rebelliously maliciously or seditiously" were mere matters of form in the indictment. It took several visits from the solicitor and attorney general to convince the jury to approve the indictment, and even then they added the caveat that Hallet had not acted rebelliously. Finally, after a court session that lasted several days longer than planned, the jury found Hallet guilty, and he was fined £350.[7]

The accounts of Hallet's case demonstrate not only the heavy-handed tactics of the government intent on gaining a conviction in a high-profile case, but also the accused planter's attempts to base his resistance to the government's actions on the time-honored rights of English subjects. Hallet's references to Magna Carta reinforce the sense that for him, as for some of the jurors, the government's power should be limited by the rights of subjects. The initial dispute turned on the right to control property. In the eyes of Governor Kendall, Hallet had insisted on placing his private profit, which he counted as "some advantage," above the need for collective defense.

Class and race are visible throughout this conflict, figuring in each move the parties made. Hallet tried to use his high standing to avoid having his land appropriated for public purposes; he deployed his servants against the slaves sent to do the work. Governor Kendall trumped both the servants and the grand jury, using all the instruments available to him to assert the government's prerogatives. The encounter between Richard Allen and Mrs. Castleton's unnamed slave came as a final coda to the interplay of class and race that ran through the entire conflict. When Hallet thrashed the governor's overseer after the confrontation on the street and the governor had him charged with treason, the two men treated the servant and slave as proxies in their contest for power. The Hallet case is remarkable because it demonstrates how ongoing conflicts within the elite could give added significance to everyday exchanges on the street. Power and authority were constituted through class and racial subordination. Asserting precedence and demanding deference from servants and slaves was a central part of that process.

Hallet was not alone among Barbados planters in resisting official orders. In 1687 William Meagher, deputy marshal to one of the militia regiments, was sent to distrain the goods of those who did not appear at musters and did not keep arms, as they were required to by the Militia Act. When he arrived at one plantation and sought to seize hogs, the slaves were ordered to resist, assaulted Meagher, and kept the hogs from him. Meagher drew his sword to defend himself "against the insolences of the Negroes." As he was leaving the plantation, he noticed a heifer and decided to seize that instead of the hogs. The overseer, who was white, attacked him with "a great long staff, which was pointed at one end and had been covered with Iron," upon which Meagher "accidentally" killed him. The incident illustrates both the quick recourse to violence on all sides and the readiness of colonists to resist the agents of government. As in Hallet's case, Meagher's conviction for murder is recorded for other reasons: because the incident took place in the performance of his duties, the Council wrote to the king requesting that he be pardoned.[8]

In both Barbados and Jamaica, disputes within the elite often played out as disputes between planters and royal governors. Because of internal divisions among the planters, governors were always able to build alliances against those they considered troublemakers. Troublemakers today might be allies tomorrow. In 1665 Lord Willoughby, the governor of Barbados, wrote home complaining of Samuel Farmer, Esq., "a great Magna Carta man and Petition of Right maker." At Farmer's instigation, Willoughby alleged, the Barbados planters were "beginning to dance after the Long Parliament's pipe," refusing to vote for anything they did not want for themselves. Farmer had begun collecting signatures on a petition to the king, presumably the one passed by the Barbados Assembly in June 1665 complaining of irregularities and abuses of the legal system. Farmer was sent home to England to be tried for treason. His defense was twofold. First, unlike Willoughby, he had been a loyal servant to Charles I during the Civil War and, when he escaped to Barbados, had opposed the supporters of Parliament. Second, he charged that Lord Willoughby not only distorted proper legal processes but also was taking funds raised in Barbados in the king's name to advance his own interests in Surinam. Two years later, Farmer had returned to Barbados and was again ensconced in the Assembly; William Willoughby, Lord Willoughby's brother, described Farmer as "Your Majesty's loyal subject."[9]

While the planters worked together to control their servants and slaves, they fought each other for property, precedence, honor and reputation, and power. Disputes within the elite were often carried on for many years. In 1683, when Sir Timothy Thornhill, a member of the Council of Barbados, was given a baronetcy, he immediately demanded precedence because of his new status. The Council, however, had traditionally based precedence on seniority in office. A furious debate ensued. When the lieutenant governor, Edwin Stede, suggested that Thornhill have precedence until instructions had been received from the king, the only dissent came from Robert Davers, Esq., son and heir of Sir Robert Davers, Bart., whose seniority ranked him above Thornhill. Stede then decided that in the absence of agreement, the existing hierarchy would hold until he received instructions from the king. At this, Thornhill stalked out of the Council.[10] This row over status held more than symbolic significance: in case of the death of the governor and lieutenant governor, executive power passed to the senior member of the Council.

Thornhill was constantly trying to claim a higher position than his fellows were willing to grant him, and he proved prickly when slighted or insulted. In 1687 he was convicted of uttering seditious words against the king. According to Richard Harwood, another councillor, Thornhill accused him of slandering Thornhill's father. Harwood insisted that he only said that Thornhill's father was a traitor for his role in turning over the island to the Parliamentary forces under Sir George Ayscue. When Thornhill retorted that Harwood's father had also been a traitor, Harwood protested that was impossible, since his father had died at the Battle of Newbury under the command of Lord Carnarvon. Thornhill responded, "Those that fought for the King in those days or pretended to fight for the King in those days were traitors," while "all that fought for the Parliament at that time were good subjects." According to another witness, Harwood admitted "that he was not of that party which their fathers were of, who had amongst them surrendered the island to Sir George Ayscue." Thornhill responded that "those who surrendered the Island at that time did the King more service than those who did oppose the enemy." Harwood informed Lieutenant Governor Stede of this exchange. When questioned, Thornhill asserted that he could not be charged with treason because there was only one witness, but his protests were unavailing.[11]

Thornhill and Harwood argued fiercely over events that had occurred nearly forty years before. The accounts of this dispute all suggest that the behavior of their fathers was central to both Thornhill's and Harwood's sense of honor. Contemporary conflicts exacerbated this dispute. One of Stede's complaints against Thornhill was that after his exchange with Harwood, Thornhill traveled around the island stirring up dissension. As Stede put it, he "makes it his business in a sort of a Monmouth's circuit to go and feast into the several quarters of the Island, thereby drawing the giddy and unsteady people to favor him, and be of his loose disposition." He allegedly told people he would use his influence to gain authority in the island and then revenge himself on anyone who did him harm.[12] The comparison to the Duke of Monmouth, so soon after the defeat of his rebellion, was designed to raise alarm in London. Thornhill remained belligerent at his trial, challenging several jurors based on earlier conflicts. He had "caned and broken the head" of one juror, and he had a legal dispute with another over the ownership of slaves.[13] Thornhill's numerous disputes with other planters demonstrate how combustible economic and social conflicts became when played out politically.

Events in Jamaica in 1683 demonstrate an even more potent combination of political and social conflicts. The chief protagonists were Sir Henry Morgan, the former privateer, now turned somewhat respectable, and the governor, Sir Thomas Lynch. According to several witnesses, Morgan and some of his followers had tried to create a riot after celebrations marking the defeat of the Rye House Plot. They sowed dissension in the Assembly, arguing against compromises that would have granted the governor revenue for a longer period in return for approval of some of the planters' favored bills. In addition, Morgan and his cronies were trying to divide Jamaica into Whigs and Tories, attacking religious Dissenters and fomenting conflict. Even a decision by a coroner's jury about the death of a sailor was portrayed as a conflict between Dissenters and the Establishment. In October of that year, Morgan was removed from the Council of Jamaica at Lynch's instigation, primarily as a result of his role in stirring up disorder in Port Royal. Furthermore, "he had on all occasions shewed dislike, and uneasiness under his [Lynch's] government." Indeed, Lynch claimed in a letter some months later, Morgan and his friends were planning to send a "factious address" to London accusing Lynch of favoring Dissenters. This was not true, Lynch insisted: while at the king's behest he had offered toleration to Dissenters, none held any "civil employment," and while a few served in the militia, that was a burden rather than a privilege. Here political conflict was expressed through drinking and brawling, as well as in debates in the Assembly and complaints about the behavior of juries.[14]

In the 1660s and 1670s, the former Cromwellian soldiers had enough land and power to be defined as a major source of Jamaica's problems. Those from established English families lamented that planters from lower social origins had no sense of how they were supposed to behave. John Style, who settled in Jamaica in 1668, was soon embroiled in a number of conflicts with his neighbors. He thought the major barriers to settlement were the soldiers, who divided the island into areas "wherein every chief exercised absolute power over all the rest as slaves either to raise money or aught else." Style clearly saw himself as above them; in another letter he wrote that "there is not one in the whole parish (myself excepted) who until he came into the Indies was either Justice of the Peace, constable, churchwarden . . . or in capacity to be any such." Style's descent down the hierarchy of offices emphasizes what he perceived as the humble origins of most colonists. Seven years later, Governor Vaughan agreed with Style's analysis. He wrote that island politics was dominated by old Cromwellian soldiers, and most of the rest "were either desperate in their fortunes, or who came over servants at first & have since crept up into estates. And among others, [there were] some who chose transporting rather than hanging & Jamaica rather than Tyburn."[15] There were few factors or merchants. The relatively humble origins of many colonists provided an explanation for corruption, incompetence, and weak government.

Although violence within the elite was not always politically motivated, members of the elite might use political connections to try to protect themselves from its consequences. In 1697 Peter Beckford, a young man from a prominent family who was receiver general in Jamaica, killed Samuel Lewis, Esq., an older man who was commissary general for the island. Both family networks went to work. Beckford fled to France, whence he sent a petition for pardon, arguing that he killed Lewis in a duel and at worst was guilty of manslaughter, not murder. The petition argued that Beckford's family "have been very faithful and serviceable to your Majesty and your government." Lewis's family was equally active in London, pointing to his years of service as justice of the peace, his peaceable disposition, and his "blameless and inoffensive life." In the end, the pardon was not granted, but the prominence of those involved allows us to see how the system operated.[16] Conflicts within the elite made it difficult for them to keep order by example among white colonists and even more difficult for them to control subordinates such as servants and slaves.

Servants, Soldiers, and Sailors

As the first source of coerced labor in the Caribbean, servants were naturally the first to challenge the authority and power of their masters. Servants had provided most labor in Barbados before the introduction of sugar cultivation in the 1640s, so they always played a larger role in Barbados than in Jamaica.[17] While white servants were desirable for their service in the militia and their supervision and control over slaves, their expectations based on the English model of service produced conflict with their masters.[18]

In 1649, according to Ligon, there was a plot by servants on the island against the planters, "their sufferings being grown to a great height, & their daily complainings to one another (of the intolerable burdens they laboured under)." The plotters were those "not able to endure such slavery." Ligon believed that a majority of the servants on the island were involved in the plot; they planned to "fall upon their Masters, and cut all their throats, and by that means make themselves not only freemen, but Masters of the Island." The plot was only discovered the day before it was to be put into execution, when one servant betrayed it to his master. Eighteen servants were executed "for example to the rest," chosen because they were "so haughty in their resolutions, and so incorrigible."[19]

Servants continued to run away and escape from the island, but the

Barbados planters never again faced such a serious threat from them. Authorities were caught between the desire to ameliorate the condition of their white dependents and the mistrust that saw harsh discipline as necessary to ensure that they were honest and biddable. In 1688 Edwin Stede wrote from Barbados that the Assembly, having revised the law of slavery, was about to take on the law relating to service. He acknowledged the need to restrain cruel masters and noted that governors had at times intervened and awarded freedom to servants who had been grossly mistreated. At the same time, "it will be impossible to keep the servants in that duty and obedience to their masters as they ought to be, and indeed with safety to this island, if there be not severe laws both to restrain and punish [them]." The problem, Stede argued, was that servants were recruited from jails, had not been accustomed to work, and therefore "run away from their masters, steal and purloin from them what they can, and many times escape off the island." The situation had been exacerbated by a recent statement by the attorney general, Sir Thomas Montgomery, that masters should not beat or whip servants at all, especially not so severely as to "break the skin"; since this pronouncement, Stede asserted, servants had become more "refractory."[20] In spite of their poor character, white servants were increasingly used to supervise slaves. The constant anxiety expressed in communications home about the shortage of servants reflected the important role they played in maintaining order on the island.[21]

Jamaica was never as dependent on servants as Barbados, so the initial threat of disorder there came primarily from English soldiers and sailors. In 1661 soldiers, who had not been paid and were badly supplied, staged a mutiny.[22] Soon afterwards the army was disbanded, and many of the soldiers received grants of land. Some stayed; others listened to the siren song of the buccaneers and sold all to participate in piracy around the Caribbean.

Sailors on shore were often sources of trouble in both islands. One of the earliest extant laws in Barbados, dating from 1652, was to "prevent frequenting of taverns and alehouses by seamen."[23] In November 1661 several of the crew of HMS *Diamond* grabbed two men celebrating Guy Fawkes Day in the streets of Bridgetown, beat them, seized their pistols, and placed them in the ship's "bilboes" [shackles] overnight. Two weeks later, the same sailors went wild in Bridgetown after they were disappointed with the available recreation. They went back to a boat and grabbed "a boathook, oars, hatchet, and brick brakes, or such like mischievous instruments, violently fell on and assaulted several persons." After injuring the constable and forcing merchants into their houses, they were finally subdued. They were bound over to keep the peace and provide security for their appearance at the next sessions, but during a wild storm their captain, Richard Whiting, sent a message to the authorities demanding their release, asserting that he had to sail that night. Whiting was himself taken into custody for his "contempt and violation of his Majesty's peace and good government," but he was released to depart two days later.[24]

Bridgetown was tame in comparison to Port Royal, one of the major ports of the Caribbean, which served not only naval vessels and the merchant fleet but also as a base for many privateers and buccaneers. As early as 1671, the new governor, Sir Thomas Lynch, reported that so much land in the town had been granted that it was "rendered unhealthy, for want of streets and public commodities."[25] The authorities in Port Royal often complained to the king of their losses from pirates and the charges the town faced in defending itself from external attack and internal disorder.[26] The busy port was known for the wide range of entertainment available there. Port Royal in 1687, according to Taylor, had several "ordinaries" where "young merchants" could lodge, as well as "many taverns, and abundance of punchy houses, or rather may be fitly called brothel houses. Here is also a coffee house." In addition, the port kept a "bull and a bear, for sport at the bear garden, and billiards, cockfighting, shooting at the target etc." Taylor characterized the town as "very loose in itself, and by reason of privateers and debauched wild blades which come hither (for all the strict restraint of the law), 'tis now more rude and antic than 'ere was Sodom." The guard that patrolled the port twice a night locking up drunks and prostitutes apparently did little good, since the "vile strumpets and common prostratures" who plied their trade were "almost impossible to civilize" and constituted a "walking plague, against which neither the cage, whip, nor ducking stool could prevail." The moral depravity of Port Royal was blamed for the destruction of much of the town in the 1692 earthquake.[27]

Taylor's account is no exaggeration. The records of the islands include numerous accounts of brawls in the taverns of Port Royal, as well as those of Spanish Town and Bridgetown; it was in these centers that insults and political gossip giving rise to disorders were exchanged. There were more taverns in Caribbean towns than in English ones: in 1670 John Style asserted that in Jamaica there were fewer than ten men "for every house that selleth strong liquors." The Jamaican authorities were sufficiently concerned about gambling in 1671 that they banned public gaming houses and barred anyone with an estate of less than £2,000 from playing cards or dice for stakes over forty shillings.[28] Jack Helyar arrived from England in 1672 after gambling away most of his stock on the journey and immediately pledged his cousin Cary's credit to get drunk in Port Royal. William Dampier was so abusive in an alehouse that "they were fain to send for the constable."[29] A 1687 letter described the escape of the pirate Bare to Havana. He was accompanied by a "strumpet" who used to dress in men's clothing and was the daughter of a "rum punch woman" in Port Royal; selling alcohol and prostitution often went together. In Havana the couple asked permission to marry, claiming that they were both loyal Catholics and that the woman was a nobleman's daughter who had fled her family. As a result of her supposed status, they had the castle guns fired in their honor.[30]

The difficulty of keeping order in Port Royal was exacerbated by the density and transience of its population, which compounded the instability created by political upheavals. During "the late disorders, passions, and miscarriages at Port Royal" of 1683, Henry Morgan was able to stir up trouble because so many sailors crowded the alehouses and other places of entertainment.[31] In early 1686 a drunken man, apparently one of the remaining Cromwellian soldiers, was provoked to assert that the Duke of Monmouth was the legitimate king. Three years later, in early 1689, a copy of the "Six Articles," clearly relating to the collapse of James II's reign, was circulating in Port Royal, brought there from London by a recent arrival who also had "the other newsletter."[32]

Complaints about disorderly sailors and pirates suggest that commanders on ships were beneficent. Yet discipline on board ships was notoriously harsh, and particularly violent commanders had to be restrained. In 1683 the captain of the *Falcon* had "whipped and ducked" his mate, who died nine days later. The Port Royal coroner's jury was inclined to find a verdict of murder, which inflamed passions in the disputes between Governor Lynch and Sir Henry Morgan and led to attacks by Morgan's supporters on Dissenters at Port Royal.[33] In 1685 the governor of Jamaica, Hender Molesworth, reported that Lieutenant Butler had become commander of the frigate *Ruby* on the death of the captain. He was generally offensive and rude, and had in an "insolent manner affronted the whole government."[34] In 1689 three ships sailed into Bridgetown harbor commanded by a Captain Hewitson, who claimed to be an admiral. Hewitson's story kept changing: was he serving James II or King William? He was also guilty of "many irregularities and unreasonable cruelties . . . towards his men" and was involved in numerous quarrels on shore. When some of his sailors had petitioned Governor Stede about his cruelty, Hewitson "threatened them all to hang them every third man with a petition about their neck." He promised to whip one young sailor to death, and he stood by with sword in hand during the whipping so that

> every stroke raised great wheals on the young man's body, and by further beating, all his skin was beaten off his body yet could not the executioner escape without three or four cuts in his head for not being severe enough in his execution . . . so that finally the poor fellow's body being all bloody and raw as a piece of beef to be broiled, he was dismissed from whipping but confined for some days and nights to a place in the ship where by cold and for want of good sustenance having nothing allowed him but a biscuit cake and water for four and twenty hours, he fell into the fever and ague and flux.

The poor sailor died later when his ship, the *Hunter*, blew up, killing seventy seamen.[35]

As the proportion of servants in the islands declined and the number of slaves increased, the planters' feared an alliance between them. Although many servants had gained positions that provided a certain amount of status, others, especially the Irish, had little standing. In 1686 some of the Irish servants in Barbados discussed a possible rebellion with slaves. But, according to Lieutenant Governor Stede, the discussions were preliminary and the slaves were the primary instigators of the plot. While none of the servants was prosecuted, at least ten planters were paid compensation for slaves executed that spring.[36]

Conflicts within the elite, public disorders, and occasional acts of overt resistance by servants and other subordinates were familiar challenges to those who governed England. Yet the context of colonial disorder was different, and those who sought to control it formed an even smaller minority on the islands than at home. Planters worried about disorder and resistance by poor whites—servants, sailors, and soldiers—largely because they were even more concerned with threats from the far larger population of slaves. The only way to control the slaves, they believed, was by ensuring that all whites worked together.

Slave Resistance

Planters and merchants in the Caribbean were plagued by fear that those they had enslaved would run away or rebel. As early as 1650, Richard Ligon thought it "a strange thing, that the Negroes, being more than double the numbers of Christians that are there and they accounted a bloody people . . . that these should not commit some horrid massacre upon the Christians, thereby to enfranchise themselves, and become masters of the Island."[37] Slave policy in both Barbados and Jamaica was driven by that fear. Slaves indeed resisted slavery both individually and collectively, committing suicide, running away, and organizing rebellions. Resistance often began on board the ships that carried slaves to the Caribbean.[38] In both islands, the most common form of resistance to enslavement was running away; more elaborate plots emerged from time to time. The differing geographies of Barbados and Jamaica shaped the nature of slave resistance. Barbados was more compact and densely settled than Jamaica. Furthermore, Jamaica's mountainous interior furnished escaped slaves with refuges where they formed autonomous communities and from which they could stage mass risings and concerted attacks on white-owned plantations. By the late 1680s, the Jamaican authorities were engaged in a continuous struggle against groups of runaway slaves. The history of slave resistance and its repression provides a window into the perspectives of slaves, while documenting how much the English were changed by planting in the Caribbean.

Barbados

The possibility of rebellion that Ligon remarked on was a continual source of anxiety to planters in Barbados. Slaves registered their resistance by running away, sometimes for a few days and sometimes for longer periods of time. They sheltered in the ravines and caves that dotted the island. Long-term survival for runaways became more difficult as the island became more densely settled, but even short absences reminded planters that their slaves did not accept slavery willingly. As early as 1648, an observer remarked on the "many hundred rebel Negro slaves in the woods" of the island.[39] The planters had to learn how to manage and police their slaves. The fear of rebellion was used in both 1666 and 1667 as an argument for having a regiment quartered on the island: the soldiers would simultaneously defend the island against the French and Dutch and against insurrection. An observer in 1667 added that impoverished and mistreated white servants could not be expected to defend the island in case of attack. Furthermore, it was increasingly difficult to recruit enough servants.[40]

In 1659 London newsbooks reported a conspiracy among the slaves in Barbados. While there is no other evidence of this conspiracy, the allegation that it was led by an African prince and that the goal was to slit the masters' throats is echoed in later plots.[41] The first well-documented plot by slaves against the planters was discovered in 1675, shortly before it was to be put into action. Slaves could organize without being noticed because their lives were largely separate from those of the planters. The pamphlet account published in London suggested as a motive for the rising "their desire of being eased from that continual work, which by being slaves, they and their posterity are liable to. . . . [N]o man labours but by necessity; or hopes at last to gain that to live on which may give him rest." The author defined the slaveholders' dilemma: how could they convince their slaves to be content without any reward for hard work? The plot in question had been in preparation for three years. The rebels were led by slaves called Coromantee by the English, who have been identified as Akan people from the Gold Coast of Africa, the single-largest ethnic group among the enslaved. Among the English, the Coromantee were reputed to be hard workers but also "warlike." The plot had been spread by the network of Coromantees throughout the island. The rebels planned to crown a "king" after summoning the slaves to action by the use of horns made of elephant tusks and gourds. The slaves were then to set fire to the sugarcanes and slit their masters' throats. The sources do not agree on whether they planned to use some of the white women as mistresses or kill them along with their husbands and fathers.[42] For at least some of the authorities, this was a plot by enslaved men against English planters, with white women as the prize.

The plot was revealed after Anne, "a house Negro woman" belonging to Justice Hall, overheard two slaves discussing it; one of them said he would not kill the "baccararoes," or white people. When she asked what they were discussing, that same slave told her of the plot. She immediately alerted her master and mistress, believing that "it was great pity so good people as her Master and Mistress were should be destroyed." Initially, seventeen slaves were convicted; six were burned alive, and eleven were beheaded and their bodies were dragged through the streets and burned. At the burning of the first six, one of the slaves appeared to be about to reveal more details of the plot, when another "jogged him and was heard to chide him in these words, 'Thou fool, are there not enough of our countrymen killed already? Art thou minded to kill them all?'" According to the pamphlet account, twenty-five more slaves were executed and five hanged themselves to avoid execution; sixty slaves were still in prison in Holetown. These numbers may be exaggerated; Governor Atkins said a total of thirty-five had been executed "for example to the rest."[43]

The scope of the plot reminded whites of their vulnerability. Their sense of insecurity was reinforced a few months later when Barbados was hit by a severe hurricane, which destroyed most of the sugar mills on the leeward side of the island and killed 200 people. Together these events were interpreted as indicators that the West Indies was an entirely different sort of place than England. One result of the conspiracy was, as we have seen, a major revision of the laws relating to slavery in Barbados, which sought to limit communication among slaves on different plantations.[44] Yet new laws did not solve the problem. In late November 1683 there were more rumors of a plot by slaves, though nothing could be substantiated. Several "insolent bold Negroes" were soundly whipped "for terror to others." One slave belonging to Madam Sharp was burned to death: he had responded to seeing "some Christians beating some Negroes" with threats, saying "that the Negroes 'ere long would serve the Christians so." His refusal to be cowed by the violence that held the slave system together posed a direct challenge to white rule. At about the same time, a paper was distributed through the fields calling on the slaves to rise a week later. Since few slaves could read, the purpose or origin of the document was unclear, but the authorities supposed that the letter was the product of some "persons of turbulent minds and unquiet dispositions to amuse the common people." The enormous panic that resulted from these relatively small incidents reveals the fear that was the planters' constant companion.[45]

The next major threat came early in 1686, in a plot that was thought to include Irish servants along with slaves. The Council promptly ordered the justices in the affected parishes to search "all the Negro houses . . . for arms, ammunition, or other dangerous weapons, and to secure all arms etc. that shall be found." They were also to try to discern how slaves had acquired any arms they might have.[46] A month later Governor Stede reported that the plot had been in its very early stages, and the Irish were not deeply involved. Still, he was concerned that the justices of the peace, as well as the planters and overseers, had not been vigilant; they had not reported weapons taken by slaves, and they had allowed gatherings of slaves where planning could take place unobserved. The execution of ten slaves indicates that however feeble the plot, the authorities were taking no chances.[47]

Anxieties about rebellion were heightened by the European wars of the 1690s. In 1690 the governor reported that the French harassed the island by "putting men on shore to steal Negroes or take prisoners, burn houses, works and canes."[48] Slaves were routinely imprisoned when it was thought they threatened the safety of the island. In 1690 Willoughby Chamberlain asked for clemency for his "Negro boys," but added, "we leave it wholly to your Honour's breast to punish them as you please." Their offence is not clear, but their imprisonment and the involvement of the governor means it was not normal misbehavior.[49]

Two years later, a far more serious plot was uncovered. The records of this plan clearly inscribed gendered ideas of race. The conspiracy described by two of the participants—after being tortured—was elaborate. Although planning had evidently begun several years earlier, any action was delayed until the soldiers were sent off the island to fight the French. In the months leading up to the plot's discovery in November 1692, the leaders had recruited enough slaves to create four regiments of foot and two of horse. Each of these regiments, modeled on the island's militia, had named officers. Most represented the skilled slaves—overseers, carpenters, bricklayers, wheelwrights, and so on. Horses and arms were to be stolen from masters and the island's magazine. While the slaves were confident of their ability to overthrow the white establishment on the island, what was to happen next was less certain, at least to the English investigators. According to the report of the court-martial, "It would have been impossible for them to have agreed in the disposal of the government, the estates of their masters, . . . or what was most desirable, the white women. They were to make wives of the handsomest, whores, cooks, and chambermaids of the others." According to a pamphlet published in London, the plot involved only slaves born in Barbados, and the plotters intended to maintain slavery as a system; all the African-born would remain slaves. Older women, white and black, were to serve as cooks and personal servants.[50]

The most important source for these details was a slave named Ben, who spent four days hanging in chains from the gibbet before he gave information. Because he was tortured, some aspects of his testimony were undoubtedly provided to satisfy the court-martial. In spite of these limitations, his account offers us a possible glimpse of slaves' desires for freedom, as well as a more certain one of planters' fears. Like the 1676 plot, this conspiracy was seen as an attack by enslaved men on white men. The goals were defined as both political—freedom from enslavement and power in the island—and sexual—access to white women. The ironies of the narrative are manifold. It charged the rebels with planning to enslave black women, although they were already enslaved; it constructed the slaves as male, when slave women did much of the field labor on the plantations. It construed the plotters' desire as focused on white women, while in fact white men were far more likely to rape enslaved women than black men were to rape white women. As white women who did not work in the fields came to be defined as separate from work, they—along with a similar freedom from work—were also seen as the goal of enslaved men. As English men told the story, the slaves were planning to participate in a classic ritual of inversion, where inferiors turned the social order upside down but kept the existing structure. This version of the plot enabled the planters to downplay the significance of resistance to enslavement.[51]

Barbados authorities took the 1692 plot very seriously. The Council paid out at least £58 for dinners and drink for those conducting the court-martial; the clerk was paid £14 for his attendance. It is not clear how many slaves were executed; there were at least three, while a pamphlet says "many." The charge for castrating forty-two slaves was £10 10s. Castration was not specified in the 1688 law, but "other pains, as their crimes shall deserve," was offered as an alternative to execution. It simultaneously preserved the lives of skilled slaves and addressed the plotters' supposed desire for white women.[52] As in 1676, the discovery of the plot led to a flurry of legislative activity. The Assembly quickly passed a bill to ensure that the militia was kept up to strength. A few months later the governor noted that no one wanted to send any soldiers off the island to fight the French, given "the dreadful apprehensions of what their slaves may attempt during their absence," and tried to reorganize plans for the war around the need to maintain soldiers in Barbados.[53] While taking steps to defend the island, the authorities sought to prevent further plots. Within a week of the court-martial, the 1676 act that had provided for the execution of any slave who ran away for more than thirty days was reinstated. The preamble argued that "by the often running away of Negroes and slaves, & by their long absence from the service of their owners, they become desperate and daily plot and commit felonies and other enormities, not only to the terror and affrightment of the neighborhood, but the danger of the island in general."[54] At the same time, the Assembly instituted penalties for selling "rum or other strong liquors" to slaves, or buying alcohol on their behalf. The penalty—a fine of twenty shillings and a whipping—shows that selling rum to slaves was an offence of poor whites, not of planters.[55] That the plot had involved neither runaways nor drunken slaves was not relevant to the authorities' response.

Barbados planters remained uncertain of the loyalty of their slaves, especially in the event of a French attack. Their agents in London asked that a regiment be stationed there permanently; they also suggested that when regiments were sent home, soldiers be given the opportunity to stay on the island to continue to provide for its defense.[56] In 1694 the new governor, Lord Francis Russell, thought it odd that there was no citadel on the island, since there were (according to his count) 50,000 slaves who "are always plotting to cut white people's throats."[57] In 1696 the Council discovered another conspiracy and quickly punished the planners.[58] In 1700 an observer argued that the presence of slaves in Bridgetown contributed to crime and enabled them to plot rebellion, "which they cannot so easily do in the country where they have hard and constant labour." The cost of his proposed remedy—planters hiring white servants for work in Bridgetown—would be paid for by the reduction in losses by theft.[59]

In spite of their continuing anxiety, by the end of the century the Barbados planters had learned to police their slaves. In 1697 a revision of the militia act provided for regular service by slaves. According to the act, "by good experience it is well known, that many Negroes and Slaves are worthy of great trust and confidence to be reposed in them." The act required that each horseman serving in the militia be accompanied by "a man slave, with a bill and lance."[60] The last feeble rumor of a planned slave uprising before the nineteenth century came in 1701; after that there was no rising planned (at least that we know of) until the first actual slave rebellion in Barbados in 1816.[61] The authorities in the island rightly continued to mistrust their slaves' loyalty, but the measures they had taken effectively eliminated conspiracies.

Jamaica

Jamaica's experience of slave resistance was dramatically different from that of Barbados for two reasons. First, Jamaica's geography meant that few people lived more than ten miles from either the coast or the mountains, both of which offered opportunities for escape. Second, unlike Barbados, Jamaica had a resident population when it was conquered. An independent community formed by former slaves of the Spanish who had intermarried with the few surviving Arawaks had lived in the east of the island for a long time. After the English invasion, some Spaniards and their slaves retreated to the interior, whence they supported attempts from Cuba to recapture the island; the former slaves remained after all the Spaniards had left. These two groups formed the core of the Maroons who continued to resist English domination. The conquest of Jamaica moved imperceptibly from a struggle against supporters of Spanish rule to a struggle against independent communities of former slaves and their descendants. As Henry Barham wrote in his 1722 history of Jamaica, the island was threatened "by the frequent rebellions of the slaves, who easily shelter themselves in the great woods, and mountains." By the 1680s the authorities were conducting almost continuous campaigns against groups of runaway slaves.[62]

The Maroons demonstrated increasing strategic sophistication in their dealings with the English. In 1660 "a party of old Spanish Negroes" commanded by Juan Lubola (or de Bola) surrendered to the English; all were given their freedom. Lubola's party was based in Lluidas Vale, north of the Guanaboa Vale; they had provided much of the food and other supplies for the Spanish resistance. There was another party of former Spanish slaves, known as Varmahaly Negroes, further inland in the Vera Ma Hollis Savanna, who were still free, but an expedition captured all but about thirty of them. Another group apparently was located further west, in the Mocho Mountains. Although William Beeston optimistically asserted that the remaining thirty Varmahaly men "by degrees were all picked up and the island left quiet to the English," in 1663 the authorities offered the remaining Varmahaly group a deal: anyone who turned themselves in and acknowledged English authority would be treated like a white person and given thirty acres of land. At the same time, Lubola was to command a militia regiment and the black community was to be essentially self-governing, aside from cases of "life and death."[63] The offer was not accepted. Instead, in November 1663, when Lubola met with the "outlying Negroes," they "cut him to pieces." Later that summer, a naval expedition went to the north side of the island to "endeavor the reducing of some outlying Spanish Negroes which still did mischief."[64]

There was peace for a few years as the Maroons retreated a bit further from English settlement, but conflict reemerged when English settlements expanded into Maroon territory. Control of women as well as territory was central to the campaign against the Maroons. In 1665 the Council announced that since the Varmahaly Negroes had begun to rob and kill, the island was in a state of war against them. The militia was called up. The Assembly raised money for the campaign to "surprise and kill those sneaking and treacherous rogues" and put prices on the heads of their leaders. Servants and slaves who captured or killed any of them would gain their freedom, a provision that would increase their interest in a successful expedition. Anyone who found their leader would receive "all the women and children and all the plunder they can find there for their reward." Those who surrendered and turned in any of their fellows would receive a pardon and freedom.[65] The Varmahaly group retreated further, but in 1668 the Varmahaly Negroes killed five white hunters who had entered their territory; the government sent an embassy to them, and their leader agreed to swear allegiance to the king.[66] This strategic move enabled the Varmahaly community to consolidate its position. Two years later, in 1670, they had "in cold blood basely murdered" six white men, again hunters who were away from major settlements. All whites on the island were now expected to be armed at all times and ready to assist in the capture of the "traitorous villains." Besides a bounty, they would receive the wives and children of any captured men as slaves. The peace of 1668 was over. While the fate of the Varmahaly community is not clear, it appears they retreated to the northeastern section of the island, where they were distant from English settlements.[67]

The Varmahaly band was an organized group and presented serious challenges to the weak state structure of early Jamaica. They were therefore treated with some respect and given numerous opportunities to become part of the society the English were trying to build. Yet their presence was never more than tolerated, their freedom always defined as a gift rather than a right. While acknowledging the Varmahalys' ability to make trouble, the English asserted their own authority. By the late 1670s, however, the Varmahaly were not the only people of African descent living in the central areas of Jamaica; a number of other groups formed, consisting both of slaves escaping from plantations and those who were shipwrecked on the island. These groups did not necessarily cooperate, and there is some evidence that the Varmahaly and other creole groups initially looked down on newcomers from Africa.[68]

The English found it easier to deal with an organized group like the Varmahaly band than with the resistance of those they had enslaved, which seemed to them more random and unpredictable. The authorities sought to limit the opportunities for resistance. In October 1663 the Council established a requirement that boat owners chain their boats at night so slaves could not use them to escape.[69] A year later, the Council complained of "certain runaway blacks from Barbados" who had landed on the north of the island and, amongst other crimes, murdered one person.[70] In 1668 the government tried to block the sale of slaves from Spanish colonies to prevent "the many mischiefs" they had done and centralized all slave sales in Port Royal.[71] In 1670, when John Style wrote a friend in London about the murder of the six hunters by the Varmahaly band, he noted that in addition to the bands "which have been long out," the planters also had to deal with "very many new Negroes run away from their masters." Style, who was imprisoned at the time, learned from a fellow prisoner, a slave from Guanaboa, "that they only watched opportunity to make themselves masters." Like the Barbados planters, Style described resistance as an inversion of the social order, not its transformation. Soon after Style's letter, some of the outlying Negroes in Guanaboa "killed ten or twelve hogs of one man's, stayed salting of them and robbed them [the household] of their arms and what else they had, and carried away besides great store of plantings."[72] Two years later,

William Grouden of St. Elizabeth was murdered by his slaves. Some of the culprits had been killed by his neighbors, but others were still on the run, so the Council offered a bounty for anyone who captured them.[73]

Given the persistence of both "petit marronage" (short-term runaways from plantations) and "grand marronage" (long-term escape from slavery that involved founding autonomous communities), Jamaican authorities were uneasy about any new slaves who might threaten order. It is impossible to tell how common the practice of running away for a short time was; it was certainly common enough that in the 1670s a list of slaves at Bybrook indicated that six had run away, while a 1709 list described one slave as a "runaway dog."[74] When Barbados deported slaves after the 1675 plot, the Council of Jamaica "seriously weighed and considered the great hazard and dangers which may accrue unto this island, and the settlers in it, by the ill government of Negroes." Their solution to the threat suggested that the problem was not ill government at all, but the character of the slaves: masters of all ships bringing slaves to the island were required to post a bond that none of the slaves on board had been transported for involvement in the Barbados plot.[75]

The problem of maintaining order, according to a report in 1677, was exacerbated by absenteeism and lack of vigilance among masters. The woods were "inviting receptacles to the slaves who by reason of the miseries they continually suffer will never be unwilling to improve such an opportunity." In December of 1675, "many families were murdered." William Whaley explained that "now at this present there is at least one hundred Negroes up in arms at the north side, and have killed several white men; burnt and destroyed most of the Plantations in St. Mary's parish." According to a proclamation, the "several insurrections and rebellions of our Negroes to the great disturbance of the peace and planting this his Majesty's island" resulted from the failure of planters to enforce existing laws. Various parties of the militia had been sent off to try to capture the rebellious slaves. When they had no success, the Council recommended that the governor raise a force of twenty men, who would be paid for two months and also receive bounties for capturing the rebels, whose leaders were identified by the size of the reward: £20 for Peter, £15 for Scanderberg and Doctor, and £5 for all the others. The party was also to be issued shoes, bread, and arms from the treasury. This unit would be joined by six Spanish Negroes, presumably from Juan Lubola's band, who would guide them in the more remote areas of the island.[76] The standard response to rebellions was developed after two decades of anxiety: a hunting party was sent to find the self-freed slaves, and any plotters were proceeded against with ruthless severity.

In 1677 the Assembly passed new laws to prevent "rebellion." In order to make masters more accountable, one law blocked compensation to owners of executed slaves if the owner had not notified the proper authorities that the slave had run away. Running away was regarded as a prelude to rebellion, and planters who tried to conceal problems with their slaves faced serious consequences.[77] Given the fear of rebellion, even "intended rebellion" was severely punished. Planters did not want slaves to think they could get away with resistance. In 1677 Joseph Bryan wrote his brother about the "cruel death" of a neighbor's slave for a planned rebellion, evidently an escape that never became a full-fledged rising: his legs and arms were broken, then "he was fastened upon his back to the ground, a fire was made first to his feet and burned upwards by degrees. I heard him speak several words when the fire had consumed all his lower parts as far as his navel the fire was upon his breast he was burning near 3 hours before he died." The slaves who had run away at the same time and were still "out in rebellion" would, he added, be treated similarly.[78]

The principal reason for the brutal punishment of rebellious slaves was the planters' own vulnerability. By the 1670s they relied on slaves not only for labor but also for defense. The 1678 orders for the militia assume the participation of slaves as the various officers saw fit, assuming they could distinguish loyal from potentially disloyal slaves.[79] These orders were issued because of a "rebellion" that, according to Joseph Bryan, began not far from Bybrook. His description is worth quoting at length:

> It was within 5 miles of Spanish Town at one Capt. Duck's plantation, they killed his wife with several more; some of the murdering rogues was presently taken and have had a just reward for their villainy there and about thirty of those which took the woods [sic] where they yet remain: there is a notable bold subtle Negro amongst them his name is Agiddy and he is their captain; this Agiddy and several more of Capt. Duck's Negroes was formerly acquainted with Sir Tho. Modyford's Negroes they living formerly together in Barbados. This Capt. Agiddy with some other of his fellow rogues being driven to the woods made up by night to the 16 mile walk to get Colonel Modyford's to go & join with them in this rebellion, to this several of Colonel Modyford's Negroes consented, the day of their rising was appointed to be last Whitsun Tuesday being the 21st of May 78.

This second phase of the plot was discovered before the slaves could carry out their design to "kill all the white men."[80] As in Barbados, the discovery of the plot led to the torture of known conspirators. One of Governor Modyford's slaves, sentenced "to have his legs and arms broke and so to be starved to death," offered evidence against eight of Helyar's slaves; another of Modyford's slaves, while being burnt, named one of the Helyars' most trusted slaves, Quashee Edoo, as a participant in the plot. Edoo had served Cary Helyar, Whaley, and the current overseer, Mr. Atcherly: "I could have put my life in his hands I judged him to be so trusty a Negro; and this Negro was one of the chiefest rogues in this conspiracy." In the end, twelve of Helyar's slaves were executed for their part in the conspiracy.[81] Whether they were really involved in planning a rebellion, or whether the accusations were part of a panic, can never be known.

Bryan's account shows the networks among slaves on distant plantations. Captain Duck's slaves knew Modyford's because they had worked together in Barbados. Those who had killed Mrs. Duck and run away were able to take advantage of the dense forests between Spanish Town and Sixteen Mile Walk to reach their fellows at Modyford's plantation. Modyford's slaves led them to Helyar's. Bryan's account also emphasizes how little owners knew of their slaves: if Quashee Edoo, trusted as he was, could be involved, how could whites know which slaves to trust? It is obvious that his feelings about enslavement were hidden from those he served. Finally, Bryan's account suggests a change in his own attitudes. A year earlier he had talked about the "cruel" punishment of slaves who were plotting to rebel; now he referred to the "just rewards" of those who had rebelled. Bryan had taken on the mentality of slave owners confronting almost constant rebellion.

The punishments that Bryan found so disturbing on his arrival were certainly different from those common in England. The English became more brutal to sustain the system of slavery. The execution Bryan described for those guilty of plotting rebellion involved the infliction of pain in multiple ways before execution, a process used in England only in the form of hanging, drawing, and quartering those guilty of treason, or burning at the stake for petty treason. Hans Sloane provided a systematic exposition of the punishments in use. For rebellion, slaves were staked to the ground and burned from the feet to the head. For crimes "of a lesser nature," they were castrated or had half a foot chopped off. Those who ran away had irons put on their feet. Whipping was the punishment for negligence. Sloane elaborated, "After they are whipped till they are raw, some put on their skins

Pepper and salt to make them smart; at other times their masters will drop melted wax on their skins, and use several very exquisite torments. These punishments are sometimes merited by the blacks, who are a very perverse generation of people, and though they appear harsh, yet are scarce equal to some of their crimes, and inferior to what punishments other European nations inflict on their slaves in the East Indies."[82] Sloane's account, like Bryan's, acknowledges the severity of punishments in Jamaica, and his use of the phrase "sometimes merited" suggests his discomfort. That uneasiness is pushed away, however, by reference to the "perverse" character of the slaves and the enormity of their crimes. They were also, his comparison to the actions of other nations suggests, intrinsic to the colonial enterprise.

The severe repression following the 1678 rising appears to have been successful, at least in the short term; no rebellions are recorded between 1678 and 1685. But the 1685 rising by the slaves belonging to Widow Guy in Guanaboa was extremely serious. The governor, Hender Molesworth, described both the coordinated actions of the slaves and the vulnerability of many plantations. His account shows how effectively the slaves were able to act and implicitly acknowledges the existence of an alternative social order among the slaves, based on traditional African practices.

> All the Widow Guy's Negroes at Guanaboa with about 20 more in the quarters (to the number in all of about 150) did rise in rebellion on a Sunday night, when they first attacked her house where there were . . . but two white men (the rest lay in out houses). They . . . killed one of the men . . . Mrs. Guy makes her escape from above out of a window to one Major Price his house a neighbor. . . . Being now armed and well provided of ammunition, they fall upon Major Price when they killed one man and wounded another, but finding a brisk opposition and having lost there one of their conjurors, upon whose encouragement they had mightily depended, they retire for a while to their breakfast, with resolution . . . to return again with all their force against the said house, not doubting but if they could cut off that family, to be masters of all Guanaboa and have a thousand Negros more to join with them, which was very probably concluded upon. A Negro of Mistress Guy's made an escape and brought the news to Town. . . . Immediately, upon the advice, I dispatched away from town about 30 troopers . . . and 40 choice foot soldiers. . . . When a party of the troop lighted to get nearer to them, . . . they betook themselves to their heels and were separated in 2 or 3 parties, but about 40 of the stoutest and best armed . . . took their way

through the mountains toward St. Ann's of the North side and, at the foot of Mount Diablo, cut off a small family that sold rum to travelers, where they killed a man, a woman, and two children when a party following them at the heels forced them to take a new path which led towards St. Mary's where one Mrs. Roe a widow . . . who having only one man in the house besides her self and two children were all cut off by those murdering villains. This (though much too much) is all the mischief they have hitherto had opportunity to do.

Molesworth mobilized both army regiments and six special parties of twenty men from the militia, and after a month the authorities had killed seven slaves and captured thirty; fifty more had turned themselves in. The rest, perhaps as many as fifty, had taken refuge in "unaccessible mountains and rocks."[83]

Over the next six months, several additional attacks were attributed to this group of former slaves. After Christmas, some of them attacked Mr. Coate's plantation in Guanaboa and killed eight or ten people. On their return toward the mountains, according to reports, they were "destroying little families they met in their way." In February 1686, the authorities were still trying to track down the remainder of the former slaves. Because "their subtlety and knowledge in the mountain paths being beyond all the rebels that ever have hitherto been in this island," the authorities worked with several parties to trap them in the mountains. In April the Council recorded the death of Cuffee, who was thought to be the leader.[84] Yet the group continued to cause problems. In June 1686, Governor Molesworth told the Assembly that the chief question of the session was "how to secure ourselves and estates (by some better provision than any hitherto made) against the barbarous treachery of our own slaves, to keep them in such due order and subjection as to render them truly serviceable unto us, and us safe with them; and in case of any sudden insurrection, to be provided with such ready means for their reducing as may not only serve to effect it speedily, but to deter all others from joining with them, or attempting the like by their example."[85]

Whatever the Assembly did was ineffective. In September, the inhabitants of St. George's in the east complained of being terrorized by a growing band of escaped slaves from the mountains, who destroyed crops and killed white colonists. These were not the slaves who had risen the previous year, who were on the western rather than the eastern end of the island. Observers suggested this group had been growing over ten to fifteen years and had its own settlements and provision grounds. The expansion of white-owned plantations infringed on the Maroons' territory. Molesworth proposed decisive actions, but to save money the Assembly first proposed that a volunteer force go after the bands. Much to the governor's disgust, this private party was accepted as a first step. The party that went to suppress the "rebels" found fewer of the blacks than they expected, but Molesworth assumed that was because the volunteers were incompetent: they had, after all, "found 15 huts with 3 or 4 cabins in each." However the English organized their expeditions, they did not usually succeed; the black communities merely changed their tactics and organization. In April 1687 the provision plantations that had supported the escaped slaves had been destroyed, but the rebels had separated into smaller groups and sheltered in the mountains where they could see any parties coming after them. The English had not yet adapted to the guerilla tactics used by the Maroons.[86] By December 1687 the threat had moved with the discovery of a planned rebellion in Sixteen Mile Walk, not far from Bybrook.[87] In March there were rumors of another rebellion, but it turned out to be only a quarrel between slaves on neighboring plantations.[88] A month later, the Assembly asked for a longer adjournment over Easter, "considering the necessity of their being at home, to keep their slaves in order these Easter holidays."[89]

Over time, rumors of rebellion and actual ones followed each other increasingly closely. While some historians have cataloged each of these as a separate rebellion, it is more useful to see these episodes as elements of chronic unrest. The authorities were unable either to keep slaves on plantations or defeat them in battle. In 1690 some 300 or 400 slaves belonging to Mr. Sutton, one of the wealthiest planters on the island, rose up and seized his weapons. The rebellious slaves were unable to convince slaves on the neighboring plantation to join them, but according to John Helyar, Sutton lost £10,000 as a result of the burning of his cane fields. Although the rebellion was effectively suppressed within a month, some of the slaves from Sutton's plantation became part of the Maroon bands and lived as free people for nearly forty more years. Governor Inchiquin was anxious, "considering the great number of the Negroes most of them Coromantees, the arms, great quantity of powder and other provisions they seized, with the great want of white men here, there being but six or seven men to that plantation to 500 Negroes." John Helyar wrote his father in response to the same events: "You may easily perceive what uncertainties estates are here."[90]

The communities of self-freed slaves in the mountains were regularly reinforced by newcomers. Many slaves ran away to join Maroon communities: running away was simpler than planning a rebellion and less likely to meet resistance from fellow slaves and authorities. The mountains in the east of Jamaica were dominated by the Spanish African Maroons, but many of the newer recruits remained in the center and west of the island and over time developed into the Leeward Maroons, who fought the English under the leadership of Cudjoe. Jamaican planters faced intransigent groups of former slaves throughout the island. More ambitious slaves might try to escape to Cuba; in 1699 Governor Beeston complained that a boat with some twenty Jamaican slaves had landed in Cuba, and the Cuban authorities had asserted that according to their law, anyone who sought the king of Spain's protection gained his freedom.[91]

Given the possibilities of escape in Jamaica and the existence of Maroon communities, the English struggled to minimize the danger and protect their estates. In 1739, after intense warfare during the 1720s, the Maroons accepted a peace that recognized their independence, at the price of returning newcomers to their masters; in other words, Maroons could remain, but they could not accept new recruits. Until then, the only protection for the English was vigilance. In 1692 militia officers were ordered to keep special watch at Christmas, when slaves were given time off and had a chance to gather.[92] In 1694 the Council had announced that any slave who had been absent more than a month was assumed to be a rebel and could be treated as such.[93] The attacks by the French throughout the 1690s raised the specter of an alliance between them and slaves. A slave provided the French with intelligence on English plans in 1694. At the same time, trusted slaves were again used as part of the defensive force; in December 1694 the expeditions sent against the escaped slaves consisted of twenty white men and twenty slaves. Jamaicans adapted their military plans to their fears. The governor rejected plans for an offensive expedition against the French in Saint-Domingue for fear that if they lost, "our blacks, who are twenty at least to our whites, and know their strength too well, might be encouraged on such a loss to attempt the reducing the place to another Guiny."[94]

The authorities sought more troops and funds for defense. In 1696 the Council asserted that they needed at least 1,500 more men in arms to protect them against both the French and the 40,000 slaves on the island. Some months earlier, the governor refused to send new expeditions against escaped slaves in the east of the island, "there being no money."[95] A year later, the Jamaica merchants in London asked for an extra 500 men to be sent immediately, asserting that "the apprehensions that many others were under of their inability to suppress a rebellion of their Negroes or repel an invasion from their neighbor enemies, have induced them to quit the island and settle themselves in some of the northern colonies." If the island were either lost to the French or "left to the mercy of the Negroes," the loss to all of the king's subjects would be enormous.[96] Where in Barbados the recruitment of new white colonists was hampered by the lack of land, in Jamaica the barrier to settlement was the lack of safety.

The reliance of planters in Barbados and Jamaica on large populations of enslaved Africans shaped the disciplinary regime of the islands in multiple ways. While the English rarely openly acknowledged slaves' everyday resistance, their severe repression of planned or merely rumored rebellions marks the insecurity they felt in the face of their slaves. In both islands, slaves routinely ran away for short periods of time; some ran away for longer periods, and others sought not just to secure their own freedom but to overturn the structures of power they confronted in the islands. Slaves, particularly in Jamaica, learned from the experience of their fellows the most effective ways to resist. As they sought to maintain their wealth and property, planters wrote new laws and instituted new forms of punishment to deter resistance. The development of systematic responses to chronic slave resistance marks the realization that slavery made the social order of the islands fundamentally different from that in England.

THE PLANTERS IN the Caribbean, having tried to replicate English society, expected order to follow. England itself was less orderly in practice than in theory, and expectations of hierarchy and obedience were routinely disappointed. But the dangers faced by planters in the West Indies when order failed were very different from those faced by elites at home. In both Barbados and Jamaica, planters developed new and increasingly violent ways to maintain social order. One dimension of this response was the fiercely repressive and punitive response to slave resistance. Another was the attempt to drive a wedge between plantations and the Maroon communities so that resistance was less desirable. The final response was a reconfiguration of status, so that race became a primary element of identity. In the islands, white people, whatever their status, could always claim to be superior to enslaved Africans, though those claims might be contested. Planters sought to have whites, however poor, define their interests as coincident with those of planters rather than slaves. This reconfiguration of the social hierarchy was never entirely successful: small planters and poor whites remained suspicious of the planters and their power. It worked just well enough to help keep order.

Yet the unity of whites against slaves was always a fiction. Economic status did matter; the interests of wealthy planters and poor planters, planters and laborers, sugar growers and ranchers were at odds with one another. White laborers were often in competition with slaves for work. At the same time, the threat that they might make common cause with slaves forced planter elites to protect poor whites more than they might otherwise have done. The acceptance of the harsh discipline that marked the control of slaves was one of the most profound changes wrought in and by English men in the West Indies. The punishments of slaves were used to create a world where slaves had no choice but to obey. It never entirely worked. It may be, however, that the Caribbean practice of discipline provided a model for English criminal law and industrial practice, as each of those turned to focus increasingly, as in the West Indies, on the protection of property and the pursuit of profit.

If Her Son Is Living
with You She Sends Her Love
The Caribbean in England, 1640–1700

Had any Negro ship arrived ere this ship had sailed I should
have sent a Negro boy and girl, but none coming you must be content
until the next summer, then God willing you shall not fail of them.
JOHN HELYAR TO WILLIAM HELYAR, 30 June 1690

Barbados and Jamaica remained closely connected with England even as the society emerging in the colonies diverged from English patterns. As the careers of Richard Ligon, John Helyar, and John Taylor attest, colonists— some successful like Helyar, others just ill like Taylor—were as likely to return to England as they were to remain in the Caribbean. Some of the wealthiest planters made multiple journeys back and forth between England and the West Indies to oversee both their plantations and their trading interests. A significant number sent their children "home" for their education, both because of the absence of appropriate schools in the islands and to ensure their children would be able to fit into English society. When Caribbean colonists traveled to England, they brought not only the exotic products of tropical agriculture but also ideas about law, social order, and race that were new in England. Equally important, they often brought African or Afro-Caribbean slaves as personal attendants. The English had changed during their time in the West Indies, and the produce, ideas, and persons that distinguished the colonies returned with them.

The two-way communication between colonists and their relatives, friends, and associates at home is visible in the Helyar letters. As Cary Helyar and his successors built the plantation of Bybrook, they did their best to educate people in Somerset about the West Indies. Their letters described life in Jamaica, plantation agriculture, and the various challenges they faced in creating a new society. Ships returning to Bristol carried goods as well as letters. Such shipments brought Cary's brother William into regular contact with merchants and sailors in Bristol. In 1670 Cary sent "some balls of chocolate, beaten up without spice, which is best and wholesomest." He advised William to "sweeten it as you please," noting that it was an excellent drink for sober men, though not for "great drinkers"; indeed, the inevitable consequence of drinking alcohol within an hour of drinking chocolate was death! William soon developed a taste for chocolate and regularly asked for more. Sugar was accompanied by such exotic crops as pimento (allspice), tamarind, limes, and green ginger. In 1682 a parrot, first mentioned by Whaley in 1672, was sent back to England by Thomas Hillyard.[1] In 1690 the colonel's son John wrote to his brother William promising to send two Negro children by the next ship to serve the household. As we have seen, at least a slave boy, Thomas, arrived; eight years later, his mother Betty wondered whether he was still in East Coker. Her question, and the love that accompanied it, is one of the few extant records of the emotional consequences of the seventeenth-century trade in humans.[2] Along with the tokens of Jamaican life that were shipped to England came African and Afro-Caribbean slaves such as Betty's son, constituting a small but visible black population in both country and city.

The Caribbean had a physical presence in late Stuart England. Colonel Drax included among his instructions for minding his plantation while he was in England orders for a wide range of tropical goods to be sent to England for his personal use, including "200 lbs. of green ginger well preserved with the best sugar . . . all the citron peels you can get be put into good brandy"; yams and potatoes; "all the orange blossoms that you can get be stilled in alembic and . . . water"; "a ten gallon runlet of Jamaica pepper well pickled in good vinegar"; and "a chest of china oranges a chest of sweet lemons."[3] The docks in London and Bristol were full of goods from the West Indies. The rapid increase in the quantity of sugar available and the consequent drop in its price made this sweetener the most ubiquitous indication of English colonization. Sugar was joined by chocolate, which became a popular drink. Along with such exotic goods came black persons, sometimes as seamen rather than domestic servants, but often as slaves. By the end of the seventeenth century, there were communities of black workers in the ports of London and Bristol, while many more blacks served in urban and provincial households across England. Slavery, too, was imported from the colonies.

The black page was an increasingly common accoutrement of the lady of fashion, whether or not she belonged to the gentry. According to *The Character of a Town Misse* in 1680, this figure of fashion, who dressed and carried herself as a lady but earned her living by prostitution, "hath always two necessary implements about her, a blackamoor and a little Dog."[4] A substantial number of late seventeenth-century portraits depict their subjects accompanied by a young black child, usually a boy. The presence of blacks in England can be tracked in a variety of records. The newspapers include an increasing number of notices for black servants who had run away. Although these advertisements contain some telling details, these slaves' acts of resistance are often the sole documentation of their existence.

We catch only glimpses of blacks in England, and much about their lives remains hidden. The cultural ramifications of slavery and race as these social relations emerged in the Caribbean magnified the significance of the small, growing presence of people of African descent, both slave and free, in late seventeenth-century England. The morality and wisdom of slavery as it was practiced in the colonies became a subject of debate. On the stage, the West Indies figured as a destination for dubious characters, who returned to England just as corrupt as they had been when they left. The colonies developed a distinct identity and a notably ambivalent set of meanings. All these—trade, fashion, portraits, plays, and people—indicate the visibility and significance of the Caribbean in England. Along with new commodities, new ideas of race and identity and new sets of social relations emerged; these colonial practices and persons figured in English society, registering the changes wrought by empire.

Questioning Slavery

As they created slave societies in Barbados and Jamaica, planters used increasingly violent methods to discipline individual slaves, attempt to control runaways, and prevent and punish rebellions. Their routine resort to naked force made English observers and newcomers to the islands uneasy. Such brutal coercion of servants by masters violated English norms, and the ownership of human beings lay outside English precedent. While Joseph Bryan and Sir Hans Sloane were both able to calm their conscience by reference to the savage and wild nature of the slaves, not everyone found this rationale satisfactory. The relative novelty of English slavery, itself a changing institution, had to be assimilated at home. Critiques of slavery emerged in dialogue with the experience of merchants, planters, and servants who had experienced the Caribbean environment. While no wholesale critiques of human bondage in principle or of slavery as an institution were published during the seventeenth century, a number of tracts criticized the practice of slavery in the West Indies, emphasizing its unchristian character and worrying about the social instability it entailed.[5] These works drew on the contrast between expectations of Christian behavior and the actual treatment of slaves, as well as the dichotomy between freedom and slavery so striking in the constitutional and legal development of the islands.

The first critical consideration of the practice of West Indian slavery came in Richard Baxter's manual for Christian living, A Christian Directory, in 1673. Baxter, a leading Presbyterian minister, discussed slavery in the context of a master's duty to his servants. Baxter argued against the contemporary practice of slavery by making punishment for crimes the only justification for enslavement. The humanity of slaves was central to his discussion: he believed the greatest sin of slaveholders to be their failure—indeed, their refusal—to convert their slaves to Christianity. He also condemned the cruel treatment of slaves, arguing that when masters treated slaves no better than beasts, they condemned themselves to damnation. He suggested that the recent fire in Bridgetown, as well as the high mortality in the islands, were plagues sent to punish planters for worshipping wealth rather than God. Throughout his discussion, Baxter emphasized the need to attend to slaves' common humanity with their masters and to ensure that they could serve God.[6] Baxter's critique, based on theological reflection rather than practical experience, shows how much work had to be done to accommodate slavery to English values.

Baxter's point is taken up and amplified in the work of Thomas Tryon, particularly in three tracts published together in 1684 as Friendly Advice to the Gentlemen Planters of the East and West Indies. The first tract concerned the adaptation of English colonists to the tropical environment, advocating the adoption of a mostly vegetarian diet of native foods because it was the best way to remain healthy in the West Indies. The second tract, "The Negro's Complaint of their hard Servitude, and the Cruelties Practiced upon them by divers of their masters professing Christianity in the West Indian Plantations," was written in the voice of a slave objecting to his treatment. Imagining himself in the position of the slave, Tryon articulates a critique grounded in the Golden Rule and English notions of service and household. The third tract, "A Discourse, in Way of Dialogue, Between an Ethiopian or Negro-Slave and a Christian, that was his Master in America," offered a slave the opportunity to question his master about the principles of Christianity and then use those principles to question the basis of slavery. While these tracts were not grounded in Caribbean slaves' own viewpoints, they constituted a powerful and subversive critique of slavery from within a Christian and English perspective, and Tryon's move to put himself and his readers in a slave's place is significant in itself.

Tryon, whose own background was modest, had lived in Barbados for seven years in the 1660s, working as a hatter and "making beavers to success"; when he returned to London, he served as a commercial agent for West Indian planters. Like Baxter, he was a Dissenter; he had moved from Anabaptism to a more mystical faith derived in part from the work of Jacob Boehme. He wrote as "Philotheos Physiologus," combining his interest in religion and natural philosophy. He was abstemious—one of the first theorists of English vegetarianism—and enormously hard working.[7] He had firsthand experience of the ways slavery transformed society in the West Indies. The planters, he asserted, were corrupted by their life of idleness, ease, and luxury; they were devoted to drunkenness, feasting, and worship of "idol Belly-God-Paunch." Indeed, they were so corrupted that they lacked common paternal care for the children they fathered on their slaves. Tryon's Negro complains:

> They deal as hardly and cruelly with their own seed, even the fruit of their own loins, as with us. For do not our Masters, to gratify their raging lusts, sometimes take our Women, and make them their concubines . . . upon whom they beget mongrel Children, that are neither white nor black, but between both which therefore are called mulattos, . . . yet the Fathers, being without natural affection, though they are their own seed, do expose them, and make them perpetual slaves, both they and their posterity. Now what can be more hellish cruelty, or greater baseness, then for men to afflict their own seed, to beget children in their drunkenness and paroxysms of lust, and then not to care what becomes of them; nay, to make themselves authors of their miseries as well as of their being, and instead of providing for, and well educating them, to enslave and tyrannize over them.[8]

Tryon points to the contradictions between the stated values of the planters and their behavior. Sexual relations between whites and blacks were not much discussed, and there was some unease about racial mixing—an unease that Tryon's use of "mongrel" suggests he shared. Cary Helyar's grant of income for his mulatto child was not unique, and some planters freed either their black mistresses or their children. Such grants were, however, individual acts, not integrated in the system.[9]

At the conclusion of "The Negro's Complaint," the Negro suggests that better treatment of slaves would increase planters' profits and, by lowering mortality, reduce the need to purchase new slaves. In return, slaves would provide loyal service to their masters in a paternalist paradise. Tryon was unable to fully accommodate slavery and the profits of empire with the demands of Christian morality. His position was more ambivalent than Baxter's: he hoped but was not certain that slavery could be transformed into a system as benign as service in England.[10]

The dialogue between the master and his slave on the nature of Christianity focuses on the divergence between Christian teachings of love, compassion, and humility and the cruel and violent treatment of slaves. The slave, who is not Christian but possesses "natural religion," points out the planters' unregulated passions and lust—precisely the opposite of the Christian virtues claimed by his master. In responding with admiration to Christian teachings, the slave argues that "we have the same Gospel that you so much talk of written in our Hearts." When the master argues that violence against slaves is occasioned by their bad behavior and their planned rebellions, the slave responds that masters should not return evil for evil. The slave's reproof finally leads the master to admit that the treatment of slaves is incongruent with Christianity. But, the master asks, "What would you have us do?" since planters could not live as they do without slaves. The slave responds that in the long run there would be more profit in moderation and kindness than cruelty. His teaching ends up convincing the master of the need to change his ways; the teacher of Christianity has himself been taught a lesson in Christian behavior.[11] For Tryon, the problem was not slavery itself, but the behavior of the masters.

Tryon elaborated his suggestions for the reform of the slave society developing in the Caribbean colonies in a series of letters published in 1700. He argued that West Indian planters should add the manufacture of cotton to the production of sugar; not only would cotton be a valuable commodity—an idea deduced by comparison with India—but it also would provide a less strenuous occupation for enslaved women and children, which in turn would improve health and allow the population of the islands to grow. While diversification would benefit the slaves, it would also benefit the planters:

"Then you may be sure that suitable returns will be made to the oppressor . . . for the groaning of him that suffereth pain is the beginning of trouble and misery to him that caused it; and it is not to be doubted, but under this black character of oppression and violence, the sugar plantations now lye under." Using biblical imagery, Tryon suggested that planters would benefit by not having to buy new slaves. Another letter argued that some land now devoted to sugar be converted to provisions. Plantations that were less dependent on imported foodstuffs would be more profitable; fewer slaves would be needed with less intensive agriculture, and better-fed slaves would live and work longer. Such changes, he argued, would make it less necessary "to be cruel and inhumane to your poor Slaves, and give them at least a kind of captivated freedom, and relaxation from their insupportable burdens laid upon them." The phrase "captivated freedom" embodies the contradiction Tryon was trying to resolve: how to create a beneficent subjection. The prosperity of planters was important to England because, as Tryon reminded his readers, "there is no one commodity [sugar] whatever, that doth so much encourage navigation, [and] advance the Kings Customs." The financial burdens on the planters, of which they complained constantly, should indeed be lightened. One argument for the lifting of impositions was the very cruelty of slavery: "If mankind were sensible how many degrees of slavery and violence the makers of sugar go through, . . . they would not only have a true value for its excellent virtues, but be eagerly intent for the discharge of the many burdensom and I may say unreasonable impositions laid upon it."[12] The conflation of slaves and planters as both "makers of sugar" maintains Tryon's divided sensibility.

Tryon's critique of slavery arose from his experiences and perspectives as a merchant and a Dissenter. When he was living in Barbados, he practiced his own trade in a free labor system and observed the slave labor regime in town and on sugar plantations. In London, his trade shaped his awareness of sugar's importance to the empire and kept him in contact with planters. As he developed his proposals for reform, he sought to advance this economic interest while ameliorating the situation of slaves. Tryon's ideal society is composed of godly households, which in the colonies include slaves as well as servants. His model for Christian behavior was common among late seventeenth-century English Dissenters: morality and self-restraint, an opposition to display and extravagance. Virtuous masters could, he suggests, advance their economic interests and the well-being of their subordinates simultaneously. Tryon's moral critique draws attention to two conjoined evils: the cruelty of the slave owners to their slaves and the corrupting effects of slavery on slave owners.

Both Baxter and Tryon were Dissenters, but Tryon was far more radical. Tryon's work was disseminated by Quaker printers, and much of the emerging critique of slavery in the seventeenth century came from Friends. But members of the established church were also concerned about the moral implications of slavery: Morgan Godwyn, an Anglican, made a passionate argument for the conversion of slaves to Christianity.[13] While Dissenters were more likely than others to be critical of slavery as an institution, the writings about the West Indies that began to appear in late seventeenth-century England register the departures from English thinking and practice that constructing a slave society in the colonies represented.

Representations: Planters and Slaves, Home and Abroad

Plays

The moral ambiguities of the wealth produced in the Caribbean were explored in popular dramas staged in London, in addition to being debated in print. Even before the English established successful colonies, the "New World," its native peoples, and Africans brought there as slaves figured in imaginative literature; Shakespeare's *The Tempest* is the best-known example.[14] As the colonies developed, the symbolic resonances offered by colonial settings and references to slavery increased. In the annual London Lord Mayor's Pageant, the late seventeenth century saw numerous representations of black people in a variety of symbolic guises. While some of these were exotic, others were more realistic: in 1672 a group of "moors" in the West Indies were depicted "gathering, carrying, setting, sorting, sowing, and ordering the Fruits and other Physical Plants of their country," while the following year "Black and Tawny Inhabitants are very actively employed, some in Working and Planting, otheres Carrying and re-carrying."[15]

A number of plays from the late seventeenth century that use the West Indies as a setting—on the stage or off—illuminate the meanings the colonies had acquired in English culture. These representations of colonial society are more grounded in concrete scenes and familiar images than the fantastic worlds projected in earlier plays. Although an air of unreality lingers around these representations, it works well dramatically. Stock characters and stereotypes about life in the colonies abound, serving as foils for virtues and values presented as English. The plays reflect on the colonies as a source of wealth and corruption, as well as sites of exploitation and cruelty. The unresolved dramatic tensions that pervade these plays indicate the difficulty of accommodating the Caribbean within English expectations or resolving the dilemmas inherent in colonialism.

William D'Avenant's opera, *The Cruelty of the Spaniards in Peru*, performed in 1658, just three years after the English conquest of Jamaica, places a historical fable in a Caribbean setting to comment critically on colonial slavery. It was presented as a series of tableaux, with speeches by the Inca Priest of the Sun, followed by choruses. After the Spanish conquer Peru and cruelly enslave the Incas, the English arrive and defeat the Spaniards. Turning the previous colonial order upside down, the English treat the Indians well but enslave the Spaniards and force them to toil in the mines. The text explains: "These imaginary English forces may seem improper, because the English had made no discovery of Peru, in time of the Spaniard's first invasion there, but yet in Poetical Representations of this nature, it may pass as a Vision discern'd by the Priest of the Sun, before the matter was extant, in order to his Prophecy."[16]

Through this fantastic, time-warping conceit, the play indirectly but pointedly probes the problems inherent in colonization that the English confront in the Caribbean. The scene is clearly not Peru but the formerly Spanish colony on Jamaica. For the "First Entry," the stage directions indicate that a landscape "of the West Indies is discerned." On the backdrop, cocoa trees, pineapples, and palms distinguish the tropical island from Europe. Monkeys, apes, and parrots are visible in the trees, and in the distance are fields of sugarcane. The Indians carry baskets filled with gold ingots and wedges of silver, but the sugarcanes in the background suggest that the cruelty of sugar plantations was as much at issue as the cruelty of mining. The play blames the European conquest of Peru on a civil war between two Inca brothers. Even more intriguingly, it attributes both the civil war and the enslavement of the Indians to greed. Before the war and conquest, the place was a paradise

> Where none did riches wish
> And none were rich by business made
> . . . .
> When none could want and all were innocent.[17]

The Inca priest, who serves as the narrator and conscience of the play, reflects on the ironies of the Spaniards' Christian faith and refers to the common assumption that Christians could not be held as slaves.

What race is this, who for our punishment
Pretend that they in haste from Heaven were sent
As just destroyers of Idolatry?
Yet will they not permit
We should our idols quit
Because the Christian law makes converts free.[18]

Audiences knew that it was the English, not the Spanish, who refused to convert slaves to Christianity. The play's displaced version of history provided an avenue for reflection on English behavior in its island colonies, especially when the profits from sugar had begun to rival those gold and silver had yielded. It also permitted reflection on the English practice of slavery, contrasting its cruelty and coercion with the ideas of freedom so central to the nation's political culture. The moral questions raised by the narrative are occluded by the conclusion, which explains the "riddle" of the Spaniards' behavior by arguing that their "heaven in caverns lies of others Gold," linking Spanish Catholicism and greed.[19] While the play contrasts Spanish cruelty with the beneficence of the English, it measures colonial practice against the ideal of Christian morality, and its critique of greed, cruelty, and slavery was as applicable to the English in the Caribbean as to the Spanish in Peru.

Aphra Behn situated *The Widow Ranter* (1688) in the British mainland colony of Virginia, then well along in the process of becoming a slave society. While offering a scathingly critical view of the planters, Behn makes their African slaves invisible. Like D'Avenant, she takes liberties with historical events. The story is loosely based on Bacon's Rebellion (1676), in which an irregular militia composed primarily of small planters and propertyless former servants led by Nathaniel Bacon, an ambitious and well-born planter, made war first against the Indians whose lands they desired for themselves and then against the Virginia elite that had excluded them from economic opportunity and political power. Bacon was extremely successful, driving the governor from Jamestown and eventually burning it, but the rebellion failed after his death from dysentery. The English were most alarmed by Bacon's offer of freedom to the servants and African slaves of those who supported the governor, the potentially fatal combination that planters in the Caribbean also dreaded.[20] Behn moves the rebellion backward in time and has Bacon fall in love with the Indian "Queen"; when he accidentally kills her in battle, he takes poison.

The Widow Ranter considers the relationship between the construction of a new social order and the multiple meanings of race in a colonial setting. As Margaret Ferguson has pointed out, Bacon's potential interracial relationship with the Indian Queen was so subversive that it had to be obliterated by death. But race refers as much to inherited property and standing as to nationality and ethnicity. Early in the play, one of the more admirable characters tells a friend newly arrived in Virginia, "This country wants nothing but to be peopled by a well-born race." In Behn's view, merely being English or white was not enough; distinctions of status mattered at least as much in the colony as in England. Dryden alerted audiences to the importance of birth and rank in his prologue to the play, where he asserts, "Now you strive about your pedigree." Such competition was the result of social mobility. Various low-born scoundrels, such as Parson Dunce, formerly a farrier, are contrasted with the virtuous and noble Bacon. Virginia had a few "noble" men but was governed by rogues and cowards. Upstart planters acquired riches but lacked good breeding, self-discipline, and the ability to govern others. Even the relatively virtuous were motivated by greed and act dishonestly to obtain marriages and fortunes.[21]

At the beginning of the play, Virginia is in chaos. Ignorance rules, corruption is rife, and justice is a farce. At the conclusion, after Bacon's tragic death, his forces defeat both the Indians and the government. This triumph, accomplished through noble leadership, provides a new basis for unity among the English, all of whom are appropriately married off to reinforce the gender and racial order. Behn's Virginia has no African slaves; they have been written out of the story. It is a peculiar omission, given that Behn wrote the play the same year she wrote her classic novel of American slavery, *Oroonoko*.[22] The 1676 rebellion advanced the racial development of Virginia, too, as poor white men were integrated into the body politic while persons of African descent were categorically excluded, just as they were relegated to oblivion in Behn's play.[23]

The Innocent Mistress, written in 1698 by Mary Pix, a successful playwright known for "ingeniously plotted" dramas, is less obviously topical than *The Cruelty of the Spaniards in Peru* and *The Window Ranter*, but it uses assumptions about the character of West Indian society as a plot device. Like *The Widow Ranter*, *The Innocent Mistress* reflects on corruption while erasing the slaves. In a comedy of extraordinary complexity even by the standards of Restoration drama, those who have been in the West Indies are uniformly corrupt. Lady Beauclair, "an ill-bred woman," is introduced as having gone to Jamaica with her husband and come back a "widow." With her late husband's fortune, she has soon remarried the virtuous Sir Charles Beauclair in a marriage of mutual unhappiness. Meanwhile, another character, Mr. Flywife, has returned to England from Jamaica with Mrs. Flywife, a stereotypical adventuress who had used her face and figure to seek her fortune in the island colony. Her story is a cliché: she attended boarding school and was orphaned at fourteen, "leaving me nothing for my portion but Pride and a few tawdry clothes; I was a forward girl, and bartering what I had not the wit to prize, a never to be recover'd fame was soon maintained in finery, idleness, and darling pleasure, but the deceitful Town grew weary of me sooner than I expected, and I sick of that, seeing other new faces preferred before me; so picking up some Moneys, and a handsome garb, I ventur'd to Jamaica." Her own history did not make her tolerant of others' efforts to rise in status: she complains that in Jamaica, "Our Beaux was the Refuse of Newgate, our merchants the Offspring of foolish plodding cits"—that is, transported criminals or shopkeepers and tradesmen, rather than gentlemen.[24]

In London, Flywife is in hiding while he sorts out his affairs. When he argues with Mrs. Flywife about her expenditures on fine clothes, she reminds him that she had refused "the richest Planters of the place, who courted me in an honest lawful way, and would have parted with their wealth, dearer than their souls, to have called me wife." Flywife responds that he had "pour'd on ye more riches than all your Husband pretenders joined together could aim at, [and] gave you such a separate fortune." She had been able to choose between a legitimate marriage and money, and she had chosen financial benefits rather than wifely subordination.[25] Mrs. Flywife takes advantage of her husband's seclusion to pursue Mr. Wildlove, who in spite of himself (his history is suggested by his name) is in love with a virtuous woman. In the final scene, Mr. Flywife is revealed to be Mr. Allen, Lady Beauclair's first husband. He reclaims both his errant wife and the part of his fortune she had brought to London: these were, presumably, the affairs he had to attend to in London. His mistress, the supposed Mrs. Flywife, is stranded, with neither husband nor fortune. Sir Charles is able to marry a virtuous young woman, and Wildlove reforms his life and also marries a virtuous lady. As in The Widow Ranter, breeding and virtue triumph, while greed and corruption flounder. Jamaica is presented as the home of vice, not virtue. The West Indies provides a shadow society. It is far enough away that people can recreate themselves on both sides of the Atlantic, and their activities on each side hidden from the other. As with Behn, Pix reminds her audience that wealth and character are separate.

Thomas Southerne's dramatic rendition of Aphra Behn's novel of slavery, Oroonoko (1688), which was first performed in 1696, also reflects on the West

Indies. The play had a wider and more varied audience than Behn's novel, making it a better guide to the cultural role of slavery in England.[26] Slavery is necessarily part of the plot, but the changes entailed in the transformation of the novel into the play dramatically illustrate the difficulties of accommodating slavery within English sensibilities. While Behn's story of the enslaved African prince who is reunited with his true love Imoinda in Surinam remains, Imoinda becomes a white woman married to Oroonoko in Africa, and Oroonoko's tragedy is framed by a comic plot with the same elements of disguise, greed, and deception that appear in The Innocent Mistress.[27] The play opens with two English sisters who arrive in Surinam at the same time that the slave ship brings Oroonoko, a captive prince. Charlotte and Lucy Welldon, like Mrs. Flywife, are ladies of the town whose charms had faded; they ventured to Surinam to get husbands. The older sister dresses as a man; soon the wealthy Widow Lackitt falls in love with "him" and insists that he marry her. He agrees, but only after he has found a husband for his sister Lucy, which he says is a promise he made to their dying father. The widow produces a grown son, who promptly marries the sister. Widow Lackitt and Charlotte Welldon are then married; the putative Mr. Welldon arranges for a man to take his place in bed on the wedding night. Welldon takes advantage of the rebellion led by the noble and defiant Oroonoko to disappear and reappear as Charlotte, who is then betrothed to a wealthy planter. Widow Lackitt is happy to accept her lover as her husband, and all are happily settled.

In the parallel Oroonoko plot, the captain of the slave ship disposes of his cargo. He warns Blandford, who acts for the governor, that Oroonoko, an Angolan prince, will be refractory. Oroonoko had come on board as the captain's guest, then been seized and imprisoned as a slave. Blandford becomes the voice of white conscience for the play. He hears from Oroonoko about his marriage to Imoinda, the daughter of a white man who had joined Oroonoko's tribe, commanded his father's armies, and taught Oroonoko the art of war. This man was killed in battle protecting Oroonoko; when Oroonoko told the daughter of her father's death, he fell in love with her. Their marriage was interrupted when Oroonoko's father wanted Imoinda as his mistress and then sold her into slavery when she refused. Imoinda is, it turns out, a slave on the plantation to which Oroonoko is sent. (The use of a white woman as a slave is unmentioned.) Blandford promises Oroonoko his freedom when the governor arrives, but Oroonoko is convinced to lead a slave escape by the prospect of his children being born into slavery. In planning the escape, Oroonoko comments on the harshness of the punishment they may expect if caught and knows that some would betray their fellows:

Who can promise for his bravery
Upon the Rack? where fainting, weary life,
Hunted thro' every limb, is forc'd to feel
An agonizing death of all its parts?
Who can bear this? resolve to be empal'd?
His skin flayed off, and roasted yet alive?
The quivering flesh torn from his broken Bones,
By burning Pincers? who can bear these pains?[28]

The escape was—as was actually often the case—betrayed by a frightened slave. In yet another act of betrayal of Oroonoko by an English man, the governor promises him his life then seizes him to kill him. Blandford secures Oroonoko's freedom again; when Oroonoko and Imoinda are reunited, Imoinda convinces him that the only way forward is death. He kills her; and then, when Blandford and the governor arrive, he kills both the governor and himself.

As the romantic farce intersects with the tragedy of Oroonoko and Imoinda, Southerne emphasizes Blandford, who has tried to protect Oroonoko, and a few other planters, who opposed the harsh treatment of the rebellious but honorable Oroonoko. Of Blandford, Oroonoko says, "For his sake, I'll think it possible / A Christian may be yet an honest man." The dishonesty of the English captain and the governor is individual, not systematic. At the same time, the virtuous love and fidelity of Oroonoko and Imoinda is contrasted with the sexual agency of Widow Lackitt and Lucy and Charlotte Welldon.[29] *Oroonoko* repeats themes that are present throughout these plays: the contrast between Christian values and slave owners' behavior, the corrupt behavior of most white settlers in the colonies, and the virtue of some English men. It adds to this a noble slave and a white slave, as well as an interracial marriage. While the implications of a white woman marrying Oroonoko are not fully developed, Imoinda's enslavement erases the racial nature of slavery.

The Restoration plays suggest how English people thought about their Caribbean counterparts during the late seventeenth century. Colonial society was represented as corrupt, even when the institution of slavery was ignored. Those who sought their fortunes in the colonies were the rejects of English society, and their behavior often degenerated further in the West Indies. Seeking their own gain in a hostile, unstable world, they treated those they met with either cruelty or disdain, and their dealings were marked by dishonesty and greed. The only possibility for those who were virtuous, like Oroonoko and Imoinda, was death. At the same time, slavery is pushed aside: D'Avenant attributes it to the Spanish, Pix and Behn render it invisible, and Southerne erases its racial character and frames it within a comic plot. What social critics and Dissenters saw as the central problem of the islands—the cruelty of slavery—was impossible to represent on the English stage. At the same time, slaves and slavery, abstracted from the work of the plantations, were integrated into the visual culture of the period.

Paintings

In 1692 Mrs. John Verney had her portrait painted with Peregrine Tyam, a young African slave belonging to her husband, John Verney (Figure 2). Verney was a successful merchant, the second son and now the heir of Sir Edmund Verney of Middle Claydon in Buckinghamshire. Among his many activities, John was a member of the Royal African Company, which engaged in the African slave trade. He had acquired Tyam by 1689, when he had the boy baptized in the parish church of Middle Claydon and stood as godfather. Mary was John's second wife, and the portrait attests to her husband's prosperity. It was painted by someone named Lenthall, not by Sir Godfrey Kneller or any of the other well-known society portraitists, but it was a large and striking painting, and the inclusion of his black page, along with the valuable jeweled brooch John had given his wife, served as a graphic display of his wealth. The collar Tyam wears—decorative but reminiscent of slave shackles—marks his status as a slave. The presence of Peregrine Tyam in this portrait alerts us to the widening group of English people who had black servants, most of whom were held as slaves.[30]

The portrait of Mary Verney is one of over seventy surviving portraits from the seventeenth century and the first decade of the eighteenth century that include a black person. In contrast to the dramatic depictions of the colonies, most of which kept slavery firmly offstage, these paintings placed slaves clearly in view. No moral qualms surrounded these representations; black servants were objects of display and enhanced the reputation of the subject. Over the course of the seventeenth century, an increasing number of portraits featured black attendants. These portraits constitute a small proportion of those painted during the period, but they make a significant statement about the African presence in England. Most of the blacks shown in portraits are young boys; a few paintings include a young girl, an adult man, and only one an adult woman. Although some, like the portrait of Mary

Verney, are not great works of art, blacks appear in portraits of leading figures by outstanding painters. The frequency of their presence has not been recognized, in part because the black figures are often omitted from the titles given by auction catalogs and museums. For example, the labels on two portraits in the collection of the National Portrait Gallery in London make no mention of the black attendant in the picture. Furthermore, most scholarly discussions of these portraits focus on the eighteenth century.[31] It is rarely possible to identify the black servant and determine whether he or she was actually associated with the sitter. Indeed, the portrait of Mary Verney with Peregrine Tyam is the only case in which the two figures can be so definitively linked. There are few portraits of black people alone.[32]

While these Africans' legal status can seldom be determined from historical records, visual clues in the portraits mark many of them as slaves and possessions. Throughout this period, the appearance of a black servant exhibits the wealth and standing of the subject—or in the case of women, their fathers and husbands. The earliest portraits present Africans as exotics. By the Restoration they are objects of display, much like the jewels with which they are often shown. By the end of the seventeenth century, black attendants appear in a wider range of portraits, domestic scenes, and conversation pieces. Through iconographic references to earlier works of art and visual connections to contemporary social life, painters and patrons engaged in a conversation about the changing meanings of race and status in England.

The paintings share important formal characteristics and iconographic features. Art historians commonly draw attention to the pictorial role the black attendants play. The blackness of their skin highlights the whiteness of the skin of the portrait's central subject; the attendants themselves are often most visible by the whites of their eyes, and sometimes their teeth. Their eyes focus on the subject's face, drawing the viewer's eyes there as well. Because of their small size and subordinate position, the children look up at the subjects they serve. For example, the black page holding Lord Byron's horse in his military portrait is dressed in a red velvet suit that matches Byron's sash and gazes admiringly at his master while Byron points toward the field of battle (Figure 3). Children are often depicted presenting something to the subject, demonstrating deference and bringing movement to the picture. Black figures are almost always on the margins, or at least to the side, of these paintings, as they were on the margins of English society. Some servants, like Lord Byron's page, wear livery, linking them visually with their wealthy masters and mistresses. In other portraits, black people wear turbans or other exotic clothing to mark their difference. The use of Middle Eastern costumes for Africans reminds us that the English often confounded the geographic origins and cultural identities of ethnic outsiders.

The earliest portraits that include black attendants depict the royal family and members of the upper aristocracy, as well as military leaders. Throughout the century, however, the vast majority of such portraits are of women. Portraits of men with black grooms or pages cluster in the 1640s and 1650s and reappear in the 1690s. Some of the subjects were engaged in the slave trade, but there are no portraits of planters recently returned from the Caribbean or of West Indian merchants that include Africans, and only two depict individuals who had strong colonial connections. The English people who had themselves painted with blacks were members of the gentry or aristocracy who possessed, or aspired to possess, black slaves. Having a black page remained a sign of conspicuous wealth, and the growing volume of the slave trade enabled a wider range of people within the English elite to display such valuable possessions. At the same time, the images helped construct an understanding of black people in England as subordinate.[33] By the turn of the eighteenth century, the visible presence of enslaved Africans reached deep into English culture.

An early example of the black as exotic is Daniel Mytens's portrait *Charles I and Henrietta Maria Departing for the Hunt* (Figure 4), dating from about 1630; three copies of this painting exist in different collections, suggesting its emblematic power. The black groom, dressed in a short wrap skirt with a leopard-skin sash over one shoulder, is bringing an elaborately equipped riding horse to the royal couple. A monkey mounted on a dog adds a bizarre touch of wildness to the foreground. On the other side of the painting, Geoffrey Hudson, Charles's dwarf, restrains two other dogs that threaten to attack the approaching horse and groom. The angel scattering flowers suggests divine blessings on the couple, while their costumes point to their fertility. Few of the later paintings make such obvious links between the black attendant, a deformed figure, the exotic, and wildness.[34] The close association of Africans with animals and nature was more common. In an extreme example, Benedetto Gennari's 1683 portrait of Hortense Mancini, Duchess of Mazarin and one of Charles II's mistresses, depicts her as Diana, goddess of the hunt, surrounded by four liveried black slaves and two large hunting dogs; three of the slaves wear collars that match those of the dogs. All are baring their gleaming teeth (Figure 5). Although they are facing in different directions, all turn their eyes toward Mancini's exposed breasts.

This portrait is excessive in its violence and flamboyant in its display of wealth and flesh. While it conforms to common visual conventions by having the slaves draw attention to the subject, its allegorical frame is unusual, as is the explicit cross-racial erotic dimension. Slaves and animals are both under the control of a predatory white goddess.

Between 1650 and 1690, almost all the portraits that included black attendants have women, not men, as their subjects; in these the blacks are decorative, like the women themselves. Two early portraits illustrate the conventional pattern. The black child offering a bowl of flowers and looking up at the subject of the painting is found in a number of Anthony Van Dyck portraits, as well as those by his followers. In a painting from Van Dyck's studio (Figure 6), the young black attendant offers a lady, said to be Queen Henrietta Maria, a bowl of flowers. A small dog plays at his feet. His eyes are directed at his mistress's face. He appears to be a bridge between nature and civilization: the dog and the flowers link him to nature, while the heavily decorated suit and his pearl earring echo the elaborate costume of his mistress.[35] Sir Peter Lely's portrait of Elizabeth Murray, Lady Dysart, circa 1651, is better known (Figure 7). In this work, the black boy steps out from behind a curtain, looks somewhat anxiously at Lady Dysart, and offers her a tray of flowers. Like the attendant in the Van Dyck, he is dressed in a European style and wears a large pearl earring that mirrors the pearl at his mistress's waist. In both portraits, the jewels underline the rarity and value of such a servant. Both Africans present their mistresses with the bounty of nature. In the case of Lady Dysart, the flowers, as well as the location of the enormous pearl at her waist, represent her fertility: this painting apparently honors the birth of her second son. As in many of these portraits, the child appears more lively than the official subject of the portrait. In all the portraits of aristocratic ladies attended by young blacks, the contrast between the Africans' dark skin and the subject's fair skin presents a sharply dichotomized view of skin color. As they emerge from the backgrounds of the painting, the children are often most clearly seen by their eyes and their teeth.[36]

A number of portraits depict Charles II's mistresses with black attendants. This monarch, popularly called "the black boy" because of his dark hair and complexion, had black pages; so did his queen, and several of his mistresses evidently had black servants as well. Four extant portraits of Louise de Keroualle, the Duchess of Portsmouth, include black attendants in conventional poses. In a 1682 portrait by Pierre Mignard (Figure 8), a black girl holds a coral in one hand and offers her a shell filled with pearls; she wears a pearl choker instead of a collar, blurring the line between the collar as a sign of possession and jewels as a sign of wealth. Gazing admiringly toward the duchess, she is the livelier figure; her mistress places an arm around her in a maternal gesture but stares fixedly at the viewer. In a 1684 Kneller portrait, a black boy holds back a drape. Although his role is to draw attention to the duchess, his face is more arresting than hers. Another portrait of Louise de Keroualle by Jacques D'Agar includes two black attendants, one of whom is holding a crown.[37] A black child also appears in a portrait of Barbara Villiers, Duchess of Cleveland; one purportedly of Nell Gwynne; and another said to be of Mary Davis, in addition to a William Wissing portrait that might be the Duchess of Mazarin.[38] Different children are portrayed in different portraits of the same subject, suggesting that these attendants, who had to be small, had short careers with the most elite mistresses.[39]

Two pairs of portraits, one by Kneller and the other by Wissing, show different elite women with blacks in not just similar but identical poses, indicating that both these artists had patterns in their studio for a portrait of a woman with a black page. One Kneller portrait is said to be of Mary Davis (Figure 9), the other of Dorothy, Lady May. The slave is not serving his mistress in any obvious way; instead, the lady is holding his chin, drawing attention to him while he admires her.[40] The Wissing pattern features an unusual pose: the subject's arm is draped around the shoulders of her black servant girl. This arrangement of the sitters undermines the usual image of service. Although this gesture seems maternal, it is also reminiscent of the ways people are portrayed with their pets, which appear even more commonly; iconographically, pets and slaves are often interchangeable. The girl holds a parrot and is picking a grape from a bunch on her mistress's lap. Both elite women and their black attendants function as objects of display; an elite woman's slave, like her pets and jewels, becomes another of the exotic goods she consumes to enhance her status.[41]

Two portraits from the early 1680s by Wissing—with similar though not identical poses—suggest the varied social status of women depicted with black servants. The young Mary Grimston was from a gentry family; her lovely portrait may have been commissioned because she was betrothed to the Earl of Essex (Figure 10). Grimston, who died when she was nine, looks older than her attendant. Her attendant does not wear a collar.[42] Wissing's portrait of Anne, Duchess of Monmouth and Buccleuch, the wife of Charles II's son the Duke of Monmouth, has an attendant with a collar, as well as a turban (Figure 11). A comparison of these two portraits suggests that, while the rules for portraying women with black pages were standardized, the attendants themselves were not stock figures but rather the actual servants of the portrait's subjects.

The conventions for portraying men with black attendants follow those in the portrait of Lord Byron. Military portraits of men often feature white as well as black attendants, while portraits of women with white attendants were unheard of. The 1690 Kneller portrait of the Duke of Schomberg, which was widely circulated as a print (Figure 12), harks back to Van Dyck's portrait of the Duc D'Aremberg and shows a black page holding Schomberg's helmet.[43] Another group of portraits represents men in ceremonial settings. In the Closterman portrait, Charles Seymour, the sixth Duke of Somerset (Figure 13), is preparing for the coronation of William and Mary in 1689; the black page carries his coronet. The military or ceremonial motif was most common in portraits of men, but several portraits of wealthy merchants with ties to the East have also survived.[44]

While the young Mary Grimston was portrayed as an adult, group portraits of white children attended by black children, which have seldom been discussed, challenge some of the conventions of the adult portraits. The contrast between the age and size of the subject and that of the attendant is less marked, reducing the visual difference in power. At the same time, it is always clear who is serving and who is being served. The anonymous 1704 portrait of Anne Stone and her brother Andrew (Figure 14) includes a young slave offering Anne fruit, which she passes on to the baby. A Jacob Huysmans portrait ca. 1680 of a pair of boys with a black attendant depicts the boys' favorite pastimes: riding, hunting, and playacting. The boys are both in costume, while the attendant wears "normal" clothes. He leads a horse; the boys are accompanied by five dogs and a peacock, and a white man in the background has a hawk on his wrist.[45] The one exception to the model of service is a 1667 Nicholas Dixon miniature, which appears to be a scene from a masque or other dramatic performance. The small black boy is in the middle, in fancy dress and holding a turban; a boy in fancy dress carrying a spear stands behind him, with his hand on the servant's head, presenting him to his older sister (Figure 15). The most sentimental and unusual grouping is a James Maubert portrait of two girls with their black nurse, an adult woman who stands behind and bends over them.[46]

By the late seventeenth century, an increasing number of paintings began to normalize the presence and work of black people in England. Black servants are still presented as objects for display, but some—like the nurse in the Maubert—are depicted doing normal work. For example, in a painting after Abraham Jansz Van Diepenbeck of the Duke of Newcastle's stables

FIGURE 2. "Lenthall," Mrs. John Verney, Née Mary Lawley
[with a black slave] (Claydon House Trust, Sir Edmund Verney;
photograph: Courtauld Photographic Survey)

FIGURE 3.
William Dobson,
John, First Lord Byron
[with black attendant]
(University of
Manchester, Tabley
House Collection;
photograph:
Photographic Survey,
Courtauld Institute
of Art)

FIGURE 4. Daniel Mytens, *Charles I and Henrietta Maria Departing*
for the Hunt (Location unknown, formerly Serlby Hall; photograph:
Photographic Survey, Courtauld Institute of Art)

FIGURE 5. Benedetto Gennari, *Hortense Mancini,*
Duchess of Mazarin, as Diana (Sotheby's Images)

FIGURE 6. Studio of Anthony Van Dyck, *Portrait of a Lady* [*with a black servant*] (Christie's Images, Ltd.)

FIGURE 7. Sir Peter Lely (1618–80), *Elizabeth Murray, Countess of Dysart, with Black Servant*, ca. 1650 (© National Trust/Angelo Hornak)

FIGURE 8. Pierre Mignard, *Louise de Keroualle, Duchess of Portsmouth, with an Unidentified Servant* (National Portrait Gallery, London)

FIGURE 9. Sir Godfrey Kneller, *Mary Davis* [*identity doubtful;
with black slave*] (Audley End; photograph: Crown Copyright NMR)

FIGURE 10. William Wissing, *Mrs. Mary Grimston*
(Gorhambury Collection, reproduced by permission of the Earl of Verulam;
photograph: Photographic Survey, Courtauld Institute of Art)

Text within image: atchefs of Monmouth / Buccleugh.

FIGURE 11. William Wissing, *Anne, Duchess of Monmouth and Buccleuch, with Her Black Page* (By kind permission of His Grace the Duke of Buccleuch and Queensberry, Knight of the Thistle)

FIGURE 12. Sir Godfrey Kneller, *Frederick, First Duke of Schomburg*
(Engraved by John Smith: National Portrait Gallery, London)

FIGURE 13. John Closterman (1660–1711), *Charles Seymour,*
6th Duke of Somerset (Petworth House, the Egremont Collection [The National Trust];
photograph: Photographic Survey, Courtauld Institute of Art)

FIGURE 14. J. H. (J. Hargrave?), *Anne Stone and Her Brother Andrew Stone with a Black Slave* (Christie's Images, Ltd. [1985])

FIGURE 15. Nicholas Dixon, *A Young Lady and Her Brother with a Black Servant* (From the Burghley House Collection; photograph: Photographic Survey, Courtauld Institute of Art)

FIGURE 16. After Abraham Jansz Van Diepenbeck (1599–1675),
Manege of Horses Belonging to William Cavendish, 1st Duke of Newcastle
(Wimpole Hall, the Bambridge Collection [The National Trust];
photograph: Photographic Survey, Courtauld Institute of Art)

FIGURE 17. Unknown artist, *Elihu Yale, the 2nd Duke of Devonshire, Lord James Cavendish, Mr. Tunstal, and a Page* (Yale Center for British Art, gift of the 11th Duke of Devonshire)

FIGURE 18. Unknown artist, detail of *Elihu Yale, the*
2nd Duke of Devonshire, Lord James Cavendish, Mr. Tunstal, and a Page
(Yale Center for British Art, gift of the 11th Duke of Devonshire)

FIGURE 19. James Worsdale, *Elihu Yale with His Black Servant*
(Yale University Art Gallery, gift of Mrs. Anson Phelps Stokes, 1910)

FIGURE 20. Gerard Soest (ca. 1600–1680?), *Cecil Calvert, 2nd Lord Baltimore, with His Grandson and Unidentified Servant* (Courtesy of Enoch Pratt Free Library, Central Library/State Library Resource Center, Baltimore, Maryland)

from the 1660s (Figure 16), each of six horses is led by a groom. Three of the grooms are black and three are white. However normal the activity, the white and black grooms wear slightly different clothing, with that of the white grooms being more conventional.[47]

Black slaves are often visible in conversation pieces, such as the anonymous portrait of Lord James Cavendish with his father, the Duke of Devonshire; his father-in-law, Elihu Yale; and an unidentified white man (Figure 17). Because Lord James received a generous income from his marriage to Yale's daughter, Yale appears at the center. The slave, who belongs to Cavendish, provides the Madeira that the men are sharing. Not only is the slave wearing a collar, but the padlock that closes it also is clearly visible (Figure 18). Yale is the only man portrayed with a slave in two paintings. In a portrait set in Bombay (Figure 19), where Yale was governor, he was painted with his slave handing him a paper. In this painting, too, the collar that marks the slave's status is clearly visible.[48]

Surprisingly, few English people associated with the colonies where slavery was taken for granted had their portraits painted with slaves. I have found only two portraits of men with direct colonial connections that include a black servant. The 1670 Gerard Soest portrait of Lord Baltimore with his grandson and a black attendant (Figure 20) is particularly interesting.[49] Baltimore and his small grandson are holding a map of his American property, Maryland. The black boy—in old-fashioned full court dress, mirroring that of Lord Baltimore—is holding a plumed hat and looking down at the younger boy. Although he is not wearing a collar, he was almost certainly a slave brought to England from Calvert's American possessions. The only other such portrait is a military portrait of Sir Charles Lyttleton, one of the first governors of Jamaica, painted soon after his return to London as a soldier, with a slave holding his helmet.[50] The slaves who were unusual and signs of display in England were commonplace in the colonies, and thus not displayed: John Trumbull included a slave in a portrait of George Washington painted in England but not the versions painted in America.[51]

These paintings followed a long artistic tradition of representing members of the European nobility with black attendants. Numerous earlier examples exist in Spain and Venice, which both had long histories of black and moorish slaves. The first individual portrait of a European notable attended by a black page is by Titian, and the iconographic tradition was picked up by Van Dyck. David Dabydeen has suggested that these images are also "a degenerate version of the religious iconography of the Madonna and Magi," a woman represented as white being attended by an African king.[52] Yet black attendants do not appear in English paintings until there actually were black slaves and servants in England; real people from Africa and the American colonies come to fill the aesthetic supporting roles projected for black subordinates within this visual tradition. The number of such paintings increased during the late seventeenth century, when the number of black people in England was growing rapidly. These paintings portray the place of black slaves and servants among the English aristocracy and gentry. What can we learn from these images about slavery and race, at least as they expressed the status and self-conceptions of white English people?

First, black servants were property—literally, as chattels, and figuratively, as exotic and expensive objects of display. This is shown not just by the frequent depiction of collars that mimic slave shackles, but also by the frequent pairing of blacks with animals and the interchangeability of black children with pets. Beyond this, what was the significance of women's preference for boys over girls as personal attendants? Especially during the Restoration, this choice indicates a complex set of meanings attached to race and gender. The power of whiteness is emphasized by giving a female subject dominance over a male one; at the same time, the woman's power is limited by placing her in a familiar role with power over a child. The black children—boys as well as girls—are powerless on account of both race and age. Finally, such paintings of women display their sexuality, even as they limit and control access to it. This is particularly clear in Gennari's portrait of the Duchess of Mazarin: she does not touch, nor is she touched by, any of her attendants. The woman dominates in every binary that divides the subjects—short/tall, child/adult, slave/free, black/white—except male/female.[53] These oppositions work in a way that parallels the meanings of the sexual and racial division of labor on plantations, simultaneously constructing "blacks" as an undifferentiated group and "white women" as a special category.

The visual conventions that shaped these paintings and the aesthetic issues implicit in these representations of black servants leave many historical questions unanswered. Why did more boys than girls serve in elite households? How many slaves, like Peregrine Tyam, were brought directly from Africa, and how many were, like Betty's son Thomas, Atlantic creoles born on the islands and sent to England? Were most of the attendants pictured in these paintings actually the possessions of the sitters? Were some of them props, added by the painter for visual and iconographic purposes or temporarily hired by the sitter for purposes of display? And what was their status? How many were legally slaves, and how many were employed as servants?

Were some black children allowed to go free when they grew up? If so, what work did they find to do? Were there really so few black women in England? How did people of African descent form families? Exploring these questions requires us to turn from representations to the recorded experiences of black residents of England during this formative period.

People

English colonists in the Caribbean continued to think of themselves as English. Governor Stede of Barbados had nothing but contempt for a man who had tried to betray the island to the French, in contrast to "true English men" (the rest of the planters) who would never have been afraid to fight the French, even when outnumbered ten to one.[54] This self-perception on the part of colonists continued despite the growing divergence between their society and that at home. Many colonists, particularly the wealthier planters, planned to return to England eventually. In the absence of schools, the sons of planters, like Christopher Codrington, were sent to England for their education; in the 1690s, one Englishman estimated that "for these last twenty years, the West-Indies have sent us back annually, about 300 persons of their offspring."[55] While some fortunate opportunists flourished in the social chaos of the Caribbean, other colonists, like John Helyar, longed only to return home and feared the tropical environment would prove fatal. Those who died in the islands were not always buried there; the earthly remains of governors, at least, might be sent home. When the Duke of Albemarle died in Jamaica in October 1688, his corpse was embalmed in pitch and sealed inside a series of coffins; in March 1689 his remains were placed on his yacht and his wife boarded a naval frigate for the journey back to England. The embarkation was attended with great ceremony, as befitted a governor and a nobleman.[56] When Lord Francis Russell, governor of Barbados, died in 1696, the Council arranged an elaborate ceremony to carry his coffin on board ship.[57] The return of children for education and bodies for burial affirmed English identity despite Caribbean residence.

Planters who returned home often brought slaves with them. In his instructions, Colonel Drax referred to "Davey and Banwick who were formerly with me in England"; these favored slaves were given the same allowances of food and clothing as white servants.[58] In 1690 the disgraced Barbados attorney general Thomas Montgomery, imprisoned for plotting treason with the French, asked not only that his brother and his clerk be sent home with him but also that he be allowed to bring "two Negroes to attend me, because of my great seasickness and my unability to help myself." Even a man imprisoned for treason expected to be accompanied by slaves on his return; he continued to expect the service he had become accustomed to.[59]

Some slaves, like Betty's son Thomas, were sent as gifts to planters' families and friends. Others, like Peregrine Tyam, were transported directly from Africa to England. The extent of this traffic is impossible to determine from the extant records since it was never entirely legitimate; those enslaved Africans who can be identified as bypassing the West Indies belonged to merchants engaged in slave-trading ventures. Information about people of African descent in seventeenth-century England is difficult to find. It is clear that the number of black residents grew steadily over time. What scattered evidence there is suggests a substantial population in London and smaller populations in port cities such as Bristol.[60] Slaves were also found in gentry households in the countryside. We know of Thomas in East Coker and Peregrine Tyam in Middle Claydon only by accident, after all. Despite the abundant anecdotal evidence of the presence of Africans in England, we have only brief, tantalizing glimpses of their lives.

In 1555 John Lok returned from a trading voyage to Africa with "certain black slaves, whereof some were tall and strong men, and could well agree with our meats and drinks."[61] The arrival of Lok's human cargo is the usual starting point for the history of Africans in England. Through the rest of the sixteenth century, small numbers of Africans were brought to England by traders, some to be trained to serve them in Africa and others to be used as domestic servants at home. Initially only those closest to the court could afford such servants. Small groups of Africans clustered in ports, including not only the cities of London, Plymouth, and Bristol but also minor ports such as Barnstaple and Weymouth. In the midst of the economic crisis of the 1590s, the African residents of England were visible enough that the authorities proposed to export them to Spain and Portugal in exchange for English prisoners held in Spain. A Lübeck merchant received a license to ship "Negroes" out of the country. The project failed, but for such an enterprise to be worthwhile, even speculatively, there must have been a substantial number of black people in England. Equally important, they remained outsiders in English eyes.[62] The number of Africans living in England grew rapidly throughout the seventeenth century, especially after the English colonies in Virginia and the West Indies came to rely on slave labor. In 1633 the Dorchester authorities seized "Mary, a blackamoor," who had run away from her master, a Weymouth sea captain. Black soldiers and sailors fought on both sides in the English Civil War.[63] As wealthy planters returning to England brought their slaves along with their fortunes, Africans came to be seen less as exotic treasures and more as ordinary, albeit valuable, commodities.

The legal status of black people in England was ambiguous, and slave traders and owners benefited from this lack of clarity. A judgment in 1569 had declared that "England was too pure an air for Slaves to breathe in." At the same time, those who imported Africans to England sold them—a procedure that never applied to English servants. By 1677 at least one court recognized that enslaved Africans were property, "being usually bought and sold among merchants, as merchandise." This ruling upholding slavery was ignored in a series of judgments beginning in 1698, when Chief Justice John Holt wrote that "as soon as a Negro comes into England he becomes free; one may be a villein in England but not a slave." Slavery was not abolished in practice, however, and during the eighteenth century Holt's rulings were reversed. Only in 1772, when Lord Mansfield ruled in the Somerset case, did the King's Bench definitively declare that, in the absence of positive legislation, the "odious" state of slavery could not be introduced for any reason and that colonial laws establishing slavery were not valid in England; the ruling did not, however, lead to freedom for slaves in England.[64]

These fluctuating legal opinions point to the unresolved contradictions between slavery's status outside the basic principles and categories of English law and the reality that Africans in England were actually held as slaves. The ideas and practices of prominent English men were as ambivalent as the legal theories. John Locke, for instance, argued that slavery was "directly opposite to the generous temper and courage of our Nation," but he invested in the Royal African Company, which between 1672 and 1698 enjoyed a monopoly in the African slave trade, and helped Lord Ashley write the Fundamental Constitutions of Carolina, which provided that "every freeman of Carolina, shall have absolute power and authority over his Negro slaves."[65] Such confusion bespeaks the unfamiliarity of Africans themselves and the strangeness of slavery as a way of organizing labor.

During the seventeenth century, these legal debates about the status of Africans in England had little effect on the common practice of holding them as slaves. At the same time, the very ambiguity of the situation generated opportunities for some Africans to evade, or even challenge, their condition of bondage. Relative to their masters, of course, slaves were at a great disadvantage: not only were they powerless, lacking property even in themselves, but they were also in an unfamiliar country and had little or no knowledge of the language, the law, or the customs regulating labor. Africans were at the mercy of their masters and any friends they might make. Those slaves who succeeded in running away appear to have found employment and lodging among the transient population in English cities; some men worked on the docks, or signed on as sailors on ships bound for foreign ports. Those few Africans who challenged their status seem to have enjoyed support from English as well as black friends, especially from religious communities.

The church, like the law, struggled to figure out how to incorporate Africans in England and to consider whether slavery was compatible with its fundamental values. Debate swirled around the relationship between Christianity and freedom. If Christians were forbidden to hold other Christians as slaves (which was not certain), did slaves who were baptized thereby become free? D'Avenant had the Priest of the Sun appeal to this notion in his condemnation of the Spaniards, and Ligon gave it as one reason why colonial planters resisted instructing their slaves in Christianity. That this idea was never formally adjudicated in civil or church law did not diminish its influence. In the West Indies, as we saw in Chapter 4, for practical reasons the planters refrained from serious efforts to convert their slaves. In England, however, such deliberate neglect was not an option; it appears that slaves brought to England were routinely baptized.[66]

Some converted Africans and their Christian friends acted on the assumption that baptism transformed slaves' position. In 1667 the Court of Aldermen in Bristol heard the case of Dinah Black, who had lived as a servant to Dorothy Smith for five years. Her mistress had recently put her aboard a ship to be sent to the plantations, but she had complained and been rescued. Because her mistress refused to take her back, Black was allowed to put herself in service until the next Quarter Sessions. Smith had treated Black as a slave, who could be sold and transported at will. Other powerful white people intervened on her behalf because she was baptized and wanted to "live under the teaching of the Gospel."[67] As Thomas Tryon and other Dissenters pointed out, Christian ideas of equality before God were essentially at odds with the practice of slavery. However, in 1680 the bishop of London asserted that emancipation was not a consequence of baptism, an opinion that was reasserted in the 1720s. The controversy fostered confusion and opened the way for Christians to convert Africans residing in England and for Africans to forge less unequal relationships with their English hosts.[68]

By the second half of the seventeenth century, glimpses of Africans in England become more frequent in the historical record. In 1669, after the departure of his cook, Samuel Pepys employed Doll, a "black-moore of Mr.

Batelier's," as a cook. She "dresses our meat mighty well." Pepys's phrasing suggests that Batelier, a wine merchant, owned Doll and hired her out, just as his counterparts in Barbados did.[69] In the 1680s, the Jenkinson family of Claxby-by-Normandy, Lincolnshire, had a black slave, whom his master later killed in a drunken rage. Twelve black families lived in Nottingham-shire in 1680.[70] In 1695 Thomas Finchly, "a blackamoor," escaped from cus-tody in Woodford, Essex, where he was being held on charges of robbery.[71]

People of African descent were part of the rural and urban landscape of late Stuart England. Any estimate of their number is at best an educated guess. The earliest reliable figures come from the 1770s; at that time, the Court of King's Bench accepted a figure of 15,000 blacks in England, while Granville Sharp, the philanthropist whose legal research was central to later challenges to slavery in England, estimated that there were 20,000.[72] Taking into account both the growth of the population and the vast expansion of imperial activity over the eighteenth century, the number of blacks living in England in 1700 is undoubtedly significantly lower, perhaps about 5,000. Whatever the number, they were highly visible in London, Bristol, and other ports and present in smaller numbers through the rest of the country.

Runaway Servants and Slaves

Whether servants or slaves, blacks in England, like their white counter-parts, did not always like their masters, and like Mary in Weymouth they were apt to run away. The most systematic source of information about black people living in England is the advertisements for such runaways that ap-peared in the newspapers of the period. The first such advertisement was published in *Mercurius Politicus* in 1659: "A Negro-boy, about nine years of age, in a gray serge suit, his hair cut close to his head, was lost on Tuesday last, August 9, at night in S. Nicholas Lane, London."[73] Whether this child "was lost" or ran away, the description matches the images presented in paintings. The *London Gazette*, which appeared after the interruption in the regular press from 1660 to 1665, initially published advertisements only about "matters of state," but by 1668 notices of lost dogs and horses, mostly belonging to the king and his family, began to appear, along with notices of prisoners who had escaped from gaol. The first notice of a runaway servant appears in 1669; these became increasingly frequent over time, and by 1673 they were a regular feature of the paper.[74]

Although most notices concern runaway servants, a few pertain to free people of African descent who were living in London. Thomas Widnel, twenty-seven, "of a short stature, black complexion, being scarred with several white scars on one side of his chin, and the lower part of his cheek, whereon no hair grows, wearing a periwig, and having under it very short black stubbed harsh hair, and a gentile [genteel] person," had run away from his father with "things of value."[75] The notice appeared because Widnel had stolen his father's property, not because he had stolen himself from a master. Such references to free black families, even fractured ones, are exceedingly rare.

In some cases, it is impossible to be certain whether someone whose absence is advertised is of African descent. Terms such as "Negro" and "blackamoor" are clear. However, the term "black" was used to describe people's complexion, not necessarily their ancestry. For instance, "A Middle sized black man, having short black brown lank hair, tawny coloured in the face" was probably not of African descent, though he may have been East Indian. Ambrose Masher, "a tall black slender man of a ruddy complexion," was also not African, nor was the Scotsman William Arnel, described as "a tall black man."[76] The "black boy of about 14 years" who had a "silver collar around his neck" was certainly of African descent; his collar, more than his color, marked him as a slave.[77]

Some descriptions are ambiguous. Thomas Blackborne, "of a black complexion, a long nose, his hair black and flaggy, and a down look," might have been African, though "flaggy" hair is straight and lank. With Morgan Auberry, "a black down looked fellow," it is difficult to tell, as it is with Mr. William Wilberson, one of the seven escaped convicts from Lancaster gaol who was a "tall black man." We know nothing about the origins of George Turner, a "tall black" with smallpox scars who kept a fencing school behind the Royal Exchange in 1692.[78] The "down look" so often described in these announcements is not unique to slaves and suggests that those who do not look you in the eye are not honest. Thus Richard Fitzgerald, alias Gerald, who was "pal'd countenanced, down-looked," was wanted for theft of money and jewels from his master.[79] Africans were generally distinguished from East Indians, although the two groups probably had a similar status. Sarah, "an Indian woman" with "tawney complexion, long black hair," was described as "strayed or spirited" from her master's house.[80] In 1686 a Turk ran away from his master, and two brothers from East India, Shackshoon and Mahomet, were "carried away" from Sir Thomas Grantham.[81] The allegation that they were stolen—"carried away," like "spirited away"—not only defines them as property but also deprives them of agency. The ads also provide early evidence of the conflation of people of African and South Asian descent as undifferentiated others; notices published in 1689 refer to an "East India black" and an "Indian black."[82]

These advertisements suggest the prevalence of black people among runaway servants. In ten sample years between 1673 and 1700, there were a total of 224 notices of runaway servants, apprentices, and slaves. Of those, thirty-seven, or 16.5 percent, were clearly of African descent; eight were identified as Indian or East Indian, and the descriptions of three were ambiguous. The proportion of Africans in the sample years ranged from a low of 10 percent to a high of more than 27 percent. Throughout the period, however, a far higher proportion of white servants were accused of theft: 56 percent of the white servants, as opposed to 5.4 percent of the black ones. Some 31 percent of the runaways *not* accused of theft were black. Black slaves were valuable property; what they stole by running away was themselves.

The notices published in the London Gazette cannot be interpreted as an indication of the proportion of Africans among runaway servants in late seventeenth-century London. Masters were much more likely to advertise for black slaves who escaped than for English servants who absconded; slaves were valuable possessions, while most servants were paid at the end of their term and forfeited their wages if they went missing. Nonetheless, these descriptions provide valuable clues to the social and legal place of blacks in English society. Of the thirty-seven black runaways mentioned, four were described as wearing collars; the portraits, too, show variations in this practice. John White, who belonged to Colonel Kirke, wore a silver collar with the colonel's coat of arms on it, similar to the collar shown on Lord James Cavendish's slave (Figure 18). Ned, who served a farrier in Lime Street, wore a brass collar. The intriguing story of William Moorfield, an eleven-year-old who ran away twice, illuminates the collar's significance. Moorfield was reported missing from his master, Mr. Thomas Lewis, in Crutch Fryers in February 1674; he had already been missing for four months when the advertisement appeared. The youth spoke English well. Six weeks later, another notice for William Moorfield revealed what had happened in the interim. When he first ran away, he had "put himself in service with Mr. Gorey," who had returned him to his master ten days previously. The next day he ran away again, but now he had "a lock and chain about his neck." The collar was not necessary initially, but after he had run away it reminded him—and anyone who saw him—of his enslaved status.[83]

The collars, which were never used on white servants, indicate that these were slaves, not servants free to make their own arrangements. Some black men had been branded, indicating their status as chattels and, perhaps, a sojourn in the West Indies. John Angola, "a blackamore man," was "iron-marked in his breast with the sign of a greyhound, and in his left side with the sign of a hawk flying."[84] Benjamin, who belonged to Theodorus Paleologus, was described simply as "branded on both shoulders."[85] The prevailing assumption that blacks, unlike other servants, were possessions is confirmed by a notice placed by Sir Thomas Janson of Tunbridge Wells in 1686. It announced that a fifteen-year-old black boy assumed to have run away from his master had been found; Janson would return him to his "owner" when he was identified.[86] Black runaways were effectively slaves, even though these notices often called them servants. The work of these slaves, alongside white servants and apprentices, made their status less evident than was slavery on the plantations, but the notices provide ample evidence that they were possessions.

Black slaves were concentrated in London, but they were found—and went missing—all over England. Joseph Bandee left his master at Plymouth, and John Angola ran away from John St. Aubyn, Esq., in St. Michael's Mount, Cornwall.[87] Lady Broughton reported a "black boy" stolen in Denbighshire.[88] Francis Smith, "a middle sized black man," served Mr. Thomas King of Chalgrave, Oxfordshire.[89] Runaways had served masters as elevated as Lady Boughton and as humble as the farrier of Lime Street. While a few served as decorative pages, like those depicted in portraits, many others, like the cook Samuel Pepys hired from Mr. Batelier, did ordinary domestic work. The most notable group of owners was comprised of sea captains and military men, who had presumably obtained their slaves in the course of their work. Captains of slaving vessels usually received some portion of the human cargo as part payment; while they sold some of them, they often kept one slave as a personal attendant.[90] Some of the runaway blacks were sailors: Pall, "a Negro man," left a ship at Ratcliff; a "tall slender Negro" ran away from the ship The Dragon.[91] William Peter, who was short and bowlegged, had recently served Captain Francis Maynard and was serving Captain Davy Breholt when he disappeared.[92]

All but one of the slaves sought by advertisements were male. The ages mentioned range from eleven to thirty-three. Fifteen were between the ages of fourteen and eighteen, while thirteen were identified as nineteen or older. While the black attendants in portraits are young boys, the blacks we can identify as runaways were somewhat older. In 1651 the Guinea Company asked its factors to provide slaves who were about fifteen years old, which coincides with the age range found in the ads.[93] The one black female runaway mentioned in the newspaper, "a tall Negro woman servant called Mary," was thirty-five.[94] As a comparison, of the 176 white runaway servants identified in the advertisements, sixteen were women and twelve were accused of theft.

The notices for runaway Africans suggest the variety of black people living in late seventeenth-century England. Richard, "a lusty Negro" who had run away from Mr. Nodens, was born in the Bermudas and spoke good English.[95] Salvador, a twenty-five-year-old "black," could not speak English; his name indicates his origins in Spanish America.[96] These advertisements also indicate the range of places where people of African descent lived and worked. Black people were no longer exotic but part of the fabric of urban and port life. Those who lived in the country, in small villages like East Coker or Middle Claydon, were more isolated. The skewed sex ratio of the black population indicates that males were more valuable commodities in England, as they were in the colonies.[97] However, there is much we do not know about the black residents of England during the seventeenth century. Black people are visible in white households, where they were isolated, but invisible when they were on their own. How many families kept their slaves for life, as the Verneys did? What did enslaved African children do when they outgrew the decorative role they had initially played? Did the ambiguous status of black servants mean that when they grew up, the boys were let go to make their way as laborers in unskilled jobs? Were black women really as scarce as they seem? Since there were more men than women in the black population, what kind of families did they join and form? Were there recognizable black communities that persisted through generations, or did black workers marry other working people in the cities, their descendants becoming part of England's working class?

BY 1700 ENGLISH COLONIZATION in the Caribbean and the slave societies constructed there had a significant impact on England. Along with the sugar and chocolate produced on West Indian plantations—and the wealth that trade yielded to the merchants and planters in London and the colonies—came English people who returned from the Caribbean and Africans who were brought to England directly or via the West Indies. The social relations that developed in the colonies, especially the slave labor system, confronted English ideas about order and liberty at every turn. A critique of colonial slavery was articulated at the same time that the institution was developing in the West Indies. The Caribbean colonies figured in plays as sites where corruption, deception, and greed ran rampant, unrestrained by stable social hierarchies or good governance—even when the moral depravity that many feared flowed from slave ownership was left out of the plot. Londoners who did not attend the theatre, read pamphlets about the colonies, or see black pages accompany members of the elite encountered enslaved or formerly enslaved Africans on the streets and the docks. At a time when one in seven people born in England lived in London at some point during their life, the concentration of blacks in the city made them familiar. In the provinces, too, people of African descent were scattered among the servants in great houses and the laborers in towns.

At the same time that the social relations of the empire produced "blackness" as an undifferentiated category, they also produced Englishness as white. As *The Widow Ranter* suggests, the English developed a sense of common identity through their confrontation with colonial "others." The increasing fixity of race that defined Africans as slaves was another product of the Caribbean that was imported to England. As D'Avenant argued in *The Cruelty of the Spaniards in Peru*, the social relations of empire were always problematic. Although the black attendants depicted in the portraits and the servants and laborers visible on the streets of Restoration London were seldom called slaves, the collars that some of them wore—especially after they had run away—make clear their status as chattels. The English had not grown comfortable enough with their empire to proclaim the benefits of slavery to the slaves, as they did later. Instead, they sought simultaneously to reinforce and disguise the social power that controlled the lives of black people living in England. Colonial planters and officials did much the same, at least in law and letters, rationalizing the violence used to control African slaves and legitimating their power by disguising it as the only source of order in a dangerously unstable environment. Slaveholding did not come easily to the English, but becoming slaveholders changed the way the English behaved, and the ways they thought about themselves and people of African descent.

Epilogue
Race, Gender, and Class Crossing the English Atlantic

We are apt to imagine that slavery is entirely abolished
at this time, without considering that this is the case only in a small
part of Europe; not remembering that all over Moscovy and all the eastern
parts of Europe, and the whole of Asia, that is, from Bohemia to the Indian
Ocean, all over Africa, and the Greatest part of America, it is still in use.
ADAM SMITH, *Lectures on Jurisprudence*

The arrival of Betty's son Thomas in East Coker was, as we have seen, only part of a larger movement between England and the Caribbean. It is relatively easy to trace the goods that traveled across the Atlantic; at least some of the people are visible. Yet the invisible trade in cultural practices and ideas is at least as significant as the visible trade. When John Helyar returned from his second stay in Jamaica, he was not the same person who had first left England eight years earlier. He brought with him a knowledge of the world and of alternative social arrangements.

To become successful planters in the Caribbean, English men had changed their social practices in multiple ways. To guarantee a supply of labor, they had used both indentured servitude and slavery; they had developed harsh regimes of labor discipline for both, and in the peak sugar production season they structured work in shifts so that production continued twenty-four hours a day. All this required changes in law that diminished the paternalistic dimensions of being a master in favor of coercive ones. The law of slavery in particular mandated harsh punishments for all offences, particularly those that even hinted at resistance. The protection of property and wealth was at the center of both the labor and legal regimes of the islands, and no cruelty was too great. As a Jamaican merchant wrote in 1709, it was only limited by "what avarice and Iniquity can suggest, or what the Caprice and Cruelty of men, bounded by no fences of human law, can invent and execute."[1] People of African descent were permanently assigned the status of chattel, to the extent that free blacks were tried not as free people, but as slaves. Freedom for Africans in the West Indies was limited. The association between African ancestry and slavery moved skin color from a source of negative stereotypes to a central aspect of identity.

In the process of making these changes, the planters had also begun to develop new ways of thinking about gender and race. With relatively few white women in the islands, their labor was less significant, and after about 1660 they did not work in the fields. Enslaved African women, on the other hand, did work in the fields. One of the distinctions between white women and black women was that there was a large difference between the work of white women and white men, while there was relatively little difference between the work of black women and black men. Over time, white women were seen as "not working" in the Caribbean. Each of these changes was largely in place by 1700. In England, by 1700 there was an image of the West Indies planter on the stage and an image of the corruption of slavery. Equally, there was a visual tradition of portraying wealthy people with their black attendants.

The eighteenth-century Caribbean consolidated the behaviors of the seventeenth century and articulated them more systematically. The fullest descriptions of work organization on plantations come from the eighteenth century, but they bear a close resemblance to seventeenth-century evidence. In 1755 William Belgrove published *A Treatise upon Husbandry or Planting* in Boston. Belgrove's work was not a general guide to agricultural methods but rather a detailed guide to planting and growing sugar, which the title page suggested would be of use "to the Planters of all the West India Islands." Belgrove designed his instructions for a large plantation of 500 acres. After providing detailed directions on planting densities and activity throughout the year, Belgrove appended what were described as the instructions from Colonel H. Drax for the management of his plantation. While the name of the addressee is different, these are substantially the same instructions as those directed to Richard Harwood in 1679 discussed in Chapter 3.[2]

Belgrove organized the instructions and numbered the items to provide structure. Several items are added to the list. Belgrove, more than Drax, worried about the consequences of idleness for the slaves. His version of the instructions therefore included notes on the use of gangs to prevent idleness and ensure that slaves did their work properly. He also created incentives for white servants while providing advice on the use of black overseers. Belgrove made explicit the concern with idleness, but it had been implicit earlier. As early as the 1640s, Ligon had described the constant work of the harvest. When the donkeys carrying canes from the field to the mill approached, several slaves met them, and "are ready to unload them, and so turning them back again, they go immediately to the field, there to take in fresh loading; so that they may not unfitly be compared to Bees."[3]

Each of the major transformations in the seventeenth-century Caribbean —in the organization of work, law, gender, and race—has a counterpart in eighteenth-century England. These English developments were not caused by the same events as in the Caribbean, but the sugar islands provided social and cultural resources that could be used as English men and women sought to respond to change. The changes necessary to sustain a slave-owning society turned out to be—in modified forms—equally useful as England developed a capitalist and increasingly industrial society.

If English agriculture was never run like a Barbadian plantation, English industrial enterprises were. The industrial enterprises of the early eighteenth century—from the Crowley iron mills to the coal mines of the northeast— were still largely paternalist in their operation. Yet in the early eighteenth century, both Crowley and the mine owners began to have skilled workers bound to serve for particular periods of time—in the case of Crowley's ironworks, an agreement that also blocked workers from plying their trade elsewhere in the region. Crowley also set up a court to punish infractions of his many rules. The pitmen's bonds ensured work in the mines for six months at a stretch. Both these arrangements bear strong resemblance to the contracts of indentured servants; this was not free labor. Later in the eighteenth century, factory owners recruited workers from workhouses, who also had limited freedom. The organization of Crowley's works apparently blended centralized industrial production in large smelters and forges and domestic production of smaller items. Like Belgrove, Crowley showed great concern with idleness, and his regulations, like those of plantations, seek to ensure industry and honesty. Throughout the eighteenth-century English economy, there are blurred divisions between free and unfree labor and tendencies to value people in terms of money. It was not only slaves who were commodities.[4]

The mature factory of the Industrial Revolution bears an even stronger resemblance to the efficient organization of the plantation. Some early factories ran twenty-four hours a day; most others took advantage of the invention of gaslight to work long into the night at intense speeds. Thus Robert Southey, visiting a factory in 1807, remarked on "the unnatural dexterity with which the fingers of these little creatures were playing in the machinery, half giddy myself with the noise and the endless motion: and when he told me there was no rest in these walls, day or night, I thought that if Dante had peopled one of his hells with children, here was a scene worthy to have supplied him with new images of torment." His focus on endless motion echoes that of Ligon a century and a half earlier.[5] Robert Owen in his memoirs remarked that one of the challenges in developing the factory complex in New Lanark was the need to develop a new labor force, made more difficult because "all the regularly trained Scotch peasantry disdained the idea of working early and late, day after day."[6]

The comparison between the idea of work in factories and that of the plantations is not a modern conceit; William Cobbett said of factory workers, "The rules which they are subjected to are such as no Negroes were ever subjected to." Furthermore, "The blacks, when carried to the West Indies, are put into a paradise compared with the situation of these poor white creatures in Lancashire, and other factories of the North."[7] Friedrich Engels argued repeatedly that industrial workers were effectively slaves to the factory owners.[8] Whether this is true or not is less important than the way in which the work of factories was linked to that of plantations. It was on the sugar plantation that the English had learned to run an industrial enterprise; slavery and the plantations remained the point of reference for those trying to understand and describe the organization and significance of the factory, just as the oppression of slaves provided an analogue for the treatment of factory workers.

Work on Caribbean plantations was accompanied by a harsh legal regime designed to protect the planters' rights of property. This was also the case in eighteenth-century England. In 1723 the English Parliament passed one of the most draconian statutes of the eighteenth century, the Waltham Black Act, one of many eighteenth-century statutes that created new capital offences. The law made it illegal for "persons armed with swords, firearms, or other offensive weapons" with "his or their faces blacked" to appear in any forest, deer park, or warren. While the blacking of faces was apparently criminal only with the other offences targeted by the act—hunting or stealing deer and poaching hares, conies, or fish—the law was soon interpreted to make blacking as a disguise itself a criminal offence. The act created at least fifty new capital offences.[9]

Looking at this legislation through the lens of English experience in the Caribbean provides a new perspective. Most intriguing is the offence of "blacking." The forests had long been known as sites of disorder, and poaching was an ancient practice. The early seventeenth century had seen many riots and disorders as Charles I sought to better exploit his forests, much as the Hanoverians did a century later. In none of those riots are people said to have blacked their faces. When they were disguised, they were disguised as women, much as the Rebecca rioters in Wales in the nineteenth century. Blacking, like the wearing of women's clothes, made someone unidentifiable. But it also linked the plight of the forest dwellers to that of slaves. Building on the political language of slavery, blacking asserted that the strict enforcement of forest laws deprived local inhabitants of their livelihoods and placed them in slavery to the owners of forests. As we have seen, "slavery" was a term with a long history in English political discourse. The experience of slavery in the Caribbean meant that it was no longer merely an abstract political concept deployed in debate; English smallholders presented themselves as black—and implicitly as slaves.[10] The drama in the forests and the legal response to it went beyond the image of blacks and slavery. The savagery of the law echoes the brutal repression of slave resistance. For the owners of the forest, as for plantation owners, any offence against their property deserved to be a capital offence. There are no direct links between West Indian planters and the landowners of the Berkshire and Hampshire forests, but there did not need to be. English men had learned how to protect property against disenfranchised people.

The move from the plantation to the factory and the development of law both show relatively straightforward echoes of Caribbean practice. The ways the Caribbean helped structure social ideas and social relations within the English imagination is more complex. The most important of these is the construction of race and gender in relation to each other. This took place over issues of work and sexuality, as well as more global ideas of racial difference.

One of the major developments of the eighteenth century was the increasing attention to women's leisure as an indicator of wealth and status. Everything we know about women in eighteenth-century England reminds us that women did work: even if not in obviously productive ways, their labor was critical to the success of the household. So the focus on women's leisure is more important as an idea than an indicator of activities. Especially among middle-class families in towns, women's work activities were increasingly isolated from the income-producing activities of the household. Even women's traditional roles came to be marginalized by scientific and technical developments in a field like dairying. That the work of housekeeping was defined as "not work" was a part of the process of distinguishing women by class.[11] So where did the idea come from that ideally, women did not work? How did it emerge? The complex interaction of race and gender in the Caribbean provides at least one part of the explanation. Where the work of slave women was not defined by sex, one characteristic of whiteness emerged from the gender divisions of white society. "Ladyhood" was envisioned as white. To put it another way, a central distinction between how West Indian society imagined blacks and whites came in the ways they thought about women.

The changes in ideas about women in England extended beyond work to sexuality. Eighteenth-century England increasingly defined women's virtue as not just chastity, but sexual passivity. Ideas about female sexual passivity came at the same time as biological theories drew increasingly sharp distinctions between the sexes. If men and women were fundamentally different, so too would be their sexual behavior and moral imperatives. This was not an easy transition; the behavior of both men and women was a subject of intense scrutiny. The debate on women's sexual nature ran through much of eighteenth-century culture. It is a central theme of Henry Fielding's *Joseph Andrews*, where Lady Booby's aggressive sexual behavior is contrasted with Fanny's purity and passivity. Lady Booby represented an earlier model of female sexuality, which accepted women's sexual appetites. By the mid-eighteenth century, these are clearly seen as inappropriate and immoral. Joseph Andrews's sister, tellingly, was the heroine of Samuel Richardson's novel, *Pamela*, now married to her erstwhile seducer.[12] Such changes in ideas of sexuality and biology carried moral imperatives for female chastity.

In 1750 Thomas Thistlewood arrived in Jamaica, where he worked as an overseer on a plantation and later owned a small plantation. In his extraordinarily detailed diaries, he provides an account of his sexual exploits. In Jamaica, he not only had a slave "wife" but also regularly raped other slave women on the plantation. He assumed slave women were always available. They had fewer opportunities to resist sexual exploitation than even a servant like Pamela had in England; when they did resist, they suffered severe punishments.[13] Stereotypes about slave women's sexual availability reflected images of open sexuality at odds with images of feminine passivity in England. But even in eighteenth-century England, men like William Byrd and

James Boswell came to see working-class women as always available for anonymous encounters: his attitude is different from that of Samuel Pepys a century earlier, whose sexual adventures were always with women he knew.[14]

I began this project when someone asked me how the rape of enslaved women by their masters might have affected the trajectory of thinking about sexual violence in England. Ten years later, I can answer that question. It is less simple than I might have hoped, but the ways in which the English practice of slavery shaped notions of race also necessarily reshaped ideas of gender, not just in the islands, but in England. In reality, it was the work of black women, and not so much the rape of black women, that changed attitudes to rape in England. White women who were "not working" were also expected to be sexually passive. With that, it became more difficult to assume that they would invent an accusation of rape. Thus, "it did not happen" would not work as a response; "she consented" would. There are sharper differences imagined between women and men and between black women and white women. The connection of race and gender also reveals a strong link between economic and sexual behavior in the European cultural imagination. Women who are economically productive have, at least in Western societies, been more likely to be imagined as sexually active or available. This applied to enslaved women in the Caribbean as well as working-class women in England. Economic activity and sexual activity go hand in hand; when women are excluded from economic activity, it becomes more difficult to imagine them as sexually active.[15]

As biological concepts of sex increasingly differentiated men and women, the development of biological theories of racial difference reflects a similar process of moving from thinking that humans are fundamentally the same with superficial differences, to defining particular groups as fundamentally distinct. The dichotomous thinking about race was fostered by the law of slavery, especially as the slave codes refused to allow free blacks in the islands the same rights as free white people. It was now race, not freedom, that determined one's place in society.[16] The eighteenth century saw the development of ideas of scientific racism, which assumed not just that blacks were in need of civilizing, but that they represented a different type of person, inherently inferior to whites. Adam Smith saw slavery as inefficient and unproductive, part of the mercantile system that depended on the domination of the weak by the strong. At the same time, David Hume wrote that "there never was a civilized nation of any other complexion than white," and that when "in Jamaica indeed they talk of one Negro as a man of parts and learning; but 'tis likely he is admired for very slender accomplishments, like a parrot, who speaks a few words plainly." As some English people challenged first the slave trade and then slavery itself, the defenders of slavery were pushed to defend it as a benefit to those enslaved.[17] The idea that all humans were descended from a common ancestor lost its significance in the defense of slavery.

The uncertain place of slavery and race in the English imagination is shown by the story of Inkle and Yarico, first told by Richard Ligon. In 1711 a version of the tale by Richard Steele was published in the *Spectator*, ostensibly as an illustration of an argument about whether men or women were more faithful. In Steele's version, Yarico had not only rescued Inkle but was also pregnant by him. The story became a favorite in the eighteenth century, using sentimentality and classical allusions to portray the end of the English relationship with the Caribs. Yarico was often portrayed as an African, not an Indian. As a story of the betrayal of a "Noble Savage" by a greedy Englishman, "Inkle and Yarico" extends the exploration of the negative dimensions of slavery and imperialism. It also included an implicit critique of native culture, given that Yarico had to hide Inkle from being murdered by her compatriots. Yet as the story, in all its versions, offered a critique of slavery, it was the individual greed of Inkle and not the system itself that was the clearest target. Equally, as in Tryon's account, what was most offensive was Inkle's willingness to sell not only the woman who had saved him, but also his own child into perpetual slavery. Greed, it seems, was an individual failing. The story appealed to the sentimental and liberal impulses of eighteenth-century culture.[18] While "Inkle and Yarico" was never told explicitly as an abolitionist story, it provided a way for English people to think about the evils of slavery.

We know enough about the world to understand now that very little of what is thought to be "human nature" is fixed; we also know that descriptions of human nature often mask behavior that differs widely from the ideal. Yet the divergence between normative descriptions of people and their behavior and experience is significant. The "heathenish, brutish and an uncertain dangerous kind of people" of the Barbados slave code of 1661 could—because of these characteristics—be coerced to work at extraordinary levels without regard to their health or well-being. The women were expected to work in the fields alongside the men and to be sexually available to their masters. At the same time, the activities of white women were totally separate from those of enslaved women—thus, "not working." Sexuality, work, and respectability were intertwined with race. And however much we reject the explicit ideas that were part of this mix, the legacy is still with us in the public policy tensions between wanting poor women to work while urging affluent women to stay home with their children.

The process of constructing slave societies explored in this book provides a critical background for many of the ways in which race and gender were connected to work, identity, and law. It also provides a source for significant aspects of eighteenth-century society. To build the institutions that supported slavery, the English had to learn entirely new ways to manage labor and organize agricultural production. The paramount goal of settlers in the West Indies was profit, not an ordered commonwealth, and much followed from that. Work was carried on with extraordinary intensity. The African slaves who were imported to the islands to work on the sugar plantations had to be defined as a different sort of people. Because they were "heathenish and brutish," there was no need to distinguish between the work of women and men. The planters in the West Indies extended and racialized the denigration of poor women's honor that Ligon described in the Cape Verde Islands, and they applied it to all black women. By the end of the seventeenth century, the distance between all white women and black women in the sugar islands supported new models of thinking about the relation of women to work. The exploitation of slaves also meant there was no need to limit the power of masters over slaves, as there was to limit the power of masters over servants. The brutal punishment of rebels was also a logical consequence of the focus on profit. It is not surprising that the English imagination saw planters in the West Indies as corrupt and immoral. The dramatic denigration of planters did not mean a vision of equality for blacks, however: only children could be presented as safe, contained within the frames of aristocratic portraits. Observers might question the cruel operation of slavery, but slavery as an institution was still accepted. In a world where people moved across the Atlantic all the time, what happened in the Caribbean was important in England.

The wealth of Barbados and Jamaica meant that few merchants in the late seventeenth century were unconnected with the trade in slaves. Yet the ease of identifying the concrete engagement of merchants with slavery may have blinded us to seeing the wider implications of slavery, and especially Caribbean slavery, in English society. The English thought of themselves as not having slavery, as Smith suggested—though, as we have seen, there was a significant slave population even in late seventeenth-century England. Racial slavery created a pattern of law and work that protected the rights of property above all else and justified incessant work in the interests of that property. It supported changing ideas of gender in English society, reserving "ladyhood" for women who did not work and who were—implicitly—white. Race became an unspoken if pervasive assumption in England. The Caribbean provided a model for a society where the bonds of paternalism had been largely abandoned. It was not just the expanding popularity of sweet drinks that mattered, but the exploitation of labor in the gendered and racial slave system that helped transform England in the century and a half following 1700.

Notes

Abbreviations

BL Add. MSS	Additional Manuscripts, British Library
CO	Colonial Office, National Archives of the United Kingdom
DD/WHh	Helyar Manuscripts, Somerset Archive and Record Service
LG	*London Gazette*
MSS Rawl. A 348	Rawlinson Manuscripts, Bodleian Library, University of Oxford
NPG	National Portrait Gallery, London
ODNB	*Oxford Dictionary of National Biography*

Introduction

1 John Helyar to William Helyar, 1690, DD/WHh 1090/3/8; Robert Hall to William Helyar, 10 March 1701, DD/WHh 1151/43; Somerset Archive and Record Service D/P/cok.e/2/1/1. The Verney family of Middle Claydon, Bucks, also baptized their slave, Peregrine Tyam. *Memoirs of the Verney Family,* 4:469–70.

2 The Helyar papers are in the Somerset Archive and Record Service, DD/WHh 1089, 1090, 1151, and Addenda Papers 12; they have been used extensively by earlier historians. See Bennett, "Cary Helyar," "William Whaley," and "William Dampier"; Dunn, *Sugar and Slaves,* esp. pp. 212–22.

3 For the laws, see Chapter 4; for rebellion, see Chapter 5. The pattern of struggle followed by integration is described by Bailyn, *Atlantic History,* p. 81. For slave societies, see Berlin, *Many Thousands Gone,* pp. 8–10; for the dominance of the Caribbean as a slaveholding region in the seventeenth century, see Philip Morgan, "The Black Experience in the British Empire, 1680–1810."

4 These issues are explored in Amussen, " 'The Part of a Christian Man,' " pp. 213–33.

5 The phrase is from Ackroyd, *London,* p. 452. For the involvement of local merchants, see, for example, Dresser, *Slavery Obscured.*

6 Williams, *Capitalism and Slavery;* Sheridan, *Sugar and Slavery,* esp. the preface by Hilary Beckles. For recent work that engages this debate, see Eltis, *The Rise of African Slavery in the Americas;* and Blackburn, *The Making of New World Slavery.* For a recent discus-

sion, see Carrington, *The Sugar Industry and the Abolition of the Slave Trade*, and the review by Matt D. Childs.

7   The most familiar sources for the eighteenth century are Equiano, *The Interesting narrative of the life of Olaudah Equiano*, and Prince, *The history of Mary Prince*; recently Carretta, *Equiano, the African*, has presented convincing evidence that Equiano was born in South Carolina rather than Africa, but this does not diminish the significance of his account of slavery. Jennifer Morgan has worked with extraordinary imagination to envision the process of slavery from the perspective of seventeenth-century slaves, but her evidence is all indirect; see Morgan, *Laboring Women*.

8   For Camden, see Kelsey, *Sir John Hawkins*, p. 271; for race and the Irish, see, for example, Smedley, *Race in North America*, pp. 52–61; compare Eltis, "Europeans and the Rise and Fall of African Slavery."

9   Brown, *Good Wives*, provides the most complete account of this, but in Virginia the changes appear to move from legal discourse to social practice rather than the other way around, as they do in Barbados and Jamaica. Morgan, *Laboring Women*, makes the argument for the ways in which race and gender interacted for enslaved women in Barbados and South Carolina and suggests that the relevant changes were present in the seventeenth century; her work does not, however, deal with white women.

10 The concept of "British" history in the seventeenth century is usually attributed to Pocock, "British History: A Plea for a Subject"; for a recent review on the subject that places the "British dimension" in a larger political context, see Samuel, " 'British Dimensions' "; for the English dimension, see Pestana, *The English Atlantic*.

11 The Harvard International Center on the History of the Atlantic World has provided critical institutional support for the concept, as has the doctoral program at Johns Hopkins University; see Bailyn, *Atlantic History*, part 1. The work of Bailyn and Greene over the course of their careers has also made a major intellectual contribution to the field. For some of the voluminous scholarship, see Armitage and Braddick, eds., *The British Atlantic World*; "AHR Forum: The New British History in Atlantic Perspective"; and Greene, "Changing Identity in the British Caribbean," esp. pp. 213–40. Linebaugh and Rediker, *The Many-Headed Hydra*, links the circulation of people and ideas in the Atlantic to the development of revolutionary ideas; Bolster, *Black Jacks*, shows a long tradition of black sailors in the Atlantic. For an excellent recent discussion of the field, see Shammas, Introduction, *The Creation of the British Atlantic World*, esp. pp. 1–6; compare Colley, "The Sea around Us."

12 Armitage, "Three Concepts of Atlantic History," esp. pp. 21–25. For the Englishness of Barbados, see, for example, Gragg, *Englishmen Transplanted*.

13 Hall, *Civilising Subjects*, p. 9; Gilroy, *Black Atlantic*, p. 17.

14 See Wheeler, Introduction, *The Complexion of Race*; Hannaford, *Race*, esp. chaps. 1, 6, and 7; Chaplin, "Race." The concept of emergent race ideas I owe to Erickson, " 'God for Harry, England, and St. George,' " esp. pp. 324–31. The classic study of the American context is Jordan, *White Over Black*; what is striking to a reader today, as Brown points out in *Good Wives*, pp. 109–10, is the way Jordan treats race as a biological reality rather than a social one.

Chapter One

1 For these developments, see, for example, Wrightson, *Earthly Necessities*, pp. 120–28, 159, 198–200, 229. For migration, see Games, "Migration," and *Migration and the Origins of the English Atlantic World*, pp. 16–20. Recent studies of migration have neglected the propaganda, which made the link between colonization and social order; for a summary, see Bridenbaugh, *Vexed and Troubled Englishmen*, pp. 397–409.

2 Wrightson, *Earthly Necessities*, p. 238; McKendrick, Brewer, and Plumb, *The Birth of a Consumer Society*, focuses on the next century but places the roots in the seventeenth century; Shammas, *The Pre-Industrial Consumer in England and America*, tracks the journey from a society based in household production to one where most goods consumed by a household were purchased.

3 Smith, *De Republica Anglorum*, pp. 38–41; Wrightson, *Earthly Necessities*, pp. 44–48, 296–97; Hill, *Society and Puritanism in Pre-Revolutionary England*, chap. 4. Canny, *Kingdom and Colony*, usefully reminds us that migration to the "new world was generally less attractive to English people than was migration to England's nearer colony, Ireland"; see esp. pp. 98–100.

4 Amussen, *Ordered Society*, pp. 35–66; Wrightson, *Earthly Necessities*, pp. 58–67; Kussmaul, *Servants in Husbandry in Early Modern England*; Guasco, "Settling with Slavery."

5 The major study of participation in the courts is Herrup, *The Common Peace*; for the range of courts available in one place, see Wrightson and Levine, *Poverty and Piety in an English Village*, esp. chap. 5.

6 Underdown, *A Freeborn People*; Hindle, *The State and Social Change in Early Modern England*.

7 Stoyle, *Soldiers and Strangers*, p. 116.

8 Underdown, *A Freeborn People*, esp. pp. 23–7, 31, 36, traces these issues in elite and popular politics; see also Pocock, *The Ancient Constitution and the Feudal Law*, esp. pp. 45–47, for the history of the idea. For the political uses of the ancient constitution, see Hill, "The Norman Yoke," in *Puritanism and Revolution*. Thomas Scott of Canterbury was particularly likely to use the term "slavery" to refer to abuses of royal power. See *Proceedings in Parliament, 1628*, 6:241; for quotes, see 2:282, 3:8, and 3:193. For other parliamentary uses, see 2:69, 2:73, and 2:153, which suggest that billeting without compensation and imprisonment without trial are marks of slavery.

9 *Proceedings in Parliament 1628*, 2:66; Dolan, "Ashes and 'the Archive,'" p. 396. For immigrants to England, see Wrightson, *Earthly Necessities*, pp. 157, 165–67; Cottret, *The Huguenots in England*; Mitchell, "'It will be easy to make money'"; and Luu, *Immigrants and the Industries of London*, pp. 3–4, 17–21, 302–8, and chaps. 4 and 5.

10 For Mandeville, see Walvin, *Black and White*, pp. 4–5; Greenblatt, *Marvellous Possessions*, chap. 2.

11 Fuller, *Voyages in Print*, pp. 1–2, 11; Walvin, *Black and White*, p. 17.

12 Morgan, "'Some Could Suckle over Their Shoulder'"; compare the fantastic historical stories in Holinshed's *Chronicles* (1587), one of Shakespeare's major sources: Hannaford, *Race*, pp. 162–64.

13 Ohlmeyer, "'Civilizinge of those Rude Partes.'" For the intellectual framework, see McGinnis and Williamson, "Britain, Race, and the Iberian World Empire"; and

Muldoon, *Identity on the Medieval Irish Frontier*, pp. 66–67, 79–81, 89–92. Muldoon suggests Ireland provided more of a model for English relations with Indians than African slaves; for a full discussion of writings on race and Africa, see Morgan, " 'Some Could Suckle over Their Shoulder.' "

14 Walvin, *Black and White*, pp. 1, 7; Milton, *Big Chief Elizabeth*, pp. 4, 64–72, 366–72; Vaughan, "Powhatans Abroad."

15 Walvin, *Black and White*, p. 31; Morgan, " 'Some Could Suckle over Their Shoulder,' " pp. 176–77. Hawkins is served by two recent biographies: Hazlewood, *The Queen's Slave Trader*, and Kelsey, *Sir John Hawkins*.

16 For a summary of the vast literature on the concept of race, see Chaplin, "Race." See also Hannaford, *Race*, esp. part 1; Loomba, *Shakespeare, Race, and Colonialism*, esp. chap. 1; Wheeler, *The Complexion of Race*, esp. the introduction; and Smedley, *Race in North America*, chaps. 1 and 2.

17 This account draws on Hannaford's magisterial *Race*; the passage from Best is quoted on page 166. For the curse on the sons of Ham and its changing relationship to ideas of race, geography, and slavery, see Braude, "The Sons of Noah."

18 Hannaford, *Race*, esp. pp. 172–84; Wheeler, *The Complexion of Race*, pp. 6–17.

19 Cary Helyar to William Helyar, 3 December 1659, DD/WHh 1151/21.

20 The classic account of these negative ideas associated with blackness is Jordan, *White Over Black*, esp. part 1. For more recent discussions, see Loomba, *Shakespeare, Race, and Colonialism*, chaps. 1 and 2; Korhonen, " 'Washing the Ethiopian White' "; Hall, *Things of Darkness*; and Parker and Hendricks, *Women, "Race," and Writing*. Goldenberg, *The Curse of Ham*, pp. 198–99, makes a distinction between aesthetic preferences and racial prejudice.

21 Pérotin-Dumon, "French, English, and Dutch in the Lesser Antilles"; Taylor, *American Colonies*, pp. 99–111; Andrews, *The Colonial Period of American History*, 1:214–16; Andrews, *Trade, Plunder, and Settlement*, esp. chap. 13; Canny, *Kingdom and Colony*, chap. 3, shows that Irish colonists engaged in agriculture, but it was not focused on a staple crop as was that in the Americas.

22 Testimony of Capt. Simon Gourdon, 25 July 1660, CO 1/14/25; compare also 1/14/31, 39, 40. Taylor, *American Colonies*, p. 207; Andrews, *Trade, Plunder, and Settlement*, esp. chaps. 6 and 13.

23 Steele, *The English Atlantic*, esp. pp. 8, 13–14, 21–27; Sobel, *Longitude*, esp. chap. 2.

24 The standard account of the early history of Barbados is Harlow, *History of Barbados*, chap. 1. More recently, see Gragg, *Englishmen Transplanted*, esp. chap. 3; and Puckrein, *Little England*, esp. pp. 7, 28–39. Campbell, *Some Early Barbadian History*, esp. chaps. 2–4, offers a more conventional political account. For the more general history of colonization, see Andrews, *The Colonial Period of American History*, vol. 2, esp. pp. 244–49; and more recently, Dunn, *Sugar and Slaves*.

25 Harlow, *Barbados*, pp. 18–19,25; Puckrein, *Little England*, pp. 37–51; Dunn, *Sugar and Slaves*, p. 49; Gragg, *Englishmen Transplanted*, pp. 29–46.

26 For the early history of Virginia, see Taylor, *American Colonies*, pp. 129–36; Ira Berlin, *Many Thousands Gone*, pp. 29–33; and Morgan, *American Slavery, American Freedom*, esp. pp. 94–95, 136.

27 "Petition of Captain Henry Powell," in "Brief Collection," pp. 36–38; Gragg, Englishmen Transplanted, p. 19.

28 Colt, "Voyage," esp. pp. 66, 69.

29 John Winthrop to Henry Winthrop, 30 January 1629, Winthrop Papers, 2:67.

30 McCusker and Menard, "The Sugar Industry in the Seventeenth Century"; Gragg, Englishmen Transplanted, pp. 88–98; Thomas Verney to Sir Edmund Verney, 10 February 1638/9, Letters and Papers of the Verney Family, pp. 192–95; Colt, "The Voyage of Sir Henry Colt," p. 69.

31 Dunn, Sugar and Slaves, pp. 53–57; Puckrein, Little England, pp. 53–55; Gragg, Englishmen Transplanted, p. 100; Richard Vines to John Winthrop, 19 July 1647, Winthrop Papers, 5:171–72.

32 McCusker and Menard, "The Sugar Industry in the Seventeenth Century," esp. pp. 297–301. There were nonsugar economies; see Shepherd, ed., Slavery without Sugar, esp. Welch, "The Urban Context of the Life of the Enslaved"; also Welch, Slave Society in the City.

33 Dunn, Sugar and Slaves, pp. 70, 74–76; Beckles, White Servitude and Black Slavery in Barbados, pp. 141–42; Gragg, Englishmen Transplanted, p. 146; Taylor, American Colonies, p. 212.

34 Sir George Downing to John Winthrop, 26 August 1645, Winthrop Papers, 5:43; McCusker and Menard, "Sugar Industry," pp. 293–95; Games, Migration and the Origins of the English Atlantic World, p. 47.

35 Taylor, American Colonies, pp. 206–7; Dunn, Sugar and Slaves, pp. 30–35; Andrews, The Colonial Period of American History, 2:258–61; Akenson, If the Irish Ran the World, esp. chap. 2; Gragg, Englishmen Transplanted, pp. 89–91.

36 Kupperman, Providence Island, esp. pp. 18–19.

37 Gragg, Englishmen Transplanted, 45–6; Puckrein, Little England, chaps. 6 and 7.

38 The classic account of the period is Davis, Cavaliers and Roundheads of Barbados; Puckrein, Little England, pp. 92–101.

39 Ligon, A True and Exact History, p. 57.

40 Handler, "Father Antoine Biet's Visit to Barbados in 1654," esp. p. 69.

41 Puckrein, Little England, esp. pp. 105–12; Gragg, Englishmen Transplanted, pp. 46–50.

42 Puckrein, Little England, esp. pp. 112–23; Gardiner, Commonwealth and Protectorate, 2:142.

43 For the 1652 laws, see Acts and Statutes of the Island of Barbados.

44 For the Navigation Acts, see Gardiner, The History of the Commonwealth and Protectorate, 2:146–50; Brenner, Merchants and Revolution, esp. pp. 625–28; Zahedieh, "Economy," in The British Atlantic World, ed. Armitage and Braddick, pp. 51–68, esp. p. 54; Mancke, "Negotiating an Empire," esp. p. 249.

45 Here I take issue with the more optimistic view of Gragg, Englishmen Transplanted; his interpretation (like Ligon's) takes the perspective of the elite, while mine is more focused on their subordinates. In comparison to Jamaica, Barbados was civilized and successful, but it was never without problems; Greene, "Changing Identity in the British Caribbean," pp. 225–27, suggests that the image of Barbados shifted in the 1660s and 1670s to one that was more civilized and more "English" than it had been earlier.

46 The most complete account of the English conquest is Taylor, *The Western Design*; for the mortality, see page 92. See also Battick, "A New Interpretation of Cromwell's Western Design"; Webb, *The Governors-General*, pp. 172–96; Robertson, *Gone Is the Ancient Glory*, pp. 38–44; Andrews, *The Colonial Period of American History*, vol. 3, esp. pp. 12–17, 22–26; and Gardiner, *The History of the Commonwealth and Protectorate*, 4:130–42. Padrón, *Spanish Jamaica*, pp. 179–216, provides an account of the conquest from the Spanish perspective.

47 Padrón, *Spanish Jamaica*, esp. pp. 24–27, 157–68.

48 Ibid., pp. 35, 148–78; Black, *History of Jamaica*, pp. 27–31.

49 For the intersections of war and settlement in the first five years in Jamaica, see Webb, *The Governors-General*, pp. 158–210; Robertson, *Gone Is the Ancient Glory*, pp. 37–44; and Sherlock and Bennett, *The Story of the Jamaican People*, pp. 79–81. For a recent account of the way the memory of the conquest was reshaped, see Robertson, "Rewriting the English Conquest of Jamaica in the Late Seventeenth Century." For the Maroons, see "Journal of Colonel William Beeston," 27 April 1660, February 1663, 1 November 1663, March 1664, BL Add. MSS 12430, fols. 23, 27, 29. See also Carey, *The Maroon Story*, pp. 95–115; see also below, Chapter 5.

50 James Knight, "History of Jamaica," 1 October 1655, 14 January 1657, BL Add. MS 12418, fols. 65v–67, 73v–74.

51 This process is recorded in the "Journal of Colonel Edward Doyley," BL Add. MS 12423, which includes notes from many meetings of the Council of War and commissioners for the island. See, for example, 10 December 1656, fol. 32v; 26 August 1656, fol. 23; 13 October 1656, fols. 26v–27; 12 September 1657, fol. 36v; 10 and 17 November 1657, fols. 40v–41; and 28 June 1658, fols. 52–v. For the promise of opportunity, see Robertson, " 'Stories' and 'Histories' in Late-Seventeenth-Century Jamaica."

52 Technically, privateers or buccaneers operated with a license from the government, while pirates were entirely outside the law.

53 Webb, *The Governors-General*, p. 185; "The Relation of Colonel Doyley on his return from Jamaica to the Lord Chancellor," ca. 1661, BL Add. MSS 11410, fols. 10v–15; Taylor, *Western Design*, pp. 131–32; Zahedieh, " 'A Frugal, Prudential, and Hopeful Trade.' "

54 For a general overview from the British perspective, see Kishlansky, *A Monarchy Transformed*, pp. 201, 237–39, 245–50; and Bridenbaugh and Bridenbaugh, *No Peace Beyond the Line*, pp. 166–82.

55 Kishlansky, *A Monarchy Transformed*, pp. 294–309, 321–25, 331–32; Marx, *Pirates and Privateers of the Caribbean*, esp. pp. 161–65; Pritchard, *In Search of Empire*, pp. 105–6; Bridenbaugh and Bridenbaugh, *No Peace Beyond the Line*, pp. 176–77, 339.

56 For this see, for example, Marx, *Pirates and Privateers of the Caribbean*, esp. chap. 5; Ritchie, *Captain Kidd and the War against the Pirates*, pp. 15–16, 22–26; Black, *Port Royal*, pp. 9–25; Zahedieh, " 'The Wickedest City in the World' "; Linebaugh and Rediker, *The Many-Headed Hydra*, pp. 156–60; and Webb, *The Governors-General*, p. 186.

57 Webb, *The Governors-General*, part 2, esp. pp. 196–210, and for the early years of royal governors, pp. 212–58; it is not until after the governorship of Sir Thomas Modyford

(1664–71) that a reasonably stable civilian government operated. Patterson, *The Sociology of Slavery*, p. 9.

58 Zahedieh, "Trade, Plunder, and Economic Development in Early English Jamaica."

59 The statistics on sugar in the early period are particularly problematic: not only did units of measurement vary (a hogshead could hold anywhere from 800 to 1,600 pounds of sugar), but also trade statistics themselves—based on customs duties paid—are incomplete in the early period. The figures here are drawn from Dunn, *Sugar and Slaves*, pp. 202–4; Sheridan, *Sugar and Slavery*, pp. 22, 493; Shammas, "Changes in English and Anglo-American Consumption from 1550 to 1800," esp. p. 182; and Mintz, *Sweetness and Power*, pp. 13–14, 76–79, 92–96, 108–13.

60 Coe and Coe, *The True History of Chocolate*, esp. pp. 167–72; Mintz, *Sweetness and Power*, esp. pp. 108–10; Pepys, *Diary*, 1:178; 3:226–27; 4:5; 5:64, 139, 329; Lillywhite, *London Coffee Houses*, pp. 108, 282–83; *London Gazette*, for example, 1695, 1698.

61 For the best recent summary of the voluminous research on trade and the colonies, see Zahedieh, "Overseas Expansion and Trade in the Seventeenth Century."

62 Eltis, "The British Transatlantic Slave Trade before 1714"; Eltis, "The Volume and Structure of the Transatlantic Slave Trade," esp. p. 43; Tattersfield, *The Forgotten Trade*, pp. 358–59, 369–70, 375–78.

63 Zahedieh, "Overseas Expansion and Trade in the Seventeenth Century"; Walvin, *Fruits of Empire*, esp. chap. 8.

Chapter Two

1 John Style to "Rt. Hon.," 24 July 1665, CO 1/19/81; Colt, "Voyage," p. 64.

2 Thomas Verney's Account of Barbadoes, Addressed to His Father, Sir Edmund, *Letters and Papers of the Verney Family*, pp. 192–96, esp. 193, 195.

3 For travel writing, see, for example, Fuller, *Voyages in Print*; The State of Jamaica, Sent by Sir Thomas Lynch, 20 September 1683, CO 138/4, pp. 212–28, esp. p. 213. Such inaccuracies are not limited to descriptions; see Robertson, "Re-writing the English Conquest of Jamaica in the Late Seventeenth Century."

4 Greenblatt, *Marvellous Possessions*, esp. pp. 76–77.

5 For the island's reputation for disease and ill health, see Kupperman, "Fear of Hot Climates"; Cary Helyar to William Helyar, 3 December 1659, DD/WHh 1151/21; Sloane, *A Voyage to the Islands*, 1:ix.

6 Ligon, *A True and Exact History*; Accounts of Robert Southwell, 11 July 1676, CO 391/21. Also in his working library were Hakluyt, John Smith, and various other histories. For references to Ligon in later printed sources, see, for example, Oldmixon, *The British Empire in America*, 2:9–10; Sloane, *A Voyage to the Islands*, 1:33.

7 For a full description of the Taylor manuscript, see Buisseret, "The Taylor Manuscript and Seventeenth-Century Jamaica"; his discussion of the failure to publish is on page 53. (Professor Buisseret is preparing an edition of volume 2 of the manuscript for publication with University of West Indies Press.) Volume 1 of Sloane's *Voyage* was published in 1707; Sloane's *Catalogus plantarum* would have provided earlier competition.

8 This summary is drawn from Campbell, "Richard Ligon," in *Some Early Barbadian His-*

tory; and "Richard Ligon," ODNB; Ligon served as executor of Coprario's will; *Calendar of the Committee for Compounding*, vol. 2, 1536; and statements in Ligon, *A True and Exact History*. There are two possible Richard Ligons of about the same age and social standing, but this one is the one whose biography best fits.

9 This discussion is drawn from Taylor's account in "Multum in Parvo," 1:1–145; Buisseret, "The Taylor Manuscript and Seventeenth-Century Jamaica"; Taylor, *Thesaurarium mathematicae*.

10 Ligon, *A True and Exact History*, pp. 1–3; the original plan was that Ligon and Modyford would continue to Antigua after a stop in Barbados.

11 This discussion is drawn from Lobban, *Cape Verde*, esp. pp. 16–27; Duncan, *The Atlantic Islands*, chaps. 8 and 9; and Bigman, *History and Hunger*, esp. pp. 71–78.

12 Ligon, *A True and Exact History*, pp. 7–8. Although the term "Portugal" is used at times to describe mulattoes, there is enough information to suggest that Mendes de Souza was European.

13 Ibid., pp. 12–13.

14 Ibid., p. 13.

15 Ibid., pp. 13–16.

16 Ibid., p. 17.

17 Ibid., pp. 20–21.

18 Taylor, "Multum in Parvo," 1:145–75, esp. pp. 147, 149–50, 162, 164, 166, 170, 175.

19 Thomas Lynch, Gov. of Jamaica, to Lords of Council, 12 June 1682, CO 138/4, pp. 69–73; Lynch to Sir Leoline Jenkins, 20 June 1682, CO 1/48/110. Lynch also found that the colony had neither a house for the governor nor revenue to support him, so he had to live off his own income.

20 Sloane, *A Voyage to the Islands*, 1:2–32.

21 Journal of Abraham Lloyd, Huntington Library HM 648, pp. 22, 47–48; a crucial page of the second log is missing, making it difficult to figure out why the sailors were so panicked about the journey to the West Indies. For middle passage mortality, see Eltis, "The British Transatlantic Slave Trade before 1714," esp. p. 185. Mortality on the crossing from Europe was lower because of the lower density of people; see Eltis, *The Rise of African Slavery in the Americas*, pp. 117–18.

22 Taylor, "Multum in Parvo," 1:170.

23 Ligon, *A True and Exact History*, p. 27; Blome, *A Description of the Island of Jamaica*, pp. 5–8; Taylor, "Multum in Parvo," 2:305, 309–10, 312; *Letters and Papers of the Verney Family*, p. 193.

24 John Scott, "Description of Barbadoes" (ca. 1667), BL Sloane MSS 3662, fol. 62.

25 James Kendall to Committee, 22 August 1690, CO 28/1, fol. 82; Sloane, *A Voyage to the Islands*, vol. 1, xiii.

26 Taylor, "Multum in Parvo," 2:512–13.

27 Deposition of Capt. Symon Gourdon, 25 July 1660, CO 1/14/25; Ligon, *A True and Exact History*, p. 59, and map; Thomas Modyford, "The Condition of Jamaica, 1 October 1664," BL Add. MSS 11410, fols. 19–21, esp. fol. 19v; Taylor, "Multum in Parvo," 2:338.

28 Thomas Modyford, "The Condition of Jamaica, 1 October 1664," BL Add. MSS 11410, fols. 19–21, esp. fol. 19v.

29 "Current State of Jamaica, by Sir Charles Lyttleton," October 1664, CO 1/18/111; "The History and State of Jamaica under Lord Vaughan," MS 159, National Library of Jamaica, p. 18; compare *The Present State of Jamaica*, p. 40.

30 "Observations on the Present State of Jamaica," 14 December 1675, CO 138/2, pp. 110–21, esp. pp. 110, 111; compare "The History and State of Jamaica under Lord Vaughan," MS 159, National Library of Jamaica, p. 8.

31 Taylor, "Multum in Parvo," 2:519–35; the section also includes discussion of potatoes, yams, and Indian provision.

32 Taylor, "Multum in Parvo," 2:306; "Inquiries Recommended to Col Lynch going to Jamaica," 16 December 1670, Sloane MSS 3984, fols. 194–95; the queries—similar to sets of queries developed by the Royal Society in that period—were based on Stubbes, "Observations," "An Enlargement of the Observations," and "The Remainder of the Observations." I am grateful to Cristina Malcolmson for making the link to the Royal Society for me. Some years later, William Whaley told Col. William Helyar that extended illnesses in Jamaica were cured by a trip to the Caymans, where one ate only turtles: William Whaley and Edm. Atcherly to William Helyar, 30 April 1676, DD/WHh 1089/3/39.

33 Ligon, *A True and Exact History*, pp. 60, 63–64; Ligon calls the gray kingbird a "counsellor."

34 Taylor, "Multum in Parvo," 2:340–41, 349, 357, 379–80.

35 Ligon, *A True and Exact History*, pp. 29, 31.

36 Thomas Verney to Sir Edmund Verney, 10 February 1639, *Letters and Papers of the Verney Family*, p. 194; Ligon, *A True and Exact History*, pp. 82, 84.

37 Taylor, "Multum in Parvo," 2:343, 345, 364–65, 388, 391–92, 396, 536, 538–39.

38 Sloane, *A Voyage to the Islands*, 1:xv–xx, xxvii–xxx; for Sloane's reflections on the varieties of foods, see xx–xxvi.

39 Tryon, *Friendly Advice*, pp. 6–7, 50–52.

40 Ligon, *A True and Exact History*, pp. 29, 43–44.

41 Ibid., pp. 85–86; Gragg, *Englishmen Transplanted*, pp. 19, 99–100; Dunn, *Sugar and Slaves*, pp. 61–64, 75–76, 85–91; Games, *Migration and the Origins of the English Atlantic World*, pp. 126–28. For the sugar revolution generally, see Higman, "The Sugar Revolution"; John Scott in 1667 placed the arrival of sugar in 1640.

42 "Observations on the Present State of Jamaica," 14 December 1675, CO 138/2, pp. 110–21, esp. p. 110.

43 Ligon, *A True and Exact History*, pp. 54–55.

44 Taylor, "Multum in Parvo," 2:252–53, 328–33; compare Robertson, "Re-writing the English Conquest of Jamaica in the Late Seventeenth Century."

45 Ligon, *A True and Exact History*, pp. 55–58; compare Cary Helyar to William, 3 December 1659, "with as much credit and splendor one may live here as at home," DD/WHh 1151/21.

46 Taylor, "Multum in Parvo," 2:400, 503–4, 511, 513.

47 Beckles, *White Servitude and Black Slavery*, p. 42; Sacks, *The Widening Gate*, pp. 252–55; the allegations of kidnapping were sufficiently common that it gave rise to the term "barbadosed" to describe such activities.

48 Ligon, *A True and Exact History*, pp. 43–45; compare Beckles, *White Servitude and Black Slavery*.

49 Taylor, "Multum in Parvo," 2:536–37.

50 Ligon, *A True and Exact History*, pp. 46, 50, 53, 57. The assertion about slaves coming from different areas of Africa was, at best, only partially true; it is a recommendation that goes back to Plato, but the planned rising in 1675 was revealed by a slave who understood the two Coromantee slaves who were discussing the plot; Plato, *The Laws*, 256–59. I am grateful to Dr. Charles Micallef for this reference.

51 Ligon, *A True and Exact History*, pp. 50, 53–54.

52 Ibid., pp. 50–51. For African beliefs, see Gomez, *Exchanging Our Country Marks*, pp. 94, 112, 128–29. Gomez suggests that the Igbo were particularly likely to commit suicide; in Works Progress Administration accounts from the Sea Islands, there are legends of slaves who "fly" back to Africa, but only African-born slaves had this power. See *Exchanging Our Country Marks*, pp. 116–20, 127–28.

53 Ligon, *A True and Exact History*, pp. 47, 50–51.

54 Ibid., pp. 44, 47, 48, 52–53; for swimming, compare Marees, *Description and Historical Account of the Gold Kingdom of Guinea* (1602), p. 26.

55 Ligon, *A True and Exact History*, pp. 48–50. This question of conversion was a long-term one in the islands; see Chapter 4.

56 Ibid., pp. 47, 51.

57 Ibid., pp. 16, 51; because Ligon's focus on breasts is not unique, it is difficult to trace it directly in seventeenth-century sources. In modern scholarship, one part of the passage is quoted, for instance, by Dunn, *Sugar and Slaves*, p. 247, as example of his positive attention to slaves; Beckles, *Natural Rebels*, p. 24, quotes the second half as a reference to women's work. The description of women working also appears in Bush, *Slave Women*, pp. 14–15. For the use of long, hanging breasts in descriptions of Africa, see Morgan, " 'Some Could Suckle over Their Shoulder,' " esp. pp. 181, 183–84, 188–89; and Marees, *Description and Historical Account of the Gold Kingdom of Guinea* (1602), p. 24.

58 For men's genitals, see, for example, Marees, *Description and Historical Account of the Gold Kingdom of Guinea* (1602), p. 29; Morgan has elaborated this argument both in " 'Some Could Suckle over Their Shoulder' " and *Laboring Women*. I differ from her only in arguing that the early discourse on Africans has not yet been racialized.

59 Neville, *The Isle of Pines*, p. 89.

60 Taylor, "Multum in Parvo," 2:539–40, 542, 544–46. While Taylor does not cite Ligon, the story is attributed to a Barbadian planter and is substantially the same as Ligon, *A True and Exact History*, pp. 50–51.

61 Taylor, "Multum in Parvo," 2:542–43; compare Morgan, " 'Some Could Suckle over Their Shoulder,' " esp. pp. 184, 188. Taylor may be drawing on Marees, who also notes that women worked the day after giving birth, and that children walked at a very young age; Marees, *Description and Historical Account of the Gold Kingdom of Guinea* (1602), pp. 23–24.

62 Taylor, "Multum in Parvo," 2:541–42, 546–47; for rebellions, see esp. pp. 548–54, 513.

63 Sloane, *A Voyage to the Islands*, 1:xlvii–liv; Rath, "African Music in Seventeenth-Century

Jamaica"; Kriz, "Curiosities, Commodities, and Transplanted Bodies." Sloane's observations about how children were carried distinguished them from the common European practice of carrying babies in front, in a sling; see Yavneh, "To Bare or Not to Bare."

64 Ligon, *A True and Exact History*, p. 53.

65 John Style to Principal Secretary, 4 January 1670, CO 1/25/1; Tryon, *Friendly Advice*. For a full discussion of Tryon's antislavery ideas (which were published not as an account of the island, but separately), see Chapter 6.

66 For the history of white slavery in the Mediterranean, which played a vivid role in the English imaginary, see Davis, *Christian Slaves, Muslim Masters*. Guasco, "Settling with Slavery," refers to the legal possibility of slavery in some sixteenth-century statutes on poverty but ignores the fact that these were never used.

67 Ligon, *A True and Exact History*, pp. 53, 54.

68 See Amussen, " 'The Part of a Christian Man.' "

69 Sloane MSS 2441, fol. 11v–12; "History and State of Jamaica," MS 159 (National Library of Jamaica), pp. 61–62; Lord Vaughan to Council for Trade and Plantations, 28 January 1676, CO 138/3, pp. 32–38; Taylor, "Multum in Parvo," 2:538.

70 "Certain Propositions for the better accommodating the foreign Plantations with servants reported from the Committee to the Council of Foreign Plantations," 1664, CO 1/18/96.

71 Ibid.; Thomas Modyford to Sir Henry Bennet, 10 May 1664, CO 1/18/65; Nine Articles Extracted from Modyford's letter of 10 May, along with Council decisions, 10 August 1664, CO 1/18/85, pp. 92, 93; "Petition of Merchants, Planters, and Masters of Ships trading to the Plantations," 12 July 1664, *Calendar of State Papers, Colonial*, no. 769, p. 220.

72 August 1672, CO 140/3, pp. 315–16; Governor Atkins to Council, 15–25 August 1676, CO 29/2, pp. 91–92, esp. p. 92; Gov. Edwyn Stede to Lords of Council, 30 August 1688, CO 29/4, pp. 7–15.

Chapter Three

1 Dunn, *Sugar and Slaves*, pp. 154, 164.

2 For the Helyar plantation, see Bennett, "Cary Helyar," "William Whaley," and "William Dampier"; and Dunn, *Sugar and Slaves*, pp. 212–22. For some more general issues around the income of sugar colonies, see Davis, *Rise of the Atlantic Economies*, esp. pp. 252–54, 259.

3 "A Moderate Calculation of the Annual Charge and Produce of a Plantation in Barbados containing 100 acres of land," 7 March 1688, BL Sloane MSS 3984, pp. 214–20, esp. p. 217.

4 Ligon, *A True and Exact History*, p. 86. The number of planters in the 1640s is unclear; estimates range from 8,300 to 11,200, making 10,000 a reasonable figure. See Handler and Lange, *Plantation Slavery in Barbados*, p. 16; and Dunn, "The Barbados Census of 1680."

5 Dunn, *Sugar and Slaves*, pp. 170–75. In one Jamaica parish in 1680, forty-eight (19 percent) of the landowners held 80 percent of the slaves (p. 174); for success on a smaller scale somewhat later, see Burnard, *Mastery, Tyranny, and Desire*, esp. chap. 2.

While there is little seventeenth-century data on other agricultural regimes in Jamaica, for the later period see the essays in Shepherd, ed., *Slavery without Sugar*; Jamaica Archives, Chancery Court 1A/3/1, Samuel Lewis vs. Samuel Man (1684), refers to cattle pens near Spanish Town.

6 Bennett, "Cary Helyar," esp. pp. 56–61; Sloane, *A Voyage to the Islands*, p. lxiv. For younger sons, see Whyman, *Sociability and Power in Late Stuart England*.

7 Cary Helyar to William Helyar, 24 September 1670, DD/WHh/ 1089/3/16a; Cary Helyar to William Helyar, 15 April 1671, DD/WHh 1089/3/18. It is likely that this calculation would have been similar to that offered by Ligon, *A True and Exact History*, esp. pp. 108–17.

8 5 July 1672, CO 1/29/5. For the cacao blight, see Bennett, "Cary Helyar," pp. 64–65; for the curse, see "The Present State of Jamaica in a letter from Mr. Nevil to the Earl of Carlisle," ca. 1677, BL Add. MSS 12429, fols. 76–85, esp. fols. 79v–80.

9 Cary Helyar to William Helyar, 15 April 1671, DD/WHh 1089/3/18.

10 Cary Helyar to William Helyar, 12 and 25 January 1672, DD/WHh 1089/3/27. Achiote seeds (from the arnotto) produced a red dye.

11 For a possible alternative outcome and the significance of the demographic lottery, see Craton and Walvin, *A Jamaican Plantation*, esp. chaps. 2 and 3. William was not the only brother to invest in the West Indies with no return; see Thomas Povey to Mrs. Povey in Barbados, 3 May 1659, BL Add. MSS 11411, fols. 80–82.

12 20 January 1659, CO 1/13/62.

13 11 July 1681, CO 1/47/27.

14 Cary Helyar to William Helyar, 10 September 1671, DD/WHh 1089/3/22; Cary Helyar to William Helyar, 12 and 25 January 1672, DD/WHh 1089/3/27. For later instances of problems, see Whaley to William Helyar, January 1675, DD/WHh 1090/2/23; and Affidavit of Charles Painter and William Draper, 28 April 1685, DD/WHh/Addenda Papers 12/29. For sugar generally, see also Higman, "The Sugar Revolution"; and Blackburn, *The Making of New World Slavery*, pp. 332–35. The organization of sugar production as it developed in the English West Indies was not the only possible structure; in Brazil, small producers brought their canes to central sugar mills. See Dunn, *Sugar and Slaves*, pp. 189–98; Mintz, *Sweetness and Power*, pp. 46–56; and McCusker and Menard, "The Sugar Industry in the Seventeenth Century," pp. 297–302.

15 Ligon, *A True and Exact History*, pp. 88–89; Dunn, *Sugar and Slaves*, pp. 191–92; MSS Rawl. A 348, p. 10.

16 Taylor, "Multum in Parvo," 2:535.

17 "Observations on the Present State of Jamaica," 14 December 1675, CO 138/2, p. 110; Henry Barham, Account of Jamaica, BL Sloane MSS 3918, fol. 39; Bennett, "William Whaley," pp. 122–23.

18 MSS Rawl. A 348, pp. 8–9; Dunn, *Sugar and Slaves*, pp. 190–92.

19 John Austin to William Helyar, 22 February 1696, DD/WHh 1089/3/69; Robert Hall to William and John Helyar, 16 April 1700, DD/WHh 1089/3/83.

20 Jamaica 3, CO 700; the map presumably dates from Lynch's second term as governor from 1682 to 1684; Dunn, *Sugar and Slaves*, pp. 212–22.

21 John Helyar to brother William Helyar, 30 June 1690, DD/WHh 1151/43. For mor-

tality generally, see Dunn, *Sugar and Slaves*, chap. 9; for slaves, see Palmer, "The Slave Trade," esp. pp. 26–28. It is possible that in the first year of arrival European mortality was higher than African; see Blackburn, *The Making of New World Slavery*, p. 315; Burnard, "Not a Place for Whites?"

22 Whaley to William Helyar, 18 January 1676, DD/WHh 1090/2/1b; in spite of Whaley's assertion, yaws is not usually considered a venereal disease. Whaley and Edward Atcherly to William Helyar, 30 April 1676, DD/WHh 1089/3/39; Whaley to Helyar, October 1673, DD/WHh 1089/3/34; also 20 June 1672, 20 May 1673, DD/WHh/Addenda Papers 12/11, 12/12; Letter of 19 March 1677, DD/WHh 1089, Bound Volume, Letter Book; Joseph Bryan to Matthew Bryan, 12 July 1677, DD/ WHh 1089/3/44; John Helyar to William Helyar, 13 October 1687, DD/WHh 1089/ 3/10. For mortality in England, see Wrightson, *Earthly Necessities*, pp. 221–22, 229–30. For most years, English mortality rates ranged between 23.5 and 28.4 per 1,000: Wrigley and Schofield, *The Population History of England*, pp. 311, 317–18.

23 For a full discussion of the diseases of the islands, see Dunn, *Sugar and Slaves*, pp. 300–311; Walvin, *Black Ivory*, pp. 56, 119, 120–22; and Blackburn, *The Making of New World Slavery*, p. 339. Seventeenth-century evidence on slave medical practice is slender, but later generations maintained African healing practices; see Bilby and Handler, "Obeah." Curtin's estimate of mortality is based on the late eighteenth century, but seventeenth-century evidence appears comparable; see Curtin, "The Sugar Revolution and the Settlement of the Caribbean," esp. p. 81.

24 10 May 1664, CO 1/18/65.

25 1 October 1664, CO 1/18/108; Dunn, *Sugar and Slaves*, p. 303.

26 18 September 1683, CO 1/60/53; Dunn, *Sugar and Slaves*, p. 306. This may be what Governor Lynch of Jamaica complained of when he wrote in 1683, "In 16 or 18 days I hardly slept, but swellings and gouty pains falling into my legs and feet eased my head, so that I was able to be carried abroad"; 22 February 1683, CO 1/51/43.

27 Taylor, "Multum in Parvo," 1:182–94, esp. pp. 193–94; Buisseret, "Taylor Manuscript." Modern scholars do not know what the dry bellyache was, though it was possibly caused in part by drinking rum processed in lead pipes; see Dunn, *Sugar and Slaves*, p. 306. Sloane frequently associates the bellyache with excessive alcohol consumption; the symptoms include vomiting and pain, as well as loss of mobility. See Sloane, *A Voyage to the Islands*, 1:cv, cviii, cxviii–cxix, cxxxvi, cxl.

28 5 January 1700, CO 138/10, pp. 28–37. For the smallpox in Barbados, see 8 January 1686, CO 1/59/7; 17 November 1685, CO 1/58/104; 21 September 1685, CO 1/58/59; and 1 October 1695, CO 31/5, pp. 68–69. See also Kiple and Ornelas, "After the Encounter," esp. p. 60.

29 12 August 1691, CO 138/7, p. 20; 29 August 1682, CO 29/3, pp. 133–40.

30 10 February 1693, CO 28/2/3.

31 23 March 1693, CO 137/3/5; Dunn, *Sugar and Slaves*, p. 163.

32 25 September 1694, CO 28/2/66.

33 Letter from Capt. Hall to Col. Lawes, in Assembly Sessional Papers for 4 June 1696, CO 140/6, p. 353.

34 This appears to be part of the complaint of Mr. Hodge in CO 29/7, pp. 217–35.

35 30 September 1680, BL Sloane MSS 2724, fol. 242v.

36 Tryon, *Friendly Advice*, pp. 50–51; Sloane, *A Voyage to the Islands*, p. ix.

37 30 January 1700, CO 29/7, p. 42; 14 May 1700, CO 28/4/46. This is an early example of the fear of "criolian contagion"; Abrahams, "Questions of Criolian Contagion," esp. p. 76.

38 Nicholas Blake to "Honored Sir," 12 November 1669, CO 1/24/94.

39 See, for example, William Dampier to William Helyar, 13 January 1675, DD/WHh 1090/2/60; Linebaugh and Rediker, in *Many-Headed Hydra*, pp. 110–11, suggest a more literal reading of such language, but they ignore the social realities of the West Indies. As in England earlier in the century, claims of equality in part reflected the uneven nature of social mobility; see Amussen, *Ordered Society*, pp. 147–48.

40 Whaley to William Helyar, 20 June 1672, DD/WHh Addenda Papers 12/11; Cary Helyar to William Helyar, 7 March 1672, DD/WHh 1089/3/24; William Whaley to William Helyar, 9 December 1675, DD/WHh 1090/2/1; Whaley to Helyar, 27 January 1675, DD/WHh 1090/2/30. Compare Cary Helyar to William Helyar, 25 January 1672, DD/WHh 1089/3/27; there is some evidence that when the land was initially cleared, white servants worked in the fields. See Bennett, "Cary Helyar," pp. 62–63; and Robert Hall to ?, 30 June 1701, DD/WHh 1090/3/4. For labor generally, see Dunn, *Sugar and Slaves*, pp. 248–49. In the early years of sugar in Barbados, white servants did the same work as slaves; see Beckles, *White Servitude and Black Slavery*, pp. 125–26, 157–59; and Beckles, *Natural Rebels*, p. 29.

41 Cary Helyar to William Helyar, 7 March 1672, DD/WHh 1089/3/24.

42 Whaley to William Helyar, DD/WHh 1090/2/1b, 18 January 1676; similarly, Whaley and Atcherly to Helyar, 30 April 1676, DD/WHh 1089/3/39; Cary Helyar to William Helyar, 15 April 1671, 22 May 1671, and Whaley to William Helyar, 9 December 1675, 1089/3/18, 20, 1090/2/1a. For continued complaints, see, for example, John Helyar to William Helyar, 30 November 1686, DD/WHh 1089/3/5; and Robert Hall to John and William Helyar, 16 April 1700, DD/WHh 1089/3/83. The skills were vital, so it was impossible to just recruit "servants"; compare Beckles, *White Servitude and Black Slavery*, esp. pp. 125–30.

43 Whaley to William Helyar, 8 December 1675, DD/WHh 1090/2/21.

44 Whaley to William Helyar, 27 January 1675, DD/WHh 1090/2/28–29; draft in DD/WHh 1090/2/24, and typescript copy in 1090/2/61. For Dampier, see Bennett, "William Dampier"; for an account of the initial discovery of the doctor's wife in London, see Thomas Hillyard to Col. William Helyar, 15 April 1674, DD/WHh 1089/3/37; William Helyar to uncle Col. William Helyar, 29 June 1677, DD/WHh/Addenda Papers 12/20; Edward Atcherly and Joseph Bryan to William Helyar, 2 March 1677, DD/WHh 1089/3/42. For the most recent biography of Dampier, see Preston and Preston, *Pirate of Exquisite Mind*.

45 John Helyar to William Helyar, 20 December 1686, DD/WHh 1089/3/7.

46 Cary Helyar to William Helyar, 12 January 1672, DD/WHh 1089/3/27. Jack arrived in Jamaica "with as many shirts as backs": Cary Helyar and Whaley to William Helyar, June 1672, DD/WHh/Addenda Papers 12/23; Whaley to Helyar, 23 September 1672, DD/WHh 1089/3/31; Whaley to William Helyar, 25 March 1675, DD/WHh 1090/2/33.

47 Letter of William Helyar to Edward Atcherly, Cousin Helyar, and Joseph Bryan, 1 July

1677, DD/WHh/1089, Bound Volume, Letter Book; Thomas Hillyard to William Helyar, 15 April 1674, DD/WHh 1089/3/37. Although the woman involved was alleged to be married to the doctor, Hillyard was skeptical about the marriage; see Whaley to Helyar, 8 December 1675, DD/WHh 1090 2/21. Eltis, *Rise of African Slavery in the Americas*, p. 50; the 1670s and 1690s featured particularly low levels of white migration to the Caribbean.

48 17 March 1674, CO 1/31/21; compare Barbados petition in CO 29/2, pp. 29–36; Beckles, *White Servitude and Black Slavery*, pp. 56–58, 63–64; and Pestana, *The English Atlantic in an Age of Revolution*, pp. 207–10.

49 15 August 1676, CO 29/2, p. 92.

50 Atkin to Committee, 26 October 1680, CO 1/46/26, fol. 63v; Sir Richard Dutton, 1681, CO 29/3, fol. 59; 1684, CO 1/56/118.

51 CO 138/3, 331–38, esp. pp. 333–34.

52 8 January 1686, CO 29/3, pp. 358–60; 26 June 1690, CO 29/4, pp. 218–27, esp. pp. 221–22; 3 June 1686, CO 140/2, pp. 82–83; 10 June 1686, CO 140/2, p. 85; 8 January 1686, CO 1/59/7. The records from Jamaica for the relevant period about the pardon are missing, but the request for delay came in a letter from Governor Kendall on 26 June 1690; see CO 29/4, esp. pp. 221–22. The act itself was later repealed, with no extension to seven years; 17 February 1691, 16–17 March 1691, CO 31/4, pp. 162–65.

53 23 March 1695, CO 28/2/81.

54 25 October 1697, CO 28/3/44, 44I; CO 138/9, pp. 79, 81, 90.

55 12 July 1698, CO 28/3/68; 5 September 1698, CO 31/5/369.

56 6 April 1676, CO 29/2, pp. 29–36; 17 March 1674, CO 1/31/21.

57 8 March 1697, CO 138/9, p. 79.

58 Tryon, *Friendly Advice*, p. 208; 28 January 1692, CO 140/2, p. 141–42.

59 This silence is common; see Dunn, *Sugar and Slaves*, pp. 225–26. Both Eltis, *The Rise of African Slavery in the Americas*, chap. 3, and Blackburn, *The Making of New World Slavery*, pp. 350–63, argue, for very different reasons, that slavery was not necessarily a rational economic choice; most recently this has been challenged by Drescher, "White Atlantic?," arguing that the costs of resistance by enslaved white labor would have been significantly higher than the costs of importing slaves.

60 Guasco, "Settling with Slavery."

61 Eltis, *The Rise of African Slavery in the Americas*, esp. chap. 3; a similar argument appears in Eltis, "Europeans and the Rise and Fall of African Slavery in the Americas."

62 Blackburn, *The Making of New World Slavery*, esp. pp. 350–63; Eltis, *The Rise of African Slavery in the Americas*; Dunn, *Sugar and Slaves*, pp. 226–29.

63 "Certain Propositions for the better accommodating the Foreign Plantations with servants," CO 1/18/96 (while this is in the records for 1664, Eltis, *The Rise of African Slavery in the Americas*, p. 62, dates it in the 1650s).

64 Cary Helyar to William Helyar, 24 September 1670, DD/WHh 1089/3/16a. Before Cary had planted Bybrook, he appears to have been a slave trader. See Bennett, "Cary Helyar," p. 55; Cary Helyar to William Helyar, 27 November 1671, DD/WHh 1089/3/21; Cary Helyar to William Helyar, 12 January 1672, DD/WHh 1089/3/27; and Cary Helyar to William Helyar, 7 March 1672, DD/WHh 1089/3/24. Ligon, *A True and Exact History*, p. 46.

65 Whaley to William Helyar, 27 January 1675, DD/WHh 1090/2/24; Whaley to William Helyar, 22 April 1675, DD/WHh, 1090/2/9; Cary Helyar/Whaley to William Helyar, June 1672, DD/WHh/Addenda Papers 12/23; Inventory of Whaley's estate, n.d., DD/WHh 1090/2/4.

66 Davies, *The Royal African Company*, pp. 41–44.

67 Petition to King, 11 May 1661, CO 31/1, fol. 24v.

68 4 April 1673, CO 1/30/19.

69 16 April 1675, CO 31/1, pp. 178–79.

70 Petition of Planters of Jamaica, 29 November 1680, CO 138/3, p. 478.

71 6 May 1683, CO 138/4, pp. 154–62, esp. pp. 156–57.

72 2 March 1698, CO 28/3/61; 5 January 1700, CO 138/10, pp. 28–37.

73 Galenson, *Traders, Planters, and Slaves*, pp. 59, 161; Davies, *The Royal African Company*, p. 363; Davies's calculations suggest that the Royal African Company shipped over 35,000 slaves to Barbados and almost 29,000 to Jamaica between 1673 and 1700; this number excludes the slaves brought by interlopers and those who arrived before 1673. Taking the whole period from 1662 to 1700, Eltis has calculated that 94,029 slaves arrived in Jamaica, while 120,113 arrived in Barbados; see Eltis, "The British Transatlantic Slave Trade before 1714," p. 48. From 1660 to 1700, just over 54,000 people came from England, again mostly to Jamaica and Barbados, yet the white population of Barbados dropped from about 30,000 in 1650 to only 15,400 in 1700; that of Jamaica only rose from 3,400 in 1660, to 7,300 in 1700. See Galenson, *Traders, Planters, and Slaves*, p. 4; compare Burnard and Morgan, "The Dynamics of the Slave Market."

74 Dunn, *Sugar and Slaves*, pp. 320–31; Whaley to William Helyar, 27 January 1675, DD/WHh 1090/2/28; William Whaley to William Helyar, 22 April 1675, DD/WHh 1090/2/9.

75 John Austin to William Helyar, 7 August 1690, DD/WHh 1089/3/57; John Austin to John Helyar, 23 August 1695, DD/WHh 1089/3/64; John Austin to William Helyar, 13 January 1698, DD/WHh 1089/3/77; Robert Hall to William and John Helyar, 16 April 1700, DD/WHh 1089/3/83. For the impact of hurricanes in general, see Mulcahy, *Hurricanes and Society*, esp. chap. 3; Mulcahy does not mention the 1687 hurricane.

76 For Helyar's attitudes, see DD/WHh 1089, Bound Volume, Letter Book, esp. William Helyar to Thomas Hillyard, 26 August 1678. There are inventories of slaves from 1678 to 1709 in DD/WHh 1089/1, nos. 1, 2, 3, 5, 6, 7, 8, 10, 12, 13; and Inventory, 16 April 1700, DD/WHh 1089/7/116. The treatment of nursing women appears unusual, but it is not clear whether the peculiarity is of the Bybrook practice or whether earlier planters also made fewer demands on nursing women.

77 Eltis, *The Rise of African Slavery in the Americas*, p. 117; Klein and Engerman, "Long-Term Trends in African Mortality"; Galenson, *Traders, Planters, and Slaves*, p. 39.

78 14 September 1685, CO 31/3, p. 122.

79 Littleton, *Groans*, p. 14; MSS Rawl. A 348, pp. 3–5 passim; for the authorship and dating of this, see Handler, *Supplement*, pp. 56–57.

80 Littleton, *Groans*, p. 18; MSS Rawl. A 348, pp. 3–5.

81 Ligon, *A True and Exact History*, pp. 37, 43–44; Taylor, "Multum in Parvo," 2:538–39; December 1696, DD/WHh 1089/3/72; "Necessaries to be sent over for Planters use

that are much wanting, from Robert Hall," ca. 1700, DD/WHh 1089/6/16; Handler, "Plantation Slave Settlements," esp. pp. 133–34. For slave commerce, see Beckles, *Natural Rebels*, pp. 77–78; and Mintz and Hall, *Origins of the Jamaican Internal Marketing System*, esp. pp. 4–13.

82 MSS Rawl. A 348, pp. 6–8; Drax is an early planter who used slaves as overseers for certain classes of work, though they were clearly subordinate to white overseers.

83 MSS Rawl. A 348, pp. 9–14; Ligon, *A True and Exact History*, pp. 89–92; Dunn, *Sugar and Slaves*, pp. 192–97.

84 Richard Smyth to John Helyar, 18 March 1690, DD/WHh 1089/2/32; Littleton, *Groans*, pp. 19–20.

85 Ligon, *A True and Exact History*, p. 91; MSS Rawl. A 348, pp. 10–11, 19.

86 Whaley to William Helyar, 9 December 1675, DD/WHh 1090/2/1a; Letters of 2 December 1678 to Thomas Hillyard and Sir Thomas Modyford, and 24 February 1679 to Thomas Hillyard, DD/WHh 1089, Bound Volume, Letter Book. The relationship may have been facilitated when Cary apparently lived at Modyford's house when first settling Bybrook; see Bennett, "Cary Helyar," pp. 62–63. The sexual exploitation of enslaved women by masters (and other white men) was common and a central component of the oppression of slaves, but evidence for it in this period is relatively sparse; Dunn, *Sugar and Slaves*, pp. 252–53; Beckles, *Centering Woman*, chap. 2, esp. pp. 23–24; Bush, *Slave Women*, esp. pp. 26, 28–29.

87 Beckles, "Social and Political Control," esp. p. 201. Craton, *Empire, Enslavement, and Freedom*, p. 169, suggests that Jamaican practice remained more flexible than the theory; in the later period it was likely that a slave owner would have made financial provision for his mistress and slave children. See, for example, Burnard, *Mastery, Tyranny, and Desire*, p. 243.

88 Whaley to Helyar, 9 December 1675, DD/WHh 1090/2/1. The precise significance of the term "Brazil Negro" beyond her origin is unclear; nor is it clear that the mother's husband was Cary's mistress's father.

89 Ligon, *A True and Exact History*, pp. 48, 50; Taylor, "Multum in Parvo," 2:540. Compare Sloane, *A Voyage to the Islands*, pp. xlvii–lii; Kriz, "Curiosities, Commodities, and Transplanted Bodies"; Rath, "African Music in Seventeenth-Century Jamaica"; Parry, "Plantation and Provision Ground"; 16 December 1690, CO 140/5, p. 70; 8 October 1680, CO 391/3, pp. 206–7; and Lord Francis Russell to Committee, 23 March 1695, CO 28/2/81.

90 Whaley to Helyar, 28 June 1675, DD/WHh 1090/2/17; Dampier to Helyar, *Somerset and Dorset Notes and Queries*, esp. p. 157.

91 "A Brief Account of what happened in . . . Jamaica . . . 1694," CO 137/1, fols. 193–96, esp. fols. 193v–194, 194v.

92 15 September 1679, CO 138/3, pp. 327–31; compare 28 January 1676, CO 138/3, pp. 32–38.

93 14 November 1679, CO 140/2, p. 52.

94 Cary Helyar to William Helyar, 10 September 1671, DD/WHh 1089/3/22; compare, for example, Cary Helyar to William Helyar, 15 April 1671 and 22 May 1671, DD/WHh 1089/3/18, 1089/3/20; and 20 May 1673, William Whaley to William Helyar, DD/WHh Addenda Papers 12/12, 12/13. Two copies of this letter survive in the archive.

95 2 December 1695, CO 137/3/96; compare 11 February 1690, CO 29/4, p. 191.

96 Letters to Thomas Hillyard from 1678 to 1686, esp. 5 September 1681, 1 September 1684, 19 January 1686, and n.d. [late August 1686], DD/WHh 1089, Bound Volume, Letter Book; 13 October 1687, DD/WHh 1089/3/10, gives the final settlement. John Helyar's observation is 27 March 1687 (really 1686), DD/WHh 1089/3/2; the accounts of the struggle are found in 16 September 1686, 1089/3/3; 28 September 1686, 1089/3/4; 15 January 1687, 1089/3/8; and 30 June 1687, 1089/3/9. See also Dunn, *Sugar and Slaves*, pp. 218–19; Jamaica 3, CO 700. Even in the eighteenth century, the possibilities of fraud remained, though then it appears to be heirs to island property living in England who were most vulnerable; see, for example, U.W.I. Library (Mona), Wilson Family Papers and Correspondence, esp. nos. 20 (20 August 1749), 27, 37 (1765), and 104.

97 MSS Rawl. A 348, fols. 13v–14; 11 July 1695, CO 28/2/105, 105i; December 1700, CO 28/4/66.

98 Gov. Atkins to Lords of Trade, CO 29/2, pp. 230–31.

99 Thomas Modyford to Secretary Bennet, 10 May 1664, CO 1/18/65; Lord Willoughby to the King, ca. July 1667, CO 1/21/89; 6 April 1676, CO 29/2, pp. 29–36, esp. pp. 34–35; and 10 November 1676, CO 29/2, esp. pp. 110–11. Another copy of the petition is found in 24 November 1675, CO 1/35/45 (i, ii); and Sir Jonathan Atkins to Sir Joseph Williamson, 3 April 1676, CO 1/36/39.

100 "The State of the Difference as it is Pressed between the Merchants and the planters in relation to Free Trade at the Caribbe Islands," BL Add. MS 11411, fols. 3v–4v, esp. fol. 4.

Chapter Four

1 3 September 1695, CO 28/2/111. For the planters in Barbados, the most important member of the Russell family had been Lord William Russell (see ODNB), a Whig leader in the 1670s and early 1680s who was executed in the Rye House plot in 1683. Governor Russell's relation to Lord William Russell is unclear.

2 For this process of negotiation, see Greene, "Transatlantic Colonization," esp. pp. 269–71.

3 This conjunction has been discussed extensively for Virginia, most notably in Morgan, *American Slavery, American Freedom*, but the process in Barbados and Jamaica was compressed since the slave population of the islands expanded early and rapidly. For the relationship between Locke's notion of freedom and subordination of women, see Pateman, *The Sexual Contract*.

4 Puckrein, *Little England*, esp. chaps. 2, 3, 6–8; Gragg, *Englishmen Transplanted*, chap. 3. See also Dunn, *Sugar and Slaves*, chap. 2, and Harlow, *History of Barbados*. For the studied neutrality of the late 1640s, see Ligon, *A True and Exact History*, p. 57; the details are also laid out in *Some Memoirs of . . . Barbados to the Year 1741*, pp. 30–32.

5 23 October 1663, Jamaica Archives 1B/5/3/1, fols. 87–89; Hanson, *The Laws of Jamaica*, fol. b4, fols. b7v–b8v; Whitson, *Constitutional Development*, pp. 8–23; Dunn, *Sugar and Slaves*, pp. 153–57.

6 Andrews, *The Colonial Period of American History*, 4:57–59, 272–91.

7 *Acts and Statutes of the Island of Barbados*.

8   16 July 1662, Jamaica Archives 1B/5/3/1, p. 51. For the 1664 statutes, see CO 139/1, fols. 44–92v. Modyford's 1670 account, "The Governor of Jamaica's Answers to the Inquiries of His Majesty's Commissioners," is found in CO 138/1, pp. 96–104. For the difficulties of governance in general and the relation of this debate to wider constitutional developments in the colonies, see Greene, *Negotiated Authorities*, chap. 1 and pp. 43–53.

9   12 June 1663, *Calendar of State Papers, Colonial*, no. 478; for the failure to send any laws, see Report Touching the Laws of Barbados, 26 June 1679, BL Egerton MSS 2395, fols. 584–86.

10   Atkins to Lords of Trade, 2/12 June 1678, CO 29/2, pp. 230–32, esp. pp. 230–31.

11   Atkins to Lords of Trade, 10/20 November 1678, CO 29/2, pp. 238–45, esp. p. 241.

12   King to Atkins, 24 July 1679, and Lords of Trade to Atkins, 26 July 1679, CO 29/2, pp. 274–77, 277–86.

13   Atkins to Lords of Trade, 16 October 1679, CO 29/2, pp. 293–97; compare Bilder, *The Transatlantic Constitution*, p. 1.

14   Report by Mr. Serjeant Baldwin re. Laws of Barbados, ca. 1680, CO 29/3, p. 6.

15   "The Governor of Jamaica's Answers to the Inquiries of His Majesty's Commissioners," ca. 1670, CO 138/1, p. 98.

16   Sir Robert Southwell to Gov. Lord Vaughan, 28 July 1676, CO 138/3, pp. 86–89.

17   Review of Laws passed by Assembly and Council of Jamaica (9 October) 1677, CO 138/3, pp. 141–54; Greene, *Negotiated Authorities*, pp. 46–48.

18   For the instructions that outline this, see CO 138/3, pp. 216–44; Whitson, *Constitutional Development*, pp. 81–83; Dunn, *Sugar and Slaves*, pp. 158–59; and Webb, *The Governors-General*, pp. 278–79.

19   Journals of the Assembly, 36 (4 October 1678) and 52 (14 November 1679), CO 140/2; E. of Carlisle to Lords of Trade, 15 September 1679, CO 138/3, pp. 327–31; Webb, *The Governors-General*, pp. 281–83.

20   4 April 1690, CO 28/1, fol. 104v; Assembly of Jamaica, 12, 19–21 April 1677, CO 140/2.

21   Sir Thomas Lynch to Dr. Worsley, 8 August 1673, CO 1/30/58; compare Hanson, *The Laws of Jamaica*, fol. B7, for the Laws of Jamaica as "by-laws."

22   Sir Jonathan Atkins to Lords of Plantations, 10/20 November 1678, CO 29/2, pp. 238–45.

23   See, for example, Council of Barbados to Lords of Trade, 2 March 1698, CO 28/3/61; Gov. Stede to Committee for Trade; 21 September 1685, CO 1/58/59; E. of Carlisle to Lords of Trade and Plantations, 20 June 1679, CO 1/43/76. Cundall, *Governors of Jamaica*, pp. 89, 90–91; Dunn, *Sugar and Slaves*, pp. 158–59.

24   Council of Barbados to Lords of Trade, 12 July 1698, CO 28/3/68; Governor Dutton speech to Barbados Assembly and response, CO 29/3, pp. 59–62; Governor Russell to Lords of Trade, 23 March 1695, CO 28/2/81; Journal of Committee for Trade and Plantations, 8 October 1680, CO 391/3, pp. 206–7; Instructions to Gov. Jonathan Atkins, CO 389/4, 28 February 1674, pp. 87–90; fol. 135, no. 31, urged him to have the assembly pass a law "restraining of any inhuman cruelty" to Christian servants. Journals of Jamaica Assembly, 25 July 1688, CO 140/2, pp. 124–25; when Albermarle was in control, a law to encourage conversion passed in one day.

25 Ligon, A True and Exact History, p. 50; Instructions to Sir Richard Dutton, CO 29/3, 30 October 1680, pp. 37–53, esp. p. 51, is the first occasion when a governor received instructions to pass a law to convert slaves to Christianity, where it is tied to a recommendation to control inhuman severity to servants. A year later, Governor Lynch was given similar instructions; CO 138/4, pp. 17–39, esp. p. 35. Thereafter it becomes a standard part of the instructions to governors: Instructions to D. of Albermarle as Gov. of Jamaica, 1687, CO 138/5, pp. 261–96, esp. p. 286; "Instructions to Lord Inchiquin," 1689, CO 138/6, pp. 247–71, esp. pp. 263–64, where he was asked to "find out the best means to facilitate and encourage the conversion of Negroes"; Instructions to William Beeston, 1692, CO 138/7, pp. 84–107, esp. p. 102; Instructions for Gov. Kendall, 1689, CO 29/4, pp. 82–103, esp. p. 99; Instructions to Gov. Russell, 1693, CO 29/4, pp. 407–31, esp. p. 428. For responses, see Council of Barbados to Lords of Trade, 12 July 1698, CO 28/3/68; and Response to speech of Governor Dutton, CO 29/3, p. 62. For the debates, see Dunn, Sugar and Slaves, pp. 104–5, 249–50; and Gragg, Englishmen Transplanted, pp. 161–64.

26 Review of laws passed by the Jamaica Assembly (9 October) 1677, April 1677, CO 138/3, p. 145.

27 Governor Atkins to Lords of Trade, 31 January 1678, CO 29/2, 224–28; for hat honor, see Stone, The Family, Sex, and Marriage in England, pp. 171–73.

28 Journal of the Committee for Trade and Plantations, 8 October 1680, CO 391/3, pp. 206–7.

29 1681, CO 29/3, pp. 59–62; 30 March 1681, CO 31/1, pp. 420–21.

30 25 July 1688, CO 140/2, pp. 124–25.

31 Lord Francis Russell to Lords of Trade, 23 March 1695, CO 28/2/81.

32 The records for Jamaica for 1688–89 are full of evidence of this conflict. See, for example, Assembly Address to King, September 1688, CO 137/2/15; Petition from Planters and Merchants from Jamaica in London, 11 January 1689, CO 137/2, no. 1; Petition from Royal African Company, 15 July 1689, CO 137/2, no. 10; Ralph Knight on behalf of the Assembly of Jamaica, 25 July 1689, CO 137/2, no. 14; Duke of Albermarle to Lords of Council, 6 March 1688, CO 138/6, pp. 88–93; Hender Molesworth to E. of Shrewsbury, 17 April 1689, CO 138/6, 166–69; Simon Musgrave, Attorney General of Jamaica, to Lords of Council, 12 May 1689, CO 138/6, pp. 210–14; Henry Barham, "History of Jamaica," BL Sloane MSS 3918, fols. 77–78.

33 Jamaica Assembly Address to King, CO 137/2, no. 15; John Helyar to Father William, 16 September 1686[7], DD/WHh 1089/3/3.

34 Petition of John Towers of Jamaica, December 1689, CO 137/2/61; Assembly Minutes, 6 April 1688, CO 140/2, p. 116; Council Minutes, 6 April 1688, CO 140/4, fol. 219v; Henry Barham, "History of Jamaica," BL Sloane MSS 3918, fol. 77v. Salus populi est suprema lex is used in Leveller tracts; see Richard Overton, "An Appeal from the Commons to the Free People" (1657), and the "Army Remonstrance of 1648," reprinted in Puritanism and Liberty, pp. 329, 456; and Brailsford, The Levellers and the English Revolution, pp. 345–46, n. 8. Mendle, Henry Parker, pp. 39–41, 43–45, 102, 108–9, shows how the slogan could be used by those on all sides in political conflict.

35 11 January 1689, CO 137/2, fol. 1; the orders went out after William had landed and James II had left London for Salisbury. The same ship that brought the letter reported

James II's departure from England, and a January petition sought to ensure that the instructions were reiterated by the new government, which they were. See also 30 November 1688 and 1 December 1688, CO 138/6, fols. 71v–72v, 73.

36 "The Governor of Jamaica's Answers to the inquiries of His Majesty's Commissioners," ca. 1671, CO 138/1, pp. 96–104; Hanson, *The Laws of Jamaica*, Preface, fols. B7v–C3v; Gragg, *Englishmen Transplanted*, pp. 59–61.

37 Council Minutes, 27 October 1692, CO 28/1, fols. 127–v; Account of Proceedings against Hallett, fols. 153–4v; Deposition of Richard Allen, fol. 155; Deposition of Sarah Young and Elizabeth Kipping, fol. 159; Exchequer Hearing on Bond of John Hallett, fol. 172; Documents for Writ of Error from Col. Hallet and Sureties, fols. 177–82. A summary of the evidence used in Hallet's trial is in CO 28/2/116 (i, ii); for other material, see CO 28/2, nos. 2, 3, 5, 13, 20, 28, 29. For a further discussion of this conflict, see Chapter 5.

38 Sir Richard Dutton to Committee of Trade, 3 January 1682, CO 1/48/1.

39 23 January 1701, CO 29/7, pp. 217–35, esp. p. 228. Hodge was trying to gain control of his father's property in Barbados. There are further discussions of the case, including responses from Barbados on 6 February 1701, CO 29/7, pp. 257–61, 286–88, 350–71, 382–432, 435–38, 445–53. The Board of Trade was not willing to take on the Barbados plantocracy to reform the administration of justice.

40 Robert Hall to William Helyar, 10 March 1701, DD/WHh 1090/3/8; Whaley to William Helyar, 28 June 1675, DD/WHh 1090/2/17; Edward Atcherly and Joseph Bryan to William Helyar, 2 March 1677, DD/WHh 1089/3/42; John Helyar to William Helyar, 30 November 1686, DD/WHh 1090/3/5; John Helyar to father William, 13–15 August 1691, DD/WHh 1089/3/58.

41 Whaley to William Helyar, 23 September 1672, DD/WHh 1089/3/31; for a summary of the dealings regarding the estate, see Bennett, "William Whaley," esp. pp. 114–15.

42 Whaley to Helyar, October 1673, DD/WHh 1089/3/34. Cary Helyar's standing on the island is suggested by the fact that his trustees were Sir Thomas Modyford, a former governor, and Molesworth, a future governor.

43 Francis Harison to William Helyar, 6 October 1673, DD/WHh 1089/3/33; Francis Harison to William Helyar, 9 October 1673, DD/WHh 1089/3/36. The situation with Cary's estate was perhaps the most dramatic set of problems with the law, but similar difficulties surrounded the purchase of 400 acres of woodland near Bybrook. The clearest summary of this is in the petition to the Crown in the case; a draft exists in DD/WHh Add. 12/4, and the original is CO 138/1, 1673/4: Petition of William Helyar, 169. Cary's letters in this case include DD/WHh 1089/3/20 and 27, 15 April 1671 and 12 January 1672; Cary Helyar and Whaley to William Helyar, DD/WHh Addenda Papers 12/23.

44 John Helyar to father William, 13 October 1687, DD/WHh 1089/3/10. Hillyard's letters are largely missing, but some of William's letters between 1678 and 1686 are in the Bound Volume, Letter Book in DD/WHh 1089.

45 For John's cultivation of his uncle's friends, see, for example, John Helyar to father William, 27 March 1687, DD/WHh 1089/3/2.

46 John Helyar to brother William Helyar, 30 June 1690, DD/WHh 1151/43. Compare John Heathcote to William Helyar, 24 October 1699, DD/WHh 1089/3/79: "An estate

there is something like a farm here which never turns to aught when he whose business it is, is not on the spot. I find it so with my own estate there."

47 Petition to Committee of Trade, 23 June 1693, CO 28/2/20.

48 1 October 1695 and 29 October 1695, CO 31/5, pp. 68–70.

49 This process is more visible in recent work on the continental colonies; see especially Berlin, *Many Thousands Gone*. The most general work covering this period in the Caribbean is Dunn, *Sugar and Slaves*; Dunn chronicles the changing nature of labor in the Caribbean but portrays slavery itself as a fixed entity.

50 Beckles, *White Servitude and Black Slavery*; Puckrein, *Little England*, esp. pp. 80–82; but compare pp. 37–39 for the earlier period. Puckrein provides a different account, which suggests greater differences between indentured servants and slaves than does Beckles. For the mainland colonies, see Berlin, *Many Thousands Gone*, pts. 1 and 2; and Morgan, *American Slavery, American Freedom*, esp. chap. 15.

51 Kussmaul, *Servants in Husbandry*, pp. 18–19, 22–23, 148–49, 168–69. For the Statute of Artificers (5 Eliz. c. 4), which governed service, see Tawney and Power, eds., *Tudor Economic Documents*, pp. 338–50; and Wrightson, *Earthly Necessities*, pp. 32–33, 58–60, 156.

52 See, for example, Wrightson, *Earthly Necessities*, p. 156; the role of Sir Thomas Smith, the commonwealthman, in developing the statute underlines its connection to concerns with order and good government.

53 Smith, *Colonists in Bondage*, esp. pp. 9–17; Beckles, *White Servitude and Black Slavery*, pp. 140–43.

54 The laws were printed in *Acts and Statutes of the Island of Barbados*. The discussion that follows is based on this set of laws.

55 Bridenbaugh and Bridenbaugh, *No Peace Beyond the Line*, p. 123.

56 *Acts and Statutes of the Island of Barbados*; the provisions regarding female servants are notable, in part because there were few of them and in part because they express gendered expectations and divisions. The move to prescribing celibacy for women servants comes later in Virginia than Barbados; see Brown, *Good Wives*, pp. 92–94, 192–93.

57 Ligon, *A True and Exact History*, pp. 43–45.

58 Ibid., pp. 29, 45–46.

59 Skinner, *Liberty before Liberalism*, esp. pp. 36–41; *Proceedings in Parliament 1628*, 2:71; Underdown, *Fire from Heaven*, p. 161; Brailsford, *Levellers and the English Revolution*, p. 344.

60 Rivers and Foyle, *England's Slavery*; the text may also be found in Burton, *Diary*, 4:255–58.

61 Ibid.; my interpretation differs substantially from that of Beckles, *White Servitude and Black Slavery*, pp. 52–54, 90; compare also Pestana, *The English Atlantic in an Age of Revolution*, pp. 210–12, for the impact in England.

62 Ligon, *A True and Exact History*, p. 44; see Goveia, *The West Indian Slave Laws of the 18th Century*, pp. 9–10; Philip Morgan, "The Poor," p. 299.

63 10 May 1676, CO 1/36/70. For servitude and its relation to slavery in the political thought of the period, see Skinner, *Liberty before Liberalism*, pp. 35, 70. The clause in question reads: "when any differences shall arise between master and servant in and

concerning the time of their servitude or terms of years": CO 139/1 (1675), fol. 136. This law is part of the bundle sent back by Sir Thomas Lynch.

64 Acts passed in the Island of Barbados, CO 30/1, p. 35.

65 31 March 1681, CO 31/2, pp. 420–21; compare 9 June 1691, CO/31/3, p. 284.

66 Dunn, Sugar and Slaves, pp. 75–76.

67 "An Act for the Better Ordering and Governing of Negroes," CO/30/2, pp. 16–26; Bush, "The British Constitution and the Creation of American Slavery." Gaspar, "With a Rod of Iron," has made a similar argument, though his analysis of the laws comes from a slightly different perspective than mine.

68 Governor Atkins to Lords of Trade, 2/12 June 1678, CO 29/2, p. 231.

69 Report of Mr. Sergeant Baldwin re. Laws of Barbados, CO 29/3, p. 6.

70 English law does have provision for "master's liability," but it is difficult to trace that before 1688; see Pollock and Maitland, The History of English Law, 2:528–29.

71 That is clause 22.

72 Although the Jamaican statute uses the word slave, the Helyar correspondence almost always refers to "Negroes" instead of slaves.

73 Beckles, Natural Rebels, p. 29; Bush, Slave Women, pp. 33–38. Compare Brown, Good Wives, pp. 83, 115, 117.

74 "An Act Declaring Negro Slaves to be Real Estate," 29 April 1668, CO 30/2, pp. 58–59; "Declarative Act upon the making Negroes Real Estate," 23 January 1673, CO 30/2, p. 105. The problem arose because, as "real estate" and chattels were treated differently in law, especially in testamentary cases, there were more constraints on the sale of real estate than chattels. For reflections on this issue, see Williams, "On Being the Object of Property."

75 An Additional Act Concerning of Detaining Negroes, 7 November 1673, CO 30/2, pp. 105–8.

76 My discussion here differs from that of Dunn in Sugar and Slaves, p. 239. I do not think that the law remained substantially unchanged after 1661; I think the changes are important and revealing. The plot itself is described in Great Newes from Barbados, pp. 9–10. Puckrein, Little England, pp. 163–64. See below, Chapter 5.

77 For the following discussion of the clauses of the act, see "A Supplemental Act to a former act for the better ordering and governing of Negroes," 21 April 1676, CO 30/2, pp. 114–25.

78 Cateau, "The New 'Negro' Business," shows that the practice only expanded as time went on; those who had the ability to travel are often crucial for resistance: Scott, Domination and the Arts of Resistance, p. 124.

79 Great Newes from Barbados, pp. 9–10. Puckrein, Little England, pp. 163–64.

80 See, for example, Minutes of Council, 4 October 1682, Lucas Transcripts, reel 2, Barbados Library (case of Alexander Cunningham), p. 454; and Minutes of Council, 13 February 1690, reel 3, p. 31, and 2 September 1690, p. 83.

81 "An Act for the Continuance of an Act entitled a supplemental act to a former act for the better ordering and governing of Negroes," 15 March 1677, CO 30/2, pp. 125–26; "An Act to Explain a branch of a former act for ordering and governing of Negroes," 13 December 1677; "An Act for the Securing the possession of Negroes and slaves," 20 February 1677, pp. 130–32.

82 Additional Instructions to Sir Richard Dutton, 3 May 1684, CO 29/3, p. 234; 30 September and 1 October 1684, CO 31/1, fols. 318v, 320. This request may have been prompted following a similar request made to Jamaica the year before; see below, note 93. For the policing nature of the legal codes, see Beckles, "Social and Political Control."

83 Edwin Stede to Lords of the Council for Trade and Plantations, 30 August 1688, CO 29/4, fols. 7–15; the Barbados law was next revised in 1823. Goveia, "West Indian Slave Laws," pp. 7–53; Handler, "Slave Revolts," p. 21.

84 "An Act for the Governing of Negroes," 8 August 1688, *Acts passed in the Island of Barbados*, no. 82, CO 30/1; while, as we shall see, the 1661 act was the basis for the Jamaican Slave Code, the 1688 act was a model for both South Carolina and Antigua. Gaspar, "With a Rod of Iron," pp. 355–59.

85 See Handler, "The Amerindian Slave Population," esp. pp. 128–31; Lepore, *The Name of War*, pp. 167–70; Breslaw, *Tituba*, chaps. 1 and 2. The evidence linking Tituba to Barbados is suggestive though not definitive.

86 On the treatment of the poor, see, for example, Wrightson and Levine, *Poverty and Piety*, pp. 182–83; and Slack, *Poverty and Policy*, pp. 193–94. See also Edwin Stede to Lords of Trade, 30 August 1688, CO 29/4, fols. 7–15.

87 Council orders 3 July 1661, CO 140/1, pp. 6–7; compare *Acts and Statutes of the Island of Barbados* (1654) for the comparison of acts.

88 15 November 1661, 1B/5/3/1, Jamaica Archives, pp. 41–42. For regulations regarding fire and servants, see Minutes, August 27 1661, 1B/5/3/1, Jamaica Archives, p. 33; Via, "A Comparison of Laws," covers only the 1683 laws, so it lacks a sense of the legal development in Jamaica.

89 For population, see Dunn, *Sugar and Slaves*, p. 155. There were 552 slaves in 1662, but since Modyford's party had included a substantial number, there were probably between 1,000 and 2,000 slaves by 1664. For the laws of 1664, see CO 139/1, fols. 44–92v; the "Act for the good Governing of Servants and ordering the Rights between Masters and Servants," CO 139/1, fols. 71v–75; "For the Better Governing of Slaves," CO 139/1, fols. 66–69v. A sentence is left out in clause 14 on fol. 68; compare CO 30/2, fol. 19v. "Freeman" was a status in Barbados but not used in the statutes on servants or slaves.

90 CO 139/2, fols. 46–55 (1672 version); CO 139/1, fols. 121–25 (1674 version). It appears that the latter remained the dominant law, as the 1696 Act for the Better Ordering of Slaves (CO 139/8, fol. 53v) specifically repeals the act of 25 Charles II, as well as that of 4 James II. The legal situation is somewhat murky, since there were perennial problems ensuring the approval of Jamaica's laws, and laws were routinely reissued.

91 CO 1/41, fols. 181v–85, esp. fol. 183v. While the 1696 act specifically repealed the 1675 act, at least some of the provisions of the 1677 act were enforced in the interim.

92 CO 139/8, fols. 49–53v. This law remained in effect until 1781. Goveia, "West Indian Slave Laws," p. 28.

93 17 February 1683, CO 138/4, pp. 128–29; 5, 12, and 20 September 1683, CO 140/2, pp. 65, 70, 72.

Chapter Five

1   Account of Proceedings against Col. John Hallet, CO 28/1, fols. 153v–154, 155, 159, 177; CO 28/2/2, 3, 5. This summary is based on the account of the attorney general of Proceedings against Col. John Hallett in CO 28/1, fols. 153–54; for all the sources for this case, see Chapter 4, note 37.

2   CO 28/1, fol. 155, for identification of Allen as "laborer"; for Hallet's account, 10 February 1693, CO/28/2/5; and for Kendall's, which identifies Allen as overseer, 18 October 1693, CO/28/2/28. For the use of "as good a man as you are," see Amussen, *An Ordered Society*, pp. 147–48.

3   "The Voyage of Sir Henry Colt," in *Colonising Expeditions*, ed. Vincent T. Harlow, p. 65.

4   See, for example, Petitions re. behavior of Capt. Richard Whiting in Bridgetown, 18 August 1662, CO 1/16/95–96. For discussion of the murder of Mr. Samuel Lewis by Peter Beckford in Jamaica, see 9 December 1697, 18 March 1698, and May 1699, CO 137/4/79, 86, 115–16.

5   Patterson, "Slavery and Slave Revolts," esp. pp. 249–50.

6   CO 28/1, fols. 127–127v, 153–54.

7   CO 28/1, fol. 154v.

8   Lt. Gov. Stede to Council, 29 July 1687, CO 29/3, fols. 427–32; Meagher was convicted of murder but at Stede's recommendation pardoned by the king (fol. 469.)

9   CO 1/19/78 (1) for articles of treason against Farmer; Francis Lord Willoughby to King, 8 August 1665, CO 1/19/92, for a summary of the complaints. Farmer's response is found in 16 March 1666, CO 1/20/28, 29; for his later career in Barbados, see William Willoughby to King, 7 May 1667, CO 1/21/43. For Farmer, who had been a Bristol merchant before becoming a planter, see Gragg, *Englishmen Transplanted*, pp. 124, 136.

10   Council Minutes, 3 October 1683, CO 31/1, fols. 294–95v; as a baronet, Davers would outrank a knight after his father's death.

11   26 November 1686, CO 1/61/14, and attachments i, ii; a detailed account of the trial is in 26 July 1687, CO 1/62/94.

12   17 March 1687, CO 1/62/11.

13   26 July 1687, CO 1/62/94.

14   18 September 1683, CO 1/32/94; 3 October 1683, CO 1/53/3; 2 November 1683, CO 1/53/32; 8 February 1684, CO 1/54/41; 12, 16, and 17 October 1683, CO 140/4, fols. 24, 26v, 27.

15   John Style to Principal Secretary of State, 4 January 1670, CO 1/25/1; John Style to Sir William Norris, 14 January 1669, CO 1/24/8; Governor Vaughan to ?, 28 May 1677, CO 1/40/93.

16   William Beeston to Lords of Council, 9 December 1697, CO 137/4/79; Petition by Benjamin Way, executor of Samuel Lewis, Esq., 18 March 1698, CO 137/4/86; Memorial of Peter Beckford, and Petition by Benjamin Way, May 1699, CO 137/4/15–16; 25 May 1699, CO 138/9.

17   Dunn, *Sugar and Slaves*, pp. 87–88, 155, 164–65.

18   See, for example, Ligon, *A True and Exact History*, p. 29.

19   Ligon, *A True and Exact History*, pp. 45–46. Sheppard, "The Slave Conspiracy that Never Was"; Handler, "Slave Revolts and Conspiracies," esp. p. 7.

20 Stede to Lords of Council, 30 August 1688, CO 29/4, pp. 7–15.

21 7 July 1675, CO 31/1, fol. 185; Council Minutes, 1686–94, 4 December 1691, CO 31/4, fols. 231–36.

22 13 August 1661, CO 140/1, p. 24; Webb, The Governors-General, pp. 206–7.

23 Rawlin, ed., The Laws of Barbados, pp. 7–8.

24 22 August 1662, CO 1/16, pp. 95–96.

25 Sir Thomas Lynch to E. of Sandwich, 14 October 1671, CO 1/27/40.

26 For example, see Petition of Justices, Churchwardens, and Vestry of Port Royal to Governor Lynch, ca. 1683, CO 1/52/47; and Zahedieh, " 'The Wickedest City in the World.' "

27 Taylor, "Multum in Parvo," 2:497, 503–4; Taylor's description is found in vol. 2, chap. 6, pp. 491–507. For the range of trade, see, for example, "The Present State of Jamaica under the Government of John Lord Vaughan," 1 January 1676, CO 138/2, esp. pp. 93–96. For Port Royal and the earthquake, see Pawson and Buisseret, Port Royal, Jamaica, esp. pp. 120–23; Dunn, Sugar and Slaves, pp. 43–44, 186–87; and Proclamation by Council of Jamaica, 28 June 1692, CO 140/5, p. 197.

28 26 October 1671, CO 140/1, pp. 250–52; John Style to Principal Secretary, 4 January 1670, CO 1/25/1; compare Clark, The English Alehouse, pp. 43–50.

29 Cary Helyar to William Helyar, 4 June 1672, DD/WHh 1089/3/29; Whaley to Helyar, January 1675, DD/WHh 1090/2/24.

30 Hender Molesworth to Mr. Blathwayt, 8 August 1687, CO 138/6, fols. 41–43.

31 12 October 1683, CO 140/4, fols. 24r–v; Lynch to Committee, 2 November 1683, CO 1/53/32.

32 Lynch to Committee, 2 November 1683, CO 1/53/32; Hender Molesworth to Mr. Blathwayt, 4 March 1686, CO 138/5, p. 145; 3 June 1686, CO 138/5, pp. 155–56; 29 January 1689, CO 140/4, pp. 263–64. Neither the "Six Articles" or "the other newsletter" can be identified.

33 Gov. Lynch to Committee, 2 November 1683, CO 1/53/32; and Gov. Lynch to Committee, 8 February 1684, CO 1/54/41.

34 Hender Molesworth to Mr. Blathwayt, 25 September 1685, CO 1/58/61.

35 16 July 1689, CO 29/4, pp. 123–26, 131.

36 16 February, 16 March, and 11–12 May 1686, CO 31/1, fols. 385v, 386–v, 388v, 394–5v; Handler, "Slave Revolts and Conspiracies," esp. pp. 20–21.

37 Ligon, A True and Exact History, p. 46. Slave resistance began even before the slaves left Africa and continued through the journey; see Richard Sheridan, "Resistance and Rebellion," pp. 181–205.

38 McGowan, "The Origins of Slave Rebellions."

39 Plantagenet, A Description of the Province of New Albion, p. 5; the best and most detailed discussion of Barbadian slave resistance is Handler, "Slave Revolts and Conspiracies."

40 "Lord Willoughby's desires for Barbados," ca. April 1666, CO 1/20/60; "Some Observation on Barbados," CO 1/21/170 (also in Journal of the Barbados Museum and Historical Society 34 (1973): 117–21).

41 Pestana, The English Atlantic in an Age of Revolution, p. 203; Pestana is the first scholar to note this conspiracy, though the newsbooks are not entirely reliable. Weekly Intel-

ligencer 18 (30 August–6 September 1659), p. 142, and (more elaborately) *Publick Intelligencer* 192 (29 August–5 September 1659), pp. 695–97.

42 *Great Newes from Barbados*, pp. 9–10; Puckrein, *Little England*, pp. 163–64; Handler, "Slave Revolts," pp. 13–16; Atkins to Sir Joseph Williamson, 3 October 1675, CO 1/35/29, fol. 231. The English terms for regions of Africa were imprecise, but those called Coromantee were known as hard workers; they also came from an area where linguistic differences among groups were limited, thus facilitating communication and resistance in Barbados. See, for example, Gomez, *Exchanging Our Country Marks*, pp. 105–07; and Thornton, "The Coromantees."

43 *Great Newes from Barbados*, pp. 11–13.

44 Atkins to Sir Joseph Williamson, 3 October 1675, CO 1/35/29, fol. 231; Atkins to Lords of Trade, 26 March 1680, CO 29/2, pp. 313–22, esp. p. 314; compare Scott, *Domination and the Arts of Resistance*, pp. 61–64.

45 Extract from letter from Barbados, CO 1/53/102, 18 December 1683.

46 16 February 1686, CO 31/1, fol. 385–v.

47 16 March 1686, 11–12 May 1686, CO 31/1, fols. 386, 394–95v.

48 Edward Stede to Committee for Trade and Plantations, 3 March 1690, CO 28/1, fol. 41v.

49 Willoughby Chamberlain to Col. Stede, 23 May 1690, CO 28/1, fol. 52.

50 CO 28/1, fols. 202, 204–6; Bohun, *A Brief but most True Relation*. The "brief relation" purports to be by a new arrival on the island; some aspects of his account, including the hundreds of arrests and executions, are clearly not accurate. Compare Brown, *Good Wives*, pp. 209–10; Fischer, *Suspect Relations*, pp. 164–65.

51 For inversion, see Natalie Davis, "Women on Top"; Underdown, *A Freeborn People*, pp. 60–61, 93, 102–106; and Underdown, "The Taming of the Scold," esp. pp. 127–28.

52 11 October 1692, 25 October 1692, and 24 January 1693, CO 31/4, pp. 377–78, 397. Deaths: Ben and Samson in CO 28/1, fols. 204v–205; Payment to Elizabeth Walrond, widow for execution of Hawgenny, boy, "found guilty in the late conspiracy," 3 October 1694, CO 31/4, p. 475. For the law, see An Act for the governing of Negroes, clause 14, 8 August 1688, CO 30/1, no. 82.

53 Kendall to Lords of Council, 10 February 1693, CO 28/2/3; Kendall to Council, CO 29/4, pp. 325–28.

54 "An Additional Act to an Act Intituled 'An Act for the Governing of Negroes,'" CO 30/3, pp. 249–51. The law applied only to slaves who had been on the island for at least a year and presumably had become accustomed to enslavement.

55 "An Act for Prohibiting the selling of rum and other strong liquors to any Negro or other slave," CO 30/3, pp. 251–52.

56 [15 March 1693], CO 28/2/9.

57 Francis Russell to Lords of Trade, 25 September 1694, CO 28/2/66.

58 20 June 1696, CO 31/5/106.

59 "Some of the Causes that are Known and others supposed to be the occasion of the continuance of the pestilential fevers and great mortality in Barbados," CO 28/4/46.

60 "Act for the Settlement of the Militia of this Island," CO 30/1, pp. 138–55, esp. p. 148.

61 Handler, "Slave Revolts and Conspiracies," pp. 29, 36; for the 1816 rebellion, see Craton, *Empire, Enslavement, and Freedom*, chap. 14.

62 For the history of indigenous people before the English conquest, see Padrón, Spanish Jamaica, pp. 152–53; Carey, The Maroon Story, esp. pp. 51–52, 61–63; "Henry Barham's Account of Jamaica," BL Sloane MSS 3918, fols. 81v–82; and Patterson, "Slavery and Slave Revolts." For Maroons and marronage in general, see Price, Introduction, in Maroon Societies, pp. 1–30. For Maroon culture, see Price, "Maroons and Their Communities"; and Webb, The Governors-General, pp. 187, 191.

63 BL Add. MSS 12430, fols. 23, 27; 1 February 1663, CO 140/1, p. 75; Campbell, The Maroons of Jamaica, pp. 17–25.

64 BL Add. MSS 12430, fol. 29; 28 July 1664, CO 140/1, p. 121.

65 15 August, 1 September, and 10 October 1665, CO 140/1, pp. 135–42.

66 29 February 1668, 28 March 1668, CO 140/1, pp. 171–76.

67 John Style to Principal Secretary, 2 May 1670, CO 1/25/29; Information of John Style, n.d., CO/1/25/30; Campbell, The Maroons of Jamaica, pp. 32–36.

68 Campbell, The Maroons of Jamaica, pp. 35–37.

69 23 October 1663, CO 140/1, p. 90.

70 9 June 1664, CO 140/1, p. 91.

71 29 February 1668, CO 140/1, p. 170.

72 Letter of John Style, 2 May 1670, and Information of John Style, CO 1/25/29, p. 30; "The Present State of Jamaica," BL Add MS 12429, esp. fols. 76–76v.

73 9 June 1672, CO 140/1, p. 305.

74 1709, DD/WHh 1089/1/5; n.d. (1670s), 1089/1/7. Carey, esp. pp. 150–52, suggests a sequence where escaped slaves first formed "self-freed African villages" and then over time developed sufficient social organization to be "pre-Maroon societies"; it was only when coordinated military activities were undertaken that these became Maroon societies. Such distinctions are helpful in understanding the histories of these communities, but they are less relevant in understanding how the English learned from slaves' resistance. For the sake of simplicity, I have called all communities of self-freed slaves "Maroon."

75 3 September 1675, CO 140/3, pp. 436–37.

76 9 December 1675, DD/WHh 1090/2/1a; 15 December 1675, CO 140/2, pp. 447–49; 23 January 1676 and 17 February 1676, CO 140/3, pp. 449–52, 453–54, 458–71.

77 Journals of House of Assembly, 11 April 1677, CO 140/2, p. 12.

78 Joseph Bryan to Matthew Bryan, 12 July 1677, DD/WHh 1089/3/44.

79 5 April 1678, CO 140/3, p. 650.

80 Joseph Bryan to William Helyar, 8 June 1678, DD/WHh 1089/3/47.

81 Ibid.

82 Sloane, A Voyage to the Islands, Introduction, p. lvii.

83 Hender Molesworth to Mr. Blathwayt, 29 August 1685, CO 138/5, pp. 87–102, esp. pp. 87–90; another description can be found in "Henry Barham's Account of Jamaica," BL Sloane MSS 3918, fols. 74–v.

84 BL Sloane MSS 3918, fol. 74v; 2 February 1686 and 8 April 1686, CO 140/4, fols. 104v–106, 108v–109.

85 Speech of Governor Molesworth, 3 June 1686, CO 140/2, pp. 82–83.

86 Hender Molesworth to Mr. Blathwayt, 28 September 1686 and 2 November 1686, CO 138/5, pp. 85–91, 199–219; 18 Sept, 24 September, and 29 November 1686, and 26

April 1687, CO 140/4, fols. 133v–34, 138, 141, 168–v. Campbell, *The Maroons of Jamaica*, pp. 37–40. The organization of the Maroon villages reflects West African practices; see, for example, Carey, *The Maroon Story*, pp. 150–51; and Patterson, "Slavery and Slave Revolts," pp. 282–83, for political side of this.

87 28 December 1687, CO 140/4, fols. 177v–78, 179v.

88 Albemarle to Lords of Committee, 6 March 1688, CO 138/6, pp. 88–93, esp. p. 92.

89 6 April 1688, CO 140/2, p. 116.

90 John Helyar to Col. William Helyar, 24 August 1690, DD/WHh 1151/52; 13–15 August 1691, DD/WHh 1089/3/58; E. of Inchiquin Gov. of Jamaica to Lords of Trade, 31 August 1690, CO 137/2/74. For the former Sutton slaves in Maroon bands, see Carey, *The Maroon Story*, pp. 146–47; and Shafer, "The Maroons of Jamaica," pp. 29–43. Patterson, "Slavery and Slave Revolts," however, argues that all the risings of the period should be seen as one event.

91 Beeston to Lords of Council, 8 February 1699, CO 137/4/108; Robinson, *The Iron Thorn*, pp. 22–23; Carey, *Maroon Story*, pp. 146–51.

92 12 December 1692, CO 140/5, p. 228.

93 10 December 1694, CO 140/5, p. 298.

94 12 February 1694, CO 137/3/28; 10 December 1694, CO 140/5, p. 298; William Beeston, "A Brief Account of . . . Jamaica . . . In 1694," CO 137/1, fols. 193–96v, esp. fols. 194v–195.

95 "Petition of Distressed inhabitants of the Windward parts of this island," 20 May 1696, CO 140/2, p. 160; 20 July 1696, CO 137/4/11.

96 27 July 1697, CO 138/9, pp. 116–17.

Chapter Six

1 Cary Helyar to William Helyar, 24 September 1670, DD/WHh 1089/3/16a; Whaley to William Helyar, 20 June 1672, DD/WHh Addenda Papers 12/11; Whaley to William Helyar, 8 December 1675, DD/WHh 1090/2/21; Edmund Atcherly, Wm. Helyar, Jos. Bryan to Col. Wm. Helyar, 28 May 1677, DD/WHh 1089/3/41; DD/WHh 1089, Bound Volume, Letter Book, passim, esp. letters of 5 September 1681 and 9 June 1682 to Thomas Hillyard.

2 John Helyar to William Helyar, 1690, DD/WHh 1090/3/8; Robert Hall to William Helyar, 10 March 1701, DD/WHh 1151/43; East Coker Parish Register, 1560–1714, Somerset Archive and Record Service D/P/cok.e/2/1/1.

3 MSS Rawl. A 348, p. 21.

4 *The Character of a Town Misse* (1680), p. 3; the "town miss" in this brief pamphlet was a lady of pleasure, not a respectable woman.

5 For a fuller discussion of these issues, see Rosenberg, "Thomas Tryon."

6 Baxter, *A Christian Directory*, pp. 557–60.

7 Tryon, *Memoirs of the Life of Thomas Tryon*, esp. pp. 40–41; ODNB, "Thomas Tryon"; Rosenberg, "Thomas Tryon."

8 Tryon, *Friendly Advice*, pp. 123, 127, 129.

9 Whaley to William Helyar, 9 December 1675, DD/WHh 1090/2/1a; Dunn, *Sugar and Slaves*, pp. 228, 252–55; Beckles, *Natural Rebels*, pp. 135–36; for later practices, see Craton, *Empire, Enslavement, and Freedom*, p. 172.

10 Tryon, *Friendly Advice*, pp. 141–42.

11 Ibid., pp. 141–42, 175–78, 189, 202–4, 208–14.

12 Tryon, *Tryon's Letters*, letters 32 to 34, esp. pp. 187, 199, 202, 221.

13 Keith, *An Exhortation and Caution to Friends*; Godwyn, *The Negro's and Indians Advocate*.

14 For a full discussion of the ways in which black people figured in imaginative economies of the period, see Hall, *Things of Darkness*; Peter Hulme, *Colonial Encounters*, esp. chap. 3; Goldberg, *Tempest in the Caribbean*.

15 Fryer, *Staying Power*, pp. 26–31, esp. pp. 28, 29.

16 D'Avenant, *Cruelty of the Spaniards*, pp. 23–24.

17 Ibid., pp. 1–2, 5–6.

18 Ibid., p. 20; for the issue of enslavement and conversion, see, for example, Shyllon, *Black Slaves*, pp. 24–25.

19 D'Avenant, *Cruelty of the Spaniards*, p. 25.

20 For Bacon's rebellion, see Taylor, *American Colonies*, pp. 149–50; and Morgan, *American Slavery, American Freedom*, pp. 254–70.

21 *The Widow Ranter* has been published as part of Behn, *Five Plays*, pp. 205–95; see Hendricks, "Civility, Barbarism, and Aphra Behn's *The Widow Ranter*"; Ferguson, *Dido's Daughters*, p. 354. I am indebted to Margo Hendricks for bringing this play to my attention.

22 Behn, *Window Ranter*, prologue, I.

23 Taylor, *American Colonies*, pp. 151–52; Berlin, *Many Thousands Gone*, pp. 109–26.

24 Pix, *The Innocent Mistress*, pp. 6–7; Pix's biography in *ODNB* does not suggest that she had any colonial connections.

25 Ibid., p. 8. It is interesting that he would give a woman who is not his legal wife the same kind of settlement that would be expected with a marriage.

26 Southerne's text was published in 1696 and 1699, reflecting performances and revivals; it was regularly revived and modified for the next century. By the 1780s, it had emerged as an abolitionist play: Iwanisziw, *Oroonoko*, pp. xiii–xvii.

27 The most recent modern edition is Iwanisziw, *Oroonoko*; the play, like the novel, is set during the brief period of English rule over Surinam in the 1660s, before Surinam was traded to the Dutch in return for Manhattan. The densely rain-forested interior provided a refuge for Maroons; see Price, *Maroon Societies*, pp. 5–8. Ferguson, *Dido's Daughters*, pp. 368–69, points out that Southerne enacts an interracial romance that parallels that of *Othello*, a romance suggested but avoided in the novel; her discussion of the historical context of the novel is on pp. 335–36.

28 *Oroonoko*, III.4.75–82.

29 Ibid., V.5.112–13. For a discussion of some of the complex implications of the changes in Behn's text, see Macdonald, "Race, Women, and the Sentimental."

30 Whyman, *Sociability and Power*, pp. 72–74; Verney, *Memoirs of the Verney Family*, 4:467, 469–70. The change in attitudes toward black people is suggested by the comment in the nineteenth-century volume that "it was one of the fashions of the day that fair Englishwomen should be served by such uncouth pages." The painter, Lenthall, is known for very few paintings; see Baker, *Lely and the Stuart Portrait Painters*, 2:206; Courtauld Institute of Art Photographic Survey, Neg. B57/1139.

31 These are the Mignard portrait of the Duchess of Portsmouth (Figure 8; NPG 497)

and an anonymous portrait of Sir John Chardin (NPG 5161); both are listed on the website only by the name of the sitter, though they can be found in a subject search under "diversity." For a general survey of these paintings, see Waterfield, "Black Servants"; for the eighteenth-century focus of recent scholarship, see Tobin, *Picturing Imperial Power*, chap. 1; Bindman, *Ape to Apollo*; and Dabydeen, *Hogarth's Blacks*.

32 There are three, though none can be dated exactly to the seventeenth century: a Kneller *Negro Trumpeter* (Yale Center for British Art photo collection); School of Kneller, *Portrait of a Negro Retainer*, Sotheby's, 14 May 1986; and School of Lely, *Black Boy*, at Knole, in Servant's Gallery. Such portraits are more common—though still rare—in the eighteenth century. This is true more generally, though well-known, non-English exceptions are Jan Mostaert, *Portrait of a Moor* (ca. 1525–30), and Diego Velazquez, *Juan de Pareja* (1650). I am grateful to Peter Erickson for assistance on this point.

33 Here I draw on Hall's sense of the possibility of simultaneously seeking a black presence in images and using images to critique the notion of race; Hall, "Object into Object?," esp. pp. 348–51.

34 Copies of the Mytens portrait are found in the Royal Collection at Hampton Court; at Serlby Hall (Courtauld Institute of Art Neg. B71/1025); and in the collection of the Duke of Buccleugh. For dating, see Kelly, "Mytens and His Portraits of Charles I."

35 The version shown was sold at Christies, 12 December 2001; another version is in the Bayerischen Staatsgemäldesammlungen and was formerly in the Alte Pinakothek, Munich; Larsen, *The Paintings of Anthony Van Dyke*, 2:502, A268. An earlier Van Dyck portrait of Elena Grimaldi (in the National Gallery of Art, Washington, D.C.), done while he was in Italy, shows how the typical English portrait developed from an Italian model. Barnes, Poorter, Millar, and Vey, *Van Dyck*, vol. 2, pl. 45; compare Henrietta of Lorraine, Barnes, Poorter, Millar, and Vey, *Van Dyck*, vol. 3, pl. 102. A less refined portrait of Susanna Poulett, Mrs. Warten, imitates the Van Dyck model but is less polished. Sotheby's, 5 February 1969, attributes this painting to Van Dyck, though this is unlikely; Yale Center for British Art, Jennings Albums, vol. 13, p. 43, attributes it to J. Hayls.

36 This portrait is dated to ca. 1651; for the connection to Van Dyck, see Oliver Millar, *Sir Peter Lely*, no. 23, p. 47–48. Millar connects this portrait to the attendant in the portrait of Henrietta of Lorraine that had been in the collection of Charles I; but it also bears a resemblance to the black attendant in the portrait of the Earl and Countess of Caernavon at Longleat, who is also seen in Plate 5.

37 The Mignard of the Duchess of Portsmouth is in the NPG; the Kneller is at Goodwood. For the D'Agar, see Hall, *Things of Darkness*, p. 250. The two Wissings are found in the photo archive at the NPG; the one that is possibly the Duchess of Portsmouth (Hall, *Things of Darkness*, p. 249, suggests it is the Duchess of Mazarin) was sold at Christie's, 21 November 1980, and the other is in a private collection and was brought to the NPG for evaluation. I am grateful to Julia Marciari Alexander for alerting me to the significance of the pearls for assessing gender.

38 Hall, *Things of Darkness*, pp. 248–50; there is a Kneller allegedly of Nell Gwynne with a black attendant.

39 Hall, *Things of Darkness* (248), cites four or five such portraits of the Duchess of

Portsmouth, and four of the Duchess of Cleveland, although I can only find one; Walvin, *Black and White*, p. 10.

40 The portrait of Mary Davis is at Audley End; that of Dorothy Lady May can be found in Farrer, *Portraits in Suffolk Houses (West)*, p. 244, no. 15. For the use of patterns, see MacLeod and Alexander, *Painted Ladies*, p. 57.

41 The Wissing pattern versions are one sold by Christie's, 21 November 1980; another version is in NPG Heinz Archive. Hall, *Things of Darkness*, pp. 240–53, esp. p. 253. More problematically, Hall also argues (p. 241) that the somewhat androgynous portrayal of the attendant allows an unproblematic construction of femininity. I find myself more convinced by Tobin, *Picturing Imperial Power*, esp. pp. 39, 55. For portraits of women with pets, see MacLeod and Alexander, *Painted Ladies*, figs. 8, 21, 22, and 39 and catalog nos. 47, 50, 52, 61, 66, 67, 98, and 100; in contrast, three of the portraits include black slaves.

42 For Mary Grimston, see Jackson-Stops, ed., *The Treasure Houses of Britain*, p. 167.

43 Stewart, *Sir Godfrey Kneller*, p. 41.

44 For a nonmilitary man attended by a slave, see the portrait of Sir John Chardin in the NPG, no. 5161; the slave holds a map, while Chardin points to Persia. Compare also below, the portraits including Elihu Yale.

45 For this painting, see Baker, *Lely and the Stuart Portrait Painters*, vol. 1, facing p. 214.

46 The Maubert, which is undated, was exhibited at the Reinhardt Galleries in New York in 1929; see Reinhardt Galleries, *Loan Exhibition of Paintings of Women and Children by Masters from the Fifteenth to the Twentieth Centuries*; it was sent by *Art News* to the library of the Frick Collection in 1942.

47 The black groom is a frequent figure in portraits, from the Paul Van Somer of Queen Anne (1617) onwards; he is also connected to the page in military portraits.

48 For a discussion of the Yale/Cavendish portrait, compare Tobin, *Picturing Imperial Power*, pp. 38–39; the other Yale portrait is the property of Yale University.

49 For the Soest, see Warner and Asleson, *Great British Paintings from American Collections*, pp. 58–59.

50 For the Lyttleton portrait, see Baker, *Lely and the Stuart Portrait Painters*, 2:3–4.

51 Waterfield, "Black Servants," p. 143.

52 Dabydeen, *Hogarth's Blacks*, pp. 30–37, esp. p. 36. Kaplan, "Titian's *Laura Dianti*," parts 1 and 2.

53 Tobin, *Picturing Imperial Power*, p. 39.

54 Governor to Sir Thomas Montgomery, 14 November 1689, CO 28/1, Entry Books, fol. 32.

55 Cited by Fryer, *Staying Power*, p. 470, n. 38.

56 Sloane, *A Voyage to the Islands*, 2:341; Cundall, *Governors of Jamaica*, pp. 115–16.

57 14 January 1698, CO 31/5/273.

58 MSS Rawl. A 348, fols. 12v, 20.

59 Thomas Montgomery to Gov. Kendall, 20 June 1690, CO 28/1, fol. 64.

60 Shyllon, *Black Slaves in Britain*, pp. 3–4; Dresser, *Slavery Obscured*, pp. 11–12, 72–81.

61 Quoted by Walvin, *Black and White*, p. 1.

62 For the early history of blacks in England, see Walvin, *Black and White*, pp. 1–10; Fryer, *Staying Power*, pp. 5–13; and Shyllon, *Black Slaves in Britain*, pp. 1–5.

63 Dorset R.O. B2/8/1, fol. 181v: I am grateful to David Underdown for this reference; Stoyle, *Soldiers and Strangers*, pp. 92–93.

64 Mansfield's actual ruling in the case was very narrow, focusing on the ability of masters to send slaves back to the West Indies without their consent; so although many people interpreted the judgment in *Somerset* to outlaw slavery in England, that was not the case, and slavery in England was not abolished. See Paley, "After *Somerset*"; Shyllon, *Black People in Britain*, p. 17; and Rushworth, *Historical Collections*, p. 468 (this case is brought forward in a debate about the punishment of John Lilburne). See Caterall, *Judicial Cases*, 1:1–5, for a summary of the legal history; for the cases, see pp. 9–19. Compare Lowe, "The Black African Presence in Renaissance Europe," pp. 20–21.

65 Davis, *The Problem of Slavery in Western Culture*, p. 118; this issue has led to extensive discussion. See Glausser, "Three Approaches to Locke and the Slave Trade."

66 Ligon, *A True and Exact History*, p. 50.

67 Latimer, *Annals of Bristol*, p. 344; the Quarter Sessions records have not survived, so Dinah Black's fate is not known.

68 Dayfoot, *The Shaping of the West Indian Church*, pp. 87–88.

69 Pepys, *Diary*, 9:510 (5 April 1669). Batelier had earlier recommended another cook to Pepys; Pepys, *Diary*, 8:419 (2 September 1667).

70 Walvin, *Black and White*, p. 11.

71 LG, no. 3103, 5–8 August 1695.

72 Walvin, *Black and White*, pp. 46–47.

73 Quoted by Walvin, *Black and White*, p. 10, from *Mercurius Politicus*, 11 August 1659.

74 LG, 1665–72, esp. no. 62; for various announcements, see nos. 42, 45, 52, 53, 214, and 282. The first notice of a runaway servant with no apparent official connection is no. 402 (20–23 September 1669). In 1670, 1671, and 1672 there are five runaway servants advertised each year; in 1673 the number jumps to twelve.

75 For Thomas Widnel, see LG, no. 654, 19–22 February 1672; the reward of £5 suggests a degree of wealth, though the person to be notified is not Widnel's father.

76 LG, no. 810, 21–25 August 1673; no. 1230, 30 August–3 September 1677; no. 2108, 28 January–1 February 1686.

77 LG, no. 1881, 26–29 November 1683.

78 LG, no. 1241, 8–11 October 1677; no. 1565, 15–18 November 1680; no. 1804, 1–5 March 1683; no. 2786, 21–25 July 1692.

79 LG, no. 2838, 23 January 1693.

80 LG, no. 1478, 15–19 January 1680.

81 LG, no. 2186, 28 October–1 November 1686; and no. 2188, 4–8 November 1686.

82 LG, no. 2513, 9–12 December 1689; compare no. 2790, 4–8 August 1692, announcement for Toby, "an East India Black."

83 LG, no. 2122, 18–22 March 1686; compare no. 1881, 26–29 November 1683; also no. 2533, 4–7 March 1689. Moorfield is no. 864, 26 February–2 March, and no. 875, 6–9 April 1674.

84 LG, no. 896, 18–22 June 1674.

85 LG, no. 2309, 10–13 October 1692. It is possible that some of the marks described, such as the man with "notches on nose and down forehead," were "country marks" made in Africa; compare Gomez, *Exchanging Our Country Marks*, esp. p. 39.

86 LG, no. 2174, 16–20 September 1686.

87 LG, no. 890, 28 May–1 June 1674; no. 896, 18–22 June 1674.

88 LG, no. 2185, 25–28 October 1686

89 LG, no. 2505, 11–14 November 1689.

90 For the payment of captains, see Shyllon, *Black Slaves*, pp. 3–4; Harms, *The Diligent*, pp. 318–19, describes an alternative, where the captain purchased slaves on his own account.

91 LG, no. 2140, 20–24 May 1677; no. 2729, 4–7 January 1692.

92 LG, no. 3050, 31 January–4 February 1695.

93 Fryer, *Staying Power*, p. 21.

94 LG, no. 3454, 15–19 December 1698.

95 LG, no. 3134, 6–10 October 1698.

96 LG, no. 2775, 13–16 June 1692; Gomez, *Exchanging Our Country Marks*, pp. 39–40, 97–98, 121–24; Blackburn, *The Making of New World Slavery*, p. 472.

97 Eltis, *The Rise of African Slavery in the Americas*, pp. 98–113. There were differences in the proportions of women shipped from different areas of Africa, and it is clear that the Royal African Company worked to maximize the number of males shipped.

Epilogue

1 *A Letter from a Merchant at Jamaica*, pp. 10–11.

2 Belgrove, *A Treatise Upon Husbandry*, pp. 55–56, 64–5; Handler, *Supplement to a Guide*, pp. 56–57; MSS Rawl. A 348, fols. 1–19; in 1758, Thomas Thistlewood borrowed Belgrove's book, and a manuscript version of the Drax instructions, from his employer, John Cope; Hall, *In Miserable Slavery*, pp. 85–86.

3 Belgrove, *A Treatise Upon Husbandry*; Ligon, *A True and Exact History*, p. 89.

4 Young, "Works Organization in the Seventeenth Century," esp. pp. 91, 93; Levine and Wrightson, *The Making of an Industrial Society*, esp. pp. 356–69; Valenze, *The First Industrial Woman*, 89–90; Valenze, *The Social Life of Money*, chaps. 6 and 7.

5 Quoted in Aspin, *The First Industrial Society*, p. 53; Engels, *The Condition of the Working Class*, p. 170; Hobsbawm, *Industry and Empire*, p. 60.

6 In Pike, *Human Documents*, p. 37.

7 Ibid., pp. 60–61.

8 Engels, *The Condition of the Working Class*, for example, pp. 93, 205.

9 Thompson, *Whigs and Hunters*, esp. pp. 21–22.

10 Sharp, *In Contempt of All Authority*, pp. 86–106; Underdown, *Revel, Riot, and Rebellion*, pp. 107–12; Manning, *Village Revolts*, pp. 285–86, 298–300. Howkins and Merricks, in " 'Wee be black as Hell,' " link blacking to the practices of the mystery plays, but it is telling that they have no instances of blacking in riots before the eighteenth century; blacking is used, along with women's clothing, as a form of disguise in the Rebecca riots.

11 Davidoff and Hall, *Family Fortunes*, esp. chap. 6; Hall, "The History of the Housewife," in *White, Male, and Middle Class*, pp. 43–71, esp. pp. 56–62; Vickery, *The Gentleman's Daughter*, esp. chap. 4; Valenze, *The First Industrial Woman*, esp. pp. 41–42, 65–67, 100, 100–109, 167–70.

12 Fielding, *Joseph Andrews*; Laqueur, *Making Sex*, 154–63; Davis, "Women on Top"; Hitchcock and Cohen, *English Masculinities*, esp. Introduction.

13 Hall, *In Miserable Slavery*, provides extensive diary excerpts; for example, see pp. 29, 31–32, 62, 67, 79–82, 84, 86, 87, 100, 105, 122, 124, 128, 150, 153, 155, 177, 184–85, 195, 198–99, 206–7, 211, 213, 221, 224, 240, 260, 264, 269, 283, 298, and 302. More analytically, see Burnard, *Mastery, Tyranny, and Desire*, esp. pp. 156–62. While Thistlewood gives little information beyond the fact of sex, the power differences and the descriptions do not suggest that his sexual activities, aside from those with his "wife," were anything other than rape.

14 Stone, *Family, Sex, and Marriage*, pp. 552–99.

15 Amussen, "The Part of a Christian Man"; Chaytor, "Husband(ry)," focuses primarily on the women's narratives but notes the general claims of innocence (p. 399). Walker, "Rereading Rape," offers a compelling critique of Chaytor and also notes the usual denial of sexual intercourse. For the later period and the argument of consent, see Clark, *Women's Silence, Men's Violence*, chap. 2.

16 The limits on free blacks were clear in the Jamaica statute of 1696; see Chapter 4, note 92; Beckles, *A History of Barbados*, pp. 65–69; and Craton, *Empire, Enslavement, and Freedom*, p. 167.

17 Young, *Economics as a Moral Science*, pp. 58, 64, 69–70, 76; Fryer, *Staying Power*, p. 152. There is a strong similarity between views like Hume's on blacks and contemporary critiques of women's intelligence; Stone, *Family, Sex, and Marriage*, pp. 356–57.

18 For an account of the eighteenth-century fortunes of the play, see Felsenstein, ed., *English Trader, Indian Maid*, esp. pp. 1–27; Hulme, *Colonial Encounters*, chap. 6, esp. p. 227.

Bibliography

Manuscript Sources

Barbados Central Library, Bridgetown
 Lucas Transcripts (microfilm)
Bodleian Library, Oxford
 MSS Rawl. A 348, "Instructions which I would have observed by Mr. Richard Harwood
  in the management of my plantations" (1679)
British Library, London
 Add. MSS 11410, "The Relation of Colonel Doyley on his return from Jamaica," ca.
  1661; Thomas Modyford, "The Condition of Jamaica, 1664"
 Add. MSS 11411, Thomas Povey, "Book of Entry of Foreign Letters," 1655–60
 Add. MSS 12429, "The Present State of Jamaica"
 Add. MSS 12430, "Journal of Colonel William Beeston"
 Add. MSS 12418, James Knight, "History of Jamaica"
 Add. MSS 12423, "Journal of Colonel Edward Doyley"
 Egerton MSS 2395, Povey Papers Relating to English Colonies in America and the West
  Indies, 1627–99
 Sloane MSS 2441, "An Account of His Majesty's Island of Barbados, and the
  Government Thereof," 1684
 Sloane MSS 3662, John Scott, "Description of Barbadoes," fols. 62–54
 Sloane MSS 3918, "Henry Barham's Account of Jamaica"
 Sloane MSS 3984, "A Moderate Calculation of the Annual Charge and Produce of a
  Plantation in Barbados Containing 100 Acres of Land"
Dorset History Centre, B2/8/1, Dorchester Court Book, 1629–37
Huntington Library, San Marino, Calif.
 HM 648, Journal of Abraham Lloyd
Jamaica Archives, Spanish Town
 1A/3/1, Chancery Court, Chancery Records, ca. 1676–84
 1B/5/3, Council Minutes, 1661–72

National Archives of the United Kingdom, Kew

CO 1/11–69, 1643–98, Privy Council and Related Bodies: America and West Indies. Colonial Papers (General Series)

CO 28/1–4, Barbados Original Correspondence, 1688–1701

CO 29/1–7, Entry Books, Barbados, 1627–1702

CO 30/1–3, Acts of Barbados

CO 31/1–5, Journal of Barbados Council and Assembly

CO 137/1–5, Original Correspondence, Jamaica

CO 138/1–10, Entry Books, Jamaica

CO 139/1–9, Acts of Jamaica

CO 140/1–6, Council, Council in Assembly Sessional Papers

CO 323/1, Misc. Correspondence

CO 324/1, Minutes, Council Meetings

CO 388/1–3, Board of Trade Original Correspondence

CO 389/1, Board of Trade Entry Books

CO 700, Maps and Plans

Jamaica 1: ca. 1674

Jamaica 3: ca. 1680

MPG 1/568, Map of Jamaica, ca. 1674

PRO 31/17/43–44, Typescript of Barbados Council Minutes, vol. 2, 1643–71

National Library of Jamaica, Kingston.

MS 105, John Taylor, "Multum in Parvo"

MS 159, "The History and State of Jamaica under Lord Vaughan," ca. 1678

Somerset Archive and Record Service, Somerset, England

D\P\co.e/2/1/1, East Coker Parish Register, 1560–1714

Walker-Heneage MSS from Coker Court

DD/WHh Addenda Papers 12: Letters and Papers

DD/WHh 1089:

/1: Lists and Inventories, 1678–1709

/2: Accounts 1687–88, 1704, 1705, also Letters

/3: Letters to William Helyar, 1662–1714

/4: "Agreements"—Land Sales, etc.

/5: Letters from 18th C Bristol re. Jamaica Trade

/6: Accounts, Receipts, Bills of Lading, Bills of Exchange, etc., 1671–1721

/7: Accounts and Receipts

/8: Deeds, Bonds, Agreements

/9: Bonds, Deeds, Agreements

/10: Letters, 1650s

/11: Accounts of Sugars Sold, etc.

Bound Volume, Letter Book of Wm. Helyar, then His Sons, 1676–87, 1696–1710 (unpaginated)

Loose Typed Pages, Carbons of Transcripts of Letters from Part 3 with Refs. to William Dampier

DD/WHh 1090

/1: Mostly Bills of Exchange, Routine Letters re. Business, ca. 1674–1714

/2: Letters, Copies of Letters and Papers, Bills of Exchange

/3: Miscellaneous Documents

/4: 19th-Century Transcripts and Copies

DD/WHh 1151, Photocopies (after originals withdrawn)

University of West Indies Library, Mona

Wilson Family Papers and Correspondence

Yale Center for British Art, New Haven, Conn.

Jennings Albums

Printed Primary Sources

Acts and Statutes of the Island of Barbados Made and Enacted Since the Reducement of the Same unto the Authority of the Commonwealth of England. London, 1654. Wing B682A.

Acts passed in the Island of Barbados, From 1643, to 1762, inclusive; Carefully revised, innumerable errors corrected; and the Whole compared and examined, with the original Acts in the Secretary's Office by the Late Richard Hall, Esq. One of the Representatives in the General Assembly for the Parish of St. Michael; and one of his Majesty's Justices of the Peace, of the said Island, near 30 years And since his Death, continued by his son, Richard Hall. London, 1764. (Also in CO/30/1.)

Baxter, Richard. *A Christian Directory.* London, 1673. Wing B1219.

Behn, Aphra. *The Widow Ranter.* In *Five Plays.* London: Methuen, 1990.

Belgrove, William. *A Treatise Upon Husbandry or Planting.* Boston, 1755.

Blome, Richard. *A Description of the Island of Jamaica, with the other Isles and Territories in America.* London, 1672. Wing B3208.

Bohun, Edmund. *A Brief but most True Relation of the late Barbarous and Bloody Plot of the Negro's in the Island of Barbados . . . in a letter to a Friend.* London, 1693. Wing B4549A.

"A Brief Collection of the Depositions of Witnesses and Pleadings of Commissioners at Law in a difference depending between the merchants and inhabitants of Barbados on the one part, and the Earl of Carlisle, Lord Willoughby, &c., on the other part." In *Colonising Expeditions to the West Indies and Guiana, 1623–1667,* edited by Vincent T. Harlow, pp. 25–42. London: Hakluyt Society, 1925.

Burton, Thomas. *Diary of Thomas Burton Esq.* Edited by John Towill Rutt. 4 vols. London: Henry Colburn, 1828. Reprinted Johnson Reprint Corporation, 1974.

Caterall, Helen T., ed. *Judicial Cases Concerning American Slavery and the Negro.* 5 vols. Washington, D.C.: Carnegie Institution, 1926–37.

The Character of a Town Misse. London, 1680. Wing C1994.

Colt, Henry. "The Voyage of Sir Henry Colt." In *Colonising Expeditions to the West Indies and Guiana, 1623–1667,* edited by Vincent T. Harlow, pp. 54–102. London: Hakluyt Society, 1925.

Dampier, William. "Letter to William Helyar." *Somerset and Dorset Notes and Queries* 23, pt. 206 (1940): 155–58.

D'Avenant, William. *The Cruelty of the Spaniards in Peru.* London, 1658. Wing D321.

Engels, Friedrich. *The Condition of the Working Class in England.* Translated by W. O. Henderson and W. H. Chaloner. Oxford: Basil Blackwell, 1971.

Equiano, Olaudah, *The Interesting narrative of the life of Olaudah Equiano, or Gustavus Vassa, the African.* London, 1789.

Felsenstein, Frank, ed. *English Trader, Indian Maid: Representing Gender, Race, and Slavery in the New World: An Inkle and Yarico Reader.* Baltimore: Johns Hopkins University Press, 1999.

Fielding, Henry. *Joseph Andrews.* Edited by R. F. Brissenden. Harmondsworth, Middlesex: Penguin Books, 1977.

Godwyn, Morgan. *The Negro's and Indians Advocate, Suing for their Admission in to the Church: Or a Persuasive to the Instructing and Baptizing of the Negro's and Indians in our Plantations.* London, 1680. Wing G971.

Great Newes from Barbados. Or a true and Faithful Account of the Grand Conspiracy of the Negroes against the English and the Happy Discovery of the same. London, 1676. Wing G1733.

Green, Mary Anne Everett, ed. *Calendar of the proceedings of the Committee for Compounding, &c., 1643–1660: preserved in the State Paper Department of Her Majesty's Public Record Office.* 5 vols. London: H. M. Stationary Office, 1889–1892.

Hakluyt, Richard. *Voyages and Discoveries: The Principal Navigations, Voyages, Traffiques, and Discoveries of the English Nation.* Edited, abridged, and introduced by Jack Beeching. Harmondworth, Middlesex: Penguin Books, 1972.

Handler, Jerome S., ed. "Father Antoine Biet's Visit to Barbados in 1654." *Journal of the Barbados Museum and Historical Society* 32 (May 1967): 56–76.

Hanson, Francis. *The Laws of Jamaica passed by the Assembly and Confirmed by His Majesty in Council, Feb 23 1683.* London, 1683. Wing J124.

Harlow, Vincent T., ed. *Colonising Expeditions to the West Indies and Guiana, 1623–1667.* London: Hakluyt Society, 1925.

Iwanisziw, Susan, ed. *Oroonoko: Adaptations and Offshoots. In The Early Modern Englishwoman, 1500–1700: Contemporary Editions,* edited by Betty Travitsky and Anne Lake Prescott. Burlington, Vt.: Ashgate Publishing Company, 2006.

Johnson, Robert C., Mary Frear Keeler, Maija Janson Cole, and William B. Bidwell, eds. *Proceedings in Parliament, 1628.* 6 vols. New Haven: Yale University Press, 1977–83.

Keith, George. *An Exhortation and Caution to Friends, Concerning the Buying and Selling of Negroes.* London, 1693. Wing K162.

Kupperman, Karen Ordahl, John C. Appleby, and Mandy Banton, eds. *Calendar of State Papers, Colonial: North America and the West Indies, 1574–1739.* CD-ROM. London: Routledge/Public Record Office, 2000.

Latimer, John. *Annals of Bristol in the Seventeenth Century.* Bristol, 1900.

A Letter from a Merchant at Jamaica to a Member of Parliament in London, Touching the African Trade. To which is added A Speech made by a Black of Gardeloupe, at the Funeral of a Fellow Negro. London, 1709.

Ligon, Richard. *A True and Exact History of the Island of Barbados.* London, 1657. Wing L2075.

Littleton, Edward B. *The Groans of the Plantations: or a True Account of their Grievous and Extreme Sufferings by the heavy Impositions upon Sugar, and other hardships, Relating More Particularly to the Island of Barbados.* London, 1689. Wing L2578.

London Gazette. London, 1665–1700.

Marees, Pieter de. *Description and Historical Account of the Gold Kingdom of Guinea (1602).* Translated and edited by Albert van Dantzig and Adam Jones. Oxford: Oxford University Press for the British Academy, 1987.

Mercurius Politicus. London, 1650–60.

Neville, Henry. *The Isle of Pines*. In *Henry Neville e l'isola de pines, col testo inglese e la traduzione italiana di The Isle of Pines*, edited by O. Nicastro. Pisa: Servizio Editoriale Universitario di Pisa, 1988.

Oldmixon, John. *The British Empire in America, Containing the History of the Discovery, Settlement, Progress and Present State of All the British Colonies on the Continent and Islands of America*. 2 vols. London, 1708.

Pepys, Samuel. *The Diary of Samuel Pepys*. Edited by Robert Latham and William Matthews. 11 vols. Berkeley and Los Angeles: University of California Press, 1970–83.

Physiologus, Philotheos. See Thomas Tryon.

Pike, E. Royston. *Human Documents of the Industrial Revolution in Britain*. London: George Allen and Unwin, 1966.

Pix, Mary. *The Innocent Mistress: A Comedy*. London, 1697. Wing P2330.

Plantagenet, Beauchamp. *A Description of the Province of New Albion*. London, 1648. Wing P2378.

Plato. *The Laws*. Translated by Trevor Saunders. Harmondworth: Penguin Books, 1970.

Powell, Henry. "Petition of Captain Henry Powell." In *Colonising Expeditions to the West Indies and Guiana, 1623–1667*, edited by Vincent T. Harlow. London: Hakluyt Society, 1925.

The Present State of Jamaica, With the Life of the Great Columbus, the first Discoverer to which is added An Exact Account of Sir Hen. Morgan's Voyage to and famous Siege and taking of Panama from the Spaniards. London, 1683. Wing P3268.

Prince, Mary. *The History of Mary Prince: A West Indian Slave, related by herself*. Edited by Moira Ferguson. Ann Arbor: University of Michigan Press, 1997.

Publick Intelligencer 192, 29 August–5 September 1659.

Rawlin, William, ed. *The Laws of Barbados, Collected in one Volume*. London, 1699. Wing B682B.

Rivers, Marcellus, and Oxenbridge Foyle. *England's Slavery: or Barbados Merchandize: Represented in a Petition to the High and Honorable Court of Parliament by Marcellus Rivers and Oxenbridge Foyle, Gentlemen, on behalf of themselves and three score and ten more Free-born Englishmen sold (uncondemned) into slavery*. London, 1659. Wing R1553.

Rushworth, John. *Historical Collections: The Second Part, containing the Principal matters which happened from the dissolution of the Parliament on the 10th of March 4 Car. I 1628/9 Until the Summoning of Another Parliament, which met at Westminster, April 13, 1640*. Vol. 1. London, 1680. Wing R2318.

Sloane, Hans. *Catalogus plantarum quæ in insula Jamaica sponte proveniunt vel vulgò? Coluntur : cum earundem synomymis & locis natalibus : adjectis aliis quibusdam quæ in insulis Maderæ, Barbados, Nieves, & Sancti Christophori nascuntur : seu Prodromi historiæ naturalis Jamaicæ pars prima*. London, 1696. Wing S3998.

———. *A Voyage to the Islands of Madeira, Barbados, Nieves, St. Christophers and Jamaica, with the Natural History of the herbs and trees, Four-footed beasts, Fishes, Birds, Insects, Reptiles &c. Of the last of those Islands*. 2 vols. London, 1707–25.

Smith, Adam. *Lectures on Jurisprudence*. Edited by R. L. Meek. Oxford: Oxford University Press, 1976.

Smith, Thomas. *De Republica Anglorum: A Discourse on the Commonwealth of England*. Edited by L. Alston. London, 1906.

Some Memoirs of the first Settlement of the Island of Barbados and the other Carribee Islands with the succession of Governors and Commanders in Chief of Barbados to the Year 1741. Bridgetown, 1741.

Southerne, Thomas. *Oroonoko: A Tragedy, As it is Acted at the Theatre-Royal.* London, 1696. Wing S4761.

Stubbes, Dr. "Observations Made by a Curious and Learned Person, Sailing from England, to the Caribe-Islands," *Philosophical Transactions* 2 (1666–67): 493–500; "An Enlargement of the Observations, Formerly Publisht, Numb. 27, Made and Generously Imparted by the Learn'd and Inquisitive Physitian, Dr. Stubbes," *Philosophical Transactions* 3 (1668): 699–709; "The Remainder of the Observations Made in the Formerly Mention'd Voyage to Jamaica, Publisht Numb. 36," *Philosophical Transactions* 3 (1668): 717–22.

Tawney, R. H., and Eileen Power. *Tudor Economic Documents: Being Select Documents illustrating the economic and social history of Tudor England.* London, 1924.

Taylor, John. *Thesaurarium mathematicae; or, The treasury of mathematicks. Containing variety of usefull practices in arithmetick, geometry, trigonometry, astronomy, geography, navigation and surveying . . .* London, 1686. Wing T534.

Tryon, Thomas. *Friendly Advice to the Gentlemen Planters of the East and West Indies.* London, 1684. Wing T3179A.

——. *Some Memoirs of the Life of Thomas Tryon, Late of London, Merchant.* London, 1705.

——. *Tryon's Letters, Domestick and Foreign, To several Persons of Quality Occasionally distributed on subjects Philosophical theological and moral.* London, 1700. Wing T3184.

Verney, Margaret, ed. *Memoirs of the Verney Family: From the Restoration to the Revolution, 1660–1696.* Vol. 4 of *Memoirs of the Verney Family.* London, 1892.

Verney Family. *Letters and Papers of the Verney Family down to the end of 1639.* Edited by John Bruce. London: Camden Society, vol. 56, 1853.

Weekly Intelligencer 18, 30 August–6 September 1659.

Winthrop Family. *Winthrop Papers, 1498–1649.* 6 vols. Boston: Massachusetts Historical Society, 1929–1947.

Woodhouse, A. S. P., ed. *Puritanism and Liberty: Being the Army Debates (1647–49) from the Clarke Manuscripts with Supplementary Documents.* London, 1951.

Unpublished Dissertation

Shafer, Daniel Lee. "The Maroons of Jamaica: African Slave Rebels in the Caribbean." Ph.D. diss., University of Minnesota, 1973.

Secondary Sources

Abrahams, Roger. "Questions of Criolian Contagion." *Journal of American Folklore* 116, no. 459 (Winter 2003): 73–87.

Ackroyd, Peter. *London: The Biography.* London: Chatto & Windus, 2001.

"AHR Forum: The New British History in Atlantic Perspective." *American Historical Review* 104, no. 2 (April 1999): 426–500.

Akenson, Donald F. *If the Irish Ran the World: Montserrat, 1630–1730.* Montreal and Kingston: McGill-Queens University Press, 1997.

Amussen, Susan Dwyer. *An Ordered Society: Gender and Class in Early Modern England*. Oxford: Basil Blackwell, 1988.

——. " 'The Part of a Christian Man': The Cultural Politics of Manhood in Early Modern England." In *Political Culture and Cultural Politics in Early Modern England*, edited by Susan Dwyer Amussen and Mark A. Kishlansky, pp. 213–33. Manchester: Manchester University Press, 1995.

Andrews, Charles M. *The Colonial Period of American History*. 4 vols. New Haven: Yale University Press, 1934–1938.

Andrews, Kenneth R. *Trade, Plunder, and Settlement: Maritime Enterprise and the Genesis of the British Empire, 1480–1630*. Cambridge: Cambridge University Press, 1984.

Armitage, David. "Three Concepts of Atlantic History." In *The British Atlantic World, 1500–1800*, edited by David Armitage and Michael Braddick, pp. 11–27. Basingstoke: Palgrave Macmillan, 2002.

Armitage, David, and Michael Braddick, eds. *The British Atlantic World, 1500–1800*. Basingstoke: Palgrave Macmillan, 2002.

Aspin, Chris. *The First Industrial Society: Lancashire, 1750–1850*. Preston, England: Carnegie Publications, 1995.

Bailyn, Bernard. *Atlantic History: Concept and Contours*. Cambridge, Mass.: Harvard University Press, 2005.

Baker, C. H. Collins. *Lely and the Stuart Portrait Painters*. 2 vols. London: P. L. Warner, 1912.

Barnes, Susan J., Nora de Poorter, Oliver Millar, and Horst Vey. *Van Dyck: A Complete Catalogue of the Paintings*. New Haven and London: Yale University Press, 2004.

Battick, John F. "A New Interpretation of Cromwell's Western Design." *Journal of the Barbados Museum and Historical Society* 34 (May 1972): 76–84.

Beckles, Hilary McD. *Centering Woman: Gender Discourses in Caribbean Slave Society*. Kingston: Ian Randle Publishers, 1999.

——. *A History of Barbados from Amerindian Settlement to Nation-State*. Cambridge: Cambridge University Press, 1990.

——. *Natural Rebels: A Social History of Enslaved Black Women in Barbados*. New Brunswick: Rutgers University Press, 1989.

——. "Social and Political Control in the Slave Society." In *Slave Societies of the Caribbean*, edited by Franklin W. Knight, pp. 194–221. Vol. 3 of *General History of the Caribbean*. London: UNESCO, 1997.

——. *White Servitude and Black Slavery in Barbados, 1627–1715*. Knoxville: University of Tennessee Press, 1989.

Bennett, J. Harry. "Cary Helyar, Merchant and Planter of Seventeenth-Century Jamaica." *William and Mary Quarterly*. 3rd series. 21, no. 1 (January 1964): 53–76.

——. "William Whaley, Planter of Seventeenth Century Jamaica." *Agricultural History* 40, no. 2 (April 1966): 113–123.

——. "William Dampier, Buccaneer and Planter." *History Today* 14 (July 1964): 469–77.

Berlin, Ira. *Many Thousands Gone: The First Two Centuries of Slavery in North America*. Cambridge, Mass.: Harvard University Press, 1998.

Bigman, Laura. *History and Hunger in West Africa: Food Production and Entitlement in Guinea-Bissau and Cape Verde*. Westport, Conn.: Greenwood Press, 1993.

Bilby, Kenneth M., and Jerome S. Handler. "Obeah: Healing and Protection in West Indian Slave Life." *Journal of Caribbean History* 38, no. 2 (2004): 153–83.

Bilder, Mary Sarah. *The Transatlantic Constitution: Colonial Legal Culture and the Empire.* Cambridge, Mass.: Harvard University Press, 2004.

Bindman, David. *Ape to Apollo: Aesthetics and the Idea of Race in the Eighteenth Century.* Ithaca, N.Y.: Cornell University Press, 2002.

Black, Clinton V. *History of Jamaica.* Kingston: Longman Caribbean, 1991.

———. *Port Royal: A History and Guide.* Kingston: Institute of Jamaica Publications, 1988.

Blackburn, Robin. *The Making of New World Slavery: From the Baroque to the Modern, 1492–1800.* London and New York: Verso, 1997.

Bolster, Jeffrey. *Black Jacks: African-American Seamen in the Age of Sail.* Cambridge, Mass.: Harvard University Press, 1997.

Brailsford, H. N. *The Levellers and the English Revolution.* Edited by Christopher Hill. Stanford: Stanford University Press, 1961.

Braude, Benjamin. "The Sons of Noah and the Construction of Ethnic and Geographical Identities in the Medieval and Early Modern Periods." *William and Mary Quarterly.* 3rd series. 54, no. 1 (January 1997): 103–42.

Brenner, Robert. *Merchants and Revolution: Commercial Change, Political Conflict, and London's Overseas Traders, 1550–1653.* Princeton: Princeton University Press, 1993.

Breslaw, Elaine G. *Tituba: Reluctant Witch of Salem.* New York: New York University Press, 1996.

Bridenbaugh, Carl. *Vexed and Troubled Englishmen, 1590–1642.* New York: Oxford University Press, 1968.

Bridenbaugh, Carl, and Roberta Bridenbaugh. *No Peace Beyond the Line: The English in the Caribbean, 1624–1690.* New York: Oxford University Press, 1972.

Brown, Kathleen M. *Good Wives, Nasty Wenches, and Anxious Patriarchs: Gender, Race and Power in Colonial Virginia.* Chapel Hill: University of North Carolina Press, 1996.

Buisseret, David. "The Taylor Manuscript and Seventeenth-Century Jamaica." In *West Indies Accounts: Essays on the History of the British Caribbean and the Atlantic Economy in Honour of Richard Sheridan,* edited by Roderick McDonald, pp. 48–63. Kingston: University of West Indies Press, 1996.

Burnard, Trevor. *Mastery, Tyranny, and Desire: Thomas Thistlewood and His Slaves in the Anglo-Jamaican World.* Chapel Hill: University of North Carolina Press, 2004.

———. "Not a Place for Whites? Demographic Failure and Settlement in Comparative Context: Jamaica, 1655–1780." In *Jamaica in Slavery and Freedom: History, Heritage, and Culture,* edited by Kathleen A. Monteith and Glen Richards, pp. 73–88. Kingston: University of West Indies Press, 2002.

Burnard, Trevor, and Kenneth Morgan. "The Dynamics of the Slave Market and Slave Purchasing Patterns in Jamaica, 1655–1788." *William and Mary Quarterly.* 3rd series. 58, no. 1 (January 2001): 205–28.

Bush, Barbara. *Slave Women in Caribbean Society.* Bloomington: Indiana University Press, 1990.

Bush, Jonathan A. "The British Constitution and the Creation of American Slavery." In *Slavery and the Law,* edited by Paul Finkelman, pp. 379–417. Madison, Wisc.: Madison House, 1997.

Campbell, Mavis C. *The Maroons of Jamaica, 1655–1796: A History of Resistance, Collaboration, and Betrayal.* Granby, Mass.: Bergin & Garvey, 1988.

Campbell, P. F. *Some Early Barbadian History.* Barbados, 1993.

Canny, Nicholas. *Kingdom and Colony: Ireland in the Atlantic World, 1560–1800.* Baltimore: Johns Hopkins University Press, 1988.

——, ed. *The Origins of Empire.* Vol. 1 of *Oxford History of the British Empire,* edited by William Roger Louis. Oxford: Oxford University Press, 1998.

Canny, Nicholas, and Anthony Pagden. *Colonial Identity in the Atlantic World, 1500–1800.* Princeton: Princeton University Press, 1987.

Carey, Bev. *The Maroon Story: The Authentic and Original History of the Maroons in the History of Jamaica, 1490–1880.* Gordon Town, Jamaica: Agouti Press, 1997.

Carretta, Vincent. *Equiano, the African: Biography of a Self-Made Man.* Athens: University of Georgia Press, 2005.

Carrington, Selwyn H. H. *The Sugar Industry and the Abolition of the Slave Trade, 1775–1810.* Gainesville: University of Florida Press, 2002.

Cateau, Heather. "The New 'Negro' Business: Hiring in the British West Indies, 1750–1810." In *In the Shadow of the Plantation: Caribbean History and Legacy,* edited by Alvin O. Thompson, pp. 100–120. Kingston: Ian Randle Publications, 2002.

Chaplin, Joyce. "Race." In *The British Atlantic World, 1500–1800,* edited by David Armitage and Michael Braddick, pp. 154–72. Basingstoke: Palgrave Macmillan, 2002.

Chaytor, Miranda. "Husband(ry): Narratives of Rape in the Seventeenth Century." *Gender and History* 7, no. 3 (November 1995): 378–407.

Childs, Matt D. "Review of Carrington, *The Sugar Industry and the Abolition of the Slave Trade.*" H-NET. <http://www.h-net.org/reviews/showrev.cgi?path=162771080787028>.

Clark, Anna. *Women's Silence, Men's Violence: Sexual Assault in England, 1770–1845.* London: Pandora Press, 1987.

Clark, Peter. *The English Alehouse: A Social History, 1200–1800.* London: Longman, 1983.

Coe, Sophie D., and Michael Coe. *The True History of Chocolate.* London: Thames and Hudson, 1996.

Colley, Linda. "The Sea around Us." *New York Review of Books,* 22 June 2006, pp. 43–45.

Cottret, Bernard. *The Huguenots in England: Immigration and Settlement, ca. 1550–1700.* Translated by Peregrine and Adriana Stevenson. Cambridge: Cambridge University Press, 1991.

Craton, Michael. *Empire, Enslavement, and Freedom in the Caribbean.* Kingston: Ian Randle Publishers, 1997.

Craton, Michael, and James Walvin. *A Jamaican Plantation: The History of Worthy Park, 1670–1970.* London: W. H. Allen, 1970.

Cundall, Frank. *The Governors of Jamaica in the Seventeenth Century.* London: The West India Committee, 1936.

Curtin, Philip. "The Sugar Revolution and the Settlement of the Caribbean." In *The Rise and Fall of the Plantation Complex: Essays in Atlantic History,* pp. 73–85. Cambridge: Cambridge University Press, 1990.

Dabydeen, David. *Hogarth's Blacks: Images of Blacks in Eighteenth Century English Art.* Athens: University of Georgia Press, 1987.

Daniels, Christine, and Michael V. Kennedy, eds. *Negotiated Empires: Centers and Peripheries in the Americas, 1500–1820.* New York: Routledge, 2002.

Davidoff, Leonore, and Catherine Hall. *Family Fortunes: Men and Women of the English Middle Class, 1780–1850.* Chicago: University of Chicago Press, 1987.

Davies, K. G. *The Royal African Company.* London: Longmans Green, 1957.

Davis, David Brion. *The Problem of Slavery in Western Culture.* Oxford: Oxford University Press, 1966.

Davis, N. Darnell. *Cavaliers and Roundheads of Barbados, 1650–1652; with some account of the early history of Barbados.* Georgetown, Guyana: Argosy Press, 1887.

Davis, Natalie Z. "Women on Top." In *Society and Culture in Early Modern France*, pp. 124–51. Stanford: Stanford University Press, 1975.

Davis, Robert C. *Christian Slaves, Muslim Masters: White Slavery in the Mediterranean, the Barbary Coast, and Italy, 1500–1800.* Basingstoke: Palgrave Macmillan, 2003.

Dayfoot, Arthur Charles. *The Shaping of the West Indian Church, 1492–1962.* Gainesville: University Press of Florida, 1999.

Dolan, Frances E. "Ashes and 'the Archive': The London Fire of 1666, Partisanship, and Proof." *Journal of Medieval and Early Modern Studies* 31, no. 2 (Spring 2001): 379–408.

Drescher, Seymour. "White Atlantic? The Choice For African Slave Labor in the Plantation Americas." In *Slavery in the Development of the Americas*, edited by David Eltis, Frank D. Lewis, and Kenneth Sokoloff, pp. 31–69. Cambridge, Mass.: Harvard University Press, 2004.

Dresser, Madge. *Slavery Obscured: The Social History of the Slave Trade in an English Provincial Port.* London: Continuum, 2001.

Duncan, T. Bentley. *The Atlantic Islands: Madeira, the Azores, and the Cape Verdes in Seventeenth Century Commerce and Navigation.* Chicago: University of Chicago Press, 1972.

Dunn, Richard. "The Barbados Census of 1680." *William and Mary Quarterly.* 3rd series. 26, no. 1 (January 1969): 3–30.

———. *Sugar and Slaves: The Rise of the Planter Class in the English West Indies, 1624–1714.* Chapel Hill: University of North Carolina Press, 1972. Paperback ed., New York: W. W. Norton, 1973.

Eltis, David. "The British Transatlantic Slave Trade before 1714." In *The Lesser Antilles in the Age of European Expansion*, edited by Robert Paquette and Stanley Engerman, pp. 182–205. Gainesville: University Press of Florida, 1996.

———. "Europeans and the Rise and Fall of African Slavery." *American Historical Review* 98, no. 5 (December 1993): 1399–1423.

———. *The Rise of African Slavery in the Americas.* Cambridge: Cambridge University Press, 2000.

———. "The Volume and Structure of the Transatlantic Slave Trade: A Reassessment." *William and Mary Quarterly.* 3rd series. 58, no. 1 (2001): 17–46.

Erickson, Peter. " 'God for Harry, England, and St. George': British National Identity and the Emergence of White Self-Fashioning." In *Early Modern Visual Culture: Representation, Race and Empire in Renaissance England*, edited by Peter Erickson and Clarke Hulse. Philadelphia: University of Pennsylvania Press, 2000.

Farrer, Edmund B. *Portraits in Suffolk Houses (West).* London: B. Quaritch, 1908.

Ferguson, Margaret. *Dido's Daughters: Literacy, Gender, and Empire in Early Modern England and France*. Chicago: University of Chicago Press, 2003.

Fischer, Kirsten. *Suspect Relations: Sex, Race, and Resistance in Colonial North Carolina*. Ithaca: Cornell University Press, 2002.

Fryer, Peter. *Staying Power: The History of Black People in Britain*. London: Pluto Press, 1984.

Fuller, Mary. *Voyages in Print: English Travel to America, 1576–1624*. Cambridge: Cambridge University Press, 1995.

Galenson, David. *Traders, Planters, and Slaves: Market Behavior in Early English America*. Cambridge: Cambridge University Press, 1986.

Games, Alison. "Migration." In *The British Atlantic World, 1500–1800*, edited by David Armitage and Michael Braddick, pp. 31–50. Basingstoke: Palgrave Macmillan, 2002.

——. *Migration and the Origins of the English Atlantic World*. Cambridge, Mass.: Harvard University Press, 1999.

Gardiner, Samuel Rawson. *The History of the Commonwealth and Protectorate, 1649–1656*. 4 vols. 2nd ed. London: Longmans, Green & Co., 1903.

Gaspar, David Barry. "With a Rod of Iron: Barbados Slave Laws as a Model for Jamaica, South Carolina, and Antigua, 1661–1697." In *Crossing Boundaries: Comparative History of Black People in Diaspora*, edited by Darlene Clark Hine and Jacqueline McLeod, pp. 343–66. Bloomington: Indiana University Press, 1999.

Gilroy, Paul. *The Black Atlantic: Modernity and Double Consciousness*. Cambridge, Mass.: Harvard University Press, 1993.

Glauser, Wayne. "Three Approaches to Locke and the Slave Trade." In *Race, Gender, and Rank: Early Modern Ideas of Humanity*, edited by Maryanne Cline Horowitz, pp. 31–48. Rochester: University of Rochester Press, 1992.

Goldberg, Jonathan. *Tempest in the Caribbean*. Minneapolis: University of Minnesota Press, 2004.

Goldenberg, David M. *The Curse of Ham: Race and Slavery in Early Judaism, Christianity, and Islam*. Princeton: Princeton University Press, 2003.

Gomez, Michael A. *Exchanging Our Country Marks: The Transformation of African Identities in the Colonial and Antebellum South*. Chapel Hill: University of North Carolina Press, 1998.

Goveia, Elsa. *The West Indian Slave Laws of the Eighteenth Century*. In *Chapters in Caribbean History*, edited by Douglas Hall, Elsa Goveia, and F. Roy Augier. Barbados: Caribbean Universities Press, 1970.

Gragg, Larry. *Englishmen Transplanted: The English Colonization of Barbados, 1627–1660*. Oxford: Oxford University Press, 2003.

Greenblatt, Steven. *Marvellous Possessions: The Wonder of the New World*. Chicago: University of Chicago Press, 1991.

Greene, Jack P. "Changing Identity in the British Caribbean: Barbados as a Case Study." In *Colonial Identity in the Atlantic World, 1500–1800*, edited by Nicholas Canny and Anthony Pagden, pp. 213–66. Princeton: Princeton University Press, 1987.

——. *Negotiated Authorities: Essays in Colonial Political and Constitutional History*. Charlottesville: University Press of Virginia, 1994.

——. "Transatlantic Colonization and the Redefinition of Empire in the Early Modern Era." In *Negotiated Empires: Centers and Peripheries in the Americas, 1500–1820*, edited by Christine Daniels and Michael V. Kennedy, pp. 267–82. New York: Routledge, 2002.

Guasco, Michael. "Settling with Slavery: Human Bondage in the Early Anglo-Atlantic World." In *Envisioning an English Empire: Jamestown and the Making of the North Atlantic World*, edited by Robert Applebaum and James Sweet, pp. 236–53. Philadelphia: University of Pennsylvania Press, 2005.

Hall, Catherine. *Civilising Subjects: Metropole and Colony in the English Imagination, 1830–1867*. Chicago: University of Chicago Press, 2002.

———. *White, Male, and Middle Class: Explorations in Feminism and History*. Cambridge: Polity Press, 1992.

Hall, Douglas. *In Miserable Slavery: Thomas Thistlewood in Jamaica 1750–1786*. Mona: University of West Indies Press, 1999.

Hall, Kim F. "Object into Object? Some Thoughts on the Presence of Black Women in Early Modern Culture." In *Early Modern Visual Culture: Representation, Race and Empire in Renaissance England*, edited by Peter Erickson and Clarke Hulse, pp. 346–79. Philadelphia: University of Pennsylvania Press, 2000.

———. *Things of Darkness: Economies of Race and Gender in Early Modern England*. Ithaca: Cornell University Press, 1995.

Handler, Jerome S. "The Amerindian Slave Population of Barbados in the Seventeenth and Early Eighteenth Centuries." *Journal of the Barbados Museum and Historical Society* 33 (1970): 111–36.

———. "Plantation Slave Settlements in Barbados, 1650s to 1834." In *In the Shadow of the Plantation: Caribbean History and Legacy*, edited by Alvin O. Thompson, pp. 123–61. Kingston: Ian Randle Publications, 2002.

———. "Slave Revolts and Conspiracies in Seventeenth Century Barbados." *Nieuwe West-Indische Gids* 56 (1982): 4–41.

———. *Supplement to a Guide to Source Materials for the Study of Barbados History, 1627–1834*. Providence: John Carter Brown Library, 1991.

Handler, Jerome S., and Frederick Lange. *Plantation Slavery in Barbados: An Archeological and Historical Investigation*. Cambridge, Mass.: Harvard University Press, 1978.

Hannaford, Ivan. *Race: The History of an Idea in the West*. Washington, D.C.: Woodrow Wilson Center, 1996.

Harlow, Vincent T. *History of Barbados, 1625–1685*. Oxford: Oxford University Press, 1926.

Harms, Robert. *The Diligent: A Voyage through the Worlds of the Slave Trade*. New York: Basic Books, 2002.

Hazlewood, Nick. *The Queen's Slave Trader: John Hawkyns, Elizabeth I, and the Trafficking in Human Souls*. New York: William Morrow, 2004.

Hendricks, Margo. "Civility, Barbarism, and Aphra Behn's *The Widow Ranter*." In *Women, "Race," and Writing in the Early Modern Period*, edited by Patricia Parker and Margo Hendricks, pp. 225–39. London: Routledge, 1994.

Herrup, Cynthia B. *The Common Peace: Participation and the Criminal Law in Seventeenth-Century England*. Cambridge: Cambridge University Press, 1987.

Higman, Barry. "The Sugar Revolution." *Economic History Review* 53, no. 2 (May 2000): 213–36.

Hill, Christopher. "The Norman Yoke." In *Puritanism and Revolution: Studies in the Interpretation of the English Revolution of the 17th Century*. London: Secker & Warburg, 1958.

———. *Society and Puritanism in Pre-Revolutionary England*. New York: Schocken Books, 1964.

Hindle, Steve. *The State and Social Change in Early Modern England, ca. 1550–1640.* Basingstoke: Macmillan Press, 2000.

Hitchcock, Tim, and Michèle Cohen. *English Masculinities, 1660–1800.* London and New York: Longman, 1999.

Hobsbawm, E. J. *Industry and Empire.* Vol. 3 of *The Pelican Economic History of Britain.* New York: Penguin Books, 1969.

Howkins, Alun, and Linda Merricks. " 'Wee be Black as Hell': Ritual, Disguise, and Rebellion." *Rural History* 4, no. 1 (April 1993): 41–53.

Hulme, Peter. *Colonial Encounters: Europe and the Native Caribbean.* London: Methuen, 1986.

Jackson-Stops, Gervase, ed. *The Treasure Houses of Britain: Five Hundred Years of Private Patronage and Art Collecting.* Washington, D.C.: National Gallery of Art, 1985.

Jordan, Winthrop. *White Over Black: Attitudes toward the Negro, 1550–1812.* Chapel Hill: University of North Carolina Press, 1968.

Kaplan, Paul H. D. "Titian's *Laura Dianti* and the Origins of the Motif of the Black Page in Portraiture." Part 1, "The Vogue for Black Servants in Renaissance Italy," and Part 2, "From Laura Dianti's Page to Othello and Van Dyck." *Antichità Viva* 21, no. 1 (1982): 11–18; and 21, no. 4 (1982): 10–18.

Kelley, F. M. "Mytens and his Portraits of Charles I." *Burlington Magazine* 37, no. 209 (August 1920): 84–89.

Kelsey, Harry. *Sir John Hawkins: Queen Elizabeth's Slave Trader.* New Haven and London: Yale University Press, 2003.

Kiple, Kenneth F., and Kriemhild C. Ornelas. "After the Encounter: Disease and Demographics in the Lesser Antilles." In *The Lesser Antilles in the Age of European Expansion*, edited by Robert Paquette and Stanley Engerman, pp. 50–67. Gainesville: University Press of Florida, 1996.

Kishlansky, Mark A. *A Monarchy Transformed: Britain, 1603–1714.* London: Penguin, 1996.

Klein, Herbert, and Stanley Engerman. "Long-Term Trends in African Mortality in the Transatlantic Slave Trade." In *Routes to Slavery: Direction, Ethnicity, and Mortality in the Transatlantic Slave Trade*, edited by David Eltis and David Richardson, pp. 36–48. London: Frank Cass, 1997.

Korhonen, Anu. " 'Washing the Ethiopian White': Conceptualising Black Skin in Renaissance England." In *Black Africans in Renaissance Europe*, edited by T. F. Earle and K. J. P. Lowe, pp. 94–112. Cambridge: Cambridge University Press, 2005.

Kriz, K. Diane. "Curiosities, Commodities, and Transplanted Bodies in Hans Sloane's 'Natural History of Jamaica.' " *William and Mary Quarterly.* 3rd series. 57, no. 2 (April 2000): 35–78.

Kupperman, Karen Ordahl. "Fear of Hot Climates in the Anglo-American Colonial Experience." *William and Mary Quarterly.* 3rd series. 41, no. 2 (April 1984): 213–40.

———. *Providence Island, 1630–1641: The Other Puritan Colony.* Cambridge: Cambridge University Press, 1993.

Kussmaul, Ann. *Servants in Husbandry in Early Modern England.* Cambridge: Cambridge University Press, 1981.

Laqueur, Thomas. *Making Sex: Body and Gender from the Greeks to Freud.* Cambridge, Mass.: Harvard University Press, 1990.

Larsen, Erik. *The Paintings of Anthony Van Dyke.* 2 vols. Freren, Germany: Luca Verlag, 1988.

Lepore, Jill. *The Name of War: King Philip's War and the Origins of American Identity*. New York: Vintage Books, 1998.

Levine, David, and Keith Wrightson. *The Making of an Industrial Society: Whickham, 1560– 1765*. Oxford: Oxford University Press, 1991.

Lillywhite, Bryant. *London Coffee Houses: A Reference Book of Coffee Houses of the Seventeenth, Eighteenth, and Nineteenth Centuries*. London: George Allen and Unwin, 1963.

Linebaugh, Peter, and Markus Rediker. *The Many-Headed Hydra: Sailors, Slaves, Commoners, and the Hidden History of the Revolutionary Atlantic*. Boston: Beacon Press, 2000.

Lobban, Richard. *Cape Verde: Crioulo Colony to Independent Nation*. Boulder, Colo.: Westview Press, 1995.

Loomba, Ania. *Shakespeare, Race, and Colonialism*. Oxford: Oxford University Press, 2002.

Lowe, Kate. "Introduction: The Black African Presence in Renaissance Europe." In *Black Africans in Renaissance Europe*, edited by T. F. Earle and K. J. P. Lowe, pp. 1–14. Cambridge: Cambridge University Press, 2005.

Luu, Lien Bich. *Immigrants and the Industries of London*. Aldershot: Ashgate Press, 2005.

Macdonald, Joyce Green. "Race, Women, and the Sentimental in Thomas Southerne's *Oroonoko*." *Criticism* 40, no. 4 (Fall 1998): 555–70.

MacLeod, Catherine, and Julia Marciari Alexander. *Painted Ladies: Women at the Court of Charles II*. London: National Portrait Gallery, 2001.

Mancke, Elizabeth. "Negotiating an Empire: Britain and Its Overseas Peripheries, ca. 1550–1780." In *Negotiated Empires: Centers and Peripheries in the Americas, 1500–1820*, edited by Christine Daniels and Michael V. Kennedy, pp. 235–65. New York: Routledge, 2002.

Manning, Roger. *Village Revolts: Social Protest and Popular Disturbances in England, 1509–1640*. Oxford: Oxford University Press, 1988.

Marx, Jenifer. *Pirates and Privateers of the Caribbean*. Malabar, Fla.: Krieger Publishing Company, 1992.

Matthew, H. C. G., and Brian Harrison, eds. *Oxford Dictionary of National Biography*. Oxford and New York: Oxford University Press, 2004.

McCusker, John J., and Russell R. Menard. "The Sugar Industry in the Seventeenth Century: A New Perspective on the Barbadian Sugar Revolution." In *Tropical Babylons: Sugar and the Making of the Atlantic World*, edited by Stuart B. Schwartz, pp. 289–330. Chapel Hill: University of North Carolina Press, 2004.

McGinnis, Paul, and Arthur H. Williamson. "Britain, Race, and the Iberian World Empire." In *The Stuart Kingdoms in the Seventeenth Century: Awkward Neighbors*, edited by Allan I. Macinnes and Jane Ohlmeyer, pp. 70–93. Dublin: Four Courts Press, 2002.

McGowan, Winston. "The Origins of Slave Rebellions in the Middle Passage." In *In the Shadow of the Plantation: Caribbean History and Legacy*, edited by Alvin O. Thompson, pp. 74–99. Kingston: Ian Randle Publishers, 2002.

McKendrick, Neil, John Brewer, and J. H. Plumb. *The Birth of a Consumer Society: The Commercialization of Eighteenth-Century England*. Bloomington: University of Indiana Press, 1982.

Mendle, Michael. *Henry Parker and the English Civil War: The Political Thought of the Public's "Privado."* Cambridge: Cambridge University Press, 1995.

Millar, Oliver. *Sir Peter Lely, 1618–1680: Catalogue of an Exhibition at the National Portrait Gallery*. London: National Portrait Gallery, 1978.

Milton, Giles. *Big Chief Elizabeth: How England's Adventurers Gambled and Won the New World*. London: Hodder & Stoughton, 2000.

Mintz, Sidney. *Sweetness and Power: The Place of Sugar in Modern History*. New York: Penguin Books, 1985.

Mintz, Sidney, and Douglas Hall. *The Origins of the Jamaican Internal Marketing System*. In Yale University Publications in Anthropology 57. New Haven: Yale University Press, 1960.

Mitchell, David. " 'It will be easy to make money': Merchant Strangers in London, 1580–1680." In *Entrepreneurs and Entrepreneurship in Early Modern Times: Merchants and Industrialists within the Orbit of the Dutch Staple Market*. Hollandse Historische Reeks. Vol. 24. Edited by C. Lesger and L. Noordegraaf, pp. 119–45. The Hague: Gegevens Koninklijke Bibliotheek, 1995.

Morgan, Edmund S. *American Slavery, American Freedom: The Ordeal of Colonial Virginia*. New York: W. W. Norton, 1975.

Morgan, Jennifer. *Laboring Women: Reproduction and Gender in New World Slavery*. Philadelphia: University of Pennsylvania Press, 2004.

———. " 'Some Could Suckle over Their Shoulder': Male Travelers, Female Bodies, and the Gendering of Racial Ideology, 1500–1700." *William and Mary Quarterly*. 3rd series. 54, no. 1 (January 1997): 167–92.

Morgan, Philip. "The Black Experience in the British Empire, 1680–1810." In *Black Experience and the Empire*, edited by Philip D. Morgan and Sean Hawkins, pp. 86–110. Oxford History of the British Empire Companion Series, no. 3. Oxford: Oxford University Press, 2004.

———. "The Poor: Slaves in Early America." In *Slavery in the Development of the Americas*, edited by David Eltis, Frank D. Lewis, and Kenneth Sokoloff, pp. 288–323. Cambridge, Mass.: Harvard University Press, 2004.

Mulcahy, Matthew. *Hurricanes and Society in the British Greater Caribbean, 1624–1783*. Baltimore: Johns Hopkins University Press, 2006.

Muldoon, James. *Identity on the Medieval Irish Frontier: Degenerate Englishmen, Wild Irishmen, Middle Nations*. Gainesville: University Press of Florida, 2003.

Ohlmeyer, Jane. " 'Civilizinge of those Rude Partes': Colonization within Britain and Ireland, 1580s–1640s." In *The Origins of Empire*, edited by Nicholas Canny. Vol. 1 of *Oxford History of the British Empire*, edited by William Roger Louis. Oxford: Oxford University Press, 1998.

Padrón, Francisco Morales. *Spanish Jamaica*. Translated by Patrick E. Bryan. Kingston: Ian Randle, 2003.

Paley, Ruth. "After Somerset: Mansfield, Slavery, and the Law in England, 1772–1830." In *Law, Crime, and English Society, 1660–1830*, edited by Norma Landau, pp. 165–84. Cambridge: Cambridge University Press, 2002.

Palmer, Colin A. "The Slave Trade, African Slavers, and the Demography of the Caribbean to 1750." In *Slave Societies of the Caribbean*, edited by Franklin W. Knight, pp. 9–44. Vol. 3 of *General History of the Caribbean*. London: UNESCO, 1997.

Parker, Patricia, and Margo Hendricks. *Women, "Race," and Writing in the Early Modern Period.* London: Routledge, 1994.

Parry, John H. "Plantation and Provision Ground." *Revista de Historia de America* 39 (June 1955): 1–20.

Pateman, Carole. *The Sexual Contract.* Stanford: Stanford University Press, 1988.

Patterson, Orlando. "Slavery and Slave Revolts: A Sociohistorical Analysis of the First Maroon War, 1665–1740." In *Maroon Societies: Rebel Slave Communities in the Americas,* edited by Richard Price, pp. 246–92. 2nd ed. Baltimore: Johns Hopkins University Press, 1996.

———. *The Sociology of Slavery: An Analysis of the Origins, Development, and Structure of Negro Slave Society in Jamaica.* London: MacGibbon & Kee, 1967.

Pawson, Michael, and David Buisseret. *Port Royal, Jamaica.* Oxford: Clarendon Press, 1975.

Pérotin-Dumon, Anne. "French, English, and Dutch in the Lesser Antilles: From Privateering to Planting, ca. 1550–1650." In *New Societies: The Caribbean in the Long Sixteenth Century,* edited by P. C. Emmer and German Carrera Damas, pp. 114–58. Vol. 2 of *General History of the Caribbean.* London: UNESCO, 1999.

Pestana, Carla Gardina. *The English Atlantic in an Age of Revolution, 1640–1661.* Cambridge, Mass.: Harvard University Press, 2004.

Pocock, J. G. A. *The Ancient Constitution and the Feudal Law: A Study of English Historical Thought in the Seventeenth Century.* Cambridge: Cambridge University Press, 1957; reissued 1987.

———. "British History: A Plea for a Subject." *Journal of Modern History* 47, no. 4 (December 1975): 601–21.

Pollock, Frederick, and William Maitland. *The History of English Law before the time of Edward I.* 2 vols. 2nd ed. Cambridge: Cambridge University Press, 1968.

Preston, Diana, and Michael Preston. *Pirate of Exquisite Mind: Explorer, Naturalist, and Buccaneer: The Life of William Dampier.* New York: Walker & Co., 2004.

Price, Richard. "Maroons and Their Communities." In *The Slavery Reader,* edited by Gad Heumann and James Walvin, pp. 608–25. London: Routledge, 2003.

———, ed. *Maroon Societies: Rebel Slave Communities in the Americas.* 2nd ed. Baltimore: Johns Hopkins University Press, 1996.

Pritchard, James. *In Search of Empire: The French in the Americas, 1670–1730.* Cambridge: Cambridge University Press, 2004.

Puckrein, Gary. *Little England: Plantation Society and Anglo-Barbadian Politics, 1627–1700.* New York: New York University Press, 1984.

Rath, Richard. "African Music in Seventeenth-Century Jamaica: Cultural Transit and Transition." *William and Mary Quarterly.* 3rd series. 50, no. 4 (October 1993): 700–726.

Reinhardt Galleries. *Loan Exhibition of Paintings of Women and Children by Masters from the Fifteenth to the Twentieth Centuries.* New York, 1929.

Ritchie, Robert C. *Captain Kidd and the War Against the Pirates.* Cambridge, Mass.: Harvard University Press, 1986.

Robertson, James. *Gone Is the Ancient Glory: Spanish Town, Jamaica, 1534–2000.* Kingston: Ian Randle Publishers, 2005.

———. "Re-writing the English Conquest of Jamaica in the Late Seventeenth Century." *English Historical Review* 117, no. 473 (September 2002): 813–39.

——. " 'Stories' and 'Histories' in Late Seventeenth-Century Jamaica." In *Jamaica in Slavery and Freedom: History, Heritage, and Culture*, edited by Kathleen E. A. Monteith and Glen Richards, pp. 25–51. Kingston: University of West Indies Press, 2002.

Robinson, Carey. *The Iron Thorn: The Defeat of the British by the Jamaican Maroons*. Kingston: Kingston Publishers, 1993.

Rosenberg, Philippe. "Thomas Tryon and the Seventeenth-Century Dimensions of Anti-Slavery." *William and Mary Quarterly* 61, no. 4 (October 2004): 609–42.

Sacks, David Harris. *The Widening Gate: Bristol and the Atlantic Economy, 1450–1700*. Berkeley and Los Angeles: University of California Press, 1991.

Samuel, Raphael. " 'British Dimensions': Four Nations History." *History Workshop Journal* 40 (Autumn 1995): iii–xxii.

Scott, James C. *Domination and the Arts of Resistance: Hidden Transcripts*. New Haven: Yale University Press, 1990.

Shammas, Carole. "Changes in English and Anglo-American Consumption from 1550–1800." In *Consumption and the World of Goods*, edited by John Brewer and Roy Porter, pp. 177–205. London: Routledge, 1993.

——. "Introduction." In *The Creation of the British Atlantic World*, edited by Elizabeth Mancke and Carole Shammas, pp. 1–16. Baltimore: Johns Hopkins University Press, 2005.

——. *The Pre-Industrial Consumer in England and America*. Oxford: Oxford University Press, 1990.

Sharp, Buchanan. *In Contempt of All Authority: Rural Artisans and Riot in the West of England, 1586–1660*. Berkeley and Los Angeles: University of California Press, 1980.

Shepherd, Verene, ed. *Slavery without Sugar: Diversity in Caribbean Economy and Society since the 17th Century*. Gainesville: University Press of Florida, 2002.

Sheppard, Jill. "The Slave Conspiracy that Never Was." *Journal of the Barbados Museum and Historical Society* 34 (March 1974): 190–97.

Sheridan, Richard. "Resistance and Rebellion of African Captives in the Transatlantic Slave Trade before becoming Seasoned Labourers in the British Caribbean, 1690–1807." In *Working Slavery, Pricing Freedom: Perspectives from the Caribbean, Africa, and the African Diaspora*, edited by Verene Shepherd, pp. 181–205. Kingston: Ian Randle, 2001.

——. *Sugar and Slavery: An Economic History of the British West Indies, 1623–1775*. 2nd ed. Kingston: Canoe Press, 1994.

Sherlock, Philip, and Hazel Bennett. *The Story of the Jamaican People*. Kingston: Ian Randle Publishers, 1998.

Shyllon, Folarin O. *Black People in Britain, 1555–1833*. London: Institute for Race Relations, 1977.

——. *Black Slaves in Britain*. London: Oxford University Press, 1974.

Skinner, Quentin. *Liberty before Liberalism*. Cambridge: Cambridge University Press, 1998.

Slack, Paul. *Poverty and Policy in Tudor and Stuart England*. London: Longman, 1988.

Smedley, Audrey. *Race in North America: Origin and Evolution of a Worldview*. Boulder, Colo.: Westview Press, 1993.

Smith, Abbott Emerson. *Colonists in Bondage: White Servitude and Convict Labor in America, 1607–1776*. Chapel Hill: University of North Carolina Press, 1947.

Sobel, Dana. *Longitude: The True Story of a Great Genius Who Solved the Greatest Scientific Problem of His Time*. London: Fourth Estate, 1996.

Steele, Ian K. *The English Atlantic, 1675–1740: An Exploration of Communication and Community.* Oxford: Oxford University Press, 1986.

Stewart, J. Douglas. *Sir Godfrey Kneller and the English Baroque Portrait.* Oxford: Clarendon Press, 1983.

Stone, Lawrence. *The Family, Sex, and Marriage in England, 1500–1700.* New York: Harper & Row, 1977.

Stoyle, Mark. *Soldiers and Strangers: An Ethnic History of the English Civil War.* New Haven: Yale University Press, 2005.

Tattersfield, Nigel. *The Forgotten Trade: Comprising the Log of the Daniel and Henry of 1700 and Accounts of the Slave Trade from the Minor Ports of England, 1698–1725.* London: Pimlico Press, 1991.

Taylor, Alan. *American Colonies.* New York: Viking Press, 2001.

Taylor, S. A. G. *The Western Design: An Account of Cromwell's Expedition to the Caribbean.* Kingston: Institute of Jamaica, 1965.

Thompson, E. P. *Whigs and Hunters: The Origin of the Black Act.* New York: Pantheon Books, 1975.

Thornton, John. "The Coromantees: An African Cultural Group in Colonial North America and the Caribbean." *Journal of Caribbean History* 32 (1998): 161–78.

Tobin, Beth Fowkes. *Picturing Imperial Power: Colonial Subjects in Eighteenth-Century Britain.* Durham: Duke University Press, 1999.

Underdown, David. *Fire from Heaven: Life in an English Town in the Seventeenth Century.* New Haven: Yale University Press, 1992.

———. *A Freeborn People: Politics and the Nation in Seventeenth-Century England.* Oxford: Oxford University Press, 1996.

———. *Revel, Riot, and Rebellion: Popular Politics and Culture in England, 1603–1660.* Oxford: Oxford University Press, 1985.

———. "The Taming of the Scold: The Enforcement of Patriarchal Authority in Early Modern England." In *Order and Disorder in Early Modern England,* edited by Anthony Fletcher and John Stevenson, pp. 116–36. Cambridge: Cambridge University Press, 1985.

Valenze, Deborah. *The First Industrial Woman.* New York: Oxford University Press, 1995.

———. *The Social Life of Money in the English Past.* Cambridge: Cambridge University Press, 2006.

Vaughan, Alden T. "Powhatans Abroad: Virginia Indians in England." In *Envisioning an English Empire: Jamestown and the Making of the North Atlantic World,* edited by Robert Applebaum and James Sweet, pp. 49–67. Philadelphia: University of Pennsylvania Press, 2005.

Via, Vicky Crow. "A Comparison of Laws Importing and Regulating the Servants of Virginia and Jamaica in the Seventeenth Century." *Journal of Caribbean History* 38, no. 2 (2004): 310–33.

Vickery, Amanda. *The Gentleman's Daughter: Women's Lives in Georgian England.* New Haven: Yale University Press, 1998.

Walker, Garthine. "Rereading Rape and Sexual Violence in Early Modern England." *Gender and History* 10, no. 1 (April 1998): 1–25.

Walvin, James. *Black and White: The Negro and English Society, 1555–1945.* London: Allen Lane, 1973.

——. *Black Ivory: Slavery in the British Empire*. 2nd ed. Oxford: Blackwell, 2001.

——. *Fruits of Empire: Exotic Produce and British Taste, 1660–1800*. Basingstoke: Macmillan Press, 1996.

Warner, Malcolm, and Robyn Asleson. *Great British Paintings from American Collections: Holbein to Hockney*. New Haven: Yale University Press, 2001.

Waterfield, Giles. "Black Servants." In *Below Stairs: Four Hundred Years of Servants' Portraits*, by Giles Waterfield and Anne French with Matthew Craske, pp. 139–51. London: National Portrait Gallery, 2003.

Webb, Stephen Saunders. *The Governors-General: The English Army and the Definition of Empire, 1569–1681*. Chapel Hill: University of North Carolina Press, 1979.

Welch, Pedro. *Slave Society in the City: Bridgetown, Barbados, 1680–1834*. Kingston: Ian Randle Publishers, 2003.

——. "The Urban Context of the Life of the Enslaved: Views from Bridgetown, Barbados, in the Eighteenth and Nineteenth Centuries." In *Slavery without Sugar: Diversity in Caribbean Economy and Society since the 17th Century*, edited by Verene Shepherd, pp. 183–98. Gainesville: University Press of Florida, 2002.

Wheeler, Roxanne. *The Complexion of Race: Categories of Difference in Eighteenth-Century British Culture*. Philadelphia: University of Pennsylvania Press, 2000.

Whitson, Agnes M. *The Constitutional Development of Jamaica, 1660–1729*. Manchester: Manchester University Press, 1929.

Whyman, Susan. *Sociability and Power in Late Stuart England: The Cultural Worlds of the Verneys, 1660–1720*. Oxford: Oxford University Press, 1999.

Williams, Eric. *Capitalism and Slavery*. Chapel Hill: University of North Carolina Press, 1944.

Williams, Patricia. "On Being the Object of Property." In *The Alchemy of Race and Rights*, pp. 216–36, 254–55. Cambridge, Mass.: Harvard University Press, 1991.

Wrightson, Keith. *Earthly Necessities: Economic Lives in Early Modern Britain*. London: Penguin, 2000.

Wrightson, Keith, and David Levine. *Poverty and Piety in an English Village: Terling, 1525–1700*. 2nd ed. Oxford: Oxford University Press, 1995.

Wrigley, E. A., and R. S. Schofield. *The Population History of England, 1541–1871: A Reconstruction*. Cambridge Studies in Population, Economy, and Society in Past Time, no. 46. Cambridge: Cambridge University Press, 1989.

Yavneh, Naomi. "To Bare or Not to Bare: Sofonisba Anguissola's Nursing Madonna and the Womanly Art of Breastfeeding." In *Maternal Measures: Figuring Caregiving in the Early Modern Period*, edited by Naomi J. Miller and Naomi Yavneh, pp. 65–81. Burlington: Ashgate Press, 2000.

Young, Jeffrey T. *Economics as a Moral Science: The Political Economy of Adam Smith*. Cheltenham: Edward Elgar, 1997.

Young, W. A. "Works Organization in the Seventeenth Century: Some Account of Ambrose and John Crowley." *Transactions of the Newcomen Society* 4 (1922–1923): 73–101.

Zahedieh, Nuala. "Economy." In *The British Atlantic World, 1500–1800*, edited by David Armitage and Michael Braddick, pp. 51–68. Basingstoke: Palgrave Macmillan, 2002.

——. " 'A Frugal, Prudential, and Hopeful Trade': Privateering in Jamaica, 1655–1689." *Journal of Imperial and Commonwealth History* 18, no. 2 (May 1990): 145–68.

——. "Overseas Expansion and Trade in the Seventeenth Century." In *The Origins of Empire*, edited by Nicholas Canny, pp. 398–422. Vol. 1 of *Oxford History of the British Empire*, edited by William Roger Louis. Oxford: Oxford University Press, 1998.

——. "Trade, Plunder, and Economic Development in Early English Jamaica." *Economic History Review*. 2nd series. 39, no. 2 (May 1986): 205–22.

——. " 'The Wickedest City in the World': Port Royal: Commercial Hub of the Seventeenth-Century Caribbean." In *Working Slavery, Pricing Freedom: Perspectives from the Caribbean, Africa, and the African Diaspora*, edited by Verene Shepherd, pp. 3–20. Kingston: Ian Randle Publishers, 2001.

Index

DATE DUE